KT-443-497

WITHDRAWN

Globalization of Food and Agriculture and the Poor

Globalization of Food and Agriculture and the Poor

Edited by Joachim von Braun and Eugenio Díaz-Bonilla

INTERNATIONAL FOOD
POLICY RESEARCH INSTITUTE

OXFORD
UNIVERSITY PRESS

YMCA Library Building, Jai Singh Road, New Delhi 110001

Oxford University Press is a department of the University of Oxford.
It furthers the University's objective of excellence in research,
scholarship, and education by publishing worldwide in

Oxford New York

Auckland   Cape Town   Dar es Salaam   Hong Kong   Karachi Kuala Lumpur
Madrid   Melbourne   Mexico City   Nairobi New Delhi   Shanghai   Taipei   Toronto

With offices in
Argentina   Austria   Brazil   Chile   Czech Republic   France   Greece Guatemala
Hungary   Italy   Japan   Poland   Portugal   Singapore South Korea   Switzerland
Thailand   Turkey   Ukraine   Vietnam

Oxford is a registered trade mark of Oxford University Press
in the UK and in certain other countries

Published in India
by Oxford University Press, New Delhi

© 2007 The International Food Policy Research Institute

The moral rights of the author have been asserted
Database right Oxford University Press (maker)

First Published 2008

Chapter 6, based partly on Thomas Reardon and C. Peter Timmer, 'Transformation
of markets for agricultural output in developing countries since 1950: How has
thinking changed?', in Handbook of Agricultural Economics, Vol. 3: Agricultural
development: Farmers, farm production, and farm markets, *Robert Evenson and*
Prabhu Pingali *(eds.), 2827–2849, copyright © 2007 Elsevier, is published with permission from Elsevier.*

All rights reserved. No part of this publication may be reproduced
or transmitted, in any form or by any means, electronic or mechanical,
including photocopying, recording or by any information storage and
retrieval system, without the prior permission in writing of Oxford University Press.
Enquiries concerning reproduction outside the scope of the above should be
sent to the Rights Department, Oxford University Press, at the address above

You must not circulate this book in any other binding or cover
and you must impose this same condition on any acquirer

ISBN-13: 978-0-19-569528 1
ISBN-10: 0-19-569528 3

Printed in India by De Unique, New Delhi 110 018
Published by Oxford University Press
YMCA Library Building, Jai Singh Road, New Delhi 110 001

Contents

Tables

Figures

Preface

Work on this volume was initiated by a workshop and policy dialogue in honor of Per Pinstrup-Andersen in recognition of his outstanding service as the International Food Policy Research Institute (IFPRI) director general from 1992 to 2002. *Therefore, this volume is in honor of Per Pinstrup-Andersen.*

The workshop was held in 2002, and Per Pinstrup-Andersen played an active role in its design with us. The chapters of this volume and the policy essays have been revised and updated thereafter, and some new chapters have been added. We are grateful for the helpful critique by anonymous reviewers through IFPRI's Publications Review Committee.

The globalization debate related to food and agriculture remains heated and controversial. IFPRI is continuously engaged in this debate with its research on markets and trade, on technology and environmental issues, and on consumption and nutrition issues and their implications for poverty. To bring out controversial aspects of the debate, and to confront it with research-based findings, this volume explicitly combines in-depth chapters written by IFPRI staff and other researchers, and the broader research community with a set of policy essays by leading experts on globalization processes in which they share their concern, extensive experiences, and insights. The essays are marked as such in the table of contents to guide the reader.

We hope that this volume furthers the debate for the benefit of rational decision-making on food and agriculture and the poor as related to globalization policy issues.

Joachim von Braun
Eurgenio Díaz-Bonilla

Abbreviations and Acronyms

AMS	Aggregate Measure of Support
AoA	Agreement on Agriculture (of World Trade Organization)
APAARI	Asia-Pacific Association of Agricultural Research Institutions
CAP	Common Agricultural Policy (European Union)
CGIAR	Consultative Group on International Agricultural Research
DRC	Democratic Republic of the Congo
EPA	Environmental Protection Agency (United States)
FAO	Food and Agriculture Organization of the United Nations
FARA	Forum for Agricultural Research in Africa
FDA	Food and Drug Administration (United States)
FDI	foreign direct investment
FORAGO	Forum for the Americas on Agricultural Research and Technological Development
FSRI	Farm Security and Rural Investment Act (United States)
GATT	General Agreement on Tariffs and Trade
GDP	gross domestic product
GFAR	Global Forum on Agricultural Research
GM	genetically modified
GTAP	Global Trade Analysis Project
HDI	Human Development Index

HIPC	Heavily Indebted Poor Countries
HVFP	high-value food product
HYV	high-yielding varieties
IARC	international agricultural research center
ICAC	International Cotton Advisory Committee
ICT	information and communications technology
IFPRI	International Food Policy Research Organization
ILO	International Labour Organization
IMF	International Monetary Fund
IPR	intellectual property rights
MDG	Millennium Development Goal
MV	modern variety
NAFTA	North American Free Trade Agreement
NARS	national agricultural research systems
NGO	nongovernmental organization
NSI	national system of innovation
ODA	official development assistance
OECD	Organisation for Economic Co-operation and Development
PPP	purchasing power parity
PRIO	International Peace Research Institute, Oslo
PSE	Producer Subsidy Estimate
R&D	research and development
SPS	sanitary and phytosanitary
TFC	transnational food company
TNC	transnational corporation
TRIPS	Trade-Related Aspects of Intellectual Property Rights Agreement (of World Trade Organization)
UNDP	United Nations Development Programme
WHO	World Health Organization
WTO	World Trade Organization

Chapter 1

Globalization of Agriculture and Food: Causes, Consequences, and Policy Implications

Joachim von Braun and Eugenio Díaz-Bonilla

The world agrifood system is becoming increasingly globalized. As the majority of the world moves into cities, and as people who remain in rural areas adopt more urbanized lifestyles when they are better connected to infrastructure, consumption of food is changing to a more varied composition yet also to greater similarity around the world. The time-saving instant noodle soup in a plastic cup in Asia, as well as the hamburger and the prepared sandwich worldwide, are indicative of this tendency. Consumption of processed foods, soft drinks, and bottled water is expanding, and foods and beverages are increasingly transported long distances, catering to changing demands. The food processing and retail industries have become global players. Farmers increasingly specialize their production as a consequence of these changing markets, which requires change upstream in the food chain—that is, in such production inputs as water, seeds, feeds, and technical equipment, which has in turn created new organizational arrangements in the food system.

This book examines how such changes are affecting the poor by looking at specific factors that are driving change. The various chapters consider different angles to the following questions: How do these changes affect the roles and powers of various actors along the food chain? How relevant are these trends to the economic developments within the global agrifood system and, in particular, to the poor segments of society? How is the globalization of foods affecting human health? How can international and national policies address possible adverse direct and indirect effects of globalization of the world's agrifood system while strengthening positive ones?

Given the rich stream of writings on globalization in recent years, and with globalization coming of age (Osterhammel and Petersson 2005), a valid question to ask is, why produce this book? A line of work has addressed, in general, the growth and poverty effects of globalization (see, for example, Rodrik 1997; Aghion and Williamson 1999; Bhalla 2002; Stiglitz 2003; Bhagwati 2004; Harrison 2006), and the debate on whether it has been beneficial or detrimental to society is ongoing and vibrant (see Chapter 2 and Essay 6). Other literature has analyzed the changes in global food markets and the effect on national agrifood systems, but not in the context of developing countries and the poor within these countries (see, for example, Regmi and Gehlhar 2005). In this book, we attempt to combine both lines of inquiry, focusing more specifically on the globalization of agrifood systems, the actual and potential effects of these trends on the poor, and the implications for food and nutrition security in developing countries.

Although it may come at the cost of a definite message and policy prescription on globalization, this volume acknowledges the uncertainties and complexities involved and attempts to do justice to the current state of research (which is expanding daily) and to expose the unresolved debates and controversies. To accommodate a variety of views, the volume is composed of nine chapters that analyze in detail the main aspects of the links between the globalization of agrifood systems and poverty, and six essays that highlight primary issues in the lively ongoing debate. Taken as a whole, the volume avoids simplistic messages about globalization being "good" or "bad." The main audience is policy advisors; civil society organizations; individuals in the private sector; and students interested in globalization, the fast-changing agrifood system, and the actions needed to influence these developments to make globalization outcomes more pro-poor.

Figure 1.1 gives an overview on the book and provides the organizing framework of the analyses presented in the various chapters and essays: four broad globalization "drivers and changes" (see columns: political context and governance; markets, capital investment, and labor; information and innovation; and health, social policies, and conflicts) are considered, and their effects on cross-cutting issues and on the elements of the food chain are addressed (see the rows in Figure 1.1).

Accordingly, after the analyses and overview on globalization and poverty in Chapter 2, the next part of this book is broadly structured along the building blocks of the food chain, with Chapters 3–7 and Essays 1 and 2 covering issues in production, marketing, processing, and consumption. Those issues are in turn embedded in the discussion of more general governance and policy issues that affect the globalization of agrifood systems and whether they can be made more pro-poor, covered in Chapters 8 and 9 and Essays 3–6. Indeed, global and national policies and institutions are important determinants of how globalization affects different segments of

Figure 1.1   Overview of issues and coverage of book chapters by drivers of globalization and the food chain

DRIVERS AND CHANGES

| Political context and governance | Markets, capital investment, and labor | Information and innovation | Health, social policies, and conflicts |

CROSS-CUTTING

Chapter 1: Globalization of agriculture and food: Causes, consequences, and policy

Chapter 2: Globalization and poverty from the perspective of agriculture and food

Essay 1: Making globalization work for the poor: Technology and trade

CONSUMPTION

Chapter 4: Globalization and smallholders: A review of issues, approaches, and tentative conclusions

Chapter 3: Implications of globalization for agricultural research

Chapter 5: Agricultural trade, globalization, and the rural poor

Essay 2: Agriculture and market power

TRADE

Chapter 6: The rise of supermarkets in the global food system

Chapter 7: Globalization of agrifood systems and the nutrition transition

Essay 3: Economic policies in developing countries to make globalization work for the poor

PRODUCTION

Chapter 8: Globalization, governance, and agriculture

Essay 4: Changing paradigms under globalization

Chapter 9: Conflict, food insecurity, and globalization

Essay 5: National government: The key to food security under globalization

CROSS-CUTTING

Essay 6: Addressing inherent asymmetries of globalization

THE AGRIFOOD CHAIN

society. Although powerful forces drive globalization in general and the agrifood system in particular, global and national policies do shape the potential benefits and risks of globalization.

This chapter provides a background for and overview of the topics covered in this book. It starts by defining the concept of globalization of agrifood systems. Subsequently, the second section provides an overview of the size and major transformations of agrifood systems resulting from globalization processes. And, drawing mainly from the essays and the other chapters in the book, the last sections look at the larger context of globalization and its implications for development and poverty reduction policies.

Because the topic of the links among globalization, agrifood systems, and poverty is so vast, this volume cannot cover all possible components. In particular, two topics, which require further research, are largely absent. First, migration issues, both nationally and internationally, have been central to the transformation of rural and agricultural economies. More recently, the growth in international remittances has further changed the economic and social dynamics in the countryside in several developing countries (see, for instance, Terry and Wilson 2005). A second important topic that is absent in this book refers to global environmental concerns—from climate change to global water management, stressed ecosystems, and losses in biodiversity.[1] These concerns are growing and will have an effect on the future sustainability of globalization of the agrifood system. In Essay 1, M. S. Swaminathan underlines the need for what he calls an "Ever-Green Revolution," whereby innovations that enable productivity improvements are developed without ecological and social harm. Costs and uncertainties should not obscure their important implications for the food security, health, and nutrition of the world's poor (see Wood 2001; Millennium Ecosystem Assessment 2005). Global climate change mainly caused by activities related to industrialized countries increases the risks and uncertainties in the agrifood system and will have increasingly adverse effects in terms of natural catastrophes and diseases that especially affect the poorest countries. Deteriorating environmental conditions may reinforce vicious cycles of conflict over resources and humanitarian crises (Chapter 9), and the poor will pay the highest price for further delays in remedial action. All countries, but industrialized countries in particular, must act responsibly to reduce the main causes of global climate change.

Defining Globalization of Agrifood Systems

There is a large body of literature on the possible nature and phases of globalization as well as a variety of definitions—from narrow notions that focus on trade liberalization to broader views, albeit still centered on economic aspects (such as the international expansion of capital, labor, and technology flows). It is important to distinguish between two very different features of globalization: the shrinkage of space and time resulting from advancements in transport and communication technologies, and the policy choices of economic and political change. As Helleiner (2001) points out, the former refers to an economic reality and is therefore a fact, whereas the latter refers to human choices. One may also distinguish globalization by its three major manifestations: first, the multiplication and intensification of economic, political, social, and cultural linkages among people, organizations, and countries at the world level; second, the tendency toward the universal application of economic, institutional, legal, political, and cultural practices; and third, the emergence of significant spillovers from the behavior of individuals and societies to the rest of the world.[2]

Whatever the scope of the definition utilized, an important distinction is between those who consider globalization as an impersonal force (driven mostly from advances in technology and other factors, such as the expansion of population)[3] from those who understand globalization as a policy choice by governments. Of course, the policy implications of emphasizing one interpretation over the other are very different, as well as the assessment of the degrees of freedom governments may have to choose among policy alternatives[4] (see also Chapter 5 and Essay 2). In this book we use the idea of globalization of agriculture and the food system in a broad sense. We would thus see increased globalization in the agrifood system[5]

- when internationally traded foods—be they raw materials or processed—increase as a proportion of production;

- when traded agricultural inputs and transborder investments expand across countries;

- when the science, knowledge, and information content of the agrifood system become increasingly internationalized;

- when standardization and the related regulatory institutions increasingly reach across borders—be they corporate organizations, such as multinational companies, or public organizations, such as the World Trade Organization (WTO);

- when consumers' tastes, and the firms and organizational forms attending to them, show growing similarities across nations and global regions;

- when agrifood systems–related health and environmental externalities have transnational or global effects; and

- when social policies related to hunger and poverty reduction become global.

In view of the diverse implications of globalization along agrifood chains, any simplistic adding up of its effects on development, distribution, and poverty should be avoided. The globalization of agrifood systems is not easily quantifiable because of the diversity of the processes involved, and because these processes do not always occur concurrently or lead in the same direction. Nonetheless, some aspects can be quantified individually, albeit imperfectly. We look first at the current size and composition of the food market and then at the evolution of some indicators of trade and foreign direct investment (FDI) in the agricultural sector, focusing mainly on developing countries.

Size and Composition of the Food Market

Historically, trade in food and agriculture has been a key driver of globalization. Long-distance trade of salt, spices, and sugar are examples from earlier centuries. The partly colonialist-driven trade in agricultural raw materials in the late nineteenth and early twentieth centuries was a central force in that early globalization episode. Today globalization of the agrifood system has a very different nature: more pervasive and deeper, less driven by raw materials, more service- and technology-intensive, and more integral to economic and societal changes.

Figure 1.2 gives an aggregate perspective of the current global agrifood system. The world population of more than 6.5 billion is served by food retailers (as well as by the restaurant industry and home production, not depicted here); the food processing and trading industry supplies the retail sector while procuring from the farm sector, which in turn is supplied by agriculture input industries. Transactions and trade occur between all these segments, and each becomes more integrated at a global scale, with big players in each of the industries (see the top five in each of the segments listed in Figure 1.2).

The value-added by the farm production sector (that is, revenue minus intermediate costs, not including factors of production) amounted to some US$1,300 billion[6] worldwide in 2003, including both food and nonfood components. Total food commercial sales (a broader concept than value-added in the food sector, but which does not include farm consumption of food products), was estimated at about US$4,000 billion around the same time (Table 1.1; Euromonitor International 2003, cited in Regmi and Gehlhar 2005).

World food sales to final consumers are in turn divided between fresh foods (about US$910 billion) and processed foods (almost US$3,200 billion; Table 1.1 from Regmi and Gehlhar 2005). About 56 percent of these sales take place at retail stores, and the rest occur in food service outlets, such as restaurants and hotels. Although these estimates exclude consumption on farms themselves (which leaves out important segments of food sales in developing countries), they do provide an approximation of the significant size of the food market at the consumer level.

Figure 1.2   The global agrifood business chain, 2006

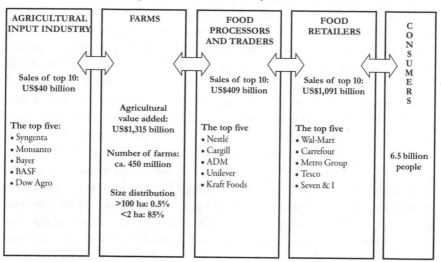

Source: von Braun (2005), updated.

Table 1.1   Global food sales (US$ billions)

Category	Retail stores	Food service	Total
Fresh food	531	382	913
Processed products	1,762	1,420	3,182
Packaged food	1,148	828	1,976
Beverages	614	592	1,206
Alcoholic drinks	316	422	729
Hot drinks	53	12	65
Soft drinks	245	167	412
Total food	2,293	1,803	4,096

Source: Euromonitor (2003), cited in Regmi and Gehlhar (2005).

The value of processed food sales is currently larger in industrialized countries (about 50–60 percent of total sales, but their population represents only 16 percent of the world total), but growth rates for food sales have been higher in middle-income countries (Regmi and Gehlhar 2005), a growth fueled by increased urbanization and rising incomes in developing regions. For instance, according to the projections of the International Food Policy Research Institute (IFPRI), by 2020, some 85 percent of the world increase in demand for cereals and meats will occur in developing countries (Rosegrant et al. 2001).

Global Trade in Agricultural Products

Table 1.2 shows the evolution of the globalization of agriculture (not the food system comprehensively), as represented by agricultural trade relative to domestic production, using the ratios of trade to agricultural production (import penetration ratio and export orientation ratio) for all agricultural products from 1961 to 2002 for different developing-country groupings.[7] Several points deserve mention. First, production for domestic use constitutes the largest component of agriculture in developing countries as a whole—that is, most of the agricultural production of developing countries is directed to their own markets. Overall, they export and import lower percentages of their production compared to industrialized countries (Díaz-Bonilla 2001).[8]

Second, the levels and trends of the import and export ratios for developing regions differ. Sub-Saharan Africa was the region with the highest initial export orientation during the 1960s but also had the deepest retraction from world export markets: the export orientation ratio stood in 2000–02 at less than half its initial value. The import penetration ratio, on the other hand, climbed from 8 percent at the beginning of the period to almost 14 percent in 2000–02. Asia has the lowest export and import ratios, and both have been trending upward very slowly until the 1980s; world integration has stopped or reversed (import penetration ratio) since then. The region consisting of Latin America and the Caribbean has become the most integrated region in world markets, surpassing Sub-Saharan Africa on both export and import ratios.

In summary, although agricultural integration in the world market (or "globalization") measured by these simple trade ratios appears to have increased for some regions and periods, the process has not been homogeneous across developing countries, with declines in international integration in some cases (such as export ratios in Sub-Saharan Africa for the whole period and imports ratios in Asia compared to the 1980s). Furthermore, local production for domestic utilization is still the dominant characteristic for the agricultural sector of developing countries as a whole. Although the above indicators show modest, rather than dramatic, changes in the integration of developing countries' agriculture in world markets, they may be too aggregated by country[9] and by product to properly assess the impact of globalization at the farm level.

Table 1.3 provides another angle to the issue of the globalization of agriculture by looking at disaggregates of export and import ratios for some of the main food products from all developing countries. Meat products, for which imports and exports represent only about 4 percent of production, appear less integrated with world markets than do cereals or, especially, vegetable oils.[10] In the case of meat and milk products, shelf life, sanitary measures, and trade protection tend to isolate domestic markets in many countries, making these products behave more like nontradables. Additionally, export ratios in meat and import ratios in milk products are currently below their peaks in the past. On the other hand, vegetable oils show a clear pattern of

Table 1.2   Agriculture trade (percent of production)

Region	1960s	1970s	1980s	1990s	2000–02
Export/production					
Latin America and the Caribbean	23.6	24.7	24.5	26.7	31.4
Sub-Saharan Africa[a]	28.5	23.0	17.2	15.3	13.2
Asia, developing	5.4	5.7	6.4	6.4	6.4
All three regions	12.1	11.8	11.3	11.0	11.6
Import/production					
Latin America and the Caribbean	6.7	8.6	11.2	14.0	15.7
Sub-Saharan Africa[a]	8.1	9.4	12.6	12.3	13.5
Asia, developing	7.1	7.7	9.2	8.9	8.8
All three regions	7.1	8.0	10.0	10.1	10.5

Source: Based on data from FAO (2006).
[a]Does not include South Africa.

Table 1.3   Developing countries' exports and imports over production (percent)

Category	1960s	1970s	1980s	1990s	2000–01
Meat					
Imports	1.4	2.4	4.1	4.1	5.4
Exports	4.9	4.6	3.8	3.7	4.4
Milk (no butter)					
Imports	7.7	11.1	15.1	11.5	10.2
Exports	0.3	0.6	0.5	1.2	1.9
Cereal					
Imports	9.3	10.5	14.2	14.7	17.3
Exports	4.7	4.0	4.3	4.7	6.1
Vegetable oil					
Imports	11.4	16.8	27.4	32.0	33.9
Exports	20.4	25.0	33.2	40.1	46.1

Source: Based on data from FAO (2006).

significant and increasing world integration. In general, world trade in processed and high-value goods expanded rapidly during the 1970s and 1980s but has somewhat stagnated since the mid-1990s, even though sales of processed food in domestic markets, both in industrialized and developing countries, has been growing strongly during the past few decades. Also, only 10 percent or so of the US$3,200 billion in sales of processed food products (representing about 78 percent of total world food sales) is traded, with the rest being produced locally, as is the case with agricultural products (Regmi and Gehlhar 2005).

All in all, these simple quantity indicators provide a more nuanced view about the extent and pace of globalization of agriculture in developing countries, which does not seem to support the common perception of dramatic across-the-board increases in world integration. However, the quantity indicators used above may not capture the extent of integration between domestic and world markets, which may be better assessed by price indicators (Knetter and Slaughter 1999). In comparing the relation between domestic and world prices, at least three issues can be distinguished (each one reflecting a progressively weaker criteria for integration with world markets, or globalization): the ratio of these prices, which is an indicator of protection and subsidization or taxation;[11] whether trends in domestic and world prices are correlated; and whether volatility of both types of prices is correlated. In most of these issues the evidence is inconclusive: although several studies show that for some countries and commodities there is greater integration with world markets in one or more of these dimensions, particularly after the policy reforms of the 1980s, the reverse can also be true, even in the same country but for different commodities (see, for example, Kherallah et al. 2000; Akiyama et al. 2003; Baffes and Gardner 2003; Rapsomanikis, Hallam, and Conforti 2003).

However, greater correlation between domestic and world prices (that is, increased globalization in some sense) may not say much about the effect on agricultural producers in developing countries of greater integration in global markets without looking at the evolution of world prices: the issue then may not be increased globalization per se, but the behavior of the world economy with which developing countries are integrating. In this regard it is important to note that since the second half of the 1980s, real world prices of agricultural products (deflated by the export unit values of industrialized countries; Figure 1.3) declined significantly (partly because of increases in subsidization and protection of agriculture in industrialized countries; see Díaz-Bonilla 2001 and Chapter 5).

World agricultural real prices have remained at a low plateau until recently, putting pressure on farmers worldwide, particularly those from nonsubsidizing countries. For instance, Akiyama et al. (2003) show that for several export commodities in Africa, the adjustments in agricultural and trade policies in the 1990s meant that producers were receiving a larger share of world prices than before (and in that sense producers were more integrated with world markets), but that net income at the producer level may not have improved because of, among other things, the decline in world prices.

So far we have looked at developments in world agricultural trade and prices to assess the extent and pace of the globalization of agriculture in developing countries. However, the process has to be considered in a broader perspective, looking at a host of global interactions with differentiated domestic implications to identify the far-reaching changes and influences on developing countries' agriculture.

Also, the past trends may not be a strong indicator of the future of agricultural globalization. New forces continuously come into play. For instance, the recent energy

Figure 1.3   World prices of agricultural products

Real world prices (index 2000 = 1)

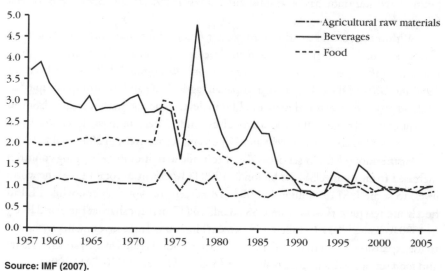

Source: IMF (2007).

price increases, which are leading to considerable interest and expansion of investments in biofuel production in many developing countries, are adding a new dimension to the globalization of agriculture through price effects. When more resources (land and water) are diverted to biofuel production, agricultural prices will be driven more by the performance of globally integrated energy sectors—with all their political and economic uncertainty. This example also shows the already strong role of integration through investment, in addition to trade, in world agriculture, a theme to which we turn next.

Financial Integration and FDI in the Agrifood Sector

The level of capital flows has increased significantly in the past decade, suggesting a greater integration in financial markets. In terms of the structure of capital flows, the largest increase has been in FDI and in portfolio investments, whereas bank lending has declined slightly (Prasad et al. 2003). Industrialized countries experienced the largest increase in their ratio of gross private capital flows to gross domestic product (GDP), from approximately 11 percent in 1990 to almost 26 percent in 2003. For developing countries as a whole, the increase was also substantial, from 6 percent in 1990 to 13 percent in 2003 (World Bank 2005; see also Chapter 8). However, this increase happened in cycles and was accompanied by increased volatility of capital flows to developing countries, generating a series of financial crises during the 1990s and early 2000s. The effects of these financial crises on world agricultural prices, competitiveness, and trade has been substantial (IMF 1999; USDA/ERS 2000; see also Chapter 8).

Within the general trend toward greater financial integration, FDI in the food and agricultural sector has increased in developing countries (including countries under the influence of the former Soviet Union): in nominal dollar value, between 1990 and 2004 FDI stock more than tripled in agriculture and roughly quadrupled in the food processing sector; the share of FDI in developing countries increased from 56 percent of world total FDI stock in agriculture and 13 percent in the food processing sector in 1990 to about 64 percent and 12 percent, respectively, in 2004 (Table 1.4).

Furthermore, FDI in services related to trade activities in developing countries increased from about US$23.4 billion in 1990 (11 percent of total FDI at the world level) to some US$190 billion in 2004 (18 percent of world share), while FDI in hotels and restaurants went from US$3.8 billion (17 percent share at the world level) in 1990 to some US$19.5 billion (24 percent) in 2004. These investments are linked to the expansion of international firms operating in food retail (mainly supermarkets) and food services (restaurants, mainly fast food, and hotels; UNCTAD 2006).

The globalization of food markets through FDI generates production and consumption dynamics that may lead to higher or lower globalization of trade, influencing the trade indicators discussed before in different directions. For instance, some characteristics of consumer-oriented FDI may seem to reduce globalization of agrifood systems from a trade standpoint, when—from the angle of FDI expansion—food firms are becoming more globalized. This divergence occurs because those firms must cater to local consumer needs, which in many cases requires sourcing products locally and/or maintaining specialized processing facilities that take into account local tastes, thus reducing (or at least not expanding) the value of trade flows (Regmi and Gehlhar 2005).

Another factor that shifts the composition of globalization from trade to foreign investment is tariff escalation (Yeats 1974; Lindland 1997; OECD 1997).[12] The practice of imposing high import taxes on processed goods and low or no tariffs on primary products (thus granting higher effective rates of protection to their own value-added) reduces significantly the processing margin of the primary producers, placing agro-industrial production at a considerable disadvantage and strongly tilting the export profile toward raw materials (Balassa and Michalopoulos 1986). This practice shifts processing investments toward the country that has demand for the processed product, leading to trade in lower value raw materials, while the higher value processed items[13] are produced locally. In terms of value, this shift may generate less trade.

Table 1.4   Foreign direct investment stock in the food and agricultural sectors, 1990 and 2004

Sector	1990			2004			
	Industrialized countries	Developing countries	World	Industrialized countries	Developing countries	South-East Europe and Commonwealth of Independent States	World
Agriculture, hunting, forestry, and fishing (US$ millions)	3,193	4,063	7,256	7,739	14,339	483	22,561
Food, beverages, and tobacco (US$ millions)	64,427	9,612	74,039	238,066	33,337	6,948	278,351
Agriculture, hunting, forestry, and fishing (percent of world)	44	56	100	34	64	2	100
Food, beverages, and tobacco (percent of world)	87	13	100	86	12	2	100

Source: Based on data from UNCTAD (2006).

Yet another trend to be considered is the expansion of food sales and services linked to hotels and restaurants and to the increased presence of supermarkets in developing countries. In this volume, Reardon and Timmer (Chapter 6) explain the explosive expansion of supermarkets in the early to mid-1990s in middle-income countries in South America and East Asia (what they call the "first wave"), where the average share of supermarkets in food retail went from roughly only 10–20 percent at the beginning of the 1990s to 50–60 percent by early in this decade. The point considered here is that retailers and food services add value to food through economic activities that, by their own nature, are nontradable. It may, however, lead to more trade in some commodities, such as fresh fruits and vegetables, when supermarkets put together a year-round supply chain.

In summary, the expansion of FDI in the agrifood system may not necessarily lead to a large expansion of trade—rather, the opposite may be the case. Therefore, the trends in quantitative indicators of trade discussed in the previous section may not detect the main channels through which globalization affects the agrifood system in developing countries. In fact, Reardon and Timmer (Chapter 6) argue that trade liberalization has not been the only factor, and probably not even the most important one, by which globalization has changed agrifood systems in developing countries since the 1990s. Instead they see fundamental restructurings of domestic food markets that were linked to changes in the processing, retail, and food service segments. These changes were in turn influenced by an increase in FDI in upstream markets, when financial markets were liberalized in many developing countries during the 1990s.

Agricultural Performance in Developing Countries during Globalization

In view of all these changes during globalization, how did agriculture perform? The agricultural performance of developing countries is uneven across regions and decades (Table 1.5). Sub-Saharan Africa had high total growth rates in the 1960s, which declined significantly in the 1970s and recovered during the 1980s and 1990s—only to drop again in the early 2000s. Asia has maintained higher total growth rates, but they declined in South Asia during 2000–04, pulling averages down. Latin America and the Caribbean has sustained total growth rates at around 3 percent except during the 1980s. Agriculture in transition economies collapsed in the 1990s during the transformation of the planned economies of the former Soviet Union and Eastern Europe. The movements in per capita agricultural rates reflect the declines in population growth in developing countries.

The simple presentation of growth statistics does not, of course, capture causality regarding the role of globalization. Many factors of political and economic changes

Table 1.5   Agricultural and food production growth, total and per capita, 1960s to 2004
(percent per year)

	1960s	1970s	1980s	1990s	2000–04	1962–79	1980–2004
Total							
Africa, developing	3.4	1.2	2.9	3.4	1.5	2.2	2.9
Sub-Saharan Africa	3.3	1.1	2.9	3.3	1.4	2.1	2.8
Asia, developing	3.0	3.1	4.1	4.1	2.9	3.1	3.9
East and Southeast Asia	3.1	3.8	3.4	2.7	3.0	3.5	3.1
South Asia	2.1	2.4	3.9	3.0	1.3	2.3	3.1
China	4.1	3.5	4.8	5.7	4.1	3.7	4.9
Latin America and the Caribbean	3.1	3.1	2.7	3.1	3.0	3.1	2.8
Transition markets	2.5	1.9	1.1	–3.9	2.6	2.2	–0.5
Developing countries	3.1	2.8	3.7	3.8	2.8	2.9	3.5
Industrialized countries	2.2	2.2	0.6	0.0	0.9	2.2	0.6
Per capita							
Africa, developing	0.8	–1.5	0.0	0.9	–0.8	–0.5	0.2
Sub-Saharan Africa	0.7	–1.7	–0.1	0.6	–1.1	–0.6	0.0
Asia, developing	0.6	0.9	2.1	2.5	1.6	0.8	2.1
East and Southeast Asia	0.6	1.5	1.4	1.0	1.6	1.1	1.3
South Asia	–0.2	0.1	1.6	1.0	–0.4	0.0	1.1
China	1.6	1.5	3.3	4.5	3.4	1.5	3.7
Latin America and the Caribbean	0.4	0.6	0.6	1.4	1.5	0.5	1.0
Transition markets	1.4	1.0	0.3	–4.0	2.8	1.2	–0.8
Developing countries	0.6	0.5	1.5	2.0	1.2	0.6	1.7
Industrialized countries	1.1	1.3	–0.2	–0.5	0.6	1.2	0.0

Source: FAO (2006).

that influenced agricultural growth were at work in the different world regions during these decades. However, a few observations based on these figures may be useful. First, since the 1980s (which many consider the period of increased globalization), agriculture grew faster in developing countries compared to the average of the 1960s and 1970s, both in the aggregate (3.5 versus 2.9 percent) and per capita (1.7 versus 0.6 percent; see the last two columns in Table 1.5). Second, growth of agricultural production in developing countries since the 1980s also surpassed that in industrialized ones, both in the aggregate (3.5 versus 0.6 percent) and per capita (1.7 versus 0.0 percent; see the last column in Table 1.5). Third, looking at individual regions, agricultural growth per capita also accelerated in all developing-country regions during 1980–2004 compared to 1962–79 (on average); the picture is mixed for per capita growth rates when 1962–79 is compared to 2000–04 (compare the bottom and top halves of Table 1.5). These trends do not seem to indicate that the developing countries have been, in general, "losers" of the globalization of agriculture, if the years since the 1980s as a whole are considered as the reference period. However, it is also clear that there was some deceleration in the first half of the 2000s. The more challenging questions are whether the changes in agricultural growth were actually related to globalization and whether such agricultural growth has been pro-poor. The next sections look at links among globalization, agriculture, and poverty in greater detail, drawing mainly from the rest of the chapters in this book.

Implications of the Globalized Agrifood System for Development and Poverty

As a result of the globalization processes, the world food system has experienced significant transformations since the 1980s. These changes can be summarized as follows:

- Innovation has accelerated, with the private sector and civil society becoming more engaged in agricultural research and development (R&D), which in turn has induced fundamental changes in the global innovation system.

- Small farmers are being immersed in more commercialized agrifood systems nationally and globally.

- Markets and retail industries are displaying important changes in trade and are defining the emergence and evolution of a global agrifood chain.

- Consumers in industrialized and developing countries are becoming a driving force for changes in the global food system, beyond their domestic markets.

This section reviews each of these major changes and gives a preview of the related chapters that address these developments and their implications. Moreover, policies and institutions are evolving at global and domestic levels and a large number of new players are shaping the globalization process of agrifood systems, and that evolution is described, too. Chapter 2 provides details on globalization–poverty linkages using a conceptual framework that traces drivers of globalization via domestic policy, institutional and market responses to community, and household poverty outcomes.

A Changing Environment for Innovation and Information

Agricultural R&D in the past has been essential to enhancing agricultural productivity, ensuring food security, and advancing economic growth in many developing countries. For instance, technological progress achieved during the Green Revolution enabled the development of high-yielding crop varieties, which in turn brought about direct benefits to consumers in the form of lower food prices and indirect benefits to landless farmers in the form of increased employment opportunities (Chapter 3). More recently, the agrifood system has become increasingly science-driven, and research and innovation have become even more vital for productivity increases along the whole food chain. The agricultural research environment has also experienced considerable change in recent decades. Chapter 3 and Essay 1 review these changes and explore the implications for poverty reduction and food security.

Pinstrup-Andersen and Mengistu (Chapter 3) highlight three trends. The first two—the growing level of involvement of the private sector in industrialized nations in agricultural R&D and the increasingly proprietary and competitive research environment—are driven by the introduction of intellectual property rights (IPR) protection for plant varieties and biotechnology products. The third trend is the slowing down of public-sector research expenditure in both developed and developing countries.

The main argument behind the extension of IPRs to plant varieties is to provide an incentive for the private sector to invest in agricultural R&D: if private firms are given exclusive rights to their innovations for a limited time, it would enable them to recover their R&D investment costs and to generate profits in the short-run. This recoupment should in turn encourage more spending on R&D that would, in the long run, be beneficial to society as a whole. The WTO's Trade-Related Aspects of Intellectual Property Rights (TRIPS) agreement, which requires that each member country of the WTO give "minimum levels of protection" to other members' intellectual property, further extends these exclusive rights across the globe, giving companies even more incentive to innovate.

However, this rationale has been subject to intense debate. At the most basic level, IPRs have been criticized as constraining the amount of innovation, because the potential of extracting profits induces firms to concentrate on filing for new patents on minor improvements to previous innovations, to the detriment of sharing and applying significant new innovations. Additionally, as the drive toward patenting each step of the innovation process intensifies, the free flow of information among researchers, which is essential to new innovations (as the latter often advance or improve on existing ones), is being curtailed. Moreover, as the number of patents accorded multiplies, the IPR system is becoming more sophisticated and costly, concentrating patents in a few large global firms and making them inaccessible to parties that do not have the know-how and resources to file for new patents and enforce their IPR (Macdonald 2001). On the global level, there is some contention that TRIPS may be highly unjust, as developed countries, where the majority of patents are awarded, historically did not abide by any type of global IPR protection when they began industrializing (Drahos and Mayne 2002).

The risk here is that this trend could not only increase corporate control over seed production and distribution, potentially creating monopolistic market structures (Boyle 2003), but also, in the context of falling public investment in agricultural R&D in developing countries, may increase the already large knowledge gap between industrialized and developing countries (Chapter 3). A related risk is that because of the shift of industrialized-country consumers on food safety and environmental issues, agricultural R&D in industrialized countries is tackling these topics, meaning that the larger part of agricultural R&D may become less pertinent to the requirements of developing countries. Pinstrup-Andersen and Mengistu (Chapter 3) emphasize the need to revisit international research priorities and implement participatory approaches to research, involving national, regional, and international research institutions as well as the private sector and farmers themselves.

In Essay 1, Swaminathan discusses the agricultural research environment in the context of the rules that govern intellectual property. He calls for the revision of TRIPS to be compatible with the equity and ethics provisions of the Convention on Biological Diversity and the International Treaty on Plant Genetic Resources for Food and Agriculture. More specifically, he calls for compulsory licensing of rights for inventions of great importance to food and health security, and for benefit sharing with the primary conservators of genetic resources and holders of traditional knowledge. He also proposes the establishment of an International Patents Bank for Poverty Eradication and Sustainable Development within the United Nations, which would encourage scientists all over the world to share their inventions by registering their patents there to make them available for the public good. Another proposed solution to the increasing knowledge gap between developed and developing countries may be differentiated IPR rules within the WTO, at least in the short-to-medium run, to allow developing countries to set up the legal infrastructure needed to implement well-functioning IPR systems (Essay 3). In particular, Ahluwalia, in Essay 3, makes the case for the revision of TRIPS to provide more flexibility for developing countries coping with public health emergencies.

The global market integration processes discussed earlier would be impossible without the revolution in information and communication technologies (ICTs). Indeed, as summarized by Muhammad Yunus (2006, xix), ICT "connects everybody and everything at a very basic level, and it is borderless, timeless, and best of all, almost costless. With all these attributes combined, ICT has enormous potential to create a new human society, and a new civilization." In the next chapter, von Braun looks at how advancements in ICTs have shaped the globalization of agrifood systems, focusing particularly on the effects on poor rural households. Many of the national telecommunications monopolies in developing countries were privatized in the 1980s and 1990s, introducing them to competition, and this stimulus, combined with ongoing technological change, prompted the development of new services in some developing countries, manifested especially in the exponential increase of cellular telephone penetration in poor countries. But this increase has not occurred in all countries; in some, the stimulus is taking effect slowly and erratically. Within countries, the inequality is even greater. Von Braun finds that even though access is still very restricted in rural areas, ICTs have had an important positive effect on rural households. Indeed, the potential benefits of ICTs include:

- economies of scale that stimulate network building and consequent spillover benefits;

- greater inclusion of individuals within networks and, even more important, increased diversity of participants by overcoming the barriers of physical distance and social standing; and

- facilitation of faster, more efficient, and ultimately better decisionmaking in all fields of endeavor, especially the integration of markets through interactive communication unhindered by distance, volume, medium, or time.

Von Braun stresses that access to information through ICTs is a question not only of connectivity but also of capability to use the new tools and relevant content provided in accessible and useful forms (Torero and von Braun 2006). Connectivity has been a priority, as a prerequisite for capability and content, but given the speed at which technologies can evolve—unconstrained by overly restrictive licenses and global patenting—costs could fall significantly, facilitating adoption. He concludes that policymakers should not overlook the need for all three "Cs" (connectivity, capabilities, and content) to progress in tandem.

Increasing Commercialization of Small Producers

Technological progress, improvements in infrastructure, and the creation of markets are facilitating the commercialization of traditional agriculture. In addition, demographic changes, such as population growth and increasing urbanization, are contributing to further commercialization (von Braun and Kennedy 1995).

In Chapter 4, Narayanan and Gulati look at the effect of globalization and more specifically the commercialization of agrifood systems on smallholders. They note that there are significant differences in the level of integration of smallholders across regions and that the effects vary. They argue that globalization, and trade liberalization in particular, could adversely affect smallholders who are net sellers of food in inefficient sectors (or in sectors where a country does not have a competitive advantage, given the trade environment and other nonprice factors). Net buyers of food working in efficient sectors in exporting countries may also face adverse circumstances if food prices go up. These smallholders can shift to other crops or livestock activities, or look for jobs elsewhere, even leaving agriculture. For instance, smallholders who have been able to successfully switch their production to high-value agriculture have gained from globalization. However, alternative choices outside of agriculture may not always be available, while deteriorating environmental conditions and low productivity gains in some resource-poor regions offer few options to shift cropping patterns.

Narayanan and Gulati observe that the winners have been smallholders who have either vertically integrated with agribusinesses (exporters or otherwise) or have devised institutional innovations (such as cooperatives or farmer companies) for collective action. Thus, it seems that greater vertical coordination with agroindustry (which can be enhanced through cooperatives, contract farming, and/or clustering) facilitates participation of small farmers in the growing processed-food trade, particularly in meeting food safety and quality standards. Also, smallholders who had access to better physical infrastructure and credit and/or those who have benefited from capacity-building activities by the public sector, private industry, or international cooperation managed to integrate successfully. Conversely, those who have failed to capitalize on the opportunities opened up by globalization or have been adversely affected were farmers who were poorly endowed in terms of natural resources, assets, and infrastructure. They lack access to markets for output, input, and land, as well as credit and insurance, and they have limited alternatives for off-farm employment, including agroindustries or other activities, in rural and urban areas. The authors note that conditions regarding these variables differ across developing regions, with Africa suffering from serious structural and institutional constraints.

Another issue that Narayanan and Gulati highlight is that in large parts of the developing world, especially Asia and Africa, average farm size decreased further in the past two decades (with average farm size in both regions reduced to about 1.5 hectares). This reduction poses a growing challenge for connecting farms to the processing and retail industries, both of which show the opposite trend of increasing size. Moreover, the growing scale of operations and recent trends in mergers both globally and nationally have drawn attention to problems with monopolistic competition all along the agrifood chain. The authors suggest that in this context, domestic policy and legislation (such as antitrust laws) may have to be established to govern monopolistic structures (see also Essay 2), while making sure that these instruments do not constrain the growth of the agribusiness sector in developing countries. And, as developing-country governments may not have the resources to invest in the required infrastructure, institutions, and capacity-building programs to facilitate smallholders' access to markets, industrialized countries can play a role by providing financial and technical support for these endeavors.

Changes in Trade and Domestic Markets: Toward a Global Agrifood Business Chain

The evolution of world and domestic food markets has important effects on growth, rural development, and poverty alleviation in developing countries. Trade and agricultural policies, which are influenced by multilateral, regional, and bilateral agreement, provide a general framework for the operation of those markets. The negotiations within WTO and a variety of regional trade agreements are redefining the parameters for trade and agricultural policies. In addition to these public-sector rules, trade patterns and the possibility of rural development and poverty alleviation will also be influenced by changes in the private rules (such as quality standards) that shape the operation of markets. Watkins (Chapter 5), Murphy (Essay 2), and Reardon and Timmer (Chapter 6) address these different aspects of public-policy and private-market changes.

Watkins discusses the agricultural trade and domestic farm policies of industrialized countries and their adverse effects on developing ones and on poor rural households (these are also mentioned in several other chapters). He notes that the United States and the European Union dominate global markets for a wide range of commodities, such as meat, dairy, sugar, and cereals, which they also subsidize or protect heavily. He argues that the subsidies and protection, besides benefiting mostly a small percentage of farmers who are already relatively rich while hurting small farmers and the environment in industrialized countries, have important negative implications for developing countries. Indeed, subsidies and protection artificially depress world prices for staple food producers and may drive them out of their own domestic markets, undermining incentives for agricultural investment, creating additional employment problems in rural areas, and promoting dependence on imports (with food imports representing significant foreign exchange costs in many low-income countries). And, according to Watkins, the potential welfare gains for consumers from lower prices, when viewed in a broader context of poverty reduction, may not compensate for the negative effects. Further, as a result of these industrialized-country practices that insulate their producers from world market trends, world prices may become more volatile. Finally, these practices also restrict market access for exports, denying opportunities for poverty reduction in developing countries by limiting opportunities for livelihood diversification and reducing incentives for investment in developing countries. The points highlighted by Watkins in his criticisms of industrialized countries' agricultural policies are crucial and have been ignored by some studies (see, for instance, Panagariya 2004), which argue that they benefit some poor countries as consumers. These studies often tend to take short-term and static views of the effects of such policies (see a more detailed discussion in Díaz-Bonilla, Frandsen, and Robinson 2006).

Watkins also warns about redefinition of subsidies that maintain substantial support for agriculture in rich countries. In particular, he criticizes so-called decoupled payments that are not truly trade neutral, to the extent that they provide liquidity that can be utilized to finance investments that increase production and shield farmers against risk, which also supports investment and production. Therefore, Watkins argues that their exclusion from future WTO disciplines may negatively affect developing countries. He calls for the progressive elimination of direct and indirect export subsidies in industrialized countries (such as the implicit subsidies and nominally decoupled support measures for production levels that exceed domestic demand).

He also recommends the recognition of the special status of developing countries, and, where necessary, he argues that they should be allowed to protect their food systems through tariffs and quotas for purposes of rural poverty reduction and food security, even when all market distortions caused by developed-country subsidies are removed. He suggests two ways of building these provisions into the world trade system rules within the WTO; either introducing a "development box," under which food security would take priority over liberalization commitments, or a special safeguards provision, to be used in the case of market shocks, such as a fall in import prices or a surge in imports. Although some of these measures may be needed to shield vulnerable subsistence farmers from catastrophic shocks, other studies have cautioned that they need to be carefully designed to avoid becoming protectionist devices that ultimately hurt the poor (to the extent that protection is mostly a privately collected tax on food). Usually, protecting the income of the poor rather than protecting a crop is better for poverty reduction and equity (see Díaz-Bonilla, Diao, and Robinson 2006).

Murphy (Essay 2) highlights the noncompetitive nature of world and domestic markets as the main basis for her conclusions about the negative effects of current agricultural trade rules (specifically, the Agreement on Agriculture [AoA] of the WTO) on developing countries and the poor. Murphy suggests that the problem with the AoA goes beyond the lack of political will to implement the agreement or the capacity of rich countries to create exceptions to the rules for themselves. She believes that even if industrialized countries ended direct export subsidies and ceased all payments to farmers, and if all countries established duty-free market access for all agricultural products, food security or decent livelihoods for those depending on agriculture would not be ensured. This failure is because (1) the AoA does not take into account that food is a basic human need and right, (2) market distortions persist in many countries, and (3) horizontal and vertical integration of the agrifood system is making the system less competitive.

To correct for the distortions in world trade, Murphy proposes the creation of a multilateral working group to discuss competition issues specifically related to international agricultural trade. She also highlights the need to document transnational agribusiness to better understand its global market reach, and to continuously evaluate the sources of market distortion, whether public or private, including the selling in world markets at prices below the cost of production prices (plus a reasonable profit). This discussion raises implicitly the issue of appropriate organizational arrangements for competition policies, such as forming a global agency or strengthening formal networks of national competition and antitrust agencies. Efficient functioning of the global agrifood system may well need such a policy framework in the future.

Murphy and Watkins focus their discussions on the public rules of world agricultural trade system and its uncompetitive nature, but Reardon and Timmer point out in Chapter 6 that although public attention is focused on public standards and market policies (such as those of the WTO), there has been a rapid rise in private standards that have reshaped markets in developing countries. In particular, Reardon and Timmer look at what they call the "supermarket revolution." The transformation of the retail sector, with multinational corporations as its key players, has important implications for consumers and farmers in developing countries. The authors find that consumers across the globe have benefited from the highly competitive supermarket supply chain. Indeed, multinational corporations have used their market power to drive down costs and, because the whole system appears competitive (or at least contestable), they have transmitted the savings to consumers through lower prices while supplying higher quality goods. However, these competitive pressures have resulted in increased pressure for farm producers to supply larger volumes of higher quality goods at lower prices. Nonetheless, this pressure has not meant the widespread exclusion of small farmers. Chapter 6 cites studies showing that, under certain circumstances, small farmers are well represented in procurement systems of large-scale agroprocessors and supermarket chains, particularly in fresh food items, such as fruit and vegetables, although they tend to operate at higher levels of physical, human, and organizational capital within that group (see also Chapter 4).

Reardon and Timmer also note that the rise of supermarkets, which took decades in industrialized countries, has occurred much faster in developing countries, making the adjustment pressures for farmers, processors, wholesalers, and traditional small-

scale retailers more severe. It has been a transformation led by multinational corporations, including global retailers and food manufacturers, which are increasingly dominant in the global food supply chain. Echoing in part the issue of imperfect markets
mentioned by Murphy, Reardon and Timmer highlight the need to pay attention to
the relative power of price determination between supermarkets and processors and
to explore price formation in oligopsonistic or oligopolistic settings.

Reardon and Timmer highlight that instigating market-oriented development
assistance programs now means dealing with multinational companies. Thus, they
urge the development community to reorient development programs and researchers to this fundamentally different reality. More specifically, although supporting
export markets remains a key policy objective, focusing development programs on
supermarkets is becoming increasingly vital, as in many cases the "supermarket market" is growing much faster than the export market. In fact they note that according
to some calculations, supermarkets in Latin America buy 2.5 times more fruits and
vegetables from local producers than do all exporters of produce in that region.
However, they warn that structuring development programs in this way to help
small farmers would not be easy because of the variety of circumstances in the
development world.

Consumer-Driven Agrifood Systems

The global change in agrifood systems was until recently largely driven by middle- to
high-income consumers in high-income countries, but in recent years consumers in
low-income countries have joined the driving forces of change. With rising incomes,
along with the greater availability of a variety of foods, consumers in high-income
countries have increasingly become specific in their demands for higher quality and
safety of food products, and they are also increasingly concerned about other attributes, such as animal welfare and the long-term environmental effects of current food
production processes. Greater food safety concerns in industrialized countries, in the
wake of animal health problems, such as mad cow disease and avian bird flu, have also
played a role, as have the risk perceptions around genetically modified organisms.
Such concerns are leading to more demands for publicly mandated or privately supplied labeling and to a greater emphasis on quality control and assurance schemes,
with requirements for traceability. Generally, the growing consumer influence in the
agrifood chain has led to the reorganization of food chains, including supermarkets
and agroprocessors, with the power shifting to the consumer, as discussed by Reardon
and Timmer in Chapter 6. More specifically, producers are going beyond their traditional focus on increasing output through productivity and efficiency gains to respond
to these consumer needs by implementing, monitoring, and enforcing production
methods to ensure food quality and safety, leading to standards stricter than legal ones

Figure 1.4   Consumer-driven agrifood systems

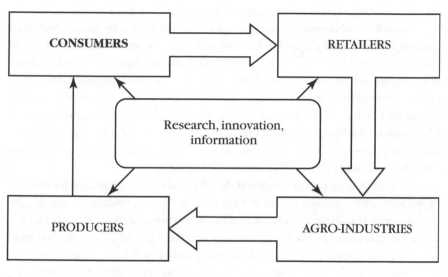

Source: von Braun and Mengistu (2004).

(Variyam and Golan 2002; Lang 2004). Narayanan and Gulati in Chapter 4 analyze the challenges these developments present for small farmers in developing countries.

Additionally, producers are trying to address consumer demands through investments in technological innovations, making all elements of the consumer-driven agrifood system increasingly affected by innovation (Figure 1.4). This trend, along with its implications for the poor in developing countries, is explored in more detail by Pinstrup-Andersen and Mengistu in Chapter 3.

There may also be pressures to move in the opposite direction, with the globalization of food markets shaping consumers' habits in developing countries. In Chapter 7, Hawkes looks at these linkages and discusses the implications for health and nutrition. While others have maintained that the increased differentiation brought about by globalization promotes good diet quality through greater diversity and perhaps lower prices, she argues that the process has led to a bifurcation of consumption habits, where poor diets among low-income groups predominate (based on mass consumption of low-quality vegetable oils, fats, and sweeteners), but a small niche market of healthy food products exists. In her view, this nutrition transition in developing countries is leading to low-quality diets associated with rising rates of obesity and diet-related chronic diseases, such as heart disease (more people now die of heart disease in developing countries than in industrialized ones), diabetes, and some cancers.

Low-quality diets are also associated with undernutrition in the form of micronutrient deficiency, which in turn lowers immunity to infectious diseases.

According to Hawkes, the changes in diets are influenced by globalization both through the associated changes in incomes and lifestyles and through alterations of the nature of agrifood systems, which modify the quantity, type, cost, and desirability of foods available for consumption. She looks at three cases that highlight channels of influence linked to global trade (liberalization of markets for vegetable oils in Brazil, China, and India), FDI (financial liberalization and U.S. agrifood investments in Mexico under the North American Free Trade Agreement [NAFTA]), and advertisement and promotion (increased consumption of oils, meats, and sweeteners along with the creation of niche health markets in Thailand).

She finds reasons for concern about the effects of market integration for the diets of the poor, although recognizing that the links between globalization and diet are complex, and that there are positive and negative implications for diet change. She also notes that although the mechanisms are operating globally, their effects depend on the specific contexts: the same globalization processes will have different outcomes for people at risk from undernutrition relative to those at risk from overnutrition, for urban compared to rural populations, and for the poor relative to the rich. Additionally, she suggests that normal business practices fostered by national and global market liberalization policies could be facilitating the uneven development of dietary habits. She highlights the risk that poor consumers are more susceptible to adopting unhealthy diets relative to wealthier consumers, who are better educated and have access to more resources and information. She therefore argues for upstream changes in the global marketplace, aimed at widespread improvement in diet quality, which would require stronger policy responses than just consumer-oriented policy options (such as education and nutrition labeling) and that also go beyond the health food sector. She points to the need for cross-sectoral response within a broader set of policy arenas involving all relevant disciplines.

Evolving National and International Policies and Institutions

In the previous section we discussed different issues, following the sequence of agrifood production, processing, marketing, and consumption, as in Figure 1.1. Here we move to the more general policies and context for the agrifood system. Such context is complex:

- The shaping of international policy is increasingly polycentric, involving more than just governments of developing countries on the one hand and multilateral and bilateral donors on the other. International institutional arrangements for the management of public goods (rights and natural resources), for IPR, and for trade have an increased prominence.

- Formal and informal networks, such as civil society organizations (which include such positive agents as credit cooperatives), parliamentary groups, social institutions, global virtual networks and forums, and anticorruption networks play an increasingly important role.

- Transnational corporations and institutional capital investors are extending their influence around the world through worldwide strategies for production, investment, and marketing.

The interactions among these actors may determine the need for regulations at the global level (such as the missing international competition policy), national levels (for instance, the management of short-term capital flows), or local levels (protection of cultural assets). They also affect the role of the state and the international community in supplying public goods, including those that are particularly significant for food security (such as infrastructure, agricultural research, education, social security programs, rule of law, and peace). Both of these sets of feedbacks often find small farmers and the rural poor in a weakened political position. But there are also opportunities that may arise from an increased freedom to operate, as market-oriented forces open up political space. Many more countries have meaningful political participation and democratic elections at the central and local level than in the 1960s and 1980s (see Chapter 8). For those individuals engaged in agrifood systems and the farming sector, elections at a decentralized level may be more relevant than central government elections in view of the special nature of agriculture. Decentralization and democratization, including of rural populations, have paralleled globalization.

These complex interactions are addressed in this section—particularly whether globalization has affected governance at the national level and whether it has affected the likelihood of conflicts. In addition, because the net effect of globalization trends on the poor depends on a variety of political, economic, and social factors specific to the circumstances of each country, the role and responsibility of national governments in ensuring food security and fostering pro-poor growth are discussed.

General Macroeconomic and Development Policies

Adequate development and macroeconomic policies at the national level, along with pro-poor policies at the international level, are also crucial to ensure that globalization helps the poor. Aziz (Essay 4) and Ahluwalia (Essay 3) debate the problems of the international trade and financial environment and discuss different domestic macroeconomic and development policies, emphasizing the need to balance the forces of globalization to include the poor.

In Essay 4, Aziz focuses his attention mainly on the international arena. He finds that the present trading and financial systems do not provide a level playing field for developing countries and poor people; aid flows and debt relief are not only inadequate but also poorly targeted to address poverty problems, and the policy prescriptions of multilateral institutions are generally inappropriate. Industrialized countries, which encourage the international financial institutions to put pressure on developing countries to pursue certain economic policies, do not practice what they preach (as in the case of protectionism in agriculture and textiles). He also condemns the disingenuous approach of industrialized countries that have created laws and institutions to address the inherent inadequacies in their domestic market (for example, laws against monopolies, taxation and social security to protect the weak and assist the poor), but at the global level, refuse to recognize that developing countries need similar compensating mechanisms and polices. Aziz calls for recognition of the role of governments: even accepting the superiority of the market system in determining resource allocation and prices, the state must play a significant role in protecting the rights and supplying the needs of the weaker and poorer segments of the population.

Aziz highlights the weakness of the Bretton Woods institutions (the International Monetary Fund [IMF] and the World Bank), particularly in the case of poverty reduction strategies that are being adopted by developing countries under their guidance. These strategies are not enough, as they focus primarily on stabilization policies (accompanied by social safety nets or targeted interventions to counter any negative fallout from these strategies on the poor) in the expectation that lower budget deficits and inflation will automatically lead to higher investment and growth. Aziz urges the international economic institutions to modify their free-market philosophies, which impose a standardized policy to achieve macroeconomic stability by reducing government spending, raising utility charges, and eliminating all subsidies. According to him, this policy results in a degree of economic liberalization in trade and financial sectors that is inconsistent with the institutions and regulatory mechanisms of the country concerned, thereby imposing heavy economic and social costs. He suggests that the focus should rather be directly on improving the incomes of the poor through mainstream interventions in the growth process and through policies that benefit the poor substantially rather than marginally—for instance, by focusing on sectors in which the poor earn their livelihoods (such as agriculture, small-scale irrigation, and livestock) and by relying on those factors of production they possess.

Ahluwalia, in Essay 3, looks mainly at domestic macroeconomic and development policies. She argues, on a somewhat different note from Aziz, that policymakers in developing countries have to prepare their economies to compete in the global marketplace. This process, according to her, often requires market-oriented reforms, sound macroeconomic policies, and—at the same time—adequate safety nets for those who are adversely affected, particularly the poor. She emphasizes the need for the public sector to focus on improvements in economic and political governance, resource mobilization, human capital accumulation, empowerment of the poor, and creation of an investment climate in which the private sector can help generate higher growth. Reforms in infrastructure and the financial sector are especially important for building a healthy investment climate for growth, as are policies and institutions that encourage R&D. At the macroeconomic level, it is important to have realistic tax rates, a very good tax administration, and an emphasis on quality for government expenditures, coupled with monetary policies that make sure that the gains in competitiveness attained through policy reforms are not eroded by high inflation rates.

Ahluwalia urges a greater engagement in international trade and trade negotiations, but cautions about a hasty or badly sequenced opening of the capital account. She adds that developing-country governments need to cut unproductive and wasteful expenditure, and concentrate on quality, which entails improving delivery of public goods and services.

In terms of the role and responsibilities of the international community, Aziz argues for the need to implement many ideas for innovative sources of financing development that have been under discussion for a long time (such as the proposal for a carbon tax on petroleum consumption, some form of the Tobin tax, and the idea of generating revenues from global commons like seabed mineral and fishing rights). Ahluwalia recognizes the need for increased aid but also urges industrialized countries to open up their trade barriers to developing countries, so as to enable them to fully exploit the new opportunities offered by globalization.

Roles and Responsibility of National Governments in Ensuring Food Security

Paarlberg (Essay 5) discusses further the general governance and policy conditions at the national level. He argues that the causes of poverty and food insecurity are highly localized. Because the causes of poverty and hunger are local rather than global, he argues that national governments have the chief responsibility for combating hunger and poverty. He considers that the greatest governance deficits are still found at the level of the nation-state: in countries where national governments have performed well in the developing world, hunger has been reduced significantly; in those with serious hunger problems, improving governance at the national level should be now the highest priority. Paarlberg argues that although democracy helps, good governance must also be measured at a more basic level: whether a government is providing basic public goods (such as internal peace, rule of law, and public investment in infrastructure and research) to all of its citizens, including those in rural areas. International organizations and donor countries should do more to help governments in poor countries finance rural roads, health and education services, and public agricultural research. He finds these investments much more important than concentrating on loans to governments in return for promises of market-oriented policy reforms. What is important is assistance for more tangible investments in doctors, clinics, teachers, schools, scientists, laboratories, irrigation maintenance, electricity, and roads.

He concludes that the localized causes of hunger are not linked in any convincing way to globalization: those countries that are most food insecure (located mainly in South Asia and Sub-Saharan Africa) still feature relatively weak connections to the international markets and private investment flows that define modern globalization. In his view the effect of globalization on food security is positive but is fairly weak, and globalization is not likely by itself to end hunger: he notes that if a poor country with high rates of illiteracy and disease, inadequate railroads, a high incidence of ethnic conflict, unstable government, and no rule of law decides to open its borders to trade and foreign direct investment, the results will be disappointing. Paarlberg considers that for poverty alleviation and food security it is better to modify the motto "think globally and then act locally" to "think locally and then act nationally."

Considering possible interventions by the international community, Paarlberg makes two main points. First, he notes that international laws and norms on state sovereignty have traditionally restricted external intervention in the domestic affairs of other states, even when those states fail to provide their own citizens with basic public goods (which reinforces his conclusion that good governance at the national level is of paramount importance if a country is to achieve food security and poverty reduction). Second, Paarlberg contends that, although improved governance at the global level is often called for, there are solid organizations operating at that level—for instance, the famine early warning and emergency food-aid system (through the World Food Programme) and international agricultural research (through the Consultative Group on International Agricultural Research [CGIAR]). He nevertheless suggests that international organizations and donor countries should do more to help governments in poor countries finance rural roads, health and education services, and public agricultural research.

These policy and institutional suggestions, as well as those mentioned in other chapters, raise a number of questions about the role of national governments and their room for maneuver under globalization. This topic is discussed next.

Governance of Food and Agriculture under Globalization

Some analysts ask whether nation-states may be losing relevance as policy and institutional centers for the advancement of their citizens' welfare, as a result of globalization. In Chapter 8, Díaz-Bonilla reviews some of the discussions of how globalization may be shaping the way governments design and implement policies and the possible effects on the agricultural sector and the poor. He looks at the effects of globalization on two dimensions of governance: first, on government's responsiveness to the needs of the people; and second, on government's effectiveness in the design and implementation of policies and programs, particularly those in support of rural and agricultural development.

The first aspect (responsiveness) is linked to institutional improvements, such as the advance of democracy, transparency, and the rule of law. Díaz-Bonilla shows data that document the advance of democracy in developing countries, particularly since the 1980s, and reviews different studies that tried to assess the links of those developments to globalization. The conclusion is that globalization, particularly in the form of increased information and communications, seems to have been associated with more open and democratic societies, which should be good for the poor.

On governments' effectiveness responding to the needs of their citizens in a more globalized economy, Díaz-Bonilla looks at some of the arguments related to legal and institutional constraints (policy space) and the availability of resources by focusing on three issues related, respectively, to trade, fiscal, and monetary policies. Regarding trade issues, he concludes from an examination of the WTO AoA that in legal terms, developing countries do not seem particularly constrained in the implementation of a range of possible investment and financial policies in support of agriculture. But industrialized countries are not that constrained either, and, as opposed to developing nations, they have the financial, human, and institutional resources to implement highly distorting policies, with significant negative effects on agriculture in many developing countries (see Chapter 5 and Essays 2–4).

In addition to formal legal constraints on the implementation of pro-poor policies, at issue is whether developing countries lack the financial resources to carry out such policies because of some limits that globalization may impose on fiscal, monetary, financial, or exchange rate policies. Regarding fiscal issues (the second area of effectiveness) Díaz-Bonilla notes that developing countries suffered fiscal retrenchment in the 1980s and 1990s, which seems to have affected agricultural expenditures during those years. The fiscal position appears to have improved somewhat in the 2000s, when government expenditures in the agricultural sector seem to have been increasingly directed toward public goods. There seems to be less explicit taxation of agriculture, at least in the form of export taxes. Whatever the opinion on the adequacy of expenditure and taxation levels related to agriculture in developing countries, it seems that at least they have been moving toward more welfare-enhancing configurations.

When exploring the effect of financial globalization on monetary, credit, and exchange rate policies and the possible implications for agriculture and rural development, Díaz-Bonilla notes the expansion of monetary aggregates and larger availability of overall credit. He finds that the effect of these developments on availability of agricultural credit is not clear. Also, increased financial globalization appears to have been accompanied by higher interest rates and an increased likelihood of bank crises (with their negative effects on agriculture), but also by other, more positive, developments, such as lower and less-volatile inflation and more flexible exchange rate regimes. Therefore, the effect of globalization on the agricultural sector of developing countries may vary. In general, the author notes that empirical studies provide a muddled image about the connections, positive or negative, of the fiscal and monetary trends and globalization, in part because of the very different indicators utilized to characterize the dependent and explanatory variables.

Conflicts and Globalization of the Agrifood System

Arguably, the greatest possible constraint to the effectiveness of governments is internal conflict and war. Paarlberg (Essay 5) calls attention to the highly localized causes of many famines, such as civil wars, and argues that such localized factors are not necessarily linked to globalization. Messer and Cohen (Chapter 9), on the other hand, look at the possible relations among conflict, food insecurity, and globalization in failed states and countries in crisis. They find that it is a complex relationship. Although it is clear that international trade in arms and "blood commodities" fosters war, they find that trade in food commodities can be a source of peace or conflict; trade sometimes contributes to conflicts when it increases price volatility of key commodities, destabilizing household and national incomes, and also when revenues from agricultural trade directly fund war activities. They further argue that conflict potential is especially high when inequalities or environmental degradation lead to extreme marginalization of large segments of populations that suffer losses of livelihoods. Additionally, they point to armed conflicts frequently becoming "food wars" when opposing factions destroy food systems and use food as a weapon, leaving a legacy of food insecurity and a source of future grievances and conflict.

Messer and Cohen recognize that developing countries need peace to ensure food security and take advantage of the new opportunities opened up by globalization. Thus, they suggest that policymakers pay more attention to low-intensity conflicts, even if they remain local, because they establish pockets of food insecurity and may become the source of future, longer, conflicts. It is important to analyze structures of production and markets and to monitor the effects of world prices for key agricultural exports of developing countries, as well as the impact of other macro, trade, and agricultural policies that determine local household livelihood options in manners that are perceived as equitable and sustainable. Additionally, they suggest the implementation of more global political and social actions, such as humanitarian operations, and human-rights norms to influence more peaceful and food-secure out-comes. Development assistance, including aid to agriculture and rural development, can play a role in this effort and can deter conflict if such aid is integrated into the construction of social contexts that promote equity.

The Larger Context of the Debate on Poverty, Hunger, and Globalization

So far we have discussed the driving forces and implications of globalization of agri-food systems. This process needs to be assessed in a broader context, as globalization of agrifood systems does not occur in isolation. As shown in Figure 1.1, several chap-ters (2, 5, and 8) and essays (1–4 and 6) take a more general view and look at cross-cutting issues. Von Braun (in Chapter 2) studies poverty, hunger, and income distri-bution trends and examines the links between these trends and globalization processes, while Birdsall (in Essay 6) looks at the general debate on globalization and explores the structural asymmetries of globalization processes.

Poverty in the context of globalization shows mixed patterns of change across developing regions (see Chapter 2): the number of people living on less than US$2 a day (purchasing power parity [PPP]) from 1981 to 2002 for all developing coun-tries has increased by approximately 164 million people, but if we take the number of people living on less than US$1 a day (PPP), poverty has decreased by approxi-mately 467 million people (World Bank 2006). These aggregate numbers also mask large regional and cross-country disparities; although the number of poor people in East Asia (particularly in China), the Pacific, and South Asia has declined substan-tially, it has increased in Sub-Saharan Africa, Europe, and Central Asia. The picture is also mixed with regard to hunger: from the early 1980s to 2004, the proportion of undernourished people in developing countries decreased from 28 to 17 percent, but 830 million people still remained food insecure in 2004, with more than 213 million of them living in Sub-Saharan Africa (FAO 2006). The nutritional situation has shown improvement outside of Sub-Saharan Africa, although the progress achieved in South Asia from 1970 to 1980 has been eroding since the 1990s (FAO 2006). In sum, hunger and food insecurity continues to decline, but not at a pace that anyone finds satisfying from a global perspective—and even less so in specific regions and countries, where the food and health sectors have been neglected by policy. Regarding income distribution, Ravallion (2003) finds that trends may depend on whether an absolute or relative definition is used. Finally, looking at the Human Development Index (HDI), it seems that the overall situation in developing countries has been improving: since 1980, the HDI has shown a continuous posi-tive trend in all developing and newly industrialized countries with large populations; the HDI for countries with the lowest human development rankings went from 0.379 in 1980 to 0.423 in 2004 (UNDP 2006). Nevertheless, since the mid-1980s and early 1990s, some countries (such as Botswana, Kenya, Russia, South Africa, Ukraine, and Zimbabwe) have been experiencing negative or stagnant HDI trends.

Looking at the relationship between these trends and globalization, the review in Chapter 2 suggests that in general globalization appears to have helped little in reducing poverty, but gainer-loser patterns are complex between and within countries. Indeed, because both globalization and poverty are multidimensional concepts, their linkages are also multidimensional. As such, globalization may affect the poor and populations in developing countries in different ways; hence, it is not surprising that assessments of the relationship between globalization and poverty vary dramatically, ranging from very negative to very positive.[14] The complexity is also evident in cases for which economic growth has had diminishing positive effects on poverty reduction because of growing inequality, for instance, in parts of Asia (such as Pakistan) and Latin America (such as Peru). Food and nutrition security does not improve under such circumstances (Chapter 2).

On the whole, these different analyses seem to lead to ambiguous conclusions, fueling the already intense debate on globalization's effects on poverty. Birdsall (Essay 6) presents conflicting views within that debate. She distinguishes three groups: cheerleaders for globalization, cynics, and worriers. The cheerleaders look at countries like China and India now, and Japan and East Asia in the past, for which integration into the global economy has brought about rapid economic growth and poverty reduction. The cynics think that global rules are rigged against the poor, to the extent that they are shaped, in good measure, by corporate and financial insiders (the best example being agricultural policies, but also the intellectual property regime and the contrast between liberalizing capital markets and restricting migration). The worriers are concerned that neither liberalization and international integration nor fairer rules may be enough. They note that China and India are exceptional cases and do not necessarily represent good examples of liberalization.

Birdsall places herself more on the side of the worriers by pointing to the structural asymmetries of globalization. One such asymmetry is linked to market imperfections and failures, as in the case of global financial markets, where volatility could lead to major crises that could be devastating for the poor and the incipient middle class in emerging markets. Ironically, the other asymmetry appears because of the proper operation of markets, which rewards those who already have productive assets (financial and human capital) and often leaves the poor, who lack those assets, behind. Birdsall concludes that, beyond the integration of poor countries within the world economy and fairer trade and financial rules, international concerted action—with strong leadership and resources provided by industrialized countries—is needed to tackle the issue of structural asymmetries.

How we define desirable outcomes (including policy objectives) is a matter of values that of course influence our judgments about whether globalization is helping to reduce poverty. Different ethical approaches emphasize the importance of considering the needs of the poor. For instance, Swaminathan (Essay 1) reminds us of two of Gandhi's simple ground rules to help the poor: *antyodaya* (which Swaminathan translates as "start with the poorest of the poor") and *sarvodaya* (interpreted as a society with high social synergy—one in which there are no winners and losers). In economic terms, Rawls's "maximin" principle of justice similarly prescribes improving the situation of the worst off first (Rawls 1971). Conversely, a general Pareto criterion suggests that reforms should be done with the objective of making some better off without leaving anyone worse off. But with Pareto optimal reforms, optimality is likely to be achieved only in the medium term, when all transitional adjustments have played out, while in the immediate aftermath of policy change, the more realistic scenario is one with both winners and losers.

What Can Be Done, Then?

Two general implications of the discussions reviewed in the previous sections are the need for complementary domestic policies in developing countries to benefit from globalization and the responsibility of industrialized countries in shaping the operation of a pro-poor world economy in general and the agriculture and food system in particular, as the poor are closely linked to agriculture. That connection works through production to poor small farmers, through wages and jobs in the food system to workers, and through spending on food to consumers (who spend a large share of their budgets on food if they are poor).

Domestic Policies and Conditions in Developing Countries

At the most fundamental level one of the important causes of poverty in some low-income countries is military and social conflict; thus, peace and security are essential for growth, poverty reduction, and food security (see Chapter 9). National policy actions and sustained international diplomatic and political engagement and financial support are therefore crucial to bringing peace and reconciliation to countries affected by conflict and to sustain fragile political transitions.

Further, a strong macroeconomic foundation and prudent macroeconomic policies[15] are necessary to promote growth and accelerate poverty reduction, as vulnerable populations tend to suffer disproportionately from increased volatility and macroeconomic crises (see Chapter 8 and Essay 3). And although growth is a precondition for tackling poverty and hunger, it is not always enough to bring about poverty reduction. Pro-poor economic growth has to be distribution-neutral, and must improve the incomes of the poor by supporting those sectors in which they earn their livelihoods (such as agriculture in many low-income countries) and expanding the demand for factors of production they possess (see Chapter 2 and Essay 4).

In effect, because three-quarters of the world's poor depend directly or indirectly on agriculture (as small farmers, artisans, small entrepreneurs, and landless rural workers), broad-based rural development needs special attention. This effort should include public good investment—especially roads, transportation, communications (including ICT), marketing institutions, and information—to reduce transaction costs, facilitate employment, and generate investments in rural areas, particularly in the rural nonfarm sector. Additionally, particular policies targeting small farmers are needed to enable them to cope with the rapidly changing agrifood supply system and its value chains (see Chapters 4 and 6). Some basic interventions include

- providing support for research and extension for products with potential for diversification;

- promoting greater vertical coordination with agro-industry and retailers and/or supermarkets through cooperatives, contract farming, and clustering;

- strengthening institutions that ensure food quality and safety;

- facilitating access to credit and to instruments to smooth incomes and manage price risk; and

- facilitating land ownership by small producers and landless workers through adequate schemes that may include agrarian reform, titling of informal settlements, and improvement in the functioning land markets (see Chapter 4).

Furthermore, implementing market-oriented reform policies that facilitate smallholder investment and avoid differential subsidies to large-scale operations is important. And, as highlighted in Essay 2, market-oriented reforms must ensure competition along the agrifood chain, where recent trends in mergers both nationally and internationally call for particular attention to problems with oligopolies and oligopsonies in key input and output markets.

Pro-poor, stable growth and a focus on rural development may not be enough. Other horizontal and targeted interventions are needed to help the poor deal with change in the short to medium run. Chapters 2 and 7 and Essay 1 point to the need for improving access to health and education services of good quality for the poor to build human capital and stress the need for adequate safety nets to reduce the vulnerability of the poor in times of economic stress. Such protection can be provided through the provision of food-related transfers (such as coupons) to ensure availability of food or through employment-generation schemes (such as rural works or food-for-work programs). Conditional cash-transfer programs, which are increasingly being implemented across the developing world, are another type of safety net program which appears to be promising.[16] Broad and comprehensive social protection programs and policies (such as old age pensions and social security systems) may be needed for the rural and urban populations when covariate risks for income and employment increase because of rising probabilities of exogenous shocks, including shocks that may result from globalization-related instabilities in markets and exchange rates.

International Policies and Institutions

Developing countries cannot confront the challenges of building a more developed and inclusive society with internal policies only. Even when they implement the best policies, some issues are global in nature and cannot be resolved until industrialized countries are more committed to building a pro-poor world economy. This requirement applies to world agriculture in particular. Thus, a number of global policy issues require attention, ranging from the architecture of global decisionmaking on the agri-food system to actions in some broad policy domains:

- Global governance architecture of the food system. The inherited organizational and institutional structure of the world food system is outdated and does not serve effectively food safety, global health, and food security of the poor. The minimum roles and structures of the global organizations serving food, agriculture, and related health issues that evolved over the past six decades (Food and Agriculture Organization of the United Nations [FAO], World Food Programme, International Fund for Agriculture Development, and World Health Organization [WHO]) require rethinking and adjustment to provide the needed global public goods (such as information; standards; emergency response; facilitation of pro-poor transformation of the smallholder farming, food, and agriculture-health linkages). The traditional roles of the global public investment agencies (World Bank and regional development banks) and the trade agency (WTO) also need consideration in this context. The architecture governing the global food system must consider the growing complexity of roles of actors in the world food system, which include (1) the current international organizations, (2) the evermore important intergovernmental and regional machinery, (3) food industry representatives, and (4) civil society (farmer and consumer representatives).

- Global trade policy reform in the interest of developing countries. Trade negotiations must reduce the combination of agricultural protectionism and high subsidies in industrialized countries that has limited agricultural growth in the developing world and weakened food security in vulnerable countries by competing with domestic production. Trade barriers between and within developing countries must be reduced as well. More, rather than less, globalization is called for in these domains. Of particular interest is a revision of the intellectual property regime to accommodate the limitations and needs of low-income countries (Chapter 3). The issue of noncompetitive markets at the international level may require a better global coordination of competition institutions at the national level and support for developing countries to establish adequate agencies for their own markets.

- International capital and aid. Although developing countries must reduce their vulnerability to global financial crises through better macroeconomic and financial policies, these may not be enough if the main industrialized countries do not foster world financial stability with adequate macroeconomic policies and help establish a more equitable international system to cope with financial crises. Although these issues may be more important for middle-income developing countries, the poorest nations, lacking access to international capital markets, need expanded aid (Essay 4). Those countries would benefit from the acceleration, extension, and proper implementation of the initiatives for debt reduction and from additional financial aid to reach the objectives of the U.N. Millennium Development Goals (MDGs) by 2015. In particular, international financial institutions should increase funding for rural and agricultural development; poverty alleviation; and health, nutrition, and education interventions.

- Employment and social policy. Most social protection and employment policies are in the domain of national policy. However, the global dimensions of food insecurity, poverty, and unemployment call for additional global actions, especially in low-income countries. However, international support will be most useful when public policies at the national level are designed to be more efficient and effective. Transnational learning about social protection policies that reach the poor and hungry in rural areas is called for. This effort warrants state–civil society cooperation.

- Global agricultural innovation and technology and environmental policy serving the poor. Expanded adaptive research for productivity-enhancing agricultural technology that is focused on the needs of poor farmers and consumers in developing countries can contribute to enhanced food security, nutrition, and health. Industrialized countries can help by fostering a serious debate on environmental, health, ethical, and equity concerns with respect to both agricultural biotechnology and agricultural research in general. Most importantly, they can provide scientific and financial support for technology development in poor countries and in Africa in particular. Similar arguments apply to research on health issues that overwhelmingly affect the world's poor.

Final Comments

The present implementation of the policies suggested above, at the national or international level, is less than adequate or complete. This inadequacy is due partly to the existing controversies around (1) the desirability of the general approach of integrating into world markets rather than trying to severe or drastically reduce the links to them, and (2) some of the specific policies (for instance, trade and IPR; see Essay 6). But there are also strong political economic reasons, both at the national and international levels, which constrain the formation of the social and political coalitions needed to implement those policies. An analysis of those forces and constraints exceeds the scope of this book.

Given the mixed results of globalization of the agrifood system for the poor, in this volume we highlight the need for a value-based approach to continue the construction of a better world. Different religious traditions and ethical approaches emphasize the importance of considering the needs of the poor. It is necessary to devise and embrace new relevant norms and values at both the national and international levels. Globalization of social policies has, to some extent, emerged with the globalization of markets, such as in the fields of economic rights (right to food, limitations on child labor), health policies, and MDGs, but lags far behind economic globalization drivers (see Chapter 2). Economic analyses of the realities of poverty and food insecurity and their causes must be coupled with ethical reflection on current social and economic structures. The process of world economic integration has indeed generated levels of wealth never seen before, potentially providing the resources with which to confront global poverty and hunger. The positive side of this process is that the accumulation of wealth supported by globalization is making possible—and therefore, morally inescapable—the previously utopian task of eliminating poverty and hunger on our planet.

Notes

1. Other topics not covered include the globalization of agro-industrial input producers and the implications of international migrations for rural poverty.

2. For a review of differing definitions, see Díaz-Bonilla and Robinson (2001); see also Lechner and Boli (2000); Guillén (2001); Waters (2001); Díaz-Bonilla (2002).

3. That the number of people on the planet has more than doubled since the 1960s is, by itself, significantly increasing the density of international economic, social, and environmental linkages (Díaz-Bonilla 2002).

4. For instance, those who believe that globalization has negative effects on society and exposure to those forces is the result of active government policies tend to call for the governments to reverse the liberalizing policies they fault, hoping the country can be isolated or "protected." On the other hand, those who think that globalization is the inexorable result of more general trends that governments do not necessarily control (such as technology) are much more skeptical about the effects of government policies that try to isolate countries and favor policies facilitating the integration into the inevitable international trends (Díaz-Bonilla 2002).

5. This list provides a broad archetype of the globalization of the agrifood system. It is not meant to unify the various definitions used by the different authors in this volume. Thus, some of the definitions in the other chapters may be slightly different from the one presented here.

6. Value-added is of course less than the market value of total agricultural production, as the former includes only payments to the factors of production (labor, capital, and natural resources) involved in the primary production.

7. All variables are from FAOSTAT (FAO 2006), measured in 1989–91 world prices. China is excluded from developing nations, because, given its size, it would dominate any indicator for that category of countries. Instead of using trade and total production over trade, value-added could have been used. For instance, World Bank (2005) shows that the average growth rate of global agricultural trade from 1985 to 2003 was 4.8 percent, while that of global agriculture value-added was only 1.9 percent, suggesting that the ratio of trade to value-added increased. FAOSTAT data for exports, imports, and production are calculated at fixed world prices in U.S. dollars for a benchmark year, avoiding all measurement issues related to value-added in domestic currency and problems of conversion with local exchange rate currencies.

8. Import penetration ratios and export orientation ratios for agricultural products in industrialized countries are noticeably larger than the corresponding values for developing countries. Also, the divergence in trade ratios between industrialized and developing countries increased during the period, particularly on the export side, as the export orientation ratio of developing countries barely moved (hovering around 15 percent), whereas the export orientation ratio for industrialized countries jumped from about 20 percent in the 1960s to about 55 percent in the 1990s (Díaz-Bonilla 2001).

9. The data on exports and imports by region are not net of the value of trade that takes place within a region (say, Latin America and the Caribbean): the regional aggregates of exports and the regional aggregate of imports refer to all destinations (including those in the region). In that sense, there is no aggregation (netting-out) problem at the country level. The aggregation problem is that, by taking the region as a whole (instead of calculating country by country and then calculating the average or median), individual cases are subsumed within regional averages that may be dominated by the larger players.

10. For a comparison of export and import ratios for industrialized and developing countries and different products, see Díaz-Bonilla (2001).

11. The price that producers receive, properly adjusted for quality and marketing costs, may be above (if the product is subsidized) or below (if taxed) the comparable world price. Thus agriculture would become more globalized to the extent that the ratio of domestic and world prices, properly adjusted by quality and transportation costs, approaches 1.

12. In particular, OECD (1997) documents important tariff escalation in coffee and cocoa products, which can in part explain the increasing share of industrialized countries in the international trade of processed goods using these raw materials.

13. It must be noted that for some products, such as fruits and vegetables, the fresh, non-processed product may be the one with higher value compared with, say, canned products.

14. Von Braun (Chapter 2) explores these issues through a literature review of empirical studies examining the poverty implications of certain aspects of globalization (particularly increased trade and FDI flows). He points to the diversity in methodological approaches and also notes the differences in methodological preferences of researchers at nongovernmental organizations (NGOs), who tend to rely mostly on case studies, versus development economists and workers at international organizations, who tend to prefer more quantitative studies based on cross-section and panel econometrics and model-based simulations.

15. Unsustainable macroeconomic policies include large and unsustainable public sector deficits, unmanaged expansions of monetary supply, unrealistic exchange rates, and trade protectionism that taxes consumers (and thus acts as a regressive tax) and/or tends to appreciate the real exchange rate (see Chapter 8 and Essay 3).

16. Conditional cash-transfer programs, which began in Latin America in the early 1990s, provide money to poor families on the condition that the families invest in human capital through, for example, sending their children to school and bringing them to healthcare centers regularly.

References

Aghion, P., and J. G. Williamson. 1999. *Growth, inequality and globalization: Theory, history and policy*. New York: Cambridge University Press.

Akiyama, T., J. Baffes, D. Larson, and P. Varangis. 2003. *Commodity market reform in Africa: Some recent experience*. Policy Research Working Paper 2995. Washington, D.C.: World Bank.

Baffes, J., and B. Gardner. 2003. The transmission of world commodity prices to domestic markets under policy reforms in developing countries. *Journal of Policy Reform* 6 (3): 159–180.

Balassa, B., and C. Michalopoulos. 1986. Liberalizing trade between developed and developing countries. *Journal of World Trade Law* 20 (1): 3–28.

Bhagwati, J. 2004. *In defense of globalization*. New York: Oxford University Press.

Bhalla, S. S. 2002. *Imagine there's no country: Poverty, inequality and growth in the era of globalization*. Washington, D.C.: Institute for International Economics.

Boyle, J. 2003. The second enclosure movement and the construction of the public domain. *Law and Contemporary Problems* 66 (1 and 2): 33–75.

Díaz-Bonilla, E. 2001. Globalization and agriculture: Some facts, interpretations, and policy issue. In *Globalization and rural development,* ed. O. Solbrig, R. Paarlberg, and F. Di Castri. Cambridge, Mass., U.S.A.: Harvard University Press.

———. 2002. Globalization, poverty and food security. In *Sustainable food security for all by 2020.* Proceedings and summary paper of the 2020 Vision International Conference, September 4–6, 2001, Bonn. Washington, D.C.: International Food Policy Research Institute. Available at http://www.ifpri.org/2020conference/PDF/summary_diaz-bonilla.pdf.

Díaz-Bonilla, E., and S. Robinson. 2001. *Shaping globalization for poverty alleviation and food security.* 2020 Vision Focus 8. Washington, D.C.: International Food Policy Research Institute.

Díaz-Bonilla, E., X. Diao, and S. Robinson. 2006. Thinking inside the boxes: Protection in the development and food security boxes versus investment in the green box. In *WTO negotiations and agricultural trade liberalization. The effects of developed countries' policies on developing countries,* ed. E. Díaz-Bonilla, S. Frandsen, and S. Robinson. Oxon, U.K., and Cambridge, Mass., U.S.A.: CAB International.

Díaz-Bonilla, E., S. Frandsen, and S. Robinson. 2006. Overview. In *WTO negotiations and agricultural trade liberalization. The effects of developed countries' policies on developing countries,* ed. E. Díaz-Bonilla, S. Frandsen, and S. Robinson. Oxon, U.K., and Cambridge, Mass., U.S.A.: CAB International.

Drahos, P., and R. Mayne. 2002. *Global intellectual property rights: Knowledge, access and development.* New York: Palgrave Macmillan.

Euromonitor International. Global market information database. Available at http://www.euromointor.com.

FAO (Food and Agriculture Organization of the United Nations). 2006. FAOSTAT. Rome. Available at http://faostat.fao.org/default.aspx.

G8 Task Force. 2001. *Digital opportunity for all: Meeting the challenge.* Report of the Digital Opportunity Task Force (DOT Force) including a proposal for a Genoa Plan of Action, May 11, Genoa.

Guillén, M. F. 2001. Is globalization civilizing, destructive or feeble? A critique of five key debates in the social-science literature. *Annual Review of Sociology* 27: 235–260.

Harrison, A. 2006. *Globalization and poverty.* NBER Working Paper 12347. Cambridge, Mass., U.S.A.: National Bureau of Economic Research.

Helleiner, G. K. 2001. Markets, politics and globalization: Can the global economy be civilized? *Journal of Human Development* 2 (1): 27–46.

IMF (International Monetary Fund). 1999. *World economic outlook (WEO): International financial contagion.* Washington, D.C.

———. 2007. *International financial statistics.* Washington, D.C. Available at http://www.imfstatistics.org.imf.

Kherallah, M., C. Delgado, E. Gabre-Madhin, N. Minot, and M. Johnson. 2000. *Agricultural market reforms in Sub-Saharan Africa: A synthesis of research findings*. Washington, D.C.: International Food Policy Research Institute.

Knetter, M., and M. J. Slaughter. 1999. *Measuring market-product integration*. NBER Working Paper 6969. Cambridge, Mass., U.S.A.: National Bureau of Economic Research.

Krueger, A. O., M. W. Schiff, and A. Valdés. 1990. *Economía política de las intervenciones de precios agrícolas en América Latina*. San Francisco: Banco Mundial, Centro Internacional para el Desarrollo Económico, afiliado al Instituto de Estudios Contemporáneos.

Lang, T. 2004. Food and health wars: A modern drama of consumer sovereignty. Cultures of Consumption Working Paper 14. London: Birkbeck College, Cultures of Consumption, and Economic and Social Research Council (ESRC)–Arts and Humanities Research Board (AHRB) Research Programme.

Lechner, F. J., and J. Boli. 2000. The globalization reader: General introduction. In *The globalization reader,* ed. F. J. Lechner and J. Boli. Malden, Mass., U.S.A.: Blackwell Publishers.

Lindland, J. 1997. The impact of the Uruguay Round on tariff escalation in agricultural products. *Food Policy* 22 (6): 487–500.

Macdonald, S. 2001. Exploring the hidden costs of patents. Notes of a talk given at Quaker House, May 16, Geneva. Mimeo.

Millennium Ecosystem Assessment. 2005. *Ecosystems and human well-being: Synthesis*. Washington, D.C.: Island Press.

OECD (Organisation for Economic Co-operation and Development). 1997. *The Uruguay Round agreement on agriculture and processed agricultural products*. Paris.

Osterhammel, J., and N. Petersson. 2005. *Globalization: A short history*. English translation ed. Princeton, N.J., U.S.A.: Princeton University Press.

Panagariya, A. 2004. The miracles of globalization. *Foreign Affairs,* 85 (5): 146–151.

Prasad, E., K. Rogoff, S.-J. Wei, and M. A. Kose. 2003. *Effects of financial globalization on developing countries: Some empirical evidence*. Washington, D.C.: International Monetary Fund.

Rapsomanikis, G., D. Hallam, and P. Conforti. 2003. *Market integration and price transmission in selected food and cash crop markets of developing countries: Review and applications*. Commodity Market Review 2003–2004. Rome: Food and Agriculture Organization of the United Nations.

Ravallion, M. 2003. The debate on globalization, poverty and inequality: Why measurement matters. *International Affairs* 79 (4): 739–753.

Rawls, J. 1971. *A theory of justice*. Cambridge, Mass., U.S.A.: Belknap Press of Harvard University Press.

Regmi, A., and M. Gehlhar, eds. 2005. *New directions in global food markets.* Agriculture Information Bulletin AIB794. Washington, D.C.: Economic Research Service, U.S. Department of Agriculture.

Rodrik, D. 1997. *Has globalization gone too far?* Washington, D.C.: Institute for International Economics.

Rosegrant, M. W., M. S. Paisner, S. Meijer, and J. Witcover. 2001. *2020 global food outlook: Trends, alternatives and choices.* Washington, D.C.: International Food Policy Research Institute.

Stiglitz, J. E. 2003. *Globalization and its discontents.* New York: W. W. Norton.

Terry, D., and S. Wilson. 2005. Beyond small change. Making migrant remittances count. Inter-American Development Bank, Washington, D.C. Mimeo.

Torero, M., and J. von Braun, eds. 2006. *Information and communication technologies for development and poverty reduction.* Baltimore: The Johns Hopkins University Press for the International Food Policy Research Institute.

UNCTAD (United Nations Conference on Trade and Development). 2006. *World investment report 2006: FDI from developing and transition economies; Implications for development.* New York: United Nations.

UNDP (United Nations Development Programme). 2006. *Human development report 2006.* New York: Oxford University Press.

USDA/ERS (U.S. Department of Agriculture/Economic Research Service). 2000. *International financial crises and agriculture. International agriculture and trade.* ERS-WRS-99-3. Washington, D.C.

Variyam, J. N., and E. Golan. 2002. New health information is reshaping food choices. *Food Review* 25 (1): 13–18.

von Braun, J. 2005. The world food situation: An overview. Paper prepared for CGIAR annual general meetings, December 6, Marrakech, Morocco.

von Braun, J., and E. Kennedy, eds. 1995. *Agricultural commercialization, economic development and nutrition.* Baltimore: The Johns Hopkins University Press.

von Braun, J., and T. Mengistu. 2004. On ethics and economics of changing behavior in food and agricultural production, consumption, and trade: Some reflections on what to do. Paper prepared for a workshop on Ethics, Globalization and Hunger, November 17–19, Ithaca, N.Y.

Waters, M. 2001. *Globalization,* 2nd ed. New York: Routledge.

Wood, S. 2001. Environment (Brief 10). In *Shaping globalization for poverty alleviation and food security,* ed. E. Díaz-Bonilla and S. Robinson. 2020 Vision Focus 8. Washington, D.C.: International Food Policy Research Institute.

World Bank. 2005. *World development indicators 2005.* Washington, D.C.

———. 2006. PovcalNet. Washington, D.C. Available at http://iresearch.worldbank.org/povcalnet/jsp/index.jsp.

Yeats, A. J. 1974. Effective tariff protection in the United States, the European Economic Community and Japan. *Quarterly Review of Economics and Business* 14 (Summer): 41–50.

Yunus, M. 2006. Foreword. In *Information and communication technologies for development and poverty reduction,* ed. M. Torero and J. von Braun. Baltimore: The Johns Hopkins University Press for the International Food Policy Research Institute.

Chapter 2

Globalization, Poverty, and Food

Joachim von Braun

O ver the past three decades, in the aggregate, the world has become much more prosperous and well fed. Nonetheless, poverty and food insecurity persist, and they have been worsening in Sub-Saharan Africa. This state of affairs is unacceptable, considering globalization and related economic and technological advances offer growing possibilities for overcoming hunger and poverty. In effect, the existence of mass poverty and widespread food insecurity are symptoms of economic policy failures. This chapter investigates the links between globalization and poverty and asks whether globalization has actually reduced poverty and food insecurity. The chapter does not go into broader issues of globalization's distributional effects (see Wade 2004 for a survey).

Defining globalization of agriculture and the food system as the global integration—across national borders—of production and processing of agriculture and food items through markets and standardizations, regulations, and technologies, this chapter traces the effects of globalization on the status of the poor and the food insecure. Policy options that may enable these vulnerable populations to better manage new risks brought about by globalization processes and to take advantage of the new opportunities are also explored.

Conceptual Framework

As globalization proceeds, poverty may or may not decline. The possibility that the two may not be strongly linked also exists, because many other things have happened in parallel with globalization and poverty reduction. Important developments in the past three decades include improved governance in some countries, the start of new conflicts and wars and the end of old ones, broadening of civil society's reach and level of organization, expansion of rural finance systems (microcredit), improved infrastructure, transformation of domestic markets (retail), improved technologies and access to them (in agriculture and communications), and far-reaching policy changes with increased devolution in many countries. Some of these changes may actually be driven by opportunities offered by globalization. Still, correlations between globalization and poverty must not be mistaken for causal relations (Bardhan 2006). Global policy shifts, such as attempted trade policy reforms under the WTO, can be interpreted as opportunities to make globalization pro-poor, and the emphasis on MDGs can be seen as a necessity to translate globalization opportunities into poverty reduction, but again, these global policy initiatives may just be correlates of globalization and may not be caused by it.

A conceptual framework that permits the separation of the key aspects of globalization from elements of domestic policy changes and initial conditions is called for. Expanding on the framework for this volume described in Chapter 1 (Figure 1.1) and focusing on the issues in this chapter, Figure 2.1 provides such a framework. The figure traces globalization–poverty linkages between three major domains of globalization drivers, domestic policies and related domestic filters, and community and household responses and outcomes:

1. globalization features that are exogenous to a country (global market change; investment and capital flows; information and innovation, be it institutional or technological; and social policies);

2. responses to the exogenous (globalization-driven) changes at national policy level and domestic filters arising from initial conditions; at this level of analysis, it is evident that globalization is no alternative to domestic development strategy (Sanchez 2003); and

3. household (and community-level) responses to the above two, and the related outcomes and effects on poverty and food security of the poor as producers, wage earners, and consumers.

A few explanations are in order to put the framework into the context of time and country specificity. Globalization can affect poverty indirectly through market and technology policies that generate growth and directly through price changes (of outputs and factors), technology, and new volatilities. The framework reflects the conclusions of growing numbers of cross-country studies—which are prone to data limitations and econometric problems of specification—and country-specific studies that the effects of globalization on the poor can only be judged comprehensively

GLOBALIZATION, POVERTY, AND FOOD 49

Figure 2.1 Conceptual framework for linkages among globalization, poverty, and food security

	MARKETS	INVESTMENT AND CAPITAL FLOWS	INFORMATION AND INNOVATION	SOCIAL POLICY
LEVEL I: GLOBALIZATION *Exogenous factors*	Expansion and increased access to outputs, inputs, and labor (migration)	Expansion of (foreign) investment and capital flows	Increased flow as a result of improved global information and communication technologies	Emergency aid; anti-discrimination human right to food; child-labor policies
LEVEL II: DOMESTIC POLICY	Market opening	Competitiveness policy; devaluation, decentralization, and privatization Political system and institutional changes (property rights, contract enforcement mechanisms, and the like)	Global innovation and intellectual property rights policies Facilitation of technology utilization and regulation Investments in public research and development	Pro-poor social interventions for vulnerable populations

RIGHTS
Land ownership, water rights, and the like

PRICES
Level and volatility

EMPLOYMENT
Level and stability

LEVEL III: HOUSEHOLDS	HOUSEHOLD ENDOWMENTS Labor and skills (human capital, health) Capital assets Land	PRODUCTION Goods Services	CONSUMPTION Food Non-food

Source: Joachim von Braun and Eugenio Díaz-Bonilla.

when the specific context is considered (see reviews by Ravallion 2004; Nissanke and Thorbecke 2005; Bardhan 2006).

The framework starts at the level of features and drivers of globalization (see level I at the top of Figure 2.1) distinguishing (1) input and output markets, (2) investment and capital flows, (3) information and innovation, and (4) social policy. The latter is limited at a global level, and the globalization of agriculture and the food system does not directly link to social policies, except perhaps in the domain of food aid and emergency assistance. But there are two avenues that call for inclusion of social policies in this review of globalization–poverty linkages: First, if the economic opportunities are expanded by globalization, public action at global and national levels may expand social policy; and second, if globalization increases risks for the poor, social policies may be increasingly employed to address these risks and thereby mitigate them.

These sorts of drivers of globalization translate through domestic policies and institutional responses (level II in the framework) into community- and household-level outcomes and effects on poverty broadly defined, including food and nutrition security and livelihoods (level III). It should be stressed that a sharp distinction between exogenous drivers of globalization and endogenous outcomes is not appropriate, as the coordinated national and intergovernmental policies also shape globalization; thus, there are also feedbacks and upward links from level II to level I of the framework.

Furthermore, the framework in Figure 2.1 does not capture the time subscripts of globalization–poverty linkages. Nevertheless, the dynamics of globalization–poverty linkages are important: because of substitution between capital and unskilled labor, and response in the demands for skills and education, a nonlinear relationship between globalization and poverty may exist; at low degrees of globalization, more and fast globalization (market opening) may hurt the poor, whereas at higher degrees of globalization, it may lead to a decline in poverty (Agénor 2002). This nonlinearity largely depends on the response to wage gaps in skilled and unskilled labor with human capital investments—be it private or public—which is inelastic in the short-to-medium run, particularly in rural areas because of deficient education systems, unfavorable attitudes toward education (especially that for girls), and strong competition for children's work time.

The effects on households of the macro-level market and institutional changes induced by globalization (at levels I and II) depend partly on whether households are net consumers or net producers of food (Orden, Torero, and Gulati 2004) and their positions in labor and asset markets. With increased openness, as cheaper imports enter domestic markets, net consumers of agricultural products benefit from a wider variety of products and reduced prices, while net producers face increased competition from imported goods, which may lead to lower prices for their products, depending on their competitiveness. More specialized net producers could also become more susceptible to higher volatility in prices of their specialty products.

In addition, the overall effect of globalization will be determined by households' ability to adjust to these changes through shifts in production and consumption patterns, such as switching production to goods whose prices have risen and consumption to those whose prices have fallen (McCulloch, Winters, and Cirera 2001). Households can also adjust through changed opportunities in labor markets, which largely depend on the location, the labor and goods markets (see, for example, the studies by Ravallion 2004 for China and Morocco; Topalova 2005 for India), and the position of the poor in the value chains of industries affected by globalization (see Jenkins 2005 for examples in horticulture, garments, and textiles in four developing countries).

The ability to make such shifts will in turn depend on households' access to markets, credit, and insurance, as well as on households' physical assets and individuals' skill sets (von Braun 2005). Additionally, access to ICT in rural areas and internationally has profound effects on labor mobility across sectors (Torero and von Braun 2006). Also, price transmission to rural markets for inputs and outputs are relevant, as there are many stages between border prices and prices faced by rural households. In effect, price transmission depends on infrastructure and transport costs, the functioning of markets, and the level of domestic taxes and regulations (Hertel and Winters 2005). Development of agriculture and the food market system are crucial in these contexts in many developing countries, as the majority of the poor spend a considerable share of their income on food and largely depend on agriculture for their food and income needs.

There is no global consensus on how to take advantage of the increased economic opportunities that globalization offers to achieve the goal of reduced poverty and hunger (Streeten 2001). Such a consensus cannot be obtained from a top-down process. It must be pursued through broad and often contentious discourse that increasingly includes the political influence of poor and food-insecure people themselves.

The next section of this chapter gives an overview of poverty and food security trends during globalization. After briefly summarizing the current debate about the overall effects of globalization on the poor, the third section explores some of the globalization–poverty linkages coming out of eight relatively large developing countries and then reviews the existing empirical literature on linkages between globalization and poverty reduction in the context of the established framework. Finally, the chapter concludes with a summary of the potential mechanisms of how globalization affects hunger and poverty.

Food Insecurity, Poverty, and Inequality during Globalization

Hunger and Food Insecurity Outcomes: Slow Progress

The proportion of the population suffering from undernourishment in developing countries shrank from 28 percent in the early 1980s to 17 percent in 2004. However, 830 million people remained food insecure in 2004, with more than 213 million of them living in Sub-Saharan Africa (FAO 2006a) (see Figure 2.2). The nutritional status of individuals in developing countries has shown improvement outside of Sub-

Figure 2.2   Food-insecurity trends in developing countries

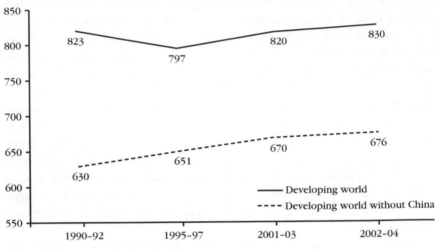

Number of undernourished people (millions)

Source: Based on data from FAO (2006).
Note: Data for 2001–03 are provisional; those for 2002–04 are preliminary.

Saharan Africa , although the progress achieved in South Asia in the 1970s and 1980s has been eroding since the 1990s (FAO 2006). Further, it is estimated that approximately 146 million children younger than 5 are underweight in developing countries (UNICEF 2006). Malnutrition is a factor in around 53 percent of all deaths of children younger than 5, and malnourished children who make it to their fifth birthdays are much less likely than well-nourished children to attain their full mental and physical potentials. They are more likely to underperform in school and to grow up to be less productive workers (UN/SCN 2004; UNICEF 2006).

The world food problem encompasses more than inadequate caloric intake. With food markets that are more integrated globally and nationally, access to healthy and diverse diets has become increasingly a matter of the income available for food expenditures and of food prices. Food prices have declined globally for staple foods (calories), but not for components of a healthy diet, such as for fruits, vegetables, fish, and pulses, in many developing countries. Consequently, micronutrient deficiencies have hardly declined among the poor. Deficiency of Vitamin A, which can lead to blindness, is a problem in at least 60 countries (including middle-income ones) and affects some 140 million preschool children, or 40 percent of preschool children in developing countries (see Figure 2.3). An estimated 35.2 percent of the world's population

Figure 2.3   Vitamin A deficiency in preschool children

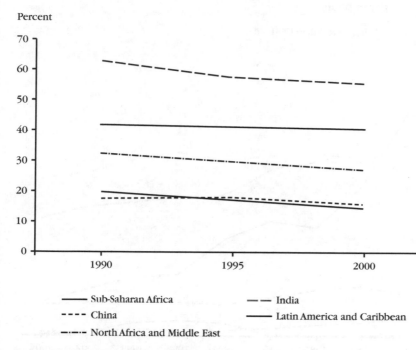

Percent

Source: Micronutrient Initiative and UNICEF (2005).

suffers from iodine deficiency. Almost 2 billion people suffer from iron deficiency, which particularly affects women and preschool children (UN/SCN 2004; Micronutrient Initiative and UNICEF 2005).

In sum, hunger and food insecurity continue to decline, but not at a pace that anyone can find satisfying from a global perspective—particularly in specific regions and countries, where the food and health sectors have been neglected by policy. Indeed, IFPRI's Global Hunger Index (GHI),[1] which captures three dimensions of hunger (essentially, availability of food, nutritional status of children, and child mortality), shows that Sub-Saharan Africa has made the least progress from 1990 to 2004, with its GHI declining by only 2.2 points, from 26.8 to 24.6. South Asia made the most progress, with its GHI declining by 7.9 points, but the hunger situation there remains almost as bad as in Sub-Saharan Africa, with an index of 24.5 in 2004 (Wiesmann 2007). Furthermore, since the 1990s, the number of food-insecure people has been increasing in both Sub-Saharan Africa and South Asia, where the majority of food-insecure people live (FAO 2006a). The persistence of hunger, despite the existence of policies and programs to address it, is one of the largest ethical dilemmas

Figure 2.4   Poverty headcount ratios at US$1 and US$2 a day purchasing power parity

Share of people living on less than US$1 a day
(percent)

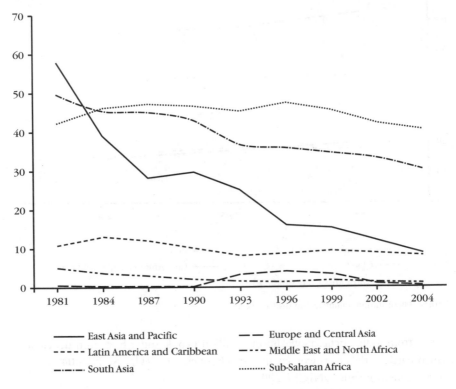

Source: World Bank (2007).

confronting our society (von Braun and Mengistu 2007). The process of setting goals has so far not yielded strong results in terms of cutting hunger at an accelerated rate. The lost opportunities of millions of people to lead productive lives, both today and in the coming decades, is one of the greatest problems caused by policy failure. Effective policy to overcome hunger has to take advantage of the opportunities offered by changed conditions and to protect those currently facing the prospect of hunger from new risks. Globalization has so far not helped to accelerate the reduction of bottom end poverty—hunger.

Mixed Evidence on Poverty and Inequality

Defined as the number of people living on less than US$2 a day (PPP), from 1981 to 2004 for all developing countries, poverty has actually increased by approximately

Figure 2.4   (continued)

Share of people living on less than US$2 a day
(percent)

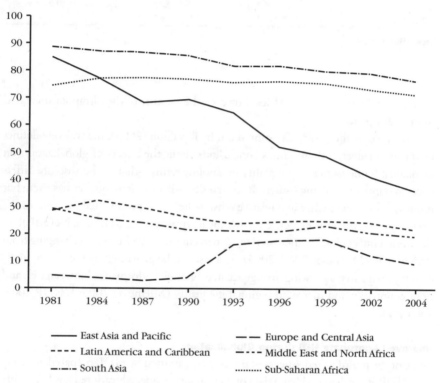

—— East Asia and Pacific   – – Europe and Central Asia
- - - - Latin America and Caribbean   – - – Middle East and North Africa
–·–·– South Asia   ·········· Sub-Saharan Africa

95 million people. But defined as the number of people living on less than US$1 a day (PPP), poverty has decreased by approximately 500 million people (Chen and Raval-lion 2007). These aggregate numbers also mask large regional and cross-country dis-parities; while the number of poor people in East Asia, the Pacific, and South Asia has declined substantially, it has increased in Sub-Saharan Africa, Europe, and Central Asia (Figure 2.4). Further, China has seen large decreases in the number of poor; from 1987 to 2004, the number of people living on less than US$1 a day (PPP) there dropped by around 182 million, and those with less than US$2 a day (PPP) decreased by almost 220 million (Chen and Ravallion 2007).

The pattern of bottom-end poverty is also changing geographically. In East Asia and the Pacific, growth and social policy have reached the ultrapoor (people living on less than half a dollar a day), and their number decreased from 1990 to 2004 (Ahmed

Table 2.1   Regional Gini coefficients

Region	1960	1980	1998
Africa	37.8	41.1	50.4
Asia	36.2	53.1	51.8
Rich countries	23.1	16.3	15.5

Source: Milanovic (2005).

et al. 2007). In Sub-Saharan Africa, however, the number of the ultrapoor increased in this same period.

For income inequality, as pointed out by Ravallion (2003), the way one defines inequality inadvertently modifies conclusions about the effects of globalization on inequality. If one thinks of inequality in absolute terms—that is, the absolute differences in standards of living—then the conclusion will be that inequality has risen; but if one thinks of inequality in a relative sense—the ratio of individual incomes to the overall mean—then the evidence on income inequality remains mixed. Nevertheless, the world Gini coefficient increased by 17 percent from 1985 to 1995, changing from 0.46 to 0.54 (Milanovic 2002, 2005). This rise can be explained by increasing inter-country inequality, a growing divergence in economic performance between rich and poor countries,[2] and increased regional inequality (Milanovic 2005; UNDP 2005; Table 2.1).

Improved Aggregate HDI during Globalization
Some of the multifaceted aspects of poverty are captured by HDI, prepared annually by UNDP. It is calculated from data on per capita income, educational levels, and life expectancy rates. It is not based on any conclusive theoretical concept, but it does provide a picture of national average living conditions.

On the basis of the more recent comparative aggregate assessment of the HDI, we can conclude that, contrary to the viewpoint frequently expressed by critics of globalization, human development during globalization in the 1980s and 1990s in fact displayed positive signs. On average, the HDI for countries with the lowest human development rankings increased from 0.379 in 1980 to 0.423 in 2004 (UNDP 2006).

Further, the most recent *Human Development Report* (UNDP 2006) indicates that since 1980, the HDI has shown a continuous positive trend in all developing and newly industrialized countries with large populations—that is, countries where the majority of the world's poor people live, including Bangladesh, Brazil, China, Egypt, India, Indonesia, Nigeria, and Pakistan. Nevertheless, since the mid-1980s and early

1990s, some countries, such as Botswana, Kenya, South Africa, and Zimbabwe, have been experiencing negative HDI trends. Ukraine and Russia also experienced similar trends in the early 1990s, but have seen their HDIs improve steadily since the mid 1990s. No data are presently available for war-stricken countries, such as Iraq and Afghanistan (UNDP 2006). In sum, human development is improving faster in middle-income than in lower-income countries.

The Effects of Globalization on Poverty and Food Security

It is estimated that half of the hungry poor are smallholder farmers and two-tenths are landless laborers who are unable to grow or buy enough food to meet their household food requirements (United Nations Millennium Project Task Force on Hunger 2005). In general, poverty is influenced by globalization but is seldom mainly caused by it. The extent and distribution of world poverty relates to the lack of access to resources and opportunities. The lack of rights of the poor (in the face of traditional local power structures), dependencies, corruption and other governance failures, and the lack of education and health care are all key factors to explaining poverty and hunger rather than globalization alone. But an analysis of globalization–poverty linkages must take the dynamics and the volatility of globalization processes into account. Given that most poor people live in rural areas and are landless laborers, small farmers, or workers in small-scale rural enterprises, globalization effects on employment and small-farm competitiveness are central to determining its influence on poverty.

A risk of globalization for poor people lies in the increased volatility of market and nonmarket institutions and the possibly reduced public and private security for specific groups affected by crises and unforeseen events. Although these risks are real, they cannot be properly estimated without a reference system for comparison. The risks of product and labor markets should be compared with the risks in nonmarket situations, such as the substantial risks poor people face in traditional subsistence economies, where bad weather or crop pests pose livelihood-threatening risks, or the risks of closed economies with heavy state involvement in markets that may result in foregone growth opportunities.

Regarding globalization effects in the small-farm economy, a key issue is the effect of increased demand for standardized outputs, stemming from the economies of scale required by increasing integration of food processing and retail industries. A complex winner/loser picture across developing regions emerges (see Chapter 4) that seems to be a result of market and nonmarket institutions facilitating lower transaction costs (such as through networks, cooperatives, or contract farming). The consequences of globalization for poor people's employment opportunities depend on labor productivity, policies (including those on education), and legal arrangements.

Additionally, in discussing the effects of globalization on poverty and food security, it is important to keep sight of the reality of poverty that lies behind the rough statistical findings—a problem that affects people of different ages, gender, and ethnic origin, in different regions, and in city slums and rural areas. The effects of globalization on the poor are as heterogeneous as their sources of employment and income, the resources at their disposal, and their political and economic environments. At the same time, poverty is not a static phenomenon. Populations affected by poverty are in a state of flux in many countries. One portion of the population may free itself from poverty, while others are newly affected or threatened by it. This mobility into and out of poverty is accelerated by the adaptation processes unleashed by globalization (World Bank 2001).

Divergent Assessments Stemming from Differing Perspectives

During the 1990s, a reversal took place in the viewpoints of industrial countries versus developing ones with respect to globalization (Bhagwati 1997). In the 1950s and 1960s, there was a great deal of skepticism in developing countries about economic openness. The "dependency thesis," a widespread paradigm of import substitution and a domestic orientation, supplied the framework for these views. In contrast, industrial countries were much more oriented toward the global market. Now, however, they fear competition from low-wage countries and outsourcing and anxiously ask whether freer trade and capital flows will result in more poverty in richer countries.

To better understand the question of whether globalization has had (or is expected to have) negative or positive consequences for poor people, it would be necessary to conduct analyses over time of both poverty and the important variables reflecting globalization. A mixed picture of developments in poverty and food insecurity during globalization emerges when different sources of data and concepts are used. This heterogeneity partly explains why the literature remains divided on the issue, especially when looking at the relationship between economic openness and poverty and those between economic growth and poverty.

Because both globalization and poverty are multidimensional concepts, their linkages are also multidimensional. Thus, globalization may affect the poor and populations in developing countries in different ways; while some aspects of poverty (such as those broadly depicted by human development indicators) have improved, progress on others (such as reducing hunger and malnutrition) has been slow at best. Consequently, assessments of the relationship between globalization and poverty vary dramatically, ranging from catastrophic to rosy and covering everything in between.

Another reason for divergent assessments of globalization–poverty linkages is the existence of a wide variety of methodological approaches to estimating the effects of globalization on the poor, which are often pursued in parallel. These can be broadly divided into three groups: econometric analyses, model-based simulations, and case studies. Each one has its advantages and limitations, and the results must be interpreted accordingly (Díaz-Bonilla et al. 2006). Also, each broad category encompasses more than one approach. For instance, among the model-based simulations, the disaggregated treatment of households (which is vital for the estimation of poverty and inequality effects) has at least three variations, even within simulations that utilize economywide models. The first one incorporates a limited number of representative households directly within the model. The second one utilizes a two-step approach in which first the economywide model is run and then the changes in prices from the model are applied to the expenditure schedules (change in good prices) and stock of factors (changes of factor prices) of a generally larger number of households. The third approach also uses a similar two-step method but allows for changes in employment conditions. In other words, it combines economywide results of prices and employment with microsimulations using a large number of households, which allows for changes in employment conditions. The diversity of results coming out of these various exercises for different aspects of globalization is elaborated on later in this chapter, when discussing the poverty implications of trade liberalization and increased levels of FDIs. It would be helpful if in future research programs on globalization, the three different approaches were employed in structured triangulations rather than disjointly and in parallel.

Critics of globalization maintain that it has contributed to increased levels of poverty and inequality (see, for example, Shiva 2000; Korten 2001; Oxfam 2002), whereas proponents maintain the opposite—that it has been instrumental in reducing poverty and the growth induced by globalization has been generally distribution-neutral (see, for example, Dollar and Kraay 2001; Bhalla 2002; Nissanke and Thorbecke 2006).[3] At the more aggregate level, a series of solid analyses now exists to help examine the evolution of worldwide poverty. Based on analyses of comprehensive random sampling, some studies conclude that there is no systematic relationship between income growth and income distribution (Deininger and Squire 1996; Birdsall and Londoño 1997; Chen and Ravallion 1997). Thus, economic growth in the context of globalization has not, in general, changed income distribution. Other researchers, however, have argued that there is a causal relationship between growth and income inequality, which may, at low growth, lead to increased poverty, although the direction of the relationship is not always agreed upon. On the one hand, Bourguignon (1981) and Li and Zhou (1998) argue that income inequality can promote growth in that the marginal propensity of rich people to save is higher than that of poor people, so investment rates in more unequal societies are greater, thus leading to higher aggregate output. On the other hand, Alesina and Rodrik (1994) and Alesina and Perotti (1996) find that as inequality increases, growth decreases, because indi-

viduals living in highly unequal societies tend to engage in activities outside legitimate markets and instability within these societies discourages investment and
accumulations.

An explanation of the causes for these differing evaluations may contribute to
clarifying the differences of opinion concerning globalization. Divergent assessments
of globalization and its effects result not only from differing evaluations of the opportunities and risks for those potentially affected. Fundamental problems lie much more
in the following factors (Kanbur 2001):

- Standards of the assessment level (aggregate versus case-specific): for instance,
  adverse case-specific examples are confronted with general, often more positive
  trends and model results about future changes at the aggregate level.

- Temporal perspective (short-term poverty crises, catastrophes, or military
  conflicts versus long-term trends): stress from short-term adjustments on poor
  segments may be weighed against long-term growth prospects.

- Divergent assessments of the functioning of markets (impeding concentration of
  markets versus efficient allocation of resources) and other institutions (democracy,
  transparency, participation) for poor people: for example, increased market risks
  are confronted with increased opportunities for participation of the poor in
  society.

Although these factors appear to be amenable to rational resolution, globalization opens up additional venues for differing perspectives. The opportunities (and
risks) posed by the use of media for communicating knowledge (and pseudo-knowl-
edge) at the global level have increased dramatically, thanks to new information technologies and the web. In a similar manner, opportunities for demagogy and the
exploitation of anxiety have expanded enormously. This media aspect and the three
factors noted above tend to get mixed up, thereby impeding rational debate and conflict resolution.

Moreover, in this debate, the huge chasm between absolute poverty in developing countries, with approximately 2.6 billion people living on the equivalent of less
than US$2 a day (Chen and Ravallion 2007), and the living standards of the lowest
income groups in industrialized countries is seldom taken into consideration. Obviously, low-income people in the industrialized countries who are grappling with
unemployment risks and living costs require policy solutions and are of great relevance for industrialized countries' globalization policies, but the difficulties they face
do not compare with the realities of poverty in developing countries.

We now return to the conceptual framework (see Figure 2.1) and review globalization effects on poverty and food insecurity along the four domains (columns) specified in the framework. Before embarking on a review of the empirical literature, the chapter presents some of the globalization and poverty trends in eight large developing countries, not as a cross-country analysis, but as an illustration of how the experiences of globalization and its effects on poverty and hunger are very much country specific. The eight countries were chosen primarily because they have (albeit at varying degrees) aggressively opened up to globalization in the past two decades and have some of the highest numbers of poor and food-insecure people in the world. Additionally, given their size, these countries have become major global and/or regional players, and, as a result, their experiences with globalization and poverty reduction are important.

Patterns in Selected Large Developing Countries
Table 2.2 presents various indicators related to the factors of globalization identified in the conceptual framework (except for social policy). It also shows some indicators of hunger and poverty reduction. When looking at the latter, a mixed picture emerges. In terms of hunger reduction, China has made the fastest relative gain, reducing hunger by almost 60 percent in the past two decades (i.e., by 12 points), whereas Indonesia, Bangladesh, and India have made the largest absolute gains, reducing their GHIs by 17, 16, and 15.5 points, respectively. Progress in Ethiopia, however, was very slow; its GHI was reduced by around 6 percent. China saw the largest reduction in the proportion of people living on less than US$1 a day, followed by Indonesia. Further, Brazil and Mexico managed to halve their proportions of poor people. In contrast, Bangladesh and Nigeria saw their shares of poor people actually increase, and Ethiopia and India made only modest progress in reducing their poverty rates.

The indicators of economic globalization reveal some homogeneity among the countries in that they all saw an improvement in their respective index of economic freedom[4] and also experienced increased trade shares in GDP. Similarly, in most of the countries (with the exception of Indonesia), the share of FDI in GDP increased. However, the indicators of globalization of innovation and information uncover a wide heterogeneity in experiences. When looking at access to ICTs (as proxied by access to mobile and fixed phones), Brazil, China, and Mexico have made great headway in the past decade, whereas Ethiopia and, to a lesser extent, Nigeria have made very little progress. A similar pattern emerges when looking at investments in innovation.

In sum, although some of the largest developing countries have taken similar paths in terms of opening up to economic globalization, the trends with regard to hunger, poverty, and other features of globalization (such as expanded access to ICTs

Table 2.2 Hunger, poverty, and globalization in selected developing countries

	Period	Bangladesh	Brazil	China	Ethiopia	India	Indonesia	Mexico	Nigeria
Indicators of hunger and poverty trends					Hunger: Global Hunger Index				
	1981	44.4	10.4	20.1	39.2	41.2	28.2	9.9	30.0
	1992	36.5	8.5	12.6	46.4	32.8	18.5	7.5	22.5
	2003	28.4	4.6	8.4	33.7	25.0	11.6	4.7	19.1
				Poverty: Share of people living on less than US$1 a day (percent)[a]					
	1980s	27.8	12.7	44.4	32.7	48.4[b]	28.2	11.1	(65.7)
	1990s	32.3	8.5	24.2	31.3	44.9[b]	16.4	8.6	(68.7)
	2000s	41.3	7.5	(14.0)	21.6	34.4[b]	7.5	4.0	(71.2)
Indicators of market opening and capital flows					Index of Economic Freedom				
	1980	3.0	3.7	3.8		4.9	5.2	5.1	3.5
	1990	4.2	3.9	4.2		4.8	6.6	5.7	3.6
	2004	5.7	5.9	5.7		6.7	6.0	6.6	5.6
				Foreign direct investment, net inflows (percent of GDP)					
	1980	0.0	0.7	0.5	0.0	0.0	0.4	1.2	1.7
	1990	0.1	1.6	3.9	1.1	0.4	1.1	2.2	4.1
	2004	0.4	3.7	3.2	5.1	0.9	–0.9	2.9	3.0
				Trade (percent of GDP)[a]					
	1980s	19.2	17.7	26.6	26.0	14.1	47.8	29.4	41.8
	1990s	25.7	18.0	40.8	30.9	21.0	57.6	49.0	79.8
	2000s	35.0	27.9	51.5	50.5	32.0	61.8	59.2	86.6
				Agriculture trade (percent of GNI)					
	1980[c]	3.8	4.7	8.4	9.1	2.2	5.3	2.4	4.8
	1990[c]	3.0	2.6	8.9	5.6	1.3	4.5	2.9	3.3
	2004	3.5	5.3	3.2	10.1	1.8	5.9	3.5	4.6
Indicators of innovation and information					Fixed line and mobile phone subscribers (per 1,000 people)				
	1990	2.1	63.0	6.1	2.5	6.0	6.1	65.1	3.2
	2004	37.0	587.2	499.4	7.8[d]	84.5	183.8	544.6	79.1
			Total public agriculture research and development (percent of agricultural output)						
	1981	0.28	1.15	0.41	0.22	0.34	0.3[e]	0.96	0.81
	1990	0.27[f]	1.65	0.32	0.44	0.48	0.3[e]	0.54	0.26
	2000	0.36[g]	1.76	0.4	0.38	0.42[e]	0.2[e]	0.87	0.38

Sources: Data compiled using IFPRI (2002, 2006), World Bank (2006, 2007), FAO (2006b), Gwartney and Lawson (2006), and Pardey, Alston, and Piggott (2006).
[a]Data represent averages calculated using available data points in the respective decade. [b]The available poverty data for India are disaggregated by rural and urban. The above data were obtained by calculating at the national level, using population estimates. [c]Data averaged for 1979–81 and 1989–91. [d]Data for 2003. [e]Data averaged for 1981–85, 1999–95, and 2001–03. [f]Data averaged for 1991–95. [g]Data for 2002.

and increased investment in R&D) are highly country specific. Thus, the heterogeneity experienced by these developing countries in the reduction of hunger and poverty seems mostly driven by domestic policies outside of the sphere of trade and FDI.

Drivers of Globalization and the Effects for Poverty

The Implications for Poverty of the Globalization of Agricultural Markets

Looking more specifically at agricultural markets, which, as stated earlier, are of particular significance because of the importance of the agricultural economy for poor people as both producers and consumers, many developing countries remain at the margin of the globalization process (see Chapter 1). Indeed, globalization has included a significant proportion of rural and urban food-insecure people into the market economy in parts of Asia and Latin America, while many of Africa's poor have been left out. Paradoxically, Sub-Saharan Africa entered the globalization era with the highest agricultural export shares among the developing regions and thus was most globalized in its agrifood system (see Table 1.2). Since then, the region has pulled back from global integration, relatively speaking, and lost competitiveness. Thus, food insecurity today predominates in the world region that participated least in the incremental globalization of agriculture.

A related concern has to do with trade policy in industrial countries. The fear is that, for the most part, large industrial countries orient their trading policies to suit their own interests. And even in the event that these countries remove tariff barriers for agricultural products, the danger that they will replace these with nontariff barriers in the guise of environmental, social, or food safety standards is strong (see Chapter 5).

For an empirical estimate of the effect of agricultural trade liberalization on the poor, most studies use computable general equilibrium models to estimate potential gains in terms of poverty reduction (for example, Cline 2004; World Bank 2004; Anderson, Martin, and van der Mensbrugghe 2005). The results of these studies are highly varied. For instance, Cline (2004) uses the Harrison-Rutherford-Tarr model, combined with the Global Trade Analysis Project (GTAP) database 5 (with base year 1997), to first estimate the change in trade flows, economic welfare, and product and factor prices as a result of full trade liberalization. He then calculates the corresponding effect on global poverty by using poverty elasticity estimates with respect to welfare changes in the aggregate. He finds that in the event of full trade liberalization, global poverty (less than US$2 a day) would be reduced by 110 million people by 2015 in the static case and by 500 million in the dynamic case (that is, taking into consideration the growth effects), and agricultural trade liberalization contributes to half of these gains. Anderson, Martin, and van der Mensbrugghe (2005) have much less optimistic results. They use the LINKAGE model combined with the GTAP database 6 (with base year 2001) and find an estimated decline in poverty (also defined as less than US$2 a day) of 52 million people by 2015 in the static case and 66 million in the dynamic case.

As analyzed by Bouët (2006), the divergent results of modeling exercises for trade effects on poor countries are largely because the studies use different experiments and data, along with models that have different behavioral parameters and theoretical features. Another issue is that developing countries' economic structures and current trade realities—that is, their trade rules, wider institutional and policy environments, standards and regulations, and domestic market development—differ, and, as a result, the effects of agricultural trade reform on households tends to be very case-specific (Imber, Morrison, and Thomson 2003). Yet another problem is that the studies use national estimates and therefore do not capture the regional disparities in incomes. Indeed, these studies make broad generalizations on the effects of trade reform on the poor. Moreover, as Ravallion (2004) and Topalova (2005) point out, cross-country analyses of the globalization (narrowly defined as increased openness to trade)–poverty linkages mask the heterogeneity of the effects of trade liberalization on different types of households. Because poverty is a multidimensional phenomenon and the poor are a very heterogeneous group, the studies fail to show the differential influences of trade reform on different households and their vulnerabilities (Reimer 2002). And, of course, they do not capture any of the nonincome elements of poverty outcomes, such as nutritional deterioration, discrimination, and lack of power to participate in society.

Current knowledge on trade reform effects at the household level is rather limited. Top-down approaches use detailed economywide data and build on the microeconomic assumption of a representative agent, whereas bottom-up approaches use detailed household expenditure data and emphasize the heterogeneity of households (Reimer 2002). In general, little consensus comes out of this literature. Hertel et al. (2003) undertake a static multicountry analysis of the effects of global trade reform on the poor in Brazil and Chile. They use a sequential two-step simulation approach while focusing on factor markets prices. They categorize households in each country in 5 groups (households within each group are divided into 20 subgroups according to income level) based on their principal income sources: transfers, agriculture, nonagricultural business, wages, and diversified income sources. Their findings indicate that in the case of full global trade liberalization, in both countries agricultural profits increase while wages and nonagricultural profits decrease. Thus, agricultural households benefit from trade reform while those specializing in nonagricultural business or depending on wages register an increase in poverty levels (less than US$1 a day;

Table 2.3   Percentage change in poverty head count in Brazil and Chile

Income source	Agriculture	Nonagriculture	Labor	Transfers	Diversified	Total
Brazil	−14.8	2.6	1.6	0.2	−2.5	−0.6
Chile	−31.2	5.0	4.0	1.2	−1.9	−1.7

Source: Hertel et al. (2003).

Table 2.3). In Brazil, for agricultural households and those depending on transfers and diversified income sources, poverty is reduced by 14.8 percent and 2.5 percent, respectively, whereas households depending on nonagricultural business and wage labor see an increase in poverty of 2.7 percent and 1.6 percent, respectively. Likewise, in Chile, poverty is reduced by 31.2 percent in agricultural households, whereas it increases in nonagricultural households and wage-dependent ones by 5 percent and 4 percent, respectively. As a result of the diverse group-specific effects, the overall effect on poverty is small (see the totals in Table 2.3).

Similarly, Ivanic (2005) conducted a multicountry analysis of the poverty effects of trade reform on different household groups. His analysis differentiates households by income sources and regions (urban and rural). He uses the GTAP model along with data from the GTAP database 6 and detailed household surveys from 15 countries. The author finds results similar to Hertel et al. (2003) for Brazil and Chile (that is, higher poverty levels in nonagricultural and wage-dependent households and lower poverty in agriculture-dependent households). However, he finds that this result does not always hold in other countries. For instance, in seven of the countries studied (Bangladesh, Colombia, Mexico, the Philippines, Uganda, Venezuela, and Zambia), full trade liberalization either increases poverty levels in agricultural and nonagricultural households or does not have any effects on poverty levels in either type of household.

Other studies use a combination of computable general equilibrium and micro-models to estimate the effects of trade liberalization on specific types of households. For instance, Cororaton and Cockburn (2006) use a computable general equilibrium microsimulation analysis to investigate the influence of trade reform (in the form of reduction of tariff rates) on rural and urban households in the Philippines. They find that tariff reductions lower consumer prices, which increases disposable income for all households. Additionally, they find that tariff cuts have a positive effect on the export-oriented manufacturing sector (because of lower costs of production and depreciation of the real exchange rate), but adversely affect the inwardly oriented agricultural sector. However, the expansion of the manufacturing sector offsets the contraction of the agricultural one, which translates into positive income effects for mobile unskilled production workers, who see the demand for their labor increase. Nevertheless, poor rural households, which largely depend on agriculture for their livelihoods, see only a nominal increase in incomes (Cororaton and Cockburn 2006).

Another study by Taylor, Dyer, and Yúnez-Navde (2005) uses a disaggregated rural economywide model to simulate the behavioral responses (farm production, labor, and migration) of rural households to market and policy shocks in the west-central region of Mexico. Specifically, they undertake two experiments whereby first, the market price of maize declines by 10 percent, and second, the market price of cash crops increases by 10 percent. In the first case, they find that in general, as a result of the decline in maize prices, commercial households decrease their production of maize by around 12 percent, which in turn decreases the demand for labor and land (by around 0.2 percent and 0.4 percent, respectively). However, they also find that because the decrease in the demand for labor and land translates into a reduction of input prices (because labor and land are also inputs), the production of subsistence maize increases. This increase results in the decrease of the "shadow" price of home-grown maize by about 0.2–0.3 percent. They conclude that the decline of maize prices has a negative income effect on both commercial and subsistence households, although it is small for the latter. In the second case of an increase in the price of cash crops, the study finds that as a result, cash-crop production increases by 3–4 percent, input prices rise (wages increase by 3.3 percent and rents by 11.8 percent), and the production of staple crops (maize in this case) declines. In terms of income effects, households owning land see the greatest increase, with their incomes increasing by 2.5–4 percent, depending on size of their landholdings; that of landless renters increases by about 2 percent (Taylor et al. 2005; see also Dyer, Boucher, and Taylor 2006 for a similar study).

In summary, despite some of these divergent findings, the overall result is that the majority of poor households will gain from trade reform while a minority will lose. Yet the results vary across countries and household types, and, according to these studies, the effect of trade openness on the incomes of poor households is not large. Thus, policymakers in each country need to consider complementary actions targeting vulnerable households to avoid potential negative effects on these populations.

Poverty Implications of the Globalization of Investment and Capital Flows

A central feature of globalization is the expansion of transborder capital investments. This trend is partly a consequence of market opening and expansion of trade, paving the way for direct engagement of global players with investments in countries that used to be only targets for trade. The question of interest here is not so much the general growth effects of FDI, but its influence on employment and income for the poor in countries receiving FDI. Important in that respect are how global changes in FDI opportunities are transforming into investment at the domestic level and how poor households, especially in rural areas, are affected (see Figure 2.1).

The theoretical literature identifies four channels by which increased FDI can affect poverty levels: employment, human capital formation, knowledge spillovers, and increased government revenue (Addison and Mavrotas 2004). When FDI flows into labor-intensive sectors, it can generate employment for unskilled workers, which would in turn increase their income level, and thus reduce poverty. However, if the FDI is either capital intensive and/or knowledge intensive, it may favor skilled over unskilled labor, which may translate into increased poverty. In the medium to long run, FDI inflows may induce growth within the economy through backward and forward linkages (that is, "crowding in" new investments) and through knowledge spillovers (Addison and Mavrotas 2004; Nguyen 2004).

Additionally, increased FDI could translate into government revenue, as the foreign firms pay corporate taxes. In the long run, when FDI flows crowd in new investments, it entails an increase in the tax base. The additional revenue could then be used to make pro-poor public investments (such as in infrastructure and public services), which would translate in poverty reduction (Addison and Mavrotas 2004).

The location of FDI (in special zones or mainly in urban areas) and the sector patterns of FDI (in the food and agriculture and related processing industries) play a role in pro-poor outcomes. FDI in agriculture and food is rather limited (see Chapter 1). FDI concentration in urban areas fosters rural–urban migration, and the effects for the rural poor are rather indirect but can be positive through remittances and wage-rate effects. FDI related to fast expansion of the retail industries can be significant for the rural poor if market innovations reach small and poor farmers, but this effect is context specific, as discussed in Chapter 6.

Although some work has been undertaken looking at the growth effects of FDI, very little empirical evidence exists on the direct influence of FDI on poverty levels. Among the few such studies, Nguyen (2004) uses a regression analysis to investigate the contributions of FDI to poverty reduction in Vietnam by looking at FDI contributions to employment, economic growth at the provincial level, and local budgets during 1996–2000. She found FDI contributed positively and significantly to provincial economic growth, and that while real growth of provincial GDP was a significant factor of poverty reduction, the direct effect of FDI on poverty at the national level was insignificant. The other channel of potential FDI contribution to poverty reduction (contribution to local budgets) was also found to be insignificant (Nguyen 2004).

The effects of globalization on employment are a major concern in industrialized as well as developing countries. The expected link is that increased trade across borders might increase pressure on wages, especially for labor with low skills. For example, one study undertaken in Indonesia used a combination of quantitative and qualitative analyses to look at the effects of FDI on gendered labor markets. The author found that although FDI increased both male and female wages, results on other factors, such as working conditions and wage gaps between men and women, varied widely by sector (Siegmann 2003). However, investigations on the effects of globalization (and particularly increased FDI) on labor markets are by no means unequivocal (Gaston and Nelson 2001). Indeed, the direct effects of FDI on salary rates and employment levels are rather small. The effects of allocating production in low-wage locations are also not conclusive with respect to salaries and employment levels. The rates of remuneration for well-trained workers, however, are rising. The consequences of globalization for poor people's employment opportunities depend on labor productivity and on policies (including education) and legal arrangements.

Implications of the Globalization of Information and Innovation on Poverty

In view of the pervasive nature of information and innovation under globalization, it is difficult to isolate their effects in the first place and even more so to relate them to poverty reduction and changes in food security. However, it would be negligent to exclude these potentially highly pro-poor developments from an assessment of globalization on poverty.

Indeed, access to information of relevance to the poor and to innovations and technology remain central for sustained poverty reduction. Global information flows, springing from media and the Internet, reach deep into poor households and influence aspirations and motivations. Today, in almost any country in the world (with very few exceptions), the poor cannot be excluded from information on political, social, and economic developments, even if some governments still attempt to block such information.

Information flows that are of relevance to the productivity and well-being of the poor are also important determinants of poor peoples' decisions and choices of livelihoods. These include information on adaptable innovations and research findings to national agricultural research systems (see Chapter 3) and the related absorptive capacity in these systems; information systems for market and price formation (see Chapter 4) and those for global health services (for example, HealthNet [http://www.healthnet.org/healthnet.php]) that facilitate inclusion of isolated medical personnel in expert advisory systems (Micevska 2005).

Although national and global agricultural and food policies are important, technologies and related policies that are exogenous to agriculture may be of much greater relevance than agricultural policies to the globalization of agriculture and its effects on the poor. Primary among those forces is the ICT revolution—the technological backbone of globalization. Indeed, as stated by professor Muhammad Yunus (2006, xix), "Every single effort for ending poverty in the world can become more effective with ICT than ever before. ICT has one great quality—we can use it for any purpose. It fits snugly into any need we want to use it for. If we want to solve the problem of hungry people finding food, ICT will help if we can come up with the right idea."

The cell phone in the hand of a poor rural woman has become the example of fundamental change brought about by globalization. Here we are not attempting to look into general ICT–development linkages during globalization (see Torero and von Braun 2006), but more specifically at ICT–agriculture and poverty linkages.

The expanding ICT infrastructure—reaching increasingly into poor rural areas—offers economies of scale that stimulate network building and have consequent spillover benefits (Torero, Chowdhury, and Bedi 2005). ICTs are not intrinsically pro-poor. Across countries, where levels of inequality differ, leapfrogging—fast-track access to new ICTs—sometimes occurs, but sometimes it does not. These different outcomes are largely determined by public action and institutional arrangements for regulation and effective privatization.

ICTs cannot be developed without strong institutions that overtly facilitate private investment. Many of the national telecommunications monopolies in developing countries were privatized in the 1980s and 1990s, introducing them to competition. This stimulus, combined with ongoing technological change, prompted the continual development of new services in some developing countries, especially the exponential increase of cellular telephone penetration in poor countries. In some countries (such as Argentina, Chile, Mozambique, Peru, Senegal, and Uganda), the government is facilitating rapid ICT progress with the help of NGOs and the private sector. In others (such as Cameroon, Ethiopia, North Korea, and Zimbabwe), the government stands in the way of reform, thus preventing access to globalization opportunities by the poor in rural areas.

Analysis of household demand for telephones in rural areas of Bangladesh and Peru and estimates of the gains in welfare from using telephones compared with alternative means of communication (such as mail, traveling, and radio communication) show a considerable gap between current prices of alternative means and the use of telephones. Just within the poorest quintile, the minimum estimated gains in welfare from local telephone calls compared with regular mail were US$0.11 and US$1.62 for Bangladesh and Peru, respectively (Chowdhury 2005). In these cases the technology and the engagement of global players has reached out to the poor and cut their costs to engage in markets for outputs, inputs, and labor, and for their access to services.

However, poor people are still excluded from many public services, and ICTs have not been adapted to the appropriate delivery of pro-poor public goods in general, such as health care and education. In many countries, a fast development of information technology–based market information systems is evolving, with commodity exchanges reaching out to small farmers, such as in India. ICTs are an opportunity for development in the context of globalization, but they are not a panacea. For the potential poverty-reduction benefits of ICTs to be realized in developing countries, many prerequisites need to be put in place: prompt deregulation, effective competition among service providers, free movement and adoption of technologies, targeted and competitive subsidies to reduce the real access gap, and institutional arrangements to increase the use of ICTs in the provision of public goods (Torero and von Braun 2006).

Implications of Global Social Policies for Poverty

One problem for hungry people is time. They cannot wait for long-term solutions, such as the economic progress that globalization offers. Overcoming poverty through economic growth alone would require decades, even with a high growth rate. For example, a per capita income of US$1 a day with a yearly growth rate of 3 percent would reach US$2 a day only after approximately 24 years. To address the time issue and to cope with emergencies, social policy is warranted.

The world does not have anything that could be called a "global social policy," and it is questionable whether one would be desirable, effective, and efficient. This question goes beyond the scope of this chapter. Global learning and adaptation of social policies across countries, however, would be a desirable feature of globalization (von Braun 2007). To the extent that social policies reach the poor and hungry, especially in rural areas, they are relevant to this review (see Figure 2.1).

Elements of a globalized social policy actually do exist, not only with the largely ineffective agenda setting at the World Summit for Social Development (in Copenhagen in 1995) and efforts to follow up on that meeting, but more realistically and gradually with efforts to establish social and economic rights at a global level.[5] A relevant example here is the human right to food (FAO 1996) and the related follow-up to a global consensus (von Braun and Cohen 2003). Another element is global emergency aid and its coordination mechanisms (for example, the Food Aid Convention [http://www.fao.org/legal/rtf/fac99-e.htm]) and the more ad hoc but coordinated responses to disasters (for example, responses to major tsunamis).

Another social policy issue to be addressed is child labor, as it is often seen in relation to globalization. The International Labour Organization (ILO) has been active since 1919 in restricting child labor and improving working conditions, among other things, by defining standards in the framework of conventions. In June 1999, the ILO adopted a convention to combat the worst forms of child labor and reached an agreement on basic standards (such as freedom of association, the right to organize and bargain collectively, freedom from forced labor, and minimum requirements with respect to wages, hours, and working conditions) that were proposed at the World Summit for Social Development in Copenhagen in 1995. According to the findings by Admassie (2001) for Ethiopia and other African countries, by far the largest proportion of child labor in the poorest countries is to be found in economic areas that have been the least touched by globalization, such as agricultural subsistence production and domestic service. Moreover, initiatives against exploitative child labor policies (for example, a recent initiative on child labor in agriculture; ILO 2007) are among recent global social policies of relevance to this review.

Also, global health policy initiatives, such as the program on Disease Control Priorities in Developing Countries and the Global Fund to fight AIDS, TB, and malaria, with new funding and operated through new networks, are significant innovations that aim to bring global scale to efforts that could change the courses of these diseases (see http://www.dcp2.org and http://www.theglobalfund.org).

Since 2000, the MDGs have been a mix of developmental and social policy objectives. They, however, do not include a comprehensive social policy agenda of social protection and insurance. And do the MDGs actually take a global view? In September 2000, the international community adopted the MDGs to guide more coherent development cooperation policies. MDG-1 is to cut the proportions of hunger and poverty in half in 2000–2015. As such, the MDGs do not offer a conceptual framework for the effects of globalization on poverty. Saith (2006, 1184, 1186) argues that "the entire MDG scaffolding and accompanying text is insufficiently global in its approach," not only because of lack of attention to structural imbalances and anti-poor policy biases but because "the goals ... have remarkably little that barks, let alone bites, in the direction of relationships between economies of the global north and south." Although the MDGs may be partly driven by globalization risks and opportunities, they are merely goals, and the appropriate set of instruments to achieve them remains a matter of great debates on development policy (for example, Sachs 2005; Easterly 2006). Nevertheless, the MDGs have created policy aspirations to address poverty and hunger more comprehensively in some countries and have stimulated new commitments in development aid.

More relevant than top-down global social policy is the influence of globalization on the spread of national social policy innovations across countries. Here, the example of the spread of the Mexican Progresa program, which focuses on building human capital in poor households through conditonal cash transfers, is important (Skoufias 2005; Levy 2006). Transnational learning about social policies and what works under what circumstances has certainly been made easier by the globalization trends of information and innovation discussed above. Such transnational learning opportunities may be relevant for a globalization of social policies, as they will from the outset build on existing institutional strength in the adopting countries, rather than building in a institutional vacuum or even undermining existing institutional arrangements that can serve as part of effective social policy.

An active search for synergy between economics and social ethics is needed to overcome the sharp conflicts accompanying globalization (von Braun and Mengistu 2007). To ensure that the poor receive a fair share of the potential gains, it is necessary to reassess the existing institutional arrangements (Sen 2002). The economic and ethical principles of social policies and inclusion of the poorest need to be translated into actual pro-poor policies at a larger scale. The ethical principles guiding institutional reform can draw on Rawls (1971), because the ethics of transnational sharing of opportunity and wealth are in principle not different from national-level considerations.

In sum, considerable innovations in social policy have sprung up over the past three decades in parallel to economic globalization and have made contributions to balance risks for the poor; increasingly—but with long delays after economic globalization—these policies have started to reach into rural areas in recent years. Although they may have helped reduce the proportions of the poor and hungry, they did not substantially reduce the absolute numbers of these population groups in many countries.

Conclusions

The effects of globalization on the poor need to be traced for different components of globalization: market integration across borders, investment capital flows across borders, information and innovation across borders, and social policies reaching into rural areas that originate at a global level or from cross-border learning. Reducing the definition of globalization to (direct or indirect) market effects only does not yield a comprehensive picture. Globalization permits poor people to either directly or indirectly access previously unavailable markets, capital, employment, knowledge, and social protection.

Poverty and hunger have not decreased commensurate with the increased resources generated by growth effects of globalization. Globalization offers opportunities for growth, but that growth alone is not a guarantee for poverty reduction. Hunger—representing a central aspect of absolute poverty—has at best been slightly reduced during the recent decades of globalization.

Trade liberalization in agriculture will allow many developing countries to deploy their comparative advantages and to actively participate in world trade. Still, a mixed picture emerges from the analyses of trade liberalization across and within developing countries. The winner–loser patterns are complex.

Trade expansion is complemented and followed by expanded capital flows (FDI) during globalization, but the record of agriculture and the rural hinterlands being touched by FDI is mixed. High-value agriculture is showing opportunities for the poor in some regions and countries.

National policy in response to globalization opportunities and risks has been of mixed effectiveness. Many countries have not shown the capability to transform globalization opportunities into poverty reduction. Adverse terms of trade, domestic institutional constraints, bad governance, and undervaluing the growth opportunities in rural areas (as revealed by lack of attention to infrastructure, rural education, and agricultural innovation) have reduced such chances.

The allocation of information, innovation, and technology in support of agricultural and rural development is a basis for self-supporting growth in low-income countries, where poverty is often concentrated in rural areas. Information and communications innovations and agricultural innovations offer opportunities during globalization, but both require public action in terms of appropriate regulations (for ICT to reach out to rural areas) and public investment (for agriculture research that has focuses on public good).

The social policy domains have thus far not been captured by a globalization trend, although various attempts are noteworthy (such as the MDGs). More relevant are cross-border learning and adaptation of social policies, as is the case with human resource–related transfer programs and the strengthening of healthcare systems in rural areas. And even more important are changes in the mindsets and institutions that focus on sharing wealth, including intellectual wealth and knowledge, as underlined in the following essay by M. S. Swaminathan. Social and political actions that seek sustainable improvement in poor people's living conditions would also foster the advancement of their social and economic rights. In principle, globalization that expands opportunities has made that utopian task of equal rights for the poor somewhat easier. The political forces of globalization have not made it more realistic.

Notes

1. The index includes three equally weighted indicators: the proportion of people who are food-energy deficient as estimated by FAO, the prevalence of underweight in children under the age of 5 as compiled by WHO, and the under-5 mortality rate as reported by UNICEF (Wiesmann, von Braun, and Feldbrügge 2000; Wiesmann 2007).

2. According to the United Nations Development Programme (UNDP), in 1960–62 the average per capita GDP of the 20 richest countries was 54 times higher than that of the 20 poorest countries, while by 2000–2002 it was 121 times higher (UNDP 2005).

3. In the past decade, many developing countries have experienced rapid economic growth, but this growth has not always translated in poverty reduction; in some cases poverty rates even increased.

Indeed, such countries as Madagascar, Peru, Bangladesh, South Africa, and the Philippines have seen their poverty rates increase, although they have been experiencing average economic growth rates of 2.5–5.6 percent a year since the mid-1990s.

4. The index, which is computed by the Frasier Institute, "measures the degree to which the policies and institutions of a country are supportive of economic freedom" Gwartney and Lawson (2007, 3).

5. INTERNATIONAL COVENANT ON ECONOMIC, SOCIAL AND CULTURAL RIGHTS, 1966

> *Article 111.* The States Parties to the present Covenant recognize the right of everyone to an adequate standard of living for himself and his family, including adequate food. . . . The States Parties will take appropriate steps to ensure the realization of this right, recognizing to this effect the essential importance of international cooperation based on free consent.

UNITED NATIONS CONVENTION ON THE RIGHTS OF THE CHILD, 1989

> *Article 24-2.* States Parties shall . . . take appropriate measures . . . to combat disease and malnutrition . . . through, inter alia, the application of readily available technology and through the provision of adequate nutritious foods.

> *Article 27.* States Parties, in accordance with national conditions and within their means . . . shall in case of need provide material assistance and support programmes, particularly with regard to nutrition.

WORLD FOOD SUMMIT PLAN OF ACTION, 1996

> *Commitment Seven.* We will implement, monitor and follow-up this Plan of Action at all levels in cooperation with the international community.

> *Objective 7.4.* To clarify the content of the right to adequate food and the fundamental right of everyone to be free from hunger, as stated in the International Covenant on Economic, Social and Cultural Rights and other relevant international and regional instruments, and to give particular attention to implementation and full and progressive realization of this right as a means of achieving food security for all.

See details for the above at http://www.fao.org/FOCUS/E/rightfood/right6.htm.

References

Addison, T., and G. Mavrotas. 2004. Foreign direct investment, innovative sources of development finance and domestic resource mobilization. Background paper for *Track II global economic agenda, Helsinki process on globalization and democracy*. Helsinki: United Nations University—World Institute for Development Economics Research.

Admassie, A. 2001. *The incidence of child labor in Africa with empirical evidence from rural Ethiopia.* ZEF Discussion Paper 32. Bonn, Germany: Zentrum für Entwicklungsforschung, Bonn University.

Agénor, P-R. 2002. *Does globalization hurt the poor?* World Bank Institute Policy Research Working Paper 2922. Washington, D.C.: World Bank.

Ahmed, A., R. Hill, L. Smith, D. Wiesmann, and T. Frahenberger. 2007. The world's poorest and hungy: Trends, characteristics and causes. 2020 Working Paper. Washington, D.C.: International Food Policy Research Institute.

Alesina, A., and R. Perotti. 1996. Income distribution, political instability, and investment. *European Economic Review* 40 (6): 1203–1228.

Alesina, A., and D. Rodrik. 1994. Distributive policies and economic growth. *Quarterly Journal of Economics* 109 (2): 465–490.

Anderson, K., W. Martin, and D. van der Mensbrugghe. 2005. Market welfare implications of Doha reform scenarios. Paper prepared for the 8th Annual Conference on Global Economic Analysis, 9–11 June, Lübeck, Germany.

Bardhan, P. 2006. Globalization and rural poverty. *World Development* 34 (8): 1393–1404.

Bhagwati, J. 1997. The global age: From a skeptical south to a fearful north. *World Economy* 20: 259–283.

Bhalla, S. 2002. *Imagine there is no country: Poverty, inequality and growth in the era of globalization.* Washington, D.C.: Institute for International Economics.

Birdsall, N., and J. L. Londoño. 1997. Asset inequality matters: An assessment of the World Bank's approach to poverty reduction. *American Economic Review* 87 (2): 32–37.

Bouët, A. 2006. *What can the poor expect from trade liberalization? Opening the "black box" of trade modeling.* IFPRI Markets, Trade and Institutions Division Discussion Paper 93. Washington, D.C.: International Food Policy Research Institute.

Bourguignon, F. 1981. Pareto-superiority of unegalitarian equilibria in Stiglitz' model of wealth distribution with convex savings function. *Econometrica* 49: 1469–1475.

Chen, S., and M. Ravallion. 1997. What can survey data tell us about recent changes in distribution and poverty? *World Bank Economic Review* 11 (2): 357–382.

———. 2007. Absolute poverty measures for the developing world, 1981–2004. Policy Research Working Paper 4211, World Bank, Washington, D.C. Mimeo.

Chowdhury, S. K. 2005. Implications of access to public telephones: The case in rural Bangladesh. In *Information and communication technologies for development and poverty reduction,* ed. M. Torero and J. von Braun. Baltimore: The Johns Hopkins University Press for the International Food Policy Research Institute.

Cline, W. R. 2004. *Trade policy and global poverty.* Washington, D.C.: Center for Global Development and Institute for International Economics.

Cororaton, C. B., and J. Cockburn. 2006. Trade reform and poverty—Lessons from the Philippines: A CGE-microsimulation analysis. *Journal of Policy Modeling* 29 (2007): 140–163.

Deininger, K., and L. Squire. 1996. A new data set measuring income inequality. *World Bank Economic Review* 10 (3): 565–591.

Díaz-Bonilla, C., E. Díaz-Bonilla, V. Piñeiro, and S. Robinson. 2006. Argentina—The convertibility plan, trade openness, poverty and inequality. In *Who gains from trade? Export-led growth, inequality and poverty in Latin America,* ed. S. R. Vos, E. Ganuza, S. Morley, and S. Robinson. New York and London: Routledge Studies in Development Economics.

Dollar, D., and A. Kraay. 2001. *Trade, growth and poverty.* Policy Research Working Paper 2615. Washington, D.C.: World Bank.

Dyer, G. A., S. Boucher, and J. E. Taylor. 2006. Subsistence response to market shocks. *American Journal of Agricultural Economics* 88 (2): 279–291.

Easterly, W. 2006. *The white man's burden: Why the West's efforts to aid the rest have done so much ill and so little good.* New York: Penguin.

FAO (Food and Agriculture Organization of the United Nations). 1996. *Final report of the World Food Summit, Part I.* Rome.

———. 2006a. *State of food insecurity in the world 2006.* Rome.

———. 2006b. FAOSTAT. Available at http://faostat.fao.org/default/aspx.

Gaston, N., and D. Nelson. 2001. *Multinational location decisions and labor markets.* ZEF Discussion Paper 37. Bonn, Germany: Zentrum für Entwicklungsforschung, Bonn University.

Gwartney, J., and R. Lawson. 2006. *Economic freedom of the world: 2006 annual report.* Vancouver: Frasier Institute.

Hertel, T. W., and A. L. Winters. 2005. Poverty impacts of a WTO agreement: Synthesis and overview. In *Poverty and the WTO: Impacts of the Doha development agenda,* ed. T. W. Hertel and A. L. Winters. Washington, D.C.: World Bank.

Hertel, T. W., P. V. Preckel, J. A. L. Cranfield, and M. Ivanic. 2003. Multilateral trade liberalization and poverty in Brazil and Chile. *Économie Internationale* 94–95: 201–234.

IFPRI (International Food Policy Research Institute). 2002. *Agriculture science and technology indicators (ASTI).* Washington, D.C.

———. 2006. *Global Hunger Index.* Washington, D.C.

ILO (International Labor Organization). 2007. *World day against child labour 2007: New global partnership against child labor in agriculture.* Geneva: ILO.

Imber, V., J. Morrison, and A. Thomson. 2003. *Food security, trade and livelihoods linkages.* Oxford: Programme of Advisory Support Services to Rural Livelihoods and Department for International Development.

Ivanic, M. 2005. The effects of a prospective multilateral trade reform on poverty in developing countries. In *Poverty and the WTO: Impacts of the Doha Development Agenda,* ed. T. W. Hertel and A. L. Winters. Washington, D.C.: World Bank.

Jenkins, R. 2005. *Globalization, production and poverty*. WIDER Research Paper 2005/40. Helsinki: United Nations University–World Institute for Development Economics Research.

Kanbur, R. 2001. Economic policy, distribution and poverty: The nature of disagreements. *World Development* 29 (6): 1083–1094.

Korten, D. 2001. *When corporations rule the world*. Bloomfield, Conn., U.S.A.: Kumarian Press.

Levy, S. 2006. Progress against poverty: Sustaining Mexico's Progresa-Oportunidades program. Washington, D.C.: Brookings Institution Press.

Li, H., and H. Zhou. 1998. Income inequality is not harmful for growth: Theory and evidence. *Review of Development Economics* 2 (3): 318–334.

McCulloch, N., A. L. Winters, and X. Cirera. 2001. Agricultural trade reform. In *The WTO and Agriculture*, vol. II, ed. K. Anderson, and T. Josling. Northampton, Mass., U.S.A.: Edward Elgar Publishing.

Micevska, M. 2005. ICT for pro-poor provision of public goods and services: A focus on health. In *Information and communication technologies for development and poverty reduction*, ed. M. Torero and J. von Braun. Baltimore: The Johns Hopkins University Press for the International Food Policy Research Institute.

Micronutrient Initiative and UNICEF (United Nations Children's Fund). 2005. *Vitamin and mineral deficiency: A global progress report*. New York: UNICEF.

Milanovic, B. 2002. True world income distribution, 1988 and 1993: First calculation based on household surveys alone. *Economic Journal* 112 (January): 51–92.

———. 2005. *World apart: Measuring international and global inequality*. Princeton, N.J.: Princeton University Press.

Nguyen, T. 2004. *Foreign direct investment and its contributions to economic growth and poverty reduction in Vietnam (1986–2001)*. New York: Peter Lang.

Nissanke, M., and E. Thorbecke. 2005. Channels and policy debate in the globalization-inequality-poverty nexus. Revised version of paper prepared for the United Nations University–WIDER project "The Impact of Globalization on the World's Poor," Helsinki.

———. 2006. The impact of globalization on the world's poor. *World Development* 34 (8): 1333–1337.

Orden, D., M. Torero, and A. Gulati. 2004. Agricultural markets and the rural poor. Draft background paper for the workshop of the Poverty Reduction Network, March 5, Washington, D.C.

Oxfam. 2002. *Global finance hurts the poor. Analysis of the impact of North-South private capital flows on growth, inequality and poverty*. Boston: Oxfam America.

Pardey, P. G., J. M Alston, and R. R. Piggott, eds. 2006. *Agriculture R&D in the developing world: Too little, too late?* Washington, D.C.: International Food Policy Research Institute.

Ravallion, M. 2003. *Debate on globalization, poverty and inequality: Why measurement matters*. World Bank PovertyNet library paper. Washington, D.C.: World Bank.

———. 2004. *Looking beyond averages in the trade and poverty debate*. Paper prepared for the United Nations University–WIDER project, "The Impact of Globalization on the World's Poor," Helsinki.

Rawls, J. 1971. *A theory of justice*. Cambridge, Mass., U.S.A.: Harvard University Press.

Reimer, J. J. 2002. *Estimating the poverty impacts of trade liberalization*. GTAP Working Paper 20. West Lafayette, Ind., U.S.A.: Center for Global Trade Analysis and Department of Agricultural Economics, Purdue University.

Sachs, J. D., ed. 2005. *Investing in development: A practical plan to achieve the Millennium Development Goals*. New York: Earthscan for the Millennium Project.

Saith, A. 2006. From universal to Millennium Development Goals: Lost in translation. *Development and Change* 37 (6): 1167–1199.

Sanchez, O. 2003. Globalization as a development strategy in Latin America? *World Development* 31 (12): 1977–1995.

Sen, A. 2002. How to judge globalism. *American Prospect* 13 (1): 2–6.

Shiva, V. 2000. BBC Reith Lectures 2000: Poverty and Globalization. Available at http://news.bbc .co.uk/hi/english/static/events/reith_2000/lecture5.stm.

Siegmann, K. A. 2003. Gender employment and equity: Effects of foreign direct investment in rural Indonesia. Ph.D. thesis, Zentrum für Entwicklungsforschung, Bonn University, Bonn, Germany.

Skoufias, E. 2005. Progresa and its impacts on the welfare of rural households in Mexico. IFPRI Research Report 139. Washington, D.C.: International Food Policy Research Institute.

Streeten, P. 2001. *Globalization: Threat or opportunity*. Copenhagen: Copenhagen Business School Press.

Taylor, J. E., G. A. Dyer, and A. Yúnez-Naude. 2005. Disaggregated rural economywide models for policy analysis. *World Development* 33 (10): 1671–1688.

Topalova, P. 2005. Trade liberalization, poverty and inequality: Evidence from Indian districts. NBER Working Paper 11614. New York and Stanford, Calif., U.S.A.: National Bureau of Economic Research.

Torero, M., and J. von Braun. 2006. Impacts of ICT on low-income households. In *Information and communication technologies for development and poverty reduction*, ed. M. Torero and J. von Braun. Baltimore: The Johns Hopkins University Press for the International Food Policy Research Institute.

Torero, M., S. K. Chowdhury, and A. Bedi. 2005. Telecommunications infrastructure and economic growth. In *Information and communication technologies for development and poverty reduction*, ed.

M. Torero and J. von Braun. Baltimore: The Johns Hopkins University Press for the International Food Policy Research Institute.

UNDP (United Nations Development Programme). 2005. *Human development report 2005.* New York: Oxford University Press.

———. 2006. *Human development report 2006.* New York: Oxford University Press.

UNICEF (United Nations Children's Fund). 2006. *Progress for children: A report card on nutrition,* no. 4. New York.

United Nations Millennium Project Task Force on Hunger. 2005. *Halving hunger: It can be done.* New York: United Nations Development Programme.

UN/SCN (United Nations System Standing Committee on Nutrition). 2004. *Fifth report on the world nutrition situation: Nutrition for improved development outcomes.* Geneva: United Nations.

von Braun, J. 2005. Agricultural economics and distributional effects. *Agricultural Economics* 32 (1): 1–20.

———. 2007. Focus on the world's poorest and hungry people: IFPRI 2006–2007 Annual Report Essay. Washington, D.C.: International Food Policy Research Institute.

von Braun, J., and M. J. Cohen. 2003. The human right to food, economic growth and development. In *The right to food and the cost of hunger,* ed. S. Arnaldi and L. Postiglione-Blommestein. Soveria Mannelli, Italy: Rubbettino.

von Braun, J., and T. Mengistu. 2007. On ethics and economics of changing behavior in food and agricultural production, consumption and trade: Some reflections on what to do. In *Ethics, hunger, and globalization,* ed. P. Pinstrup-Andersen and P. Sandøe. Dordrecht, The Netherlands: Springer.

Wade, R. H. 2004. Is globalization reducing poverty and inequality? *World Development* 32 (4): 567–589.

Wiesmann, D. 2006. A Global Hunger Index: Measurement concept, ranking of countries, and trends. FCND Discussion Paper 212. Washington, D.C.: International Food Policy Research Institute.

———. 2007. *The challenge of hunger 2007: Global Hunger Index; Facts, determinants, and trends.* Washington, D.C., and Bonn: International Food Policy Research Institute and Deutsche Welthungerhilfe, Concern Worldwide.

Wiesmann, D., J. von Braun, and T. Feldbrügge. 2000. *An international nutrition index—Successes and failures in addressing hunger and malnutrition.* ZEF Discussion Paper 26. Bonn, Germany: Zentrum für Entwicklungsforschung, Bonn University.

Winters, A. L., N. McCulloch, and A. McKay. 2004. Trade liberalization and poverty: The evidence so far. *Journal of Economic Literature* 42 (1): 72–115.

World Bank. 2001. *World development report 2001.* New York: Oxford University Press.

————. 2004. *Global economic prospects 2004: Realizing the development promise of the Doha agenda.* Washington, D.C.

————. 2006. *PovcalNet.* Washington, D.C. Available at http://iresearch.worldbank.org/PovcalNet/jsp/index.jsp.

————. 2007. *World development indicators 2007.* Washington, D.C.

Yunus, M. 2006. Foreword. In *Information and communication technologies for development and poverty reduction*, ed. M. Torero and J. von Braun. Baltimore: The Johns Hopkins University Press for the International Food Policy Research Institute.

Making Globalization Work for the Poor: Technology and Trade

M. S. Swaminathan

This essay focuses on two aspects of the links between globalization and the poor: technology and trade. The spectacular progress of science and technology has resulted in an increasing technological divide between industrialized and developing countries. If access to technology has been a major cause of economic inequity in the past, the challenge now lies in enlisting technology as an ally in the movement for social and gender equity. I also refer briefly to how to build a sustainable trade security system for the poor, because increasingly, agriculture has become a gamble in the market. In my country, India, we used to say that agriculture is a gamble on the monsoon, but at least now with irrigation and other infrastructure, the influence of changing weather on crop production can be minimized, to some extent. However, the difficulty of trade is still there.

Before going to the two issues mentioned, there are some broad principles regarding what needs to be done if globalization is truly to help the poor. First, there must be a global commitment to eliminate unsustainable lifestyles and unacceptable poverty. If the commitment is not there, the goal is going to be very difficult to attain. Second, project design must aim at social inclusion. Third, it is important to change the mindset from patronage to partnership. Referring to the poor as "target groups" (a phrase that I dislike profoundly) is a reflection of a patronage mentality that must be modified if we want to achieve poverty reduction. Safety net programs should not compromise human dignity. Fourth, there must be a shift from unskilled to skilled work. So long as people are unskilled, the maximum they can expect is to receive the minimum wage, which is more than most people get in a majority of developing countries. Finally, it is clear that we must promote job-led economic growth, particularly in population-rich but land-hungry countries. As Gandhi put it, "production by masses is the need of the hour and not just mass production."

Another general point that must be emphasized is that the best safety net against hunger and poverty, particularly in countries where a large percentage of the population still lives in rural areas, is broad agriculture progress, including crop and animal husbandry, fisheries, forestry, and agroprocessing. For instance, studies in India have shown that wherever there is agriculture progress, poverty reduction is quite steep. That is why I endorse those who emphasize the need to give agriculture a higher priority in the national agenda, including attention to technology, training and capacity building, techno-infrastructure, and trade and asset reform.

Technology

Small Farms Can Be Highly Productive

The Indian Green Revolution was started by many small farmers, most of whom were introduced to the new opportunities through national demonstrations. Farming in the world today, however, is becoming divided into two cultures: large agribusinesses supported by heavy inputs of technology, capital, and subsidies and small farmers operating one or two hectares, who face many difficulties. Here I want to differentiate between a small farmer and a small farm. A small farm is ideal for intensive ecological agriculture and can be highly productive. But the small farmer is a euphemism for a producer who suffers from severe economic and technological handicaps, such as lack of access to credit and to markets, a mismatch between production and postharvest technology, and related problems.

The other important feature, particularly in India, but also partly true in other countries (for example, China), is that most farms—and not only small ones—resort to mixed farming/mixed cropping. This practice is a coping mechanism against calamities and failure of income opportunities. The crop–livestock integration is very important, both for household nutrition security and for additional sources of income. For instance, India produced close to 92 million tons[1] of milk in 2003 (FAO 2006); dairy production provides supplementary income to more than 70 percent of rural households, and women carry out more than 90 percent of the activities related to care and management of dairy animals (Delgado, Narrod, and Tiongco 2004).

As Marcel Proust put it, "the real voyage of discovery does not consist of seeking new landscape but in having new eyes." When discussing poverty and globalization, more important than having a new thesis is to look with the eyes of the people involved and to look at their concerns. Then one can see that if small producers are given the power of scale through cooperatives to achieve assured and remunerative marketing, production can go up speedily. Such a dramatic increase is evidenced in the dairy sector in India, where milk production rose from about 20 million tons in the 1960s to close to 92 million tons, largely produced by small farms of one to two buffaloes or two cows. By the end of the 1990s, India surpassed the United States in milk production (Figure E1.1).

But how did this happen? The most important thing is that small producers were allowed access to the power of scale in processing and marketing. As stated earlier, the small farm is ideal for intense ecological agriculture, even though the small farmer is affected by many handicaps. Similarly, in the case of

Figure E1.1   Milk production, India and United States, 1961–2003

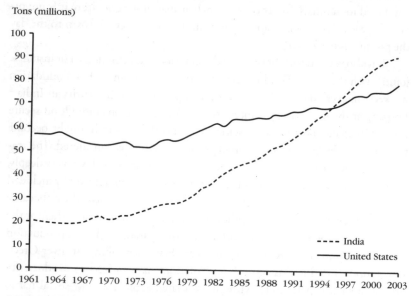

Tons (millions)

- - - - India
—— United States

Source: FAO 2006.

animal production, if farmers are provided the services needed, such as health care, marketing, and particularly fodder and feed, then they can overcome at least some of those handicaps. And that is what the cooperative movement in India did. The lesson I want to convey is that the poor should be helped by the power of scale at both the production and marketing levels. In other words, decentralized production supported by key centralized services—services such as plant and animal health care, in this particular case—can trigger greater progress.

From Green Revolution to Ever-Green Revolution

Another problem in most developing countries is a mismatch between production and postharvest technologies. Many times, production technology is advanced, but postharvest technology has lagged. A vast amount of biomass is produced by the plants: after all, if the harvest index is, say, one-third, that means that two-thirds are the other parts of that plant. In Punjab, for example, more than 10 million tons of rice straw are burned because farmers have to harvest their rice speedily if they are to plant their wheat on time. At the same time, in neighboring Rajasthan there is a tremendous shortage of fodder and feed. Taking the rice straw and enriching it with urea and molasses can create good feed for animals. In other words, when analyzing agriculture it is important to have an end-to-end approach from the day the seed is sown to the day the product is marketed.

It is also very important to take a dynamic look at technology. For instance, jointly with the World Food Programme, the M. S. Swaminathan Foundation worked on a very detailed analysis and mapping of food insecurity in India.[2] Looking at the maps, what is interesting is that the regions more food secure now, such as Punjab and other states in the north and south, might become food insecure by 2020 if sustainability of food security is considered. The reason is that the soil is overexploited, the groundwater has gone down very deeply, and there is extensive salinization. The crop rotation, which normally included at least one legume, now has given way to a sequence of rice-wheat, because there is a ready market for both products and the government buys them at the support price. Therefore, it is important to have a paradigm shift in production technology from Green Revolution to what I have been calling an "Ever-Green Revolution." I define this term as a revolution that can lead to productivity improvements in perpetuity without associated ecological and social harm, provided the proper mix of technology and public policy is employed. The difference in approach is that the Green Revolution has been commodity centered, whereas the Ever-Green Revolution must center on integrated natural resources management. This notion is very aptly captured by Edward O. Wilson (2002) in *The Future of Life:*

> The problem before us is how to feed billions of new mouths over the next several decades and save the rest of life at the same time without being trapped in a Faustian bargain that threatens freedom from security. The benefits must come from an evergreen revolution. The aim of this new thrust is to lift production well above the levels attained by the Green Revolution of the 1960s, using technology and regulatory policy more advanced and even safer than now in existence.

I want to emphasize that an Ever-Green Revolution is also possible, based on the synergy between technology and public policy. Without appropriate public policy, the technology will just lie without sprouting on the ground. It is important to underscore the interaction between technology and public policy, for an Ever-Green Revolution requires even better public policies involving management of groundwater to avoid overexploitation, conservation of prime farmland for agriculture, promotion of integrated pest management, and so on.

This broad view allows the reconciliation of approaches that have sometimes been presented as antagonistic when they should not be so: organic farming and biotechnology. "Biotechnology" is a broad term. Productivity can be improved in perpetuity without associated ecological harm if an organic farming approach is adopted that requires support from a number of aspects of the broad area of biotechnology, from vermiculture and biofertilizers to greater carbon sequestration (Figure E1.2). Adoption of organic farming, which can ensure that high productivity is maintained in perpetuity, requires support from a whole series of biotechnologies.

Sustainable food security involves first defending the gains already made. This is where the biotic and abiotic stresses and probable effects of climate change must be considered. First, a rise in sea level is a real possibility, according to the Intergovernmental Panel on Climate Change, and therefore, an anticipatory program must be implemented for meeting such an eventuality. Second, the gains achieved to date must be extended to rainfed and marginal environments, and third, new gains must be made for farming systems through diversification and value addition.

Figure E1.2   The Ever-Green Revolution:
Synergy between organic farming and biotechnology

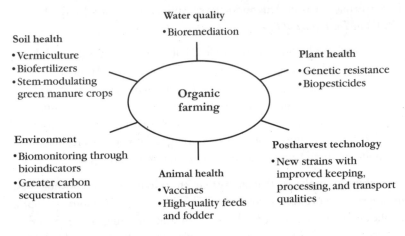

Source: Author.

Let me give you an example with mangroves, wonderful plants found along the estuaries in many countries. About a century ago most of the coastal areas, including the U.S. coast, had numerous mangroves. Many of them have gone, but now people are starting to realize the great importance of mangroves for carbon sequestration, soil stabilization, prevention of coastal sea erosion, and sustainable fisheries. The M. S. Swaminathan Foundation in Madras has initiated a large program on mangroves along the East Coast—significant amounts of carbon are sequestered from the atmosphere by the mangrove plant, apart from their biomass contribution. There is also a U.S. group, the Seawater Forest Initiative, that has taken up a large program in Eritrea on planting mangroves, along with shrimp farming. They plant trees (mangroves, casuarinas, and other trees), and consequently, along the creeks one can harvest prawns, fishes, and so on. Thus, there are extensive opportunities for seawater farming, involving integrated attention to culture and capture fisheries and to forestry and agroforestry.

Another important issue is integrating genetic diversity and genetic efficiency (Figure E1.3). Most CGIAR centers, such as the International Rice Research Institute and the International Maize and Wheat Improvement Center, function as prebreeding centers. They try to generate novel genetic combi-

Figure E1.3   Integrating genetic efficiency with genetic diversity

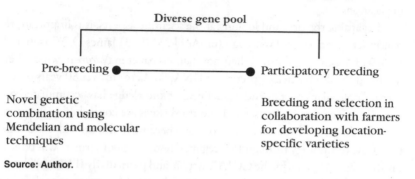

Source: Author.

nations. Another example comes from the M. S. Swaminathan Foundation, where we have taken genes from mangroves for seawater tolerance, put them in rice, some millets, and mustard. We plan to give them to the local people for breeding, using participatory breeding approaches. In this way, one attains genetic diversity without losing genetic efficiency. In other words, if there is a problem of genetic homogeneity, possibly leading to genetic vulnerability to diseases and pests, it can be overcome by having a series of varieties available through participatory breeding programs carried out with the cooperation of farmers.

Genetically Modified Crops in the Ever-Green Revolution

Perceptions vary greatly in governments and nongovernmental or civil society organizations with regard to risks and benefits associated with genetically modified (GM) crops. Let me quote two statements from the World Food Summit Plus 5 of June 10–13, 2002, one from the official declaration and the second from civil society organizations. The government declaration stated, "We are committed to study, share, and facilitate the responsible use of biotechnology in addressing development needs" (FAO 2002, 86), while the civil society organizations said, "Genetically modified organisms represent a threat to family farmers, other food producers, the integrity of genetic resources, and human and environmental health. They will affect particularly the rural poor who cannot afford this costly alternative." In my opinion the second statement has several issues mixed up: first, what is wrong with the science; second, who controls the science; and third, who will have access to products of science. Unless these issues are disaggregated, it will be impossible to clarify the analysis and policy implications.

Regarding the first and looking at the scientific aspects, it is important to remember that about 50 years ago (on April 25, 1953) James D. Watson and Francis H. C. Crick published their now famous paper in *Nature* in which they described the double helix structure of DNA. So there are over 50 years of science in molecular genetics and a great deal of knowledge has accumulated on the scientific part of it. The second and third issues are control of science and access to the technology. The concern is that because multinationals have control of the technology through IPR regimes, resource-poor farmers will be at a disadvantage. That is why the CGIAR system, and particularly IFPRI, has been dealing with biotechnology policy—to ensure beneficial outcomes for all farmers and society. Unless the stakeholders disaggregate the issues involved in the GM organism debate and deal with them separately, acceptable solutions will not be found. And without regulatory mechanisms that are transparent, involve multiple stakeholders, and inspire confidence on the objectivity of the risk-benefit analysis mechanisms, this technology will not take off.

I am not surprised at the reactions against biotechnology, because even Mendel's Laws, published in 1865, were not accepted for 35 years. It was only in 1900 that Mendel's work was rediscovered. I do not think one should worry too much about many of these reactions, but what is important is to look at all problems in a fair and objective way. This approach will involve greater investments of public funds for research in the public good.

Managing Change

As a result of globalization, we are in an era of change in agriculture. Managing change has become exceedingly important. Many countries are not ready to manage change, and that is the problem.

Changes come in many forms. There is a demographic challenge, largely because most developing countries are predominantly young, considering the age of their populations. In India, for example, 50 percent of the population is below the age of 21. Now, where are the jobs for them? Are they going to live in rural areas? Are they going to continue agriculture as a profession or a vocation? Unless agriculture becomes knowledge intensive, intellectually stimulating, and economically rewarding, young people are not likely to be attracted to agriculture. This area is where modern scientific agriculture and technology-based agriculture have become important.

There are also technological challenges in information technology, the genetic divide, and the digital divide. Ecological challenges, including the climate and biodiversity conventions, are also important. Many economic challenges need to be mentioned, including those posed by the WTO AoA, but there are also ethical challenges relating to TRIPS. And finally there are equity challenges in relation to gender and other underprivileged social groups.

The management of change in technology requires looking at the heritage of Watson and Crick: in my view, progress in transgenic technologies is proceeding at a pace faster than the human capacity to digest its implications and to manage current and future risk and benefits. Greater efforts must be made in promoting the public understanding of the new genetics. Francis Fukuyama (2002), in *Our Post-Human Future,* argues that human biotechnology differs substantially from agricultural biotechnology insofar as it raises a host of ethical questions related to human dignity and human rights (mostly in relation to cloning), and that existing regulatory institutions in the United States, such as the Food and Drug Administration (FDA), Environmental Protection Agency (EPA), and the Department of Agriculture, are not proving adequate to meet this challenge. I mentioned this not because I fear that the FDA or EPA may not be competent to deal with these challenges, but to emphasize that if in a country like the United States there are doubts, imagine the case of most developing countries, where adequately informed or competent regulatory mechanisms do not exist.

Linking Global and Local Knowledge

In addition, regarding IPR, there is a debate between individual and community rights related to knowledge and genetic resources. In the case of traditional IPR (for example, patents), many of them are individual rights that can be granted separately, but most traditional wisdom and traditional conservation material is community-based and difficult to attribute to one individual. Therefore, a major challenge is how to develop mechanisms for recognizing and rewarding community contributions in addition to individual ones. This issue has become important in the post–Doha Declaration period.

Take, for example, the debate in India regarding medicinal plants, which may also apply to other developing countries. Medicinal plants are taken away and commercialized by people from outside the original communities who found that the plants had medicinal properties. But those plants may be very important for regions, such as Kerala: in spite of declining prices of rubber, pepper, and so on, the activity that has been keeping Kerala's economy growing is health tourism. Another example is the rice variety Navara, which is used for arthritis, one of the most potent local treatments. So there is an enormous amount of indigenous knowledge, and instead of biopiracy there should be biopartnership.

It is important to keep on working at the local level all the way up to the global level to ensure that conservation and commercialization are mutually reinforcing. Otherwise, the genetic base of crops involved in food and health security will become increasingly narrow. There are now six plants dominating much of the food security system of the world, when in the past there were 200–300 plants in that system. In India, the government has enacted legislation, the Protection of Plant Varieties and Farmers' Rights Act, which for the first time provides opportunities for recognizing and rewarding the work of local people who generate knowledge on biological material and conserve biodiversity. This law is based on a principle called *antyodaya,* a term coined by Mahatma Gandhi more than 70 years ago to refer to the poorest of the poor. He said that one should "recall the face of the poorest and the weakest person you have seen, and ask yourself if the steps you contemplate are going to be of any use to him."

The above considerations led to the birth of the biovillage movement in Pondicherry, India, and the expansion of information centers at the local level, which try to bridge the digital and gender divides. Experience has shown that women-managed, user-driven, computer-aided, and Internet-connected rural knowledge centers can help bridge these divides simultaneously. For example, when women in a coastal village were asked what kind of information they needed in their lives, one concern that came out was sea conditions, as their husbands, and sometimes their children, were going to sea in small boats, and the women were worried that they could not come back. They wanted to know whether there was a way to find out what the conditions of the sea will be. We found out that the U.S. Naval Oceanography Office maintains a database from which one can calculate the state of the local sea. So every evening the rural knowledge centers unload the information, determine the state, and then announce through loudspeakers information regarding the state of the sea. After 3 years of doing this, they reported that the information had been highly accurate: the sea behaved exactly as predicted in terms of the wave heights and so on. The system can and must be expanded to include tsunami early warning and early response capabilities.

Based on these experiences, we, at the M. S. Swaminathan Foundation, are establishing a Virtual Academy for Food Security and Rural Prosperity following a hub-and-spokes model, linking data collectors, data users, and data managers into a cooperative grid. They all form a consortium. There is a meteorological satellite, METSAT, from which rural knowledge managers download information on weather, and then all generic information is converted into location-specific information by people with local knowledge. Because the generic information shown in satellite pictures is of no use to rural inhabitants, there are three sets of information tools. One is the hub-and-spokes model, connected to the Internet; the second set of tools is a group of cable TV networks operating in a large number of local languages (it is very important to use the local language); the third set is the community and local radio. In this way the community radio, cable TV channel, and the Internet provide an uncommon opportunity to reach everyone, every family—"to reach the unreached."

Take another example. It is said that factor productivity in India is very low, and that it is one of the reasons why the cost of production is high. Farmers always want higher prices, but in a globalized economy one has to be competitive. If I want to improve the productivity of fertilizers, a very important input, I need to consider the right choice of fertilizer, the right quantity, the right method, the right time, and the right positive interactions with other operations, such as tillage, water, and weed management. This is knowledge-intensive agriculture, the kind of agriculture that can fascinate the younger generation. We have now started a whole series of agri-clinics and agribusiness centers operated by farm graduates, home science graduates, and so on. We must think of more ways and methods to bridge the technological divide. Research on technology delivery systems must be specific to culture and locality.

Trade

WTO AoA

Let me say a word about the ongoing negotiations on the revision of the AoA. Trade should not only be free, it must also be fair, which means the elimination of trade-distorting subsidies. Today the Blue and Green Boxes (respectively, subsidies tied to programs limiting production, and subsidies that in theory must not distort trade, including direct income support payments and environmental protection and regional development programs) are being abused.

Members of the Organisation for Economic Co-operation and Development (OECD) spend more than US$1 billion a day in support of their agricultural sectors, but then somebody from the World Bank comes to India and says, "You are giving too many subsidies to fertilizer." How does one reconcile the two situations? At the same time, more than 50 percent of the population in developing countries depends on agriculture for their livelihoods. These are the poor people, they are in the marginal areas, and they are in remote areas. There has to be some method of protecting them, or they will not be able to compete. Now there is no level playing field at all.

Therefore, in the ongoing trade negotiations, it may be useful to consider the two alternatives. First, all boxes (that is, the categories of subsidies classified according to their presumed distorting effects on trade) should be abolished and the rules with reference to trade distortion and unfair trade practices should be spelled out in clear and unambiguous terms. Second, as an alternative negotiating principle, a separate box relating to Sustainable Livelihoods (a Livelihood Security Box) should be introduced to allow developing nations, facing the challenge of providing livelihoods to their rural populations, to place restrictions on imports when there is convincing evidence that such imports will erode job or livelihood opportunities in their countries. The percentage of population dependant on agriculture for their livelihoods should be the major criterion for eligibility to use the provisions of this proposed Livelihood Security Box. The minimum could be 50 percent of the population. Globally, the continuation of the present situation—a few million farm families in industrial countries, supported by heavy inputs of technology, capital, and subsidy, competing with more than a billion small farmers who have little access to technology, credit, and adequate postharvest infrastructure—will not help to make free trade an instrument of poverty eradication.

In addition, other measures can be considered. For instance, market access should be provided for the crops produced by low-income and resource-poor farmers, while allowing higher levels of domestic support for these farmers in keeping with Article 6.2 of the AoA. All nontariff barriers standing in the way of access to the markets of industrialized countries should be reviewed and removed where logical. At the same time, assistance should be extended to developing countries to improve their capacity in the area of sanitary and phytosanitary (SPS) measures, as well as in the adoption of *Codex Alimentarius* standards of food safety. Unrealistically high SPS standards are often used to create nontariff trade barriers against developing-country exports. India and other developing countries must become a part of the process in which SPS standards are determined.

Trade-Related IPR

The revised TRIPS should be compatible with the equity and ethics provisions of the Convention on Biological Diversity and the International Treaty on Plant Genetic Resources for Food and Agriculture. In particular, it should contain provisions for the compulsory licensing of rights in the case of inventions of great importance to food and health security, as well as for benefit sharing with the primary conservers of genetic resources and holders of traditional knowledge. This consideration will help avoid fear and accusations of biopiracy and promote mutually beneficial biopartnerships.

It is also necessary to reflect on methods of giving meaning and content to the ethical obligations of scientists in relation to society. The World Conference on Science held at Budapest in 1999 called for a new social contract between scientists and society. With a rapidly expanding emphasis on IPR in scientific laboratories, the products of scientific inventions may become increasingly exclusive, with access limited only to those who can afford to pay. The rich–poor divide will then increase, because currently unattended agricultural products will remain orphans with reference to scientific attention.

How can policymakers develop a knowledge management system that will ensure that inventions and innovations of importance to human health, food, livelihood, and ecological security benefit every child, woman, and man, and not just the rich? I propose that the United Nations explore the possibility of establishing an International Patents Bank for Poverty Eradication and Sustainable Development. Scientists and technologists from all parts of the world should be encouraged to assign their patents to such a bank, so that the fruits of scientific discoveries are available for public good. Such an institution would stimulate scientists to consider themselves as trustees of their intellectual property, sharing their inventions with the poor, in whose lives they may make a significant difference for the better.

The French mathematician Marquis de Condorcet, who was a contemporary of Thomas Malthus, said more than two centuries ago that the human population would stabilize itself if "children are born for happiness and not just existence." Making all well-to-do members of the human family regard themselves as trustees of their financial and intellectual property will be essential for fostering a human happiness movement. There already are many philanthropic organizations for harnessing financial resources. An International Bank for Patents for Poverty Eradication and Sustainable Development will help scientists and technologists practice what the great Indian spiritual and intellectual leader Swami Vivekananda advocated as the true pathway to human fulfillment: "In this life, give everything you can—give money, give food, give love or anything else you can—but do not seek barter."

Conclusion

I mentioned earlier that there must be some ground rules if we really want globalization to help the poor. I think Gandhi gave three simple ground rules. He mentioned *antyodaya:* start with the poorest of the poor. Nowadays this approach is called bottom-up rather than trickle-down. The second rule is *sarvodaya:* a high social synergy society—a society in which there are no winners and losers. And finally the concept of trusteeship, which I mentioned earlier in relation to the patents. It is important that we hold our brains—not only funds and materialist financial wealth but also intellectual wealth—as trustees, not owners, so that they are available to those who need them.

There are methods of making globalization work for the poor. We want to ensure that everybody has access to a reasonable quality of life, that everyone has an opportunity for a productive and healthy life. Technology and trade can become powerful allies in the movement for social and gender equity only if ethical principles underpin the international agreements relevant to bridging the growing rich–poor divide.

Notes

1. In this volume, all references to "tons" are to metric tons.

2. The information has been included in three documents (available on CD-ROM), all produced by the M. S. Swaminathan Research Foundation (MSSRF) and the World Food Programme of the United Nations: Food insecurity atlas of rural India (Cheannai: MSSRF, 2003); Food insecurity atlas of urban India (Cheannai: MSSRF, 2003); and Atlas on sustainability of food security in India (Cheannai: MSSRF, 2004).

References

Delgado, C., C. Narrod, and M. Tiongco. 2004. Implications of the scaling-up of livestock production in a group of fast-growing developing countries. In *Livestock and livelihoods:*

Challenges and opportunities for Asia in the emerging market environment, ed. V. Ahuja. Anand, India, and Rome: National Dairy Development Board and Food and Agriculture Organization of the United Nations.

FAO (Food and Agriculture Organization of the United Nations). 2002. *Declaration of the World Food Summit: Five years later.* Rome.

———. 2006. FAOSTAT. Rome.

Fukuyama, F. 2002. *Our post-human future: Consequences of the biotechnology revolution.* New York: Farrar, Straus, and Giroux.

Wilson, E. O. 2002. *The future of life.* New York: Knopf.

Chapter 3

Implications of Globalization for Agricultural Research

Per Pinstrup-Andersen and Tewodaj Mengistu

A s discussed in earlier chapters, globalization—the expanded cross-border flows of capital, goods and services, information, technology, and labor—has transformed the economic situation of many nations and people around the world. Traditional state boundaries have weakened with widespread market liberalization, privatization, and decentralization. Through significant advancements in ICTs and transportation infrastructure, economies around the world have become more integrated, with increased global communications and trade.

Agricultural research has also evolved in this context, experiencing changes in both supply and demand. On the supply side, the advances in ICTs and transportation infrastructure, increased trade opportunities, and the changes in the institutional domain of intellectual property in the 1990s have introduced new incentives for undertaking agricultural research. Indeed, agricultural research, once dominated by the public sector, is now being increasingly undertaken by the private sector, particularly in industrialized countries. There is also a tendency for more research to be done by the private sector using public funds. Other actors, such as nonprofit organizations, are also getting involved. Further, improved ICTs and the expansion of labor and capital movements have enabled a greater exchange of knowledge and technology across national boundaries.

On the demand side, changes in the lifestyles of consumers in industrialized countries and income growth in developing countries have affected the nature of

The authors gratefully acknowledge comments received from Philip Pardey and Ruben Echeverría.

agricultural research. Rising incomes and falling staple crop prices have enabled consumers to demand more quality and diversification in their food choices. Higher-income consumers have become more conscientious about the food safety and ethical ramifications of current food production processes. Producers have responded by investing in technological innovations that would meet these needs. And with more trade, competition among producers has intensified, resulting in producers having to adopt new technologies to maintain their competitiveness in world markets. This competition has also affected farmers in developing countries, as increased global trade has made them more connected to producers and consumers in industrialized nations.

The MDGs represent an international consensus on tackling issues of poverty, malnutrition, hunger, and other key constraints to development. Agricultural research targeting the poor has an immense potential to help achieve these goals. It can contribute to alleviating hunger and malnutrition by increasing poor farmers' productivity and improving the quality of their produce. The agricultural growth thus induced could have a direct influence on the surrounding community by providing landless laborers and other farmers greater employment opportunities and higher wages, and it may subsequently lead to employment and income multipliers in other areas, both urban and rural. In the long run, this growth could give small-scale farmers better access to the decisionmaking process by increasing their capacity for collective action and reducing their vulnerability to income shocks through asset accumulation. For consumers, the outcomes of research can lead to lower prices and more nutritious foods (Hazell and Haddad 2001). Furthermore, agricultural research can contribute to reducing child mortality, improving maternal health, and ensuring environmental sustainability—all goals that were agreed upon at the Millennium Summit held in 2000 at the United Nations in New York.

Despite this potential, many poor people have not been reached by agricultural R&D. One reason is that institutional arrangements guiding research and dissemination of research results to farmers in developing countries have not evolved at the same pace as research itself and have not adapted to the changing global context. Since the 1960s, national agricultural research systems (NARS) and international agricultural research centers (IARCs) have tended to follow a linear, top-down approach of undertaking research. Under these arrangements, significant progress has been achieved in terms of crop genetic improvements, creation of gene banks, and knowledge sharing between NARS and IARCs (Roseboom 2004). But these institutions tend to be supply driven and inward looking, concentrating mostly on research capacity, knowledge output, and diffusion. As a result, they have lacked effective external linkages and have sometimes overlooked the technology needs of smaller farmers (Peterson, Gijsbers, and Wilks 2003; Roseboom 2004; World Bank 2005).

Further, throughout the past four decades many NARS have been plagued by the lack of a performance and evaluation culture, along with bureaucratic procedures and insufficient resources (Peterson, Gijsbers, and Wilks 2003). NARS are, of course, not homogeneous systems across developing countries. They are merely concepts that include all public and private elements of research that may or may not function as a system. Some systems are very strong in a few developing countries (perhaps 10–20 of them), whereas they are less strong in many others and really do not exist in many of the poorest developing countries.

Many research systems are recognizing these problems and experimenting with new institutional arrangements that would make agricultural research more effects oriented. Some are adopting an innovation systems approach, which emphasizes the interdependence and the interaction of the different actors and institutions that participate in the process of innovation—producers (farmers and food processors), supporters (governments, infrastructure providers, research institutions, universities, and so on), and influential institutions (such as NGOs and consumers; Hartwich 2005).

This chapter assesses how globalization has affected agricultural research and identifies policy options to achieve more impact-oriented agricultural R&D in an era of globalization. In the first section we elaborate on the pro-poor potential of agricultural research by looking at the achievements of the Green Revolution and reviewing the example of rice research in India and China. In the second section we describe how globalization has affected agricultural research and explore the implications in terms of achieving food security and poverty reduction. Finally, in the third section, we look toward the adoption of a new institutional framework that would enable agricultural R&D to be more pro-poor, and we elaborate on the role of key public-sector stakeholders in this process.

The Effects of Research on Food Security and Poverty Reduction

Starting in the early 1960s, high-yielding varieties (HYVs) were developed and adapted to the agroecologies of developing countries, resulting in dramatic gains in crop yields in some developing countries—so much so that the experience was dubbed the Green Revolution (Pardey and Beintema 2001). Indeed, the achievements of the Green Revolution meant that countries, such as India and China, that had previously experienced major famines became food secure at the national level, although many households remained food insecure.

The Green Revolution experience has been surrounded by intense controversy, however, with many critics asserting that it promoted the use of scale-biased technologies and environmentally unfriendly practices and therefore worsened the poverty situation of rural populations (Hazell and Haddad 2001)—a conclusion we believe to be refuted by available empirical evidence.

The Effect of the Green Revolution

The need for innovations in agricultural production in developing countries became clear in the 1960s, as land and water resources were being used excessively in the face of rapid population growth. Widespread hunger was predicted for Asia. Thus, the primary objective of research at the time was to increase yields and expand food production.

The IARCs, together with partner institutions, were the initiators of the Green Revolution. Each center specialized in one or a small set of commodities or a particular climatic zone and worked with NARS to adapt improved varieties to local agroecologies. Among the IARCs, the International Rice Research Institute and the International Maize and Wheat Improvement Center, both created in the early 1960s, were the most important actors of the Green Revolution (Evenson and Gollin 2003).

With improved varieties, complemented by heavy use of pesticides and fertilizers, over the next four decades the Green Revolution produced a tremendous increase in productivity, especially for crops with good water management (Figure 3.1). In addition, because of the success of the first phase, the adoption rate for modern varieties (MVs) increased steadily through the next four decades (Table 3.1). Subsequent generations of MVs, requiring fewer inputs, were adapted to different agroecologies and socioeconomic niches (Hazell and Haddad 2001).

Despite this progress, the Green Revolution has attracted its share of critics. The main concern was that only large farms had the capacity to take advantage of the new technologies, because they had access to irrigated lands, mechanization, and other expensive inputs, such as purchased seeds, fertilizers, and pesticides. These farmers were able to increase their productivity and therefore reduce unit costs. In contrast, the argument went, small-scale farmers did not have the necessary capital to adopt new technologies and therefore were either unaffected by the revolution or worse off, because the price of their produce declined (Lipton and Longhurst 1985; Hazell and Ramasamy 1991). Other arguments against the Green Revolution include that it was limited to a small number of crops in certain agroecological zones and that its benefits largely eroded after the 1980s because of environmental degradation (Evenson and Gollin 2003).

Although some of these concerns are relevant to the earlier phase of the Green Revolution, many of them emerged from ideas in studies conducted too soon after the release of the new technologies (Hazell and Ramasamy 1991). As noted by Even-

Figure 3.1   Yields for selected crops in developing countries

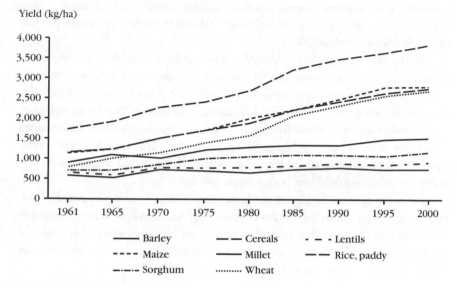

Source: Evenson and Gollin (2003).

Table 3.1   Adoption rate of modern varieties across all crops (percent)

1970	1980	1990	1998
7	29	46	63

Source: Evenson and Gollin (2003).

son and Gollin (2003, 12), "the Green Revolution is better understood as a forty year history of steady productivity gains rather than as a one-time event," and the technologies continued to be improved throughout the 1980s and the 1990s as researchers produced more high-yielding crops for different types of agroecologies. Further, many of these earlier studies neglected the benefits that higher yields brought to poor consumers in both rural and urban areas in the form of reduced food prices, as well as the indirect benefits, such as increased employment opportunities for poor landless laborers (Lipton and Longhurst 1985; Hazell and Haddad 2001). Also, with regard to the argument that the Green Revolution technologies were scale-biased, many small-scale farmers were later able to benefit from HYVs within a relatively short time

(Lipton and Longhurst 1985). Thus, on the whole, the Green Revolution made important contributions in some countries to food security and economic growth through income and employment multipliers induced by higher agricultural productivity (Hazell and Haddad 2001).

Furthermore, using IFPRI's IMPACT model,[1] Evenson (2003) presents counterfactual scenarios that show that farmers and consumers in developing countries would have been substantially worse off in the absence of the Green Revolution. He finds that in developing countries food prices would have been 29–61 percent higher, agricultural production would have been 10–18 percent lower, and the area cropped would have been 3–5 percent higher. This situation would have resulted in per capita food consumption being 10–13 percent lower than it is now, and around 30–40 million more children would have been malnourished.

However, as noted by Lipton and Longhurst (1985, iii), in some cases, the "propoor potential (of Green Revolution technologies) has been lost due to (a) insertion of MV into social systems favoring urban groups and big farms who supply them, (b) demographic dynamics making labor cheaper relative to land, (c) research structures prioritizing fashionable topics rather than genuine needs of the poor."

Evidence from Rice Research in India and China

In 1966 a new high-yielding rice variety (IR 8) was introduced in India, and by 1998 some 75 percent of that country's rice area was planted with HYVs. In China, high-yielding rice was introduced in the mid-1960s and, by 1991 61 percent of rice production there consisted of HYVs (Fan et al. 2003). In both countries the technologies translated into rural economic growth (Table 3.2). They also enhanced food security by improving food availability and access to food, and they made significant contributions to poverty reduction (Tables 3.3 and 3.4).

In rural areas of China, poverty was reduced through increased rural GDP, and in urban areas, poverty declined through a reduction of food prices. Indeed, Fan, Zhang, and Zhang (2002) estimate that the reduction of food prices stemming from agricultural research investments accounted for 18–30 percent of the reduction in urban poverty between 1992 and 1998. The situation was similar in India, where investment in R&D had a larger influence on urban poverty reduction than did any other public investment and the second largest effect on rural poverty (next to investments in rural roads; Table 3.4).

Further, the Green Revolution reduced caloric and protein deficiencies of the poor. Through a survey of villages in North Arcot, India, Pinstrup-Andersen and Jaramillo (1991) found that villages in the area had substantially increased their caloric intake from its level in 1971, because they had more income available for food and also because of increased rice production.

Table 3.2 Returns to rural GDP from public investments in China (yuan, per yuan expenditure)

Investment	Return (average for all regions)
R&D	9.59
Roads	8.83
Education	8.68
Telephone system	6.98
Irrigation	1.88
Electricity	1.28

Source: Fan, Zhang, and Zhang (2002).

Table 3.3 Returns to poverty reduction from public investments in China (number per 10,000 yuan)

Investment	Reduction in number of poor (average for all regions)
Education	8.8
R&D	6.79
Roads	3.22
Electricity	2.27
Telephone system	2.21
Irrigation	1.33
Poverty loans	1.13

Source: Fan, Zhang, and Zhang (2002).

Table 3.4 Returns to poverty reduction from public investments in India, 1995 (number per million Rs)

Investment	Reduction in number of urban poor	Reduction in number of rural poor	Total reduction in poor
Agricultural research and development	72.11	84.5	156.61
Rural roads	28.39	123.8	152.19
Rural education	7.43	41.0	48.43
Irrigation	7.31	9.7	17.01
Rural development	5.87	25.5	31.37
Soil and water conservation	5.15	22.6	27.75
Rural health care	4.55	17.8	22.35
Rural electricity	1.44	3.8	5.24

Source: Fan (2002).

Trends in Agricultural Research in the Context of Globalization

In general, globalization is affecting the framework for setting agricultural research priorities by better identifying comparative and competitive advantages of the different stakeholders regionally and internationally. This framework is very different from the one that exists in a closed-country setting. Globalization also tends to focus the debate around agricultural research more on management and governance issues, particularly when cross-country comparisons can be made. Some specific manifestations of these trends in the agricultural R&D environment can be summarized as:

- New actors have emerged with the introduction of incentives for private-sector research in the form of IPRs in the 1980s and 1990s. This emergence has made the agricultural R&D environment increasingly competitive and proprietary. Other new actors include NGOs and farmer organizations.

- The growth in publicly funded agricultural research expenditure has slowed in recent years in both developing and industrialized countries. In the latter, the private sector has significantly expanded agricultural R&D, whereas in the former the reduction in public expenditure has translated into a decline of agricultural research in many developing countries and only a slow growth in others. For developing countries, however, regionalism—which may be a part of globalization—opens up new opportunities for cooperative arrangements among small countries.

- In recent years molecular biology has taken center stage in agricultural research. It presents tremendous potential benefits for the poor, but may also present yet unknown risks for human health or the environment. The use of biotechnology has therefore sparked intense debate on whether its potential benefits are worth the risks.

- Consumers in the developed world have become increasingly vocal about their concerns about food safety and biodiversity risks of current food processes, as well as about ethical issues and animal welfare. And as supermarkets and other retail and wholesale industries become dominant features of the supply chain in both industrialized and developing countries (see Chapter 6), supermarkets are responding to consumers' concerns (especially in industrialized countries and urban areas in developing countries) and are therefore increasingly influencing research priorities. As a result, agricultural research, especially in the developed world, has expanded the research agenda to include food safety and environmental and social issues.

This section looks at these four points in more detail and maps out the types of opportunities and challenges the agricultural research sector may face in terms of its effects on food security, malnutrition, and poverty reduction.

IPR and Private Agricultural Research

IPR and implications for nonprofit research.   IPRs in the form of patents or plant breeders' rights for plant varieties and biotechnology products were linked to trade in 1995 with the TRIPS agreement of the WTO. All 148 members of the WTO must comply with the TRIPS agreement, which states that patent rights should be made "available for any invention, whether product or processes, in all fields of technology, provided that they are new, involve an inventive step and are capable of industrial applications" (article 27.1). Patent rights apply for 20 years from the date of filing but only in the legal jurisdiction where they were filed. For plant varieties, WTO members are required to provide IPR protection through either patents and/or a sui generis system, such as the International Union for Protection of New Varieties of Plants, which was designed to provide "intellectual property protection which has been specifically adapted for the process of plant breeding" (UPOV 2002; WTO 2005).

The rationale behind providing exclusive rights protection for plant varieties and biotechnology products is to provide better incentives to innovate in socially beneficial technologies and to facilitate other innovations by requiring disclosure of patented technologies (Pardey et al. 2003). In so doing, TRIPS attempts to "strike a balance between the long-term benefits and possible short-term costs to society" of technological innovation (WTO 2005). Thus, in theory, because the provision of exclusive rights enables companies to extract profits from innovations resulting from their investments in R&D, patents and/or plant breeders' rights provide a strong incentive for them to invest in R&D. In the long run, when these exclusive rights run out, society as a whole is able to benefit from these innovations.

However, this rationale has been criticized more generally on the basis that granting IPRs may actually limit the level of innovation, as the free flow of information, which is central to improving on existing products, may be curtailed by patenting and other forms of IPR protection (Macdonald 2001). In the specific case of plants and seeds, one concern is that if one company owns multiple patents and/or plant breeders' rights, it may lead to concentrated innovation systems, leading in turn to the concentration of the seed supply industry (Louwaars et al. 2005). The current IPR system has also been criticized as being unjust, in that for-profit institutions can obtain free plants or seeds from public institutions, such as CGIAR, or from farmers, make small modifications, and patent them for profit (NAS 2000).

In practice, there is a wide variety in IPR systems around the world, with developing countries having the least advanced systems. Additionally, the key technologies protected by patents are held by a small number of multinational firms in the Western world, and although many developing countries do not have the capacity to use these technologies, international research systems, such as CGIAR, have used them to make crop improvements benefiting the poor. The problem with increasing IPR protection is the possible risk to freedom-to-operate for researchers in nonprofit sectors. At this point, however, freedom-to-operate has not proved to be a serious limitation for nonprofit researchers, because rights to intellectual property are confined to the jurisdiction in which they are granted, and most developing countries do not have many patented technologies. Further, private multinational corporations concentrate on a small number of high-value crops, which currently do not greatly affect trade and food security in developing countries. In fact, exports of CGIAR crops from developing to industrialized countries are insignificant compared to total agricultural exports from developing countries and to domestic agricultural production (Nottenburg, Pardey, and Wright 2002; Pardey et al. 2003).

Nevertheless, lack of freedom-to-operate by developing-country research institutions may become an issue in the future as more patents are filed in developing countries and international trade in agricultural commodities increases, especially for such crops as bananas, soybeans, and rice (Pardey and Beintema 2001; Pardey et al. 2003). In addition, as the agricultural research sector becomes increasingly competitive and proprietary, the cost of research in the nonprofit sector might increase. As more patents are given out to different parties, it will become increasingly costly for researchers to get licenses to conduct research using preexisting knowledge, thus reducing the incentives for engagement in R&D. This fragmentation of IPRs will have important implications, especially in agriculture, because technologies in agriculture have to be adapted to local environments (Phillips and Dierker 2001; Kremer and Zwane 2005).

Engagement of the private sector in agricultural research. The introduction of IPRs for plant varieties and biotechnology products in the mid-1990s changed the incentives of undertaking research. In industrialized countries, the private sector is increasingly taking on research that was previously done by the public sector, with private firms often bidding for publicly funded projects, and some functions of public research being explicitly privatized. Further, industrial nations are encouraging universities and public research institutions to file patents and are providing incentives to collaborate with the private sector to innovate (Phillips and Dierker 2001). With the introduction of competitive grant processes, this trend has been complemented by a shift in funding processes from long- to short- and fixed-term contracts (Alston, Pardey, and Taylor 2001). Other factors, such as market size, the general business climate, and the ability of public-sector research to come up with new knowledge, also affect the level and type of private-sector involvement in agricultural R&D (Pray 2002).

The private sector has had a very limited engagement in R&D in developing countries, and where it has been involved, the outcomes of research have benefited the poor only to a limited extent, as R&D investments were mainly targeted toward highly commercialized agricultural sectors in large developing countries (Spielman and von Grebmer 2004). The prospect that the private sector would engage in research benefiting smallholders in the near future remains bleak for several reasons. First, the private sector tends to concentrate its research agenda on technologies that have potential for high economic gains and therefore produces technologies more suited for capital-intensive commercial farmers, who are usually located in industrialized countries and a few developing countries, such as Argentina, Brazil, and South Africa. Technology transfers to developing countries may not be appropriate, because many of these technologies are suitable only for crops in temperate climates and therefore do not apply to some staple crops that grow in tropical climates, such as cassava and millet (Kremer and Zwane 2005).

Second, protecting intellectual property is very difficult in developing nations because of the lack of institutional infrastructure. Plants and seeds self-multiply, enabling farmers to reuse or sell seeds, which ultimately will reduce the price of the seed close to marginal costs, making it difficult for private firms to recover the cost of R&D. Also, it is difficult to prohibit the sale or reuse of seeds, as farmers in developing countries are usually scattered on small and remote plots (Kremer and Zwane 2005).

Third, there is little incentive for governments in developing countries to enforce IPRs—for the private company developing the technology, the research process is costly and risky, but once the product is developed, it can be produced at low cost, which is ideal for governments. Further, because of the public goods nature of agricultural research, the benefits of research outcomes cannot be confined within the national boundaries of a single country, so governments may be reluctant to protect IPR (Kremer and Zwane 2005). And fourth, most developing countries lack important market structures (such as rural infrastructure; access to credit for farmers and traders; and functioning markets for seeds, fertilizers, and agricultural outputs), which would enable a more widespread diffusion of new technologies (Pinstrup-Andersen 2001).

Another problem in developing countries is that the boundaries between breeders and farmers are not as clear as in industrialized nations. Seed requirements in developing countries are usually met through farmer-to-farmer exchange. Western-style intellectual property protection regimes are not well suited for this type of informal innovation process. Some developing countries are trying to solve this problem by having systems that balance farmers' rights to save, reuse, and exchange seeds with breeders' rights of intellectual property protection (Ramanna 2003). India was the first developing country to come up with such a system, in the Protection of Plant Varieties and Farmers' Rights Act of 2001.

Developments in Publicly Funded Research

Importance of public research for socially beneficial outcomes.   Market mechanisms do not always lead to socially optimal outcomes because of market failures, such as externalities and the free-rider problem. In agricultural R&D, the private sector will under-invest in areas where the potential for externalities and free-riders is the highest. Externalities arise when the benefits of research spill over to parties (such as consumers and farmers) other than the party that invested in the R&D (the private sector, for instance). Similarly, private research institutions will underinvest in technologies that could benefit the environment, as such technologies may not provide private profits. The free-rider problem arises when new knowledge produced through R&D cannot be excluded from parties that are unable or unwilling to pay for the new technology because of the public goods nature of the new knowledge (Alston and Pardey 1999; Pinstrup-Andersen 2001). But even when the research output is not of a public goods nature, the private sector may not be able to capture a sufficiently large share of the social gains to cover research costs, because farmers are poor and they have no or little access to credit to help them pay for improved technology. Without effective credit programs or public research funding, large potential social benefits are forgone, and poor farmers do not escape poverty.

Governments can try to reduce these market failures through improvements in property rights protections and more explicit incentives for private research, such as subsidies, tax breaks, and the provision of public funds for private research (Alston and Pardey 1999). But even with these measures, the private sector would still underinvest in agricultural R&D, especially in basic scientific research, which is by nature more difficult to appropriate privately compared to more applied (or near-market) research. Because applied research is based on the achievements of basic research, public involvement in basic R&D is essential (Pinstrup-Andersen 2001).

In developing countries with little private investment to begin with, public research plays an important role, and the potential for economic gains from agricultural R&D is high. Moreover, because some types of R&D produce technologies that are relevant to a number of countries/regions (that is, they produce global public goods), and increasingly so in the context of globalization, public research should not be confined to national institutions but extended to international (such as CGIAR) and regional institutions (Pinstrup-Andersen 2001; Dalrymple 2002).

Public research trends. In the aftermath of World War II public agricultural research expenditure grew rapidly in both developing and industrialized countries. But in the 1980s and 1990s there was widespread decline in the growth of public expenditure in agricultural research (Pardey and Beintema 2001). Such expenditures in developing countries stagnated between 1981 and 1991 and declined between 1991 and 1996, while public expenditure growth in industrial countries declined from 2.2 percent in 1986–91 to 0.2 percent in 1991–96. International public research expenditure growth, in real terms, stagnated to around US$390 million (in 2003 dollars) beginning in the early 1990s (Pardey and Beintema 2001; Beintema, pers. comm., 2005). Since 2002 stagnation has been replaced by some growth. Contributions to international public research have followed similar trends: from the mid-1980s to 2001 there was steady decline in total contributions to CGIAR, but there was some recovery starting in 2002 (Figure 3.2).

Figure 3.2   Total CGIAR contributions, 1972–2004

2004 US$ (millions)

Source: Beintema (2005).

Not all developing countries reduced their expenditure on agricultural research, however; there is a wide disparity among them. In Latin America and China, the growth of public investment in agriculture research during the 1990s was significant, whereas there was a reduction in Sub-Saharan Africa and stagnation or only very limited growth in the rest of the world (Pardey and Beintema 2001).

The widespread slowdown in public expenditure growth in the 1980s and 1990s can be explained by the decline in the importance of agriculture relative to other sectors of the economy as perceived by policymakers, especially in industrial nations, where consumers have access to a wide range of foods at low prices. In addition, because of the success of the Green Revolution in increasing yields of some major crops, international donors and aid agencies reduced their support to agricultural research in developing countries in the mid-1980s to concentrate on other issues, such as macroeconomic affairs, health and education service provision, gender inequalities, and environmental protection. Also, as pointed out by Alston, Pardey, and Taylor (2001, 9), donors "increasingly seem to view agricultural R&D as a means of directly and rapidly tackling poverty problems rather than as an activity best suited to stimulating productivity and growth over the longer term, with poverty reduction brought about as a consequence of that growth." Many national agricultural research institutions suffered as a result, especially in Sub-Saharan Africa (Pinstrup-Andersen and Schiøler 2003). Furthermore, since the 1980s developing-country governments themselves have neglected rural and agricultural sector development and have therefore not regarded agricultural research as a priority (Pinstrup-Andersen 2001).

New opportunities for international and regional cooperation. There is growing recognition that the confinement of research within the borders of one nation may not be optimal in the context of increasing globalization (Roseboom 2004). Regional cooperation in agricultural R&D can alleviate some of the resource constraints that many NARS face and can also allow for important knowledge spillovers in neighboring countries. For instance, using IFPRI's DREAM model,[2] Abdulai, Diao, and Johnson (2005) carried out ex ante simulations for some key commodities in East and Central Africa and showed that the spillover multiplier from technology transfers and adoption can be as high as three or four. Another reason for advancing regional or subregional research programs relates to the potentially better use of research infrastructure. This possibility is particularly important in the case of small countries that would benefit the most by pooling current and future resources with other countries instead of attempting to maintain a complete research program on their own.

Many developing countries are creating regional research organizations to provide an institutional background to enable cooperation in agricultural R&D at the subregional, regional, and international levels and to better facilitate knowledge spillovers. The establishment of regional organizations is supported by the Global Forum on Agricultural Research (GFAR), an international initiative that "facilitates and promotes cost-effective partnerships and strategic alliances among agriculture research and development stakeholders in their efforts to alleviate poverty, increase food security, and promote the sustainable use of natural resources" (GFAR 2005).

Biotechnology Research in Agriculture

Modern biotechnology encompasses such techniques as tissue culture and fermentation, marker-assisted breeding, genetic engineering, and functional genomics, which enable crops to resist biotic and abiotic stresses (Qaim, Krattiger, and von Braun 2000). The most contentious of these technologies have been GM or transgenic crops. At present, the principal GM crops are soybeans, with 57 percent of the global area planted in GM crops; maize, with 25 percent; cotton, with 13 percent; and canola, with 5 percent. The dominant traits are herbicide tolerance and insect resistance (James 2006). Over the past decade, the number of countries growing GM crops has increased tremendously, as has the global acreage planted with GM crops, with an annual growth rate of 13 percent in 2006 and 11 percent in 2005 (James 2005, 2006; Table 3.5). And in 2004, for the first time, the absolute growth in the biotech area was

Table 3.5   Genetically modified (GM) crops around the world

Measure	1992	1996	1997	1998	1999	2002	2004	2005	2006
Number of countries growing GM crops	1	6	—	9	12	—	17	21	22
Global area planted with GM crops (millions of ha)	—	1.7	11	27.8	39.9	67.2	81	90	102

Source: James (2002, 2004, 2005, 2006).
Note: — indicates no data available.

Table 3.6   Average net revenue for all surveyed farmers in northern China (US$ per ha)

	1999		2000		2001	
Type of cotton	Bt	Non-Bt	Bt	Non-Bt	Bt	Non-Bt
Net revenue	351	–6	367	–183	277	–225

Source: Pray et al. (2002).

higher in developing countries (a growth of 7.2 million hectares) than in industrial countries (6.1 million hectares). This growth is largely restricted to China, India, Argentina, Brazil, and South Africa (James 2004).

Some developing countries, such as India, China, Brazil, and South Africa, are now growing large areas with GM crops, especially cotton, soybeans, and maize. And, particularly in the case of China and India, small-scale cotton farmers have benefited greatly. Indeed, according to James (2006), out of the 10.3 million farmers growing biotech crops in 2006, 9.3 million were poor farmers from developing countries, the majority of whom planted Bt cotton. In terms of benefits, a survey conducted in northern China over 3 years (1999–2001) found that, despite higher prices of Bt seeds relative to non-Bt seeds, the average Bt cotton farmers' net revenues were much higher in all 3 years than those of farmers who planted non-Bt varieties, largely because Bt varieties reduced the use of other inputs, such as pesticides and labor (Pray et al. 2002; Table 3.6). Similarly, a recent study comparing 9,000 Bt and non-Bt cotton farmers in India's Maharashtra State showed significant economic gains for farmers who planted Bt varieties (see Bennett et al. 2004).

So far, most of the biotechnology research has been undertaken by a select group of private multinational firms, known as life-science companies, located in industrialized countries, and most of the resulting crops are found predominantly on large farms (Pinstrup-Andersen and Cohen 2000b). Nevertheless, CGIAR has been gradually increasing its biotech work, with an emphasis on tissue culture and marker-assisted breeding. For instance, the International Rice Research Institute, using both traditional breeding and biotechnology, is making significant advances in developing new rice hybrids with 15–20 percent higher yields than existing HYVs (IRRI 2006).

Until recently, other developing countries, especially low-income ones, for multiple reasons, have done very little in the domain of biotechnology research. Indeed, biotechnology research requires human and financial resources that many developing countries do not have. Additionally, developing countries do not have the institutional capacity to ensure biosafety. And, as seen earlier, incentives for private-sector research through IPR protection are lacking. There is also a fear that some industrialized countries (mainly in the European Union) that are important trade partners would put up trade barriers against the GM produce of developing nations (Qaim, Krattiger, and von Braun 2000; Juma 2001).

Molecular biology–based research presents tremendous opportunities for agriculture. First and foremost for developing countries, technologies developed through biotechnology can enhance yields by making plants more productive, limiting losses with disease- and insect-resistant crops, and improving tolerance to adverse weather and soil conditions. Further, biofortification (which can use transgenic or conventional breeding) can be used to increase the nutritional content of foods consumed in developing countries without having to resort to vitamin and other types of nutritional supplements, which would be costly to poor-country governments and difficult to manage. In fact, significant progress has already been achieved in this area. For instance, to combat Vitamin A deficiency, which causes blindness in an estimated 500,000 children and 1–2 million deaths every year, the Golden Rice Project developed rice fortified with beta carotene, which stimulates the production of vitamin A in the human body (Golden Rice Project 2007). Another promising initiative comes from CGIAR's HarvestPlus program, which is making important headway in developing nutrient-fortified staple crops, such as beans, cassava, rice, maize, and sweet potatoes (HarvestPlus 2007). For industrialized-country consumers, such research can be used to provide better quality foods and thus provide more choices—for example, sweeter tomatoes or potatoes with high starch content. In addition, as shown in the case of Bt cotton, biotechnology has the potential to produce more environmentally friendly outcomes by reducing the use of pesticides and insecticides while increasing yields (Pinstrup-Andersen and Schiøler 2003).

But biotechnology may also present some risks, in that its effects on human health and the environment are not fully understood. Therefore, the potential for adverse effects exist, although no evidence has surfaced to date. Nevertheless, when assessing the risks for developing countries, one needs to approach the problem in a different light from that of high-income countries. Being plagued by food insecurity and malnutrition, many consumers in developing regions do not have the luxury of a wide variety of nutritious and healthy foods, as do consumers in industrial countries, nor do they have the money to pay for such items. They therefore have a different risk perception than do people in the West (Juma 2001).

The debate regarding the use of genetic engineering has focused on potential risks instead of on a benefit-risk assessment. Although no negative health effects have been identified for GM foods, the use of genetic engineering in human medicine—which is opposed by very few—applies a benefit-cost assessment.

Concerns about Threats to Biodiversity and Food Safety

The current rapid rate of species extinction may be a serious threat to future agricultural productivity and, therefore, to human livelihoods. As for food safety risks, which include biological contaminants (bacteria, viruses, and parasites), concern stems from the emergence of new antibiotic-resistant pathogens and the potential, but unproven, risks to human health posed by genetically modified organisms (Unnevehr 2003).

Biodiversity.   Biodiversity—the source of all crops and animals—plays a vital role in agriculture. Throughout history, it has enabled scientists and farmers to improve plant and animal varieties through breeding of natural varieties (Evenson and Wright 2001; Heal et al. 2002). Currently, global biodiversity comprises more than 14 million species, but the rate of species extinction has accelerated and has surpassed the natural rate of extinction by a factor of 50–100. At this rate, it is estimated that between 5,000 and 150,000 species are becoming extinct every year (CBD/UNEP 2000; Iwanaga and Watson 2003). This rapid rate of extinction is linked to population growth and the expansion of agriculture, infrastructure, and human settlements.

Increased food demand stemming from population growth has led to the overexploitation of lands and animals, as well as to land clearing and deforestation. Research that facilitated the intensification of agricultural production has improved yields per unit of land and therefore reduced the pressure to acquire new lands for farming and protected biodiversity. But some detrimental effects to the environment and biodiversity have also occurred because of the use of agrochemicals and of irrigation without adequate drainage, which has led to increased water pollution, soil degradation, and a loss in coastal biodiversity (Pinstrup-Andersen 2002; Scherr 2003). Further, increased trade has translated into an expansion of commercial agriculture, which has meant increased use of modern varieties and a preference for monocropping over traditional farming methods, as well as more logging and deforestation (Heal et al. 2002; Scherr 2003).

To respond to the loss of biodiversity, many medium- and long-term germplasm storage facilities were established in the 1970s. The CGIAR centers play an important role in this function. Together, CGIAR centers hold 600,000 accessions of more than 3,000 crops, forage, pastures, and agroforestry species (Pinstrup-Andersen and

Cohen 2000a). This storage is a key global public good that supports sustainable world food security.

Food safety.   In industrialized nations, following a series of food-related scares in the 1990s, consumers have become more aware of food safety issues, and consequently public interest groups have been heavily involved in advocating for stringent food safety requirements. And in some developing nations (mostly middle-income countries), growing urbanization has led to an increased demand for processed foods and improvements in food safety. On the supply side, the food chain has become more complex, with expanding international trade and multinational corporations becoming dominant features of the food system. To satisfy the demands of consumers in the developed world, multinationals are entering into direct partnerships with smallholders and retailers in developing countries. Further, as urban populations in developing countries increase, multinational supermarket chains are entering that market and addressing the needs of urban consumers. Accordingly, these multinational firms are paying more attention to food safety, to differentiate themselves from competitors and to protect their brands (FAO 2003; Lang 2004).

Although food safety issues have come to the forefront of policymakers' agendas in recent years because of increasing concerns expressed by consumers, more complex food chains and fiscal constraints have reduced governments' capacity to ensure food safety. Thus, most governments have relegated this responsibility to multinational firms, which has led to a privatization of quality control and safety insurance (FAO 2003; Lang 2004).

Implications of Current Agricultural R&D Trends

In developing countries, the slow growth in public expenditure has meant a general drop in agricultural research growth, whereas in industrial countries the private sector has taken charge of the bulk of R&D (Pardey and Beintema 2001). This trend has some serious implications in terms of widening the already considerable knowledge gap between the developed and developing worlds, especially considering that public research intensities[3] in industrial countries are 4.2 times higher than those in developing countries (Pardey and Beintema 2001).

Another serious problem related to a more competitive and proprietary environment in agricultural research is the risk that developing countries will become isolated from the new developments in science, because most of them do not yet have the capacity to utilize modern scientific methods or to implement intellectual protection. As Serageldin (2001, 19) puts it, a "scientific apartheid, whereby 80 percent of humanity in the developing world is increasingly locked out of the most recent advances of modern science" may be emerging. This possibility is especially pertinent to research in biotechnology, where the increasing involvement of the private sector in industrialized nations, the inability of developing-country national research institutions to engage in such research, and the insufficient involvement of international agricultural research institutions have left most developing countries out of important developments in molecular biology–based research.

The nature of agricultural R&D is also changing. In industrialized nations, agricultural research has been directed toward basic research, while funding for public near-market research has been cut. In addition, because of the decline of the farming sector relative to other economic sectors and to the food supply chain, general agricultural research has broadened its scope to include more prefarming and postharvest technologies, such as food processing (Alston, Pardey, and Taylor 2001). As noted earlier, consumer concerns in industrialized countries have shifted toward food safety and environmental issues arising from the use of new technologies, thus shifting the attention of public research institutions in these countries to these topics. These research outcomes are relatively less relevant to the needs of the poor in developing countries, where research aimed at improving agricultural productivity is still a priority (Alston, Pardey, and Smith 1999).

For food safety issues, there is a concern that the privatization of food safety assurance may lead to negative distributional effects, in that only consumers with adequate economic resources would have access to safe foods (FAO 2003; Lang 2004). Further, on the supply side, although new partnerships between big corporations and smallholders have created opportunities for some small farmers, many others who do not have the resources to meet the necessary quality standards are marginalized in the production chain (Kirsten and Sartorius 2002; Unnevehr 2003). Public research, including policy research in the area of food safety, is therefore needed to establish more universal quality standards and improve public regulatory systems.

Toward Sensitizing Agricultural R&D in Developing Countries to the Needs of the Poor

Future agricultural research must focus on a number of emerging challenges, including but not limited to those associated with globalization. Continued population pressures and poor land and water use practices are also important current and future challenges to which agricultural research can contribute significantly. Opportunities created by modern science as well as new opportunities and risks associated with an increasingly globalized market and changing consumer preferences add to the set of challenges facing agricultural research. To effectively contribute to the MDGs within the context of these and related future challenges, it is critically important that research priorities and institutional arrangements are both appropriate. As the agricultural R&D environment in industrialized countries advances and becomes increasingly removed from the realities and needs of the poor in developing countries, institutions involved in agricultural R&D in the latter countries need to start relying on themselves and on one another to develop pro-poor technologies (Pardey, Alston, and Piggott 2006). In this section, we highlight some of the initiatives that are being undertaken to achieve this goal. We focus particularly on two trends: reorganizing research institutions using an innovation systems approach and setting priorities for agricultural research at the regional level. Subsequently we look at the roles and responsibilities of the main stakeholders in implementing these changes.

Institutional Arrangements of Agricultural R&D

In recent years, many agricultural research systems have recognized the need for institutional innovation to pursue more participatory and bottom-up research. Many have also realized that the process of technological innovation involves a range of stakeholders outside the research institution itself. However, the implementation of institutional innovations has been slow and spotty.

Innovation systems are multistakeholder platforms where participants interact to produce a new technology that is disseminated and then adopted by the prospective beneficiaries. To better capture these interactions and produce more useful and more widely adapted technologies, some research organizations are looking into the national system of innovation (NSI) as a new institutional arrangement for conducting research. An NSI is "a system or network of private and public sector institutions whose interactions produce, diffuse and use economically useful knowledge" (Hall et al. 2001, 793). The emphasis here is on the interdependence of the actors and institutions involved in producing new knowledge, as well as the interaction among the different actors and the complex relationships formed to produce new knowledge (Roseboom 2004; Hartwich 2005).

One advantage of an NSI is that it takes into account a country's socioeconomic and political contexts. An NSI also recognizes that innovations can happen outside formal research (that is, in NARS) from learning processes in the agricultural production chain that are shared through interaction (Roseboom 2004; Hartwich 2005). Further, an NSI is a dynamic system that is able to adapt to changes and new opportunities (Roseboom 2004).

However, because innovation systems in public agricultural R&D in developing countries are relatively new, the adoption of such an approach remains at the analytical stage. Models and best practices often do not exist, so the establishment of such a system will take time and require an extensive "learning by doing" process (Hartwich 2005). Further, the adoption of an innovation-system approach requires complementary investments, such as the development and strengthening of farmer organizations, the development of strategic public–private partnerships, the decentralization of regional innovation centers, and improvements in technology transfer mechanisms, as well as technology-sharing mechanisms between research centers (World Bank 2005). Nevertheless, this approach has a great potential to focus research effectively on the needs of poor farmers living in a globalizing world.

Regional Priorities for Agricultural Research and Development

With the support of GFAR, regional prioritization exercises are currently being carried out. The GFAR supports five regional initiatives: the Forum for Agricultural Research in Africa (FARA), the Asia-Pacific Association of Agricultural Research Institutions (APAARI), the Forum for the Americas on Agricultural Research and Technological Development (FORAGRO), the Association of Agricultural Research Institutions in the Near East and North Africa, and the Association of Agricultural Research Institutions of Central Asia and the Caucasus region. This section provides brief descriptions of the research priorities in different regions. It also highlights the need for agricultural research organizations to deal with cross-regional issues. To illustrate this, we take the example of how agricultural research has an important role to play in dealing with the health threats to agriculture and rural development posed by HIV/AIDS and malaria.

Research priorities in Sub-Saharan Africa. Sub-Saharan Africa is experiencing high population growth. It is also the region least affected by the Green Revolution, partly because, unlike Asia, there is no dominant farming system, and most crops are rainfed rather than irrigated. Indeed, at least 17 major farming systems exist in Sub-Saharan Africa, and these systems are usually characterized by high fragility and declining soil fertility caused by increasing population and lack of appropriate technology. Further, African agricultural research has been largely donor-dependent; with donor withdrawal from the agricultural sector, research organizations in Africa have suffered, as funding has become increasingly scarce and irregular. As a result, investment in R&D is declining (Beintema and Stads 2004).

Thus, in terms of setting priorities for research, FARA has adopted the Integrated Agricultural Research for Development approach in the proposal currently being developed for a Sub-Saharan Africa Challenge Program to produce demand-driven and effects-oriented agricultural research (Jones 2004). FARA's strategy is to first identify problems and potential solutions through an ecological approach for four priority farming systems (maize-mixed system, cereal/root crop–mixed system, irrigated system, and tree crop–based system) that have shown most promise in increasing food security on the continent. To that end, FARA promotes the development of close relationships between farmers and scientists to better detect problems and find appropriate solutions.

FARA also advocates more effective regional and international networking and collaboration in research and funding for research. Another priority area for FARA is the formation and maintenance of human capital for agricultural R&D in Africa. This goal requires extensive investments in higher education in science and the creation of an incentive structure for scientists within NARS to stay and work in their countries. These incentives could be in the form of adequate pay and the institution of merit-based systems (InterAcademy Council 2004).

Research priorities in Asia.   As for FARA, one of the main research priorities for APAARI in Asia is to create a more client-oriented approach in agricultural research, linking farmers to research organizations and markets. To strengthen the links between farmers and NARS, APAARI has concentrated on the use of information and communications technologies and has established the Asia-Pacific Research Information System. As for strengthening the link between farmers and markets, APAARI is facilitating access to available information on postharvest technologies (APAARI 2004).

Biotechnology has also been identified as a priority research area in Asia. In 2004, the Asia Pacific Consortium on Agricultural Biotechnology was established to facilitate biotechnology research in the region through public awareness programs, capacity building, research partnerships, and information dissemination (APAARI 2004).

Research priorities in Latin America.   The problem in Latin America is that of adequate access to food for all people rather than inadequate levels of production. Thus one of FORAGRO's research priorities is to reduce regional imbalances by concentrating on regions that are most in need. These are the Meso-American region, the Andean region, and the Amazonian low humid tropics (FORAGRO 2001). Another problem in Latin America comes from the entrance of multinational firms into local markets. These firms have entered into partnerships with some small farmers but have left out many other smallholders who are not able to keep up with stringent quality standard requirements. Thus, many small farmers have been displaced (Drugger 2004). The challenge is to promote competitiveness and increase the capacity of the displaced farmers to engage in partnership with the large multinational firms. This effort will require credit markets to give smallholders resources to improve the quality of their produce and technical expertise for farmer cooperatives (Drugger 2004).

Research priorities in other regions.   In Central Asia and the Caucasus and in the Near East and North Africa, research emphasis is on improving productivity in a more sustainable way. Some of the research priorities include improving crops' adaptability to biotic and abiotic stresses, minimizing the use of chemical fertilizers and pesticides, and implementing natural resources management in terms of more-efficient use of water resources and soil conservation (AARINENA 2000; CGIAR 2002).

An example of cross-regional research needs.   HIV/AIDS and malaria epidemics have had devastating effects on the agricultural sector in developing countries, mainly in Sub-Saharan Africa but also in Asia. Households are affected in many ways when their members are infected by HIV, including income loss, loss of assets that must be sold to cover the costs of illness, and the loss of skills as people with knowledge of farming die from the disease. In the long run, the epidemic is forecast to lead to a reduction in area cultivated, a shift in the types of crops cultivated from labor-intensive cash crops into less labor-intensive ones (such as cassava or sweet potatoes), and lower yields because of a shortage of weeding labor and lack of resources to invest in agricultural inputs. These changes would reduce crop productivity, thus leading to increased poverty and hunger (Jayne et al. 2005).

Malaria is another serious health problem, with 300–500 million people developing the disease worldwide each year, and 1.5–2.7 million of them dying from it. Sub-Saharan Africa suffers the greatest burden, but malaria is also a major challenge in other parts of the world. In many parts of Asia, for instance, the management of irrigation water has induced a spread of mosquitoes, which has increased the incidence of malaria. The disease poses a major threat to food security and poverty reduction, as it is most prevalent during the rainy harvest season, when worker productivity needs to be at its highest, and it therefore inhibits agricultural production significantly. The incidence of malaria is growing because of insecticide and antimalarial drug resistance and environmental changes, such as heavier rain patterns and the creation of new mosquito breeding grounds around dams and irrigation projects (Egan 2001).

Agricultural research communities need to take these serious health threats into consideration when developing new technologies. These institutions need to conduct research on the relationship between these diseases and agricultural productivity to determine what kind of technologies would be optimal in such contexts. Labor-saving technologies, for example, may be appropriate, especially for land preparation and weeding. Also, it is essential to improve information channels available to farmers, because HIV/AIDS and malaria are hampering the transfer of accumulated knowledge and skill from one generation to the next. One option would be to improve the skills of extension workers so they could help transfer relevant skills and knowledge (Jayne et al. 2005). Research on more-efficient water use and drip irrigation can also help in the management of the malaria epidemic, in that such practices may lead to fewer mosquitoes and therefore reduce outbreaks.

Role and Responsibility of Key Public-Sector Stakeholders

National governments.   National governments continue to play a central role in agricultural R&D. Their various responsibilities include focusing on the agricultural sector as a source of development, ensuring the sociopolitical and economic environments to promote innovation, providing adequate financial and technical support to

NARS, ensuring a suitable environment to enable multistakeholder platforms for public research organizations, and providing incentives for private-sector engagement in research.

The most urgent action needed by national governments in developing countries is to reestablish the focus of the government's agenda on rural development and the agricultural sector. Indeed, most poor people live in rural areas and get most of their incomes from agriculture. Because technological innovation is the key to agricultural development, governments have to invest in their research institutions, providing them with better financial and technical support. Further, for technologies to be successfully adopted by small farmers, agricultural research needs to be complemented with investments in human capital (particularly improved access for poor people to primary education and health care) and infrastructure (such as roads).

Governments can also play a role in motivating different actors to participate in the agricultural innovation. Policymakers can encourage the private sector to engage in R&D that would benefit the smallholders through alternative funding mechanisms such as "pull" funding programs that pay for research output rather than "push" programs that fund research inputs. Under pull funding, policymakers and donors only pay for concrete research outputs. Thus, in cases where policymakers can identify a specific desired technology and its social value, pull funding programs may be appropriate. Payment could also be tied to adoption rates, rewarding developers according to the degree to which the new products are actually adopted by farmers (Kremer and Zwane 2005).

Governments can also engage the private sector through the promotion of public–private partnerships. In the current context of globalization, such partnerships can offer multinational private firms access to farmers in emerging markets as well as the opportunity to improve corporate image and reputation, while they can give public agencies access to financial resources to conduct pro-poor research and access to new technologies, knowledge, and expertise (Spielman and von Grebmer 2004). Further, as private-sector involvement in the food and agricultural sector grows, there will be increased opportunities for the public and private sectors to collaborate on research projects (van der Meer 2002).

To increase farmer participation in the innovation process, national governments can strengthen farmers' organizations by ensuring their freedom of association and supporting outreach and educational programs.

NARS. Most NARS presumably see their principal role as producing or adapting technologies that would contribute to food security and poverty alleviation. In some regions of the developing world, this function entails creating knowledge and technologies to increase crop productivity and the nutritional content of foods; in others, it is more about creating knowledge and technologies that improve the links between farmers and markets. To achieve these goals and thus better meet the needs of target groups, NARS are moving toward more focused, participatory, and demand-led research. This emphasis entails setting specific research priorities based on the potential effects of the end results of the research endeavor. Further, NARS are trying to ensure a high quality standard for their research, maintaining scientists who are highly motivated and accountable for their results.

Regional and subregional organizations can assist NARS in refining research priorities, promoting a more cohesive regional research program, securing funding for research endeavors, and forging better partnerships with other research institutions in the region and internationally, as well as with farmers' organizations, nonprofit organizations, and the private sector. Regional and subregional research efforts, including the so-called centers of excellence, may help compensate for the inability of small, low-income countries to make the necessary investments in national systems.

IARCs and the international community. The overall goal of the research carried out by CGIAR and its partners continues to be to improve the livelihood of low-income people in developing countries and to help assure the sustainable management of natural resources there. The 15 centers sponsored by CGIAR continue to play an essential role in the creation of international public goods knowledge and technology that benefit millions of people in developing countries through improved food security and reduced poverty. Similarly, the centers are playing a major role in generating international public goods knowledge on sustainable natural resource management.

The niche for IARCs is that of generating knowledge and technology of a public goods nature that will benefit many countries. Thus, the outputs from IARCs serve as inputs into national agricultural research. As already discussed, this mechanism does not necessarily imply a linear approach to agricultural research, in which the international agricultural research system produces knowledge that is then disseminated to national institutions, which in turn disseminate the adopted technology to farmers. The generation of the knowledge and technology may well be undertaken in innovation systems that include researchers from CGIAR, NARS, and the private sector, as well as from NGOs and farmers' associations. What is important is that each of these groups focuses on its comparative strengths. In the case of CGIAR, that means the generation of international public goods rather than attempting to substitute for NARS by producing national public goods. It also implies that the CGIAR centers should not enter into development activities but should focus on their comparative advantage in research.

A recent effort to establish forward-looking research priorities within CGIAR resulted in five priority areas, with each including four priorities for research. The five priority areas are

- sustaining biodiversity for current and future generations;

- producing more and better food at lower costs through genetic improvements;

- reducing rural poverty through agricultural diversification and the exploitation of emerging opportunities for high-value commodities and products;

- alleviating poverty and managing water, land, and forest resources sustainably; and

- improving policies and facilitating institutional innovation to support the sustainable reduction of poverty and hunger.

The priorities embodied in these five areas will be pursued by the Future Harvest centers sponsored by CGIAR in partnership with NARS, the private sector, and NGOs.

The international community has a role to play in setting and enforcing international laws, especially in the domains of IPRs, biosafety regulations, and food quality standards. In terms of IPRs, issues of access to patented technologies for nonprofit research need to be resolved. Although freedom-to-operate for nonprofit research is not currently a major problem for most NARS, it could become one in the future as trade in agricultural commodities increases and more patents are filed in developing countries. Thus, a clearer picture of the complexities formed by the growing number of IPRs and their fragmentation is needed. The challenge here is to balance the need to protect intellectual property (to improve the incentive to innovate) with the need to gain access to preexisting knowledge by nonprofit research (to produce socially beneficial outcomes and protect farmers' rights to use seeds from their own harvests).

In the domain of biosafety regulations, the relationship between the Cartagena Protocol on Biosafety and the WTO's Agreement on the Application of Sanitary and Phytosanitary Measures (SPS) needs to be clarified. Indeed, although both agreements allow a country to use the precautionary principle when deciding whether to import a GM food product based on sufficient scientific evidence, the biosafety protocol is more detailed and less ambiguous than the SPS agreement. Thus, there is a need to harmonize these agreements to facilitate trade in agricultural products, in particular, those containing GM organisms.

There is also a need to harmonize food quality standards to promote trade in agricultural produce. To that effect, the Codex Alimentarius Commission created by the FAO and the WHO could play a central role. Last but not least, the industrial countries should recognize the importance of agricultural development for poverty alleviation and the critical role of agricultural research, and they should allocate future development assistance accordingly.

Conclusion

Agricultural R&D has the potential to boost agricultural productivity, promote sustainable managment of natural resources, and alleviate food insecurity and malnutrition through the development of new technologies that are geared toward the needs of the poor in developing countries. Globalization has changed the agricultural research environment, making it more competitive and proprietary. It has also induced research to focus on competitiveness and on issues that have more relevance to industrialized countries, such as food safety and biodiversity. This emerging agricultural R&D environment has critical implications for the poor in developing countries, in that the agricultural R&D needs of the poor may become increasingly neglected, especially in the context of weakened capacity of public research institutions in these countries.

Nevertheless, rapid developments in science—including molecular biology, nanotechnology, and information and communications—are opening up new and exciting opportunities for helping poor people to escape poverty, hunger, and malnutrition. For instance, new technologies enhancing plant productivity and those enabling the improvement of the nutritional content of staple crops are now available or are being developed.

The agricultural research environment in developing countries needs to adapt to these changes to have an effect on hunger and malnutrition. Public research institutions are therefore undergoing major changes to produce research outcomes that are more results oriented. The current trend is to move toward multistakeholder research approaches through the involvement of all actors in the innovation system. Another trend is the development of regional frameworks to improve regional cooperation among the different national research institutions. The challenge here is to create new knowledge that would benefit poor farmers while also integrating them within the new, more globalized agricultural research environment.

Notes

1. The International Model for Policy Analysis of Agricultural Commodities and Trade (IMPACT) model was developed to provide insights into the management of the "dynamic risks and forces that shape the factors affecting people's access to food and the links with malnutrition" through appropriate policy actions. It allows the exploration of the potential effects of different policy alternatives to manage hunger, malnutrition, commodity prices, demand, cereal yields, production, and net trade by projecting future global food scenarios to 2050 (von Braun et al. 2005, vii).

2. The Dynamic Research Evaluation for Management (DREAM; IFPRI 2005) model is used to evaluate the economic effects of agricultural research investments. It enables simulations of a "range of market, technology adoption, research spillover, and trade policy scenarios based on a flexible, multimarket, partial equilibrium model."

3. Research intensity is a relative measure that compares total agricultural research investment to the value of agricultural output.

References

AARINENA (Association of Agricultural Research Institutions in the Near East and North Africa). 2000. AARINENA in 2000 and beyond: A framework for action (2000–2005). Document discussed and adopted at AARINENA's Seventh General Conference, March 20–23, Beirut, Lebanon.

Abdulai, A., X. Diao, and M. Johnson. 2005. *Achieving regional growth dynamics in African agriculture.* Development Strategy and Governance Division Discussion Paper 17. Washington, D.C.: International Food Policy Research Institute.

Alston, J. M., and P. G. Pardey. 1999. The economics of agricultural R&D policy. In *Paying for agricultural productivity*, ed. J. M. Alston, P. G. Pardey, and V. H. Smith. Baltimore: The Johns Hopkins University Press.

Alston, J. M., P. G. Pardey, and V. H. Smith. 1999. *Paying for agricultural productivity.* Baltimore: The Johns Hopkins University Press.

Alston, J. M., P. G. Pardey, and M. J. Taylor. 2001. *Agriculture science policy: Changing global agendas.* Baltimore: The Johns Hopkins University Press.

APAARI/FAO (Asia-Pacific Association of Agricultural Research Institutions/Food and Agriculture Organization of the United Nations). 2004. *APAARI Newsletter* 13 (June). Bangkok, Thailand: FAO, Regional Office for Asia and the Pacific.

Atanassov, A., A. Bahieldin, J. Brink, M. Burachik, J. I. Cohen, V. Dhawan, R. V. Ebora, J. Falk-Zepeda, L. Herrera-Estrella, J. Komen, F. C. Low, E. Omaliko, B. Odhiambo, H. Quemada, Y. Peng, M. J. Sampaio, I. Sithole-Niang, A. Sittenfeld, M. Smale, Sutrisno, R. Valyasevi, Y. Zafar, and P. Zambrano. 2004. *To reach the poor—Results from ISNAR-IFPRI Next Harvest study on genetically modified crops, public research, and policy implications.* Environment and Production Technology Division Discussion Paper 116. Washington, D.C.: International Food Policy Research Institute.

Beintema, N. M., and G.-J. Stads. 2004. *Investing in Sub-Saharan African agricultural research: Recent trends.* 2020 Africa Conference Brief 8. Washington, D.C.: International Food Policy Research Institute.

Bennett, R. M., Y. Ismael, U. Kambhampti, and S. Morse. 2004. Economic impact of genetically modified cotton in India. *AgBioForum* 7 (3): 96–100.

CBD/UNEP (Secretariat of the Convention on Biological Diversity/United Nations Environment Programme). 2000. *Sustaining life on earth: How the Convention on Biological Diversity promotes nature and human well-being.* Montreal: CBD.

CGIAR (Consultative Group on International Agricultural Research). 2002. *Collaborative research program for sustainable agricultural development in Central Asia and the Caucasus.* Washington, D.C.

———. 2007. CGIAR Annual Report 2006: Focus on partnerships for effective research. Washington, D.C.

Cosbey, A., and S. Burgiel. 2000. *The Cartagena Protocol on Biodiversity: An analysis of results.* IISD Briefing Note. Winnipeg, Manitoba, Canada: International Institute for Sustainable Development.

Dalrymple, D. G. 2002. International agricultural research as a global public good: A review of concepts, experience and policy issues. In *Proceedings of the Warren E. Kronstad Symposium,* ed. J. Reeves, A. McNab, and S. Rajaram. Mexico, D.F.: Centro Internacional de Mejoramiento de Maiz y Trigo.

Drugger, C. W. 2004. The food chain: Survival of the biggest; supermarket giants crush Central American farmers. *New York Times (International),* December 28.

Egan, A. 2001. Malaria. In *Health and nutrition: Emerging and reemerging issues in developing countries,* ed. R. Flores and S. Gillespie. 2020 Focus 5. Washington, D.C.: International Food Policy Research Institute.

Evenson, R. E. 2003. Modern variety (MV) production: A synthesis. In *Crop improvement and its effect on productivity: The impact of international agricultural research,* ed. R. E. Evenson and D. Gollin. Cambridge, Mass., U.S.A.: CAB International.

Evenson, R. E., and D. Gollin, eds. 2003. *Crop improvement and its effect on productivity: The impact of international agricultural research.* Cambridge, Mass., U.S.A.: CAB International.

Evenson, R. E., and B. D. Wright. 2001. The value of plant biodiversity for agriculture. In *Agricultural science policy: Changing global agendas,* ed. J. M. Alston, P. G. Pardey, and M. J. Taylor. Baltimore: The Johns Hopkins University Press.

Fan, S. 2002. *Agricultural research and urban poverty in India.* Environment Production Technology Division Discussion Paper 94. Washington, D.C.: International Food Policy Research Institute.

Fan, S., L. Zhang, and X. Zhang. 2002. *Growth, inequality and poverty in rural China: The role of public investments.* Research Report 225. Washington, D.C.: International Food Policy Research Institute.

Fan, S., C. Chang-Kang, K. Qian, and K. Krishnaiah. 2003. *National and international agricultural research and rural poverty: The case for rice research in India and China.* Environment and Production Technology Division Discussion Paper 109. Washington, D.C.: International Food Policy Research Institute.

FAO (Food and Agriculture Organization of the United Nations). 2003. FAO expert consultation on food safety: Science and ethics. Proceedings from expert consultation, September 3–5, 2002, Rome.

FORAGRO (Forum for the Americas on Agricultural Research and Technology Development). 2001. Pilot project for the study of agricultural research priorities in Meso-America and to consolidate strategic alliances around them. Prepared by the Technical Secretariat of FORAGRO/IICA and the Executive Secretariat of GFAR based on the conclusions of the Mexico meeting, May 2–3, El Batan, Mexico.

GFAR (Global Forum on Agricultural Research). 2005. About GFAR. Available at http://www.egfar .org/egfar/website/aboutegfar.

Golden Rice Project. 2007. Golden Rice Project website. Available at http://www.goldenrice.org/. Accessed March 2007.

Hall, A., G. Bockett, S. Taylor, M. V. K. Sivamohan, and N. Clark. 2001. Why research partnerships really matter: Innovation theory, institutional arrangements and implications for developing new technology for the poor. *World Development* 29 (5): 783–797.

Hartwich, F. 2005. Innovation systems theory and agricultural development. Paper presented at the International Food Policy Research Institute Brown Bag Series, January 25, Washington, D.C.

HarvestPlus. 2007. HarvestPlus website. Available at http://www.harvestplus.org/. Accessed March 2007.

Hazell, P., and L. Haddad. 2001. Agriculture research and poverty reduction. Food, Agriculture, and the Environment Discussion Paper 34. Washington, D.C.: International Food Policy Research Institute.

Hazell, P., and C. Ramasamy. 1991. Introduction. In *The Green Revolution reconsidered: The impact of high-yielding rice varieties in South India*, ed. P. Hazell and C. Ramasamy. Baltimore: The Johns Hopkins University Press.

Heal, G., B. Walker, S. Levin, K. Arrow, P. Dasgupta, G. Daily, P. Ehrlich, K.-G. Maler, N. Kautsky, J. Lubchenco, S. Schneider, and D. Starrett. 2002. Genetic diversity and interdependent crop choices in agriculture. Nota Di Lavoro (Working paper) 100. Milan: Fondazione Eni Enrico Mattei.

———. 2005. DREAM: A tool for evaluating the effects of agricultural R&D. Available at http:// www.ifpri.org/dream.htm.

InterAcademy Council. 2004. *Realizing the promise and potential of African agriculture: Science and technology strategies for improving agricultural productivity and food security in Africa.* Amsterdam.

IRRI (International Rice Research Institute). 2006. *Annual report of the director general 2005–2006.* Los Baños, the Philippines.

Iwanaga, M., and D. Watson. 2003. Food production and biodiversity. Paper prepared for the Mexico Action Summit, June 2–3, Mexico City, Mexico.

James, C. 2002. *Preview—Global status of commercialized transgenic crops: 2002.* International Service for the Acquisition of Agri-Biotech Applications (ISAAA) Brief 27. Ithaca, N.Y., U.S.A.: ISAAA.

———. 2004. *Global status of commercialized biotech/GM crops: 2004.* ISAAA Brief 32. Ithaca, N.Y., U.S.A.: International Service for the Acquisition of Agri-Biotech Applications.

———. 2005. *Global status of commercialized biotech/GM crops: 2005*. ISAAA Brief 34. Ithaca, N.Y., U.S.A.: International Service for the Acquisition of Agri-Biotech Applications.

———. 2006. *Global status of commercialized biotech/GM crops: 2006*. ISAAA Brief 35. Ithaca, N.Y., U.S.A.: International Service for the Acquisition of Agri-Biotech Applications.

Jayne, T. S., M. Villareal, P. Pingali, and G. Hemrich. 2005. HIV/AIDS and the agricultural sector in Eastern and Southern Africa: Anticipating the consequences. Background report for a plenary presentation at the International Food Policy Research Institute/Regional Network on AIDS, Livelihoods and Food Security International Conference on HIV/AIDS, Food and Nutrition Security, April 14–16, Durban, South Africa.

Jones, M. 2004. *Strengthening agricultural research in Africa*. 2020 Africa Conference Brief 9. Paper prepared for the conference on Assuring Food and Nutrition Security in Africa by 2020: Prioritizing Actions, Strengthening Actors, and Facilitating Partnerships, April 1–3, Kampala, Uganda. Washington, D.C.: International Food Policy Research Institute.

Juma, C. 2001. Modern biotechnology. In *Appropriate technology for sustainable food security*, ed. P. Pinstrup-Andersen. 2020 Vision Focus 7. Policy Brief 4. Washington, D.C.: International Food Policy Research Institute.

Kirsten, J., and K. Sartorius. 2002. Linking agribusiness and small-scale farmers in developing countries: Is there a new role for contract farming? Department of Agricultural Economics Working Paper 13, University of Pretoria, Pretoria, South Africa.

Kremer, M., and A. P. Zwane. 2005. Encouraging private sector research for tropical agriculture. *World Development* 33 (1): 87–105.

Lang, T. 2004. Food and health wars: A modern drama of consumer sovereignty. Cultures of Consumption Working Paper 14. London: Cultures of Consumption and Economic and Social Research Council–Arts and Humanities Research Board Research Programme.

Lipton, M., and R. Longhurst. 1985. Modern varieties, international agricultural research, and the poor. Study Paper 2. Washington, D.C.: World Bank.

Louwaars, N. P., R. Tripp, D. Eaton, V. Henson-Apollonio, R. Hu, M. Mendoza, F. Muhhuku, S. Pal, and J. Wekundah. 2005. *Impacts of strengthening intellectual property rights on the plant breeding industry in developing countries: A synthesis of five case studies*. Report commissioned by the World Bank. Wageningen, The Netherlands: Centre for Genetic Resources.

Macdonald, S. 2001. Exploring the hidden costs of patents. Notes of a talk given at Quaker House, May 16, Geneva.

NAS (National Academy of Sciences). 2000. *Transgenic plants and world agriculture*. Washington, D.C.: National Academies Press.

Nottenburg, C., P. G. Pardey, and B. D. Wright. 2002. Accessing other people's technology for non-profit research. *Australian Journal of Agricultural and Resource Economics* 46 (3): 389–416.

Pardey, P. G., and N. M. Beintema. 2001. *Slow magic: Agricultural R&D a century after Mendel*. Food Policy Report 31. Washington, D.C.: International Food Policy Research Institute.

Pardey, P.G., J. M. Alston, and R. Piggott, eds. 2006. *Agricultural R&D in the developing world: Too little, too late?* Washington, D.C.: International Food Policy Research Institute.

Pardey, P. G., B. D. Wright, C. Nottenburg, E. Binenbaum, and P. Zambrano. 2003. *Intellectual property and developing countries: Freedom to operate in agricultural biotechnology*. Biotechnology and Genetic Resources Policies Brief 3. Washington, D.C.: International Food Policy Research Institute.

Peterson, W., G. Gijsbers, and M. Wilks. 2003. A new approach to assessing organizational performance in agricultural research organizations. ISNAR Briefing Paper 63. The Hague: International Service for National Agricultural Research.

Phillips, P. W. B., and D. Dierker. 2001. Public good and private greed: Realizing public benefits from privatized global agrifood research. In *The future of food: Biotechnology markets and policies in an international setting*, ed. P. G. Pardey. Washington, D.C.: International Food Policy Research Institute.

Pinstrup-Andersen, P. 2000. Strengthening partnership in agricultural research for development in the context of globalization. Keynote address on policy management and institutional development, Global Forum on Agricultural Research, May 21–23, Dresden, Germany.

———. 2001. Is research a global public good? *Entwicklung + Ländlicher Raum* 34 (2): 4–6.

———. 2002. Towards a sustainable global food system: What will it take? Keynote presentation for the Annual John Pesek Colloquium in Sustainable Agriculture, Iowa State University, March 26–27, Ames, Iowa, U.S.A.

Pinstrup-Andersen, P., and M. J. Cohen. 2000a. Biotechnology and the CGIAR. Paper presented at the International Conference on Sustainable Agriculture in the Next Millennium: The Impact of Modern Biotechnology on Developing Countries, May 28–31, Brussels.

———. 2000b. Modern biotechnology for food and agriculture: Risks and opportunities for developing country food security. *International Journal of Biotechnology* 2 (1–3): 145–163.

Pinstrup-Andersen, P., and M. Jaramillo. 1991. The impact of technological change in rice production on food consumption and nutrition. In *The Green Revolution reconsidered: The impact of high-yielding rice varieties in South India,* ed. P. Hazell and C. Ramasamy. Baltimore: The Johns Hopkins University Press.

Pinstrup-Andersen, P., and E. Schiøler. 2003. *Seeds of contention—World hunger and the global controversy over GM crops*. New Delhi: Oxford University Press.

Pray, C. 2002. The growing role of the private sector in agricultural research. In *Agricultural research in an era of privatization*, ed. D. Byerlee and R. G. Echeverría. Cambridge, Mass., U.S.A.: CAB International.

Pray, C. E., J. Huang, R. Hu, and S. Rozelle. 2002. Five years of Bt cotton in China—The benefits continue. *Plant Journal* 31 (4): 423–430.

Qaim, M., A. F. Krattiger, and J. von Braun, eds. 2000. *Agricultural biotechnology in developing countries: Towards optimizing the benefits for the poor.* Boston: Kluwer Academic.

Ramanna, A. 2003. *India's plant variety and farmers' rights legislation: Potential impact on stakeholder access to genetic resources.* Environment and Production Technology Division Discussion Paper 96. Washington, D.C.: International Food Policy Research Institute.

Roseboom, J. 2004. Adopting an agricultural innovation system perspective: Implications for ASARECA's strategy. ASARECA Strategic Planning Paper 5. Entebbe, Uganda: Association for Strengthening Agricultural Research in Eastern and Central Africa.

Scherr, S. J. 2003. Hunger, poverty and biodiversity in developing countries. Paper prepared for the Mexico Action Summit, June 2–3, Mexico City, Mexico.

Serageldin, I. 2001. Changing agendas for agricultural research. In *Agricultural science policy,* ed. J. M. Alston, P. G. Pardey, and M. J. Taylor. Baltimore: The Johns Hopkins University Press.

Spielman, D. J., and K. von Grebmer. 2004. *Public-private partnership in agricultural research: An analysis of challenges facing industry and the consultative group on international agricultural research.* Environment and Production Technology Division Discussion Paper 113. Washington, D.C.: International Food Policy Research Institute.

Unnevehr, L. J. 2003. *Food safety in food security and food trade.* 2020 Focus 10. Washington, D.C.: International Food Policy Research Institute.

UPOV (International Union for the Protection of New Varieties of Plants). 2002. Mission statement. Available at http://www.upov.int/en/about/mission.html. Accessed March 2007.

Van der Meer, K. 2002. Public-private cooperation in agricultural research: Examples from the Netherlands. In *Agricultural research policy in an era of privatization,* ed. D. Byerlee and R. G. Echeverría. Cambridge, Mass., U.S.A.: CAB International.

von Braun, J., M. W. Rosegrant, R. Pandya-Lorch, M. J. Cohen, S. A. Cline, M. A. Brown, and M. S. Bos. 2005. *New risks and opportunities for food security: Scenario analyses for 2015 and 2050.* 2020 Discussion Paper 39. Washington, D.C.: International Food Policy Research Institute.

———. 2005. Enhancing agricultural innovation: How to go beyond the strengthening of research systems. Concept note, January 13. Washington, D.C.: Agricultural innovation systems.

WTO (World Trade Organization). 2005. Intellectual property: Protection and enforcement. Available at http://www.wto.org/english/thewto_e/whatis_e/tif_e/agrm7_e.htm.

Chapter 4

Globalization and Smallholders: A Review of Issues, Approaches, and Tentative Conclusions

Sudha Narayanan and Ashok Gulati

This chapter surveys recent studies that evaluate the effects of globalization on smallholders. Our objective is fourfold:

- to map the different factors that would affect smallholders in the changing context of agriculture in developing countries;

- to review the literature and summarize the different approaches and methodology used to assess the impact of globalization on smallholders and identify areas that have been under-researched;

- to draw some conclusions, from the literature review, about the effects of globalization on smallholders; and

- to explore policy options that could help smallholders ride the wave of globalization rather than be swept away by it.

This chapter is based on Narayanan and Gulati (2002).

The authors benefited from the comments of several colleagues, including Chris Delgado, Eugenio Díaz-Bonilla, Arie Kuyvenhoven, Nick Minot, and Per Pinstrup-Andersen from IFPRI; Jock Anderson; Shawki Barghouti; Kevin Cleaver; Sushma Ganguly; John Nash; Felicity Proctor; Garry Pursell; and Dina Umali-Deininger. We are also grateful to two anonymous reviewers for their suggestions.

The underlying motivation of this chapter is that, although there has been much discussion on globalization and poverty in general, the smallholder question has not commanded as much attention. Perhaps reflecting this focus, reviews of literature pertaining to trade liberalization and poverty are many (for example, McCulloch, Winters, and Cirera 2001; Reimer 2002), as is true of those focusing on specific issues—such as linkage between trade liberalization and wages (Wood 1995; Slaughter 1999), globalization, and agro-industrialization (Reardon and Barrett 2000). In contrast, few have put smallholders in the spotlight. This chapter attempts to do exactly that.

In the first section we characterize smallholders and explain why they deserve special attention. We also discuss the factors that operate to shape smallholders' environment in the context of globalization. In the second section we review the literature on the effects of globalization trends on smallholders, with a particular focus on trade expansion. We also identify areas that require more research and comment on the limitations of the different methodologies. Finally, in the third section, we draw on these studies to map out policy options that would allow smallholders to gain more than they lose in the process of globalization.

Smallholders in a Globalizing World

Why Are Smallholders Important?

Smallholders merit special attention for a number of reasons.[1] First, smallholders often represent a large share of agricultural production, with almost 85 percent of all farms being smaller than 2 hectares (von Braun 2004). In countries like Bangladesh, most of the cultivated land is operated by farmers whose holdings are a mere 0.3 hectares (Gulati 2001). And in India, farmers with less than 2 hectares were responsible for 41 percent of total food grain production in 1990–91 (compared with 34 percent in 1980–81) and possessed the highest share of livestock population in 1998–99 (Singh and Kumar 2002). Further, in Sub-Saharan Africa smallholders account for about 90 percent of agricultural production (Spencer 2001).

Second, 75 percent of the estimated 1.1 billion people in the world who live on less than US$1 a day live and work in rural areas, and many are small farmers (World Bank 2004). In fact, in Africa they account for a majority of the rural poor (estimated at 73 percent; European Commission 2002), whereas in Asia they represent about 49 percent of the functionally poor.[2]

Third, smallholders face a set of unique problems. On the one hand, unlike larger farmers, they are typically constrained by resources that limit their ability to absorb shocks or even negotiate their participation in a new globalized context. On the other hand, unlike other groups of rural poor (such as agricultural laborers and landless

Table 4.1   Global drivers and meta-trends

Global drivers: What drives globalization?	Meta-trends: Global and local trends independent of globalization
• Trade expansion and trade liberalization • Intellectual property rights • Food safety and quality standards • Foreign direct investment • Scale of agroprocessing and retail industry	• Technological change • Urbanization, increasing incomes, and population pressure • Shifts in food consumption patterns • Environmental trends (such as climate change and soil quality)

Source: Authors.

workers), smallholders' relative advantage in possessing both labor and land implies they are better positioned not only to take advantage of opportunities but also to make decisions that are much more complex and wide-ranging. Although smallholders might be successful while remaining small, technological and market changes provide opportunities for smallholders to grow—for example, to scale up or (if their farms remain small, which is very likely in the short to medium run) to move to high-value agriculture or initiate off-farm activities as household time is reallocated. To some extent, what happens to rural poverty depends on which way the smallholders go.

Issues Affecting Smallholders

From the point of view of smallholders, the elements of globalization most likely to have strong repercussions can be organized into two broad categories: global drivers and meta-trends (see Reardon and Barrett 2000; Table 4.1). Global drivers refer to such factors as multilateral trading agreements that have led to fundamental and large-scale changes in the policy orientation of hitherto closed economies. Meta-trends refer to changes taking place all over the world, independently of the globalization process, yet shaping the nature of globalization and occurring both globally and locally.

Global drivers. Trade expansion consequent to trade liberalization is the most important global driver.[3] The direct effect of trade liberalization is usually through change in prices of commodities that have been liberalized (that is, the impact effect). However, it also triggers a whole range of second-round effects through factor prices, income, investment, employment, and demand linkages. In the short run, the effect depends on the production and consumption profile—considering whether the products are importables, exportables, or nontradables and whether liberalization affects imports, exports, or both.

In this analysis, several other aspects need to be considered when establishing any link between price changes and welfare effects:

- Whether price transmission actually occurs. Price transmission depends on the mechanism and structure of the distribution sector, the government's role in marketing and distribution, costs and constraints of marketing, infrastructure, domestic taxes and regulation, and markets for inputs.

- The small-farm household's response to price signals in terms of substitution between commodities in the consumption and production bundles, marketed surplus, and labor allocation decisions. These may differ widely, depending on the individual circumstance of households. Among the factors that determine this response are access to public services and goods, inputs, credit, and the demographic profile (labor endowments) of the household. These could be classified as institutional and structural constraints.

- Significant second-round effects in operation that come from linkages with other nonfarm activities within and outside the rural economy. The ways in which second-round effects operate are difficult to gauge, primarily because they depend on opportunities available and performance in the nonfarm sector.

- The long-run effects, which may be less obvious, of government transfers. Transfers are influenced by changes in revenue from trade taxes, incentives for investment and innovations, and changes in terms of trade.

Other global drivers also have important implications for small farmers. The establishment of IPR under the Trade-Related Aspects of Intellectual Property Rights Agreement of the WTO could affect smallholders' access to new technologies, or smallholders may face higher prices for critical inputs resulting from more oligopolistic or monopolistic seed industry structures. A similar challenge is posed by increasingly stringent food safety and quality standards (SPS measures) in industrialized countries, and by similar trends domestically, which might impinge on smallholders' ability to exploit opportunities for high-value exports to these countries. Also, the liberalization of capital flows results in an increase in cross-country investment in agrifood industries, leading in part to larger scale operations and a growing concentration in the agrifood chain (inputs, processing, retailing, trading, and so on).

Meta-trends.   Population pressures in developing countries, particularly in rural areas, affect landholding patterns; consequently, smallholders could proliferate, and their farms could get even smaller. Urbanization and rising incomes have led to shifts in demand away from unprocessed staples to more processed foods (Bennett's Law), opening up some areas of opportunity for small farmers.

Another important trend is the rapid technological changes that are dramatically affecting agro-industries as well as the distribution channels from farm to table (information technology, packaging, storing, and transport). Depending on the extent to which these technologies have scale bias, they can affect smallholders' institutional environment significantly.

Other factors include environmental degradation, particularly in resource-poor regions, and a gradual shift in political economy toward neo-liberal regimes that reinforce trends in globalization and greater cross-country integration. Although each of these factors has important implications for the smallholder, for the purpose of this chapter, trade expansion consequent to liberalization is the central focus.[4]

Key Questions

The fundamental question is whether smallholders can take advantage of the opportunities presented by globalization while surviving its threats. A related issue is the increased exit of smallholders from the agricultural sector. This trend may be expected in the normal course of development in globalization, but it is important to ask why. Do pull factors represented by opportunities in the nonfarm sector, notably the industry and service sectors, attract them away from farming? Or are they forced to quit farming in the face of adverse circumstances (because of push factors) as a result of trade liberalization or other globalization processes? Naturally, these scenarios are two very different things; the latter in particular should be of grave concern to policymakers.

What implications does this exit of smallholders from farming have for policy? Should there be an effort to keep smallholders on their farms, or should they be encouraged to quit farming? If the latter, what are the exit options that can be made available to the smallholder, and how can the transition be smoothed? If not, what mechanisms can be devised to protect smallholders who are particularly vulnerable to the effects of globalization? It is also important in this context to determine whether these policy levers should merely ensure that small farmers are not disfavored vis-à-vis large farmers or whether they should be explicitly supported through special benefits. This issue is especially critical for regions where smallholders form the backbone of agriculture and are instrumental in driving growth in the agricultural sector. A broader question relates to how the current political disempowerment of smallholders can be redressed so that they count in the decisionmaking process in developing countries.

Review of Select Literature

So far, studies evaluating the implications of liberalization on poverty in general far outnumber those focusing exclusively on the situation of the smallholder. However, to the extent that smallholders constitute a substantial part of the rural poor, these studies may be relevant.

Three broad approaches have been used to study the effects of agricultural trade liberalization (and more generally globalization) on small farmers (McCulloch, Winters, and Cirera 2001). They can be described broadly as the descriptive (qualitative) approach,[5] data-based or survey methods,[6] and the modeling approach,[7] although some studies have attempted to combine different approaches in addressing the issue. There is, however, considerable diversity in emphasis and methodology even within these categories.

The first two approaches—descriptive and data-based or survey methods—can be thought of as bottom-up approaches, which focus on micro-level details (Reimer 2002). Modeling, in contrast, particularly those of the general equilibrium kind, is typically a top-down approach. Drawing on a macro-level algebraic framework of the economy, an attempt is made to capture the effects of exogenous shocks to the system on different agents (usually a representative agent). Recent innovations have attempted to marry the two approaches in what is termed a "micro-macro" synthesis (see Chapter 2 for results that emerge from these studies). Given the tremendous diversity in approaches, it is natural that they all address issues and make assumptions that are equally diverse.

The Debate

The debate on how the smallholder would fare in a liberalized agricultural context follows two main strands. On one hand, some people believe that price increases in response to liberalization would have a favorable effect on small farmers, because they would benefit from higher producer prices and incomes. This argument implies an optimistic future for small farmers, especially in the high-value sector, which offers these individuals opportunities to participate in the globalized system. On the other hand, there are those who claim that, because smallholders are often net consumers of food, adjustment programs that increase the prices of tradable commodities (food) would squeeze real incomes of small farmers who are net buyers, thus suggesting that smallholders may "retreat into subsistence." In this reasoning, when the effect of liberalization is to decrease rather than increase the price of staples, it creates negative production outcome but a positive consumption-price outcome. Still others acknowledge that the effects of adjustment or liberalization cannot be determined by looking merely at the consumption bundle or relative prices in isolation. It would also be important to see how price changes affect the production basket and to consider second-round effects on wage rates, given that many smallholders work on others' fields. It is thus the net effect on the production, consumption, and wage income of smallholders that needs to be considered.

Literature on the Impact of Trade Liberalization on Smallholders

The issue that has been addressed most often is the effect on the smallholder of trade liberalization and concomitant price changes and second-round effects. Indeed, these effects are the most visible aspect of globalization.

Assessing impact effects.   In assessing impact effects, studies have generally been concerned with two sets of issues: relative price changes with trade liberalization and price volatility. The impact effect is the immediate short-term consequence of relative price changes at the border following export liberalization (removal of a quota), import liberalization (reducing tariffs, freeing up imports), or other policy changes, such as currency devaluation. Two main, contradictory arguments emerge from studies. If domestic prices are less than export parity prices, liberalization has the effect of pushing up domestic prices. Because smallholders are typically net buyers of food, many studies contend that liberalization is inimical to them. On the other hand, if domestic price levels remain higher than import parity prices, liberalization would lead to domestic prices declining to world levels. In this case, liberalization leads to cheap imports, which, studies claim, destroys the livelihoods of small farmers (Watkins 1997 for corn in the Philippines and Mexico; Nadal 2000a,b for corn in Mexico; Rojjanapo 2000 for Thailand). Ahmad and Tawang (2000), in their econometric analysis of Malaysia's palm oil and paddy sectors, emphasize that these effects are sector specific: whereas smallholder palm producers are likely to benefit, rice farmers could see farm incomes decline by 15–60 percent.

Assessing the impact effect of liberalization and the consequent change in prices requires, however, that both the consumption and the production of the commodity in question be considered. This requirement is because even within a given group, such as smallholders, there may be gainers and losers, depending on the individual household's status as a net seller or a net buyer. Most qualitative studies do not take this factor into account in a rigorous manner. The data-based studies that do take it into account come up with different prognoses for different countries. For instance, although the effects on welfare are positive for rice price increases in Thailand and Indonesia (Deaton 1989; Budd 1993), they are negative in Madagascar (Barrett and Dorosh 1996).

It is clear from this set of studies that accounting for marketed surplus is important. Even so, many of these studies typically focus on a single commodity sector, which is restrictive. In reality, the evidence is that smallholders in developing countries have highly diversified income profiles and there is a whole range of goods, exportables, importables, and nontradables—both agricultural and nonagricultural—in their consumption and production baskets.

The need for detailed analysis of data on the structure of household incomes, consumption bundles, and output has been recognized but has not led to detection of an unequivocal pattern of change in the real welfare of smallholders across countries (Sahn and Sarris 1991).[8]

The comprehensive coverage of the production and consumption baskets still misses out on two issues. First, within the smallholder group, studies often do not distinguish household types; welfare implications may be very different for small-holders with different production and consumption profiles. And second, models of the kind just described do not allow for substitution possibilities in production and consumption in the long run. All in all, focus on estimating welfare effects of price changes in the short term and on a single commodity tends to, as Barrett and Dorosh (1996) admit, somewhat circumscribe the policy implications of the analysis.

Household response to price change is crucial to determine whether the small-holder benefits. It is expected that in the medium and long terms, cropping patterns of smallholders would shift to crops with higher relative profitability; on the consumption side they would try to substitute among commodities in favor of products with lower relative prices. In particular, decisions regarding what they produce for self-consumption and what they buy and sell in the market are critical, as is the response of marketed surplus. In short, the response to changes induced by liberalization would determine whether the smallholder retreats into subsistence or rides the globalization wave.

Studies suggest that either could happen (Barrett 1998; Nadal 2000a,b). Barrett (1998), for instance, proposes an "immiserized growth hypothesis," whereby small farmers retreat into subsistence. Somewhat in contrast are findings that most of the poor, rural, and self-employed would either benefit from higher farm prices or remain unaffected by hypothetical price changes (Glewwe and de Tray 1988 for Côte d'Ivoire; Gulati and Kelly 1999 for India; Minot and Goletti 2000 for Vietnam).

Household response is the factor that has been most effectively integrated into several modeling frameworks. Data-based approaches have limited scope for such a comprehensive characterization of household behavior. Agricultural household models, on the other hand, offer scope for a formal treatment of household response, usually through incorporation of a supply response function, a marketed surplus response function, and a consumption function (Singh, Squire, and Strauss 1986). There have been several studies analyzing pricing policies for several countries (Braverman and Hammer 1986 for Senegal; Braverman, Hammer, and Ahn 1986 for Korea; Singh and Subramanian 1986 for Nigeria and Korea); many stress the importance of linking up different commodity markets that allow for substitution possibilities. The findings are again fairly diverse, with many suggesting a favorable influence on real incomes (Minot and Goletti 1998; Gulati and Kelly 1999) but not always on inequality.

The other anticipated consequence of trade liberalization is price volatility. Removal of border protection (particularly any that is similar to quantitative restrictions) exposes domestic agricultural sectors to world prices, so that greater fluctuations in world prices consequent to trade liberalization get transmitted to domestic prices. For small farmers with limited means to safeguard against downswings, such volatility could push them to the brink of destitution. Such fears have been articulated in several assessments of the impact effect (Nayyar and Sen 1994; Barrett and Dorosh 1996 for rice prices in Madagascar; Nadal 2000a,b for Mexico; Rojjanapo 2000 for Thailand; Karanja 2002 for small coffee growers in Kenya). Empirical estimates of international price volatility, however, tend to conclude differently. Although prices are volatile, there is no indication that they are systematically linked to trade liberalization (Sarris 1997 for cereals; Valdés and Foster 2002) in a way that would lead one to conclude that liberalization contributes to volatility, something that is borne out in other studies as well. The upside of exposure to international prices is insurance against the consequences of local price shocks (such as local crop failures) that international markets provide. Whether this protection happens in reality is, however, open to question.

Perhaps more than volatility, the problem faced by farmers in developing countries is the prolonged periods of low international prices (Valdés and Foster 2002).[9] The reasons are several, the most important of which is the presence of industrialized-country policies that offer countercyclical emergency assistance to farmers when world prices fall. This intervention has the effect of deflecting the downswing in prices back to international markets instead of absorbing them domestically. In such a situation, small farmers in developing countries have few options to tide them over during periods of low prices. Although there may be feasible solutions for price risk management in the short run—indeed, there have been several success stories in price risk management in developing countries, chief of which is the role of financial markets that reduce price volatility (Karanja 2002)—they may not help for prolonged downswings in prices. Here what may be more important is the streamlining of distortionary agricultural policies of industrialized countries in WTO negotiations.

Structural and institutional constraints.   Assessments of the impact effect of trade liberalization, specifically, quantitative assessments that use the modeling approach, often assume away problems of price transmission and structural and institutional constraints in the smallholders' environment. These can, however, be extremely important determinants of how smallholders in developing countries fare, and they therefore merit special attention.

Most studies that evaluate the effect of trade liberalization tend to assume that price changes at the border are transmitted down to the farmer. But typically in developing countries there is a large difference between the border prices and prices faced by the smallholder, reflecting weak price transmission (Quiróz and Soto 1995; Sarris

1997). The extent of price transmission varies, depending on a range of factors—from domestic and external policies to structural and institutional considerations.

Weak price transmission could have two very different effects. On one hand, rural low-income households may be somewhat isolated from the cash economy—the insulation could protect them from the adverse effect of price changes at the border. On the other hand, there could be asymmetric price transmission, wherein farmers pay more for what they buy, be it inputs or other importables, but may not be able to gain from higher prices for their output, as in Rwanda (Minot 1998). Or it could be that market power among buyers of produce could effectively prevent net-selling smallholders from benefiting from price rises. Alternatively, as Nadal (2000a,b) claims, small maize farmers as buyers do not benefit from reductions in maize prices, because tortilla industry cartels prevented the passage of 50 percent price reductions to consumers of corn products, although they would still benefit from reduced prices if they were to buy corn directly from the market.

Another neglected aspect is that smallholders often sell in a buyer's market when prices are low, and they may buy off-season in a seller's market when prices are high. In such cases, it is the traders who benefit and not the smallholder farmer. In Malawi, traders have emerged as important players, buying food commodities from farmers and selling them to urban consumers or exporters (Parris 1999).

Closely related to the question of price transmission are institutional and structural constraints. A burgeoning literature, much of which is informed by the New Institutional Economics perspective, has highlighted structural and institutional factors that result in high transactions costs, often constraining the smallholder from exploiting opportunities opened by trade or intensifying the adverse effects (see Delgado 1999; Kydd et al. 2001; McCulloch, Winters, and Cirera 2001). It is therefore important to know what these constraints are, how they affect smallholders, and what experience developing countries have had in tackling these constraints.

Incorporating second-round effects: Factor earnings. So far, the focus has been on assessments of impact effects and on several caveats related to aspects that are often neglected in impact studies. In the long run, however, the initial effect itself may be dissipated, overturned, or exacerbated by second-round effects operating primarily through linkages within rural economies and the urban sector. Such effects are also likely to influence direct upstream and downstream production linkages, investment linkages, and indirect consumption or expenditure linkages, among others (Delgado 1998; Kydd et al. 2001; McCulloch, Winters, and Cirera 2001).

Of all the linkages, factor earning is a critical component in assessing the effects on welfare of trade liberalization (Reimer 2002). Even if small farmers were to lose in the short run (with benefits received mainly by larger farmers), in the long run they could benefit from farm and nonfarm activities through greater employment opportunities. This benefit could happen through greater aggregate employment; more gainful employment; or higher wage earnings, which would come from rural on-farm wages, rural nonfarm incomes, and urban earnings. Naturally, this possibility is contingent on factors that may affect the nonfarm sector quite independently of the agricultural sector.

For smallholders, on-farm income from agricultural wages is often an important supplemental earning. If higher food prices were to stimulate food production, which increases demand for agricultural labor, it could push up wages. Under such circumstances, although net buyers of food would be adversely affected by food price increases in the short run, they could gain through wage increases over a longer time period, highlighting the need to gauge the responsiveness of wages with respect to (output) prices (Ravallion 1990; Warr 2001; Rashid 2002).[10]

Data also suggest that rural nonfarm income may be quite important—more so in Latin America and Africa than in Asia. In the late 1990s, in Latin America as much as 46 percent of rural household income in selected countries on average came from nonfarm sources (with a weighted average proportion of 40 percent). The proportion was close to 45 percent in Africa and 35 percent in Asia. And this share may be increasing, particularly in Latin America, both in absolute and relative terms. Similarly, urban wages could also be a significant part of smallholder income. For instance, seasonal rural–urban migration is common among small farmers in many developing countries—more common in Asia than in Latin America or Africa, where, contrary to popular belief, migration income is far outweighed by nonfarm incomes (Reardon, Berdegué, and Escobar 2001). In such Asian countries as China, part-time farming is widespread (Taylor 2003), whereas in India and Thailand, urban centers are recipients of seasonal labor from the countryside.

Rural factor markets have been effectively integrated into multimarket models (Barnum and Squire 1979; Braverman, Hammer, and Ahn 1986; Gulati and Kelly 1999), offering a more complete treatment of the link between prices and rural wages. The expansion of models to include nonfarm sectors (rural and urban), on the other hand, leads to general equilibrium modeling that captures not only rural nonfarm linkages but also economy-wide ones. These models are sensitive to the assumptions made regarding closures, specification of relationships, and the number of representative agents identified. Given the diversity in the models, the predicted outcomes of policy shocks representing liberalization are equally diverse (see also Chapter 2). However, the major findings are:

- When trade liberalization alone is undertaken, it often has adverse effects on the rural poor (although these models are run with full-employment specifications that mute the employment-multiplier effects). But complementary policies undertaken simultaneously have the potential to overturn the adverse influences. These models thus emphasize the importance of complementary policies (land redistribution, self-targeted rural works programs, and restructuring of government expenditures and taxation; see Bautista and Thomas 1998, 2000; Löfgren, El-Said, and Robinson 1999).

- When rural households have highly diversified incomes, they are less prone or vulnerable to shocks (see, for instance, Löfgren et al. 2001).

- When trade liberalization is undertaken, it is possible that apart from (or rather than) changes in wage rates, there may be overall positive effects on aggregate employment (see Gerard et al. 1998).

Although these results from modeling exercises are instructive, it is essential to go beyond mere numbers and see what motivates the rural poor to diversify their sources of income. Are push factors at work? Or do pull factors dominate? It is immediately obvious that the two imply very different things as far as the welfare of smallholders is concerned. Studies in Africa and Latin America suggest that, although rural nonfarm income and employment are important in both cases, in Africa they tend to be driven more by push factors and in Latin America by pull factors (Barrett, Reardon, and Webb 2001; Reardon, Berdegué, and Escobar 2001).

The dynamics of smallholder livelihood strategies needs special attention, and it is unlikely that models studying trade liberalization—however sophisticated—manage to capture the various dimensions in all their complexity. Similarly, capturing the effects of other global drivers, such as IPR, food safety standards, FDI, and the scale of agroprocessing and retail industry, on smallholders is equally difficult. These problems have been discussed in detail by Narayanan and Gulati (2002).

Synthesis on the Effects of Trade Liberalization

At the outset, the complex dimensions of smallholders' new context induced by trade liberalization and other global drivers and meta-trends were emphasized. Understandably, no study reviewed has been so comprehensive as to cover the whole canvas of issues. It is evident that studies on different aspects of globalization and the smallholder have varying focuses and use diverse approaches with different points of departure. Their results are as mixed and varied as the methods they employ.

One important feature that emerges is that studies focusing on trade liberalization alone (operating through price changes) and those that address broader issues of globalization (such as the changing structure of the food and retail industry and new relationships in the interface of farm and firm, SPS issues, and so on) have run somewhat parallel to each other, whereas a greater integration of the two would be more valuable.

Methodological approaches may have something to do with this apparent dichotomy. Modeling, used so commonly in trade liberalization studies, has a limited scope in capturing structural changes that typify the broader issues of globalization. Such studies also tend to assume away critical factors, such as institutional constraints and global drivers and meta-trends (such as SPS, IPR, and FDI in the food and retail industry). Qualitative approaches, on the other hand, although useful for focusing on particular aspects, fail to capture the net effects of the different changes in a rigorous way. In particular, those dealing with such issues as quality standards and technological change are usually devoid of the context of price changes induced by trade liberalization. It seems that a survey-based approach, in conjunction with qualitative studies, offers the best alternative to assess the predicament of the smallholder in the context of globalization.

Apart from greater integration of the two streams of literature, there are several areas that are significantly under-researched and deserve attention. These include the implications of IPR (particularly the changing structure of the seed industry), compliance costs of SPS, the implications of different kinds of technological advances, and the concentration of food-related industry and its implications for smallholders. In particular, it would be useful to have rigorous and data-based evidence on these areas.

Finally, another issue is that almost all the studies reviewed addressed smallholders often only peripherally in discussions of larger issues, such as technological change, trade liberalization, or food safety and quality standards. It would be useful instead to allow smallholders to be the subject of the research. This practice is really the key to understanding how globalization affects smallholders and what policy options are available to deal with the issue.

Overall, from the literature reviewed, it is apparent that trade liberalization could adversely affect some agricultural activities in particular countries rather severely, as the prognosis for maize in the Philippines and Mexico and for rice in Malaysia suggests. To generalize, smallholders who are net sellers in inefficient sectors (or those whose country does not have competitive advantage, given the trade environment and other nonprice factors) lose out, and net-buyer smallholders in efficient sectors in exporting countries face similarly adverse circumstances.

But then adjustment processes come into play: smallholders can shift to other crops or livestock activities or look for jobs elsewhere, even leaving agriculture. Alternative choices outside of agriculture may not be available, however, and deteriorating environmental conditions and low productivity gains in some resource-poor regions offer few options for shifts in cropping patterns. Where the possibility of changing agricultural activities exists, high-value agriculture for exports, and increasingly for urban domestic markets, seems to offer opportunities for smallholders in developing countries. Some of those activities are often labor-intensive or are suitable for marginal lands (poultry raising, for example). Smallholders who are able to switch to high-value agriculture successfully would, it seems, gain substantially from globalization. Indeed, there have been instances of small farmers everywhere benefiting from such exports to other countries or even other regions within the country (cut flowers from China, for instance, or fish from Bangladesh and horticulture from Kenya and Zimbabwe).

It is instructive that in all these cases the winners have been smallholders who

- are vertically integrated with agribusinesses (exporters or otherwise) or have devised institutional innovations (such as cooperatives or farmer companies) for collective strength;

- have access to better physical infrastructure and credit; and

- have benefited from capacity-building activities by the public sector, private industry, or international cooperation.

On the other hand, those who have failed to capitalize on the opportunities opened up by globalization or have been adversely affected are poorly endowed in terms of natural resources, assets, and infrastructure; lack access to markets for output, input, land, and also credit and insurance; and have limited alternatives for employment (off-farm) in rural and urban areas—in agro-industries or otherwise.

To sum up the evidence, it is apparent that global drivers and meta-trends pose a big challenge to small farmers, ironically precisely in areas that offer them the greatest opportunity—namely, high-value agriculture. However, there are also clear indications that these challenges can be met, and where this has happened it has usually been through a combination of vertical coordination with processors and agro-industry and a proactive public sector or government (whether in research or in establishing certifying and testing procedures).

Policy Implications

Appropriate policies to protect smallholders would have two related objectives: to enable them to take advantage of opportunities where there are constraints preventing them from doing so and to deal with and minimize adverse effects on smallholders in the globalization process. To work toward achieving these goals, it is useful to think of two broad groups of policy instruments: enabling factors that help farmers

Figure 4.1   Policy implications: A two-pronged approach

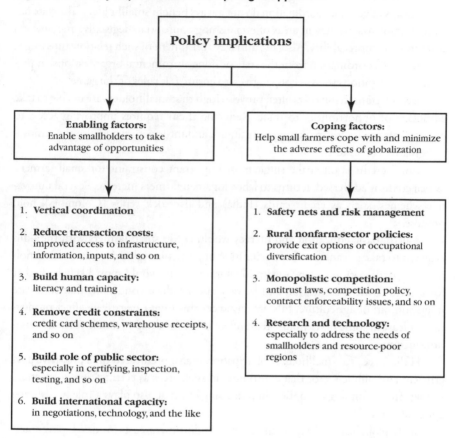

Source: Authors.

ride the globalization wave and coping factors that protect them from being swept away (Figure 4.1).

Enabling Factors

If smallholders are to take advantage of the opportunities presented by globalization, many constraints they face must be removed. Six areas are critical. First, greater vertical coordination with agro-industry facilitates participation of small farmers in the growing processed-food trade, particularly in meeting food safety and quality standards. This coordination can be achieved through institutional innovations, such as cooperatives, contract farming, and clustering. There is legitimate concern that the mechanisms of vertical coordination do not always benefit smallholders. The state has an important role to play in areas of establishing appropriate legislative frameworks and contract enforceability. Also, the initial establishment of such relationships might require some coordination from the state or nongovernmental organizations, in particular in institutions such as cooperatives, to ensure fair rules of the game.

Second, transaction costs often prove so high that smallholders are unable to take advantage of opportunities to trade. Reducing them requires improving access to physical infrastructure, marketing institutions, and information and also the removal of legislative constraints.

Third, credit is often the single-most important constraint for small farmers. When credit is addressed, returns to labor for small farmers increase. Several innovative schemes, such as credit cards (India) and livestock repos (Colombia), hold promise.

Fourth, basic education and literacy would equip small farmers with the skills required to take advantage of opportunities. In particular, adoption rates of technology and participation in new institutional innovations would most likely be higher for literate farmers. Education and literacy also produce conditions that stimulate migration out of agriculture. In some instances this might negatively affect production, at least in some households. Yet it offers scope for diversification of rural household incomes.

Fifth, successful smallholder participation is also predicated on a proactive government and public sector that contributes in such areas as certification, inspection, testing, and technology adoption in processing but that also plays a role in fostering agro-industry.

Sixth, globalization may entail significant adjustment costs for developing countries, which are also financially less capable. It is necessary to support international capacity-building measures that help developing countries cope with the many challenges that globalization poses. This assistance can occur at different levels. One is institution and infrastructure building, so that developing countries can exploit opportunities opened up by trade. Examples include China's cut flower exports and Bangladesh's marine exports. A greater scale of such activities in partnership with national and local governments is essential, particularly in the resource-poor least-developed regions, where private initiative is least likely to penetrate. Another is political empowerment to foster a greater degree of representation of smallholder interests in the political decisionmaking processes. Finally, at the level of international negotiations, it is essential to build capacity in developing countries to have a more active involvement in the multilateral trade negotiations and in decisionmaking processes of standard-setting bodies (such as FAO's Codex).

Coping Factors

Protective instruments are needed to minimize the adverse effects that inevitably accompany the globalization process. For small farmers, there are four main issues. First, price volatility and, more importantly, persistence of low prices have surfaced as critical threats for small farmers. Given their low capital and resource base, it is important that smallholders have access to price risk management instruments and safety nets. Unlike industrialized countries, which can offer safety nets, developing countries' modest treasuries underscore the need to have other alternatives. There have been several successes in evolving schemes that help small farmers cope with price risks—ranging from commodity and futures exchanges to warehouse receipts systems. Several financial instruments act both as price risk management instruments and as a means of getting credit. As far as safety nets are concerned, ensuring availability of food and the use of food coupons or stamps could be very important. Also, given that employment is the best safety net, complementary policies, such as rural works or food-for-work programs, would be necessary. These programs would have to be complemented with border protection policies based on automatic triggers, such as the new Special Safeguard now being discussed in WTO negotiations and price floors or price band systems that are compatible with the WTO Agreement on Agriculture. Automatic triggers, however, pose the danger of forcing other (nonproducer or subsistence and/or semi-subsistence producer) households into poverty by raising their consumption costs, which needs to be factored in when developing such instruments.

Second, rural nonfarm employment is an important source of income for small farmers, yet it does not appear prominently in policy discussions (Haggblade, Hazell, and Reardon 2002). This omission would have to be redressed, which can be achieved through overhauling financing of such activities, providing infrastructure in rural areas, streamlining land legislation or other restrictive laws so that agro-industries and other nonfarm activities are promoted, and raising the skills of small farmers. Educational attainment and physical access to markets seem to be particularly important.

Third, the growing scale of operations and recent trends in mergers both globally and nationally have drawn attention to problems with monopolistic competition all along the agrifood chain. Under the circumstances, domestic policy and legislations (such as antitrust laws) may have to be established to govern monopolistic structures (this tactic has been effectively used in the United States to control retail mergers), while making sure that these do not constrain the growth of the agribusiness sector in developing countries.

Fourth, as technology research geared to address small farmers specifically is unlikely to be undertaken by the private or even the public sector, political disempowerment could relegate these important issues to the periphery. There is a need for more focused research, particularly on inexpensive, small-scale technologies and those for resource-poor regions (typically unirrigated, rainfed areas). It is also important to ensure the transfer of these technologies to small farmers, who may have problems gaining access to them.

Policies Working in Tandem

More often than not, enabling and coping policies will have to operate in tandem and produce a coupling effect to address the problem in the most effective manner possible. The speed with which events associated with globalization can alter the landscape emphasizes the need for countries to have anticipatory or proactive policies rather than reactive ones. Needless to say, the relative importance of different policy instruments will vary across regions. It is therefore critical to identify which battery of policies is appropriate, depending on the unique circumstances of each region.

Notes

1. There exists no precise or universally accepted definition of "smallholder." The term is commonly linked to the size of the landholding or livestock owned: for instance, one with holdings of less than 2–5 hectares and about 10–20 head of livestock. However, there are a series of well-known problems with this type of definition: what is considered small depends on the agricultural activity; a strict definition based on size ignores the quality of the natural resources and whether there is irrigation. In addition, the notion varies widely across different regions of the world, because the concept is defined primarily in relation to the average landholding size in a given region. Thus, rather than defining the term "smallholder," for the purpose of this review, we characterize the smallholder as a farmer (crop or livestock) practicing any combination of commercial and subsistence production in which the family provides the majority of labor and the farm provides the principal source of income. It could happen that a considerable number of farmers who fit this description actually possess little land and only a few livestock compared to the regional average.

2. It is important to remember, however, that there are exceptions. For instance, small commercially oriented farms that draw on family labor growing high-value crops, such as cut flowers and produce for export, or those growing vegetables in peri-urban areas could in fact be counted among the more prosperous farmers.

3. Although this expansion may be attributed to liberalization policies, increased trade has often occurred even within the structure of existing protectionist practices.

4. Studies relating to the effects of other global drivers on smallholders are reviewed in Narayanan and Gulati (2002).

5. Descriptive studies give an account of trade policy reforms and the manner in which these reforms affect rural populations, in this case the smallholder. Typically, studies that are qualitative describe the changes in policy scenario and try to evaluate their effects by comparing the circumstances of the smallholder before and after the policy change in question.

6. The data-based approach uses primary surveys or, sometimes, secondary data. Usually some hypothesis with respect to the link between liberalization (typically represented as change in prices) and incomes of farmers is tested and often complemented with descriptive statistics.

7. Modeling entails the construction of a theoretical framework that captures linkages between trade liberalization and the smallholder, trying to reflect the conditions of the economy. Its empirical basis derives from the parameters used in the model, which are often obtained from analysis of actual data. This umbrella category encompasses models that vary across several socioeconomic dimensions.

8. Sahn and Sarris's (1991) study of five African countries—Côte d'Ivoire, Ghana, Malawi, Madagascar, and Tanzania—shows that across these five countries, the share of nonagricultural income earned is 13–58 percent whereas agricultural income ranged between 39 percent and 81 percent. Also, an interesting feature is that a very high share of total agricultural income was from nontradable goods, a major portion of which was sold locally.

9. For instance, Cashin, Liang, and McDermott (2000) observe that low prices endure for more months than do high prices. For wheat, international price shocks have a median half-life of 44 months. There is a probability of 50 percent that prices prevail below the expected value (declining over time) for more than 44 months.

10. In a study of a proposed rice export tax in Thailand, Warr (2001) found that the resultant decline in domestic rice prices would also drive down wages of unskilled labor, which is employed extensively in the rice industry. The outcome for the rural (and urban) poor, who derived 40 percent of their income from unskilled employment, is interesting—the consumption benefit of a decline in rice prices was outweighed by a negative income effect of depressed unskilled wages.

References

Ahmad, T. M. A. T., and A. Tawang. 2000. Evaluating the effects of trade liberalization on Malaysian agriculture with emphasis on the palm oil and paddy subsectors. In *Proceedings of the seminar on repositioning of the agriculture industry in the next millennium, Serdang, Malaysia, July 13–14, 1999,* ed. A. Radam and F. A. Mohd. Selangor, Malaysia: UPM Press.

Barnum, H., and L. Squire. 1979. A model of an agricultural household: Theory and evidence. World Bank Staff Occasional Paper 27. Washington, D.C.: World Bank.

Barrett, C. 1998. Immiserized growth in liberalized agriculture. *World Development* 26 (5): 743–753.

Barrett, C., and P. Dorosh. 1996. Farmers' welfare and changing food prices: Nonparametric evidence from rice in Madagascar. *American Journal of Agricultural Economics* 78 (August): 656–669.

Barrett, C., T. Reardon, and P. Webb. 2001. Nonfarm income diversification and household livelihood strategies in rural Africa: Concepts, dynamics and policy implications. *Food Policy* 26 (4): 315–331.

Bautista, R. M., and M. Thomas. 1998. Does trade liberalization enhance income growth and equity in Zimbabwe? The role of complementary policies. Trade and Macroeconomics Division Discussion Paper 32. Washington, D.C.: International Food Policy Research Institute.

———. 2000. Macroeconomic and agricultural reforms in Zimbabwe: Policy complementarities toward equitable growth. Trade and Macroeconomics Division Discussion Paper 57. Washington, D.C.: International Food Policy Research Institute.

Braverman, A., and J. Hammer. 1986. Multimarket methodology for analyzing agricultural pricing policies in an operational context: A background note. Economics and Policy Division, Agricultural and Rural Development Department Working Paper 121. Washington, D.C.: World Bank.

Braverman, A., J. Hammer, and C. Y. Ahn. 1986. Multimarket analysis of agricultural pricing policies in Korea. In *Theory of taxation for developing countries,* ed. N. Stern and D. Newbery. New Delhi: Oxford University Press.

Budd, J. W. 1993. Changing food prices and rural welfare: A nonparametric examination of the Côte d'Ivoire. *Economic Development and Cultural Change* 41 (April): 587–603.

Cashin, P., H. Liang, and J. McDermott. 2000. How persistent are shocks to world commodity prices? Staff Paper 47 (2). Washington, D.C.: International Monetary Fund.

Deaton, A. 1989. Rice prices and income distribution in Thailand: A non-parametric analysis. *Economic Journal* 99 (395): 1–37.

Delgado, C. 1998. Sources of growth in smallholder agriculture in Sub-Saharan Africa: The role of vertical integration of smallholders with processors and marketers of high value-added items. Paper presented at the Inter-Conference Symposium of the International Association of Agricultural Economists, August 10–16, Badplaas, South Africa.

———. 1999. Sources of growth in smallholder agriculture in Sub-Saharan Africa: The role of vertical integration of smallholders with processors and marketers of high value-added items. *Agrekon* 38 (May): 165–189.

European Commission. 2002. *Rural development policy.* Brussels: European Commission.

Gerard, F., I. Marty, F. Lançon, and M. Versapuech. 1998. Measuring the effects of trade liberalization: Multilevel analysis tool for agriculture. Working Paper 30. Bogor, Indonesia: Centre for Alleviation of Poverty through Secondary Crops' Development in Asia and the Pacific.

Glewwe, P., and D. de Tray. 1988. The poor during adjustment: A case study of Côte d'Ivoire. LSMS Working Paper 47. Washington, D.C.: World Bank.

Gulati, A. 2001. The future of agriculture in South Asia: W(h)ither the small farm? Paper prepared for the International Conference on Sustainable Food Security for All by 2020, September 4–6, Bonn, Germany.

Gulati, A., and T. Kelly. 1999. *Trade liberalization and Indian agriculture.* New Delhi: Oxford University Press.

Haggblade, S., P. Hazell, and T. Reardon. 2002. Strategies for stimulating poverty-alleviating growth in the rural nonfarm economy in developing countries. Environment and Production Technology Division and Rural Development Department Discussion Paper 92. Washington, D.C.: International Food Policy Research Institute and World Bank.

Karanja, A. M. 2002. Liberalization and smallholder agricultural development: A case study of coffee farms in Kenya. Ph.D. thesis, Wageningen University, Wageningen, the Netherlands.

Kydd, J., A. Doward, J. Morrison, and G. Cadisch. 2001. *The role of agriculture in pro-poor economic growth in Sub-Saharan Africa.* Kent, U.K.: Imperial College of Science, Technology and Medicine at Wye.

Löfgren, H., M. El-Said, and S. Robinson. 1999. *Trade liberalization and complementary domestic policies: A rural-urban general equilibrium analysis of Morocco.* Trade and Macroeconomics Division Discussion Paper 41. Washington, D.C.: International Food Policy Research Institute.

Löfgren, H., O. Chulu, O. Sichinga, F. Simtowe, H. Tchale, R. Tseka, and P. Wobst. 2001. *External shocks and domestic poverty alleviation: Simulations with a CGE model of Malawi.* Trade and Macroeconomics Division Discussion Paper 71. Washington, D.C.: International Food Policy Research Institute.

McCulloch, N., A. Winters, and X. Cirera. 2001. *Trade liberalization and poverty: A handbook.* London: Center for Economic Policy and Research.

Minot, N. 1998. Distributional and nutritional impact of devaluation in Rwanda. *Economic Development and Cultural Change* 46 (January): 379–402.

Minot, N., and F. Goletti. 1998. Export liberalization and household welfare: The case of rice in Vietnam. *American Journal of Agricultural Economics* 80 (4): 738–749.

———. 2000. *Rice market liberalization and poverty in Vietnam.* Research Report 114. Washington, D.C.: International Food Policy Research Institute.

Nadal, A. 2000a. *The environmental and social impacts of economic liberalization on corn production in Mexico.* Oxford, U.K., and Gland, Switzerland: Oxfam GB and the World Wide Fund for Nature.

———. 2000b. Corn and NAFTA: An unhappy alliance. Available at http://www.grain.org/seedling/?id=14. Accessed June 2005.

Narayanan, S., and A. Gulati. 2002. *Globalization and the small holders: A review of issues, approaches and tentative conclusions.* Markets and Structural Studies Division Discussion Paper 50. Washington, D.C.: International Food Policy Research Institute.

Nayyar, D., and A. Sen. 1994. International trade and agricultural sector in India. In *Economic liberalization and Indian agriculture,* ed. G. S. Bhalla. New Delhi: Institute for Studies in Industrial Development.

Parris, B. 1999. *Trade for development—Making the WTO work for the poor.* World Vision Discussion Paper. East Burwood, Australia, and Geneva, Switzerland: World Vision International.

Quiróz, J., and R. Soto. 1995. *International price signals in agricultural prices: Do governments care?* Documento de Investigacion 88. Santiago, Chile: Programa de Postgrado en Economia, Instituto Latinoamericano de Doctrina y Estudios Sociales/Georgetown University.

Rashid, S. 2002. *Dynamics of agricultural wage and rice price in Bangladesh: A re-examination.* Markets Structural Studies Division Discussion Paper 44. Washington, D.C.: International Food Policy Research Institute.

Ravallion, M. 1990. Rural welfare effects of food price changes under induced wage responses: Theory and evidence for Bangladesh. *Oxford Economic Papers* 42 (3): 574–585.

Reardon, T., and C. Barrett. 2000. Agroindustrialization, globalization, and international development: An overview of issues, patterns, and determinants. *Agricultural Economics* 23 (3): 195–205.

Reardon, T., J. Berdegué, and G. Escobar. 2001. Rural nonfarm employment and incomes in Latin America: Overview and policy implications. *World Development* 29 (3): 395–409.

Reimer, J. J. 2002. *Estimating the poverty impacts of trade liberalization.* West Lafayette, Ind., U.S.A.: Purdue University, Center for Global Trade Analysis and Department of Agricultural Economics.

Rojjanapo, P. 2000. *Trade liberalization: Impact on small farmers in Thailand.* Cork, Ireland: International Famine Center.

Sahn, D., and A. H. Sarris. 1991. Structural adjustment and rural smallholder welfare: A comparative analysis from Sub-Saharan Africa. *World Bank Economic Review* 5 (2): 259–289.

Sarris, A. H. 1997. Risk management in cereal and oilseed markets. Paper prepared for the Commodity Risk Management Group, World Bank, Washington, D.C. Mimeo.

Singh, I., and Subramanian J. 1986. Agricultural household modeling in a multicrop environment: Case studies in Korea and Nigeria. In *Agricultural household models, extensions, applications and policy*, ed. I. Singh, L. Squire, and J. Strauss. Baltimore: The Johns Hopkins University Press.

Singh, I., L. Squire, and J. Strauss. 1986. *Agricultural household models, extensions, applications, and policy.* Baltimore: The Johns Hopkins University Press.

Singh, R. B., and P. Kumar. 2002. Empowering the small farmers: Fight against hunger and poverty in India. Rome: FAO. Mimeo.

Spencer, D. 2001. Will they survive? Prospects for small farmers in Sub-Saharan Africa. Paper presented at the International Conference on Sustainable Food Security for All by 2020, September 4–6, Bonn, Germany.

Taylor, J. E. 2003. The microeconomics of globalization: Evidence from China and Mexico. In *Agricultural trade and poverty—Making policy analysis count.* Proceedings of the Global Forum on Agriculture, Trade Reform, Adjustment and Poverty, Organisation for Economic Co-operation and Development, May 23–24, 2002, Paris.

Valdés, A., and W. Foster. 2002. Reflections on the policy implications of agricultural price distortions and price transmission for producers in developing and transition economics. Background Paper CCNM/GF/AGR(2002)7. Global Forum on Agriculture, Trade Reform, Adjustment and Poverty, Organisation for Economic Co-operation and Development, May 23–24, Paris.

von Braun, J. 2004. Small farmers in a liberalized environment. Prepared for Ministry for Foreign Affairs and Ministry of Agriculture and Forestry of Finland's Seminar on Agriculture Producers in a Liberalized Trade Environment, October 18–19, Helsinki, Finland.

Warr, P. G. 2001. Welfare and distributional effects of an export tax: Thailand's rice premium. *American Journal of Agricultural Economics* 83 (4): 903–920.

Watkins, K. 1997. Globalization and liberalization: Implications for poverty, distribution, and inequality. Occasional Paper 32. New York: United Nations Development Programme.

Wood, A. 1995. How trade hurt unskilled workers. *Journal of Economic Perspectives* 9 (3): 51–80.

World Bank. 2004. *World development indicators 2004.* Washington, D.C.

Chapter 5

Agricultural Trade, Globalization, and the Rural Poor

Kevin Watkins

The coexistence of rising prosperity, mass poverty, and growing inequality is one of the hallmarks of globalization. One of the expressed aims of the Doha round of world trade talks was to change this picture. More equitable sharing of the benefits of world trade was identified as one of the ends of the negotiations—and agricultural trade reform as a means to that end. Outcomes have failed to live up to the "development round" billing.

Under the right conditions, agricultural trade could act as a powerful force for poverty reduction. Although the links between trade and rural poverty are complex, granting access to developed-world markets and providing protection against subsidized exports from the European Union and the United States have the potential to support national poverty-reduction efforts. Unfortunately, the Doha negotiations have failed to address these problems. The world's economic superpowers may preach open markets, but when it comes to agriculture, different rules apply. Industrialized-country policies continue to encourage agricultural overproduction and export dumping, destroying the local markets of smallholder farmers and denying poor countries an opportunity to benefit from trade. By undermining the dynamism of rural economies, agricultural policies of the developed world not only generate short-term costs, they also obstruct the powerful multiplier effects that agricultural growth can generate for poverty reduction.

This chapter is based on a speech given in December 2002 at the International Food Policy Research Institute, Washington, D.C.

The first section of this chapter looks at some trends in world agricultural trade and their implication for the rural poor (including the decline in real prices of commodities and the internationalization of food processing firms and supermarkets). It argues that globalization is reinforcing the structures of disadvantage at the heart of rural poverty. The main focus in this chapter is on the poverty of small and poor farmers, but it is noted that poor consumers (including small farmers as consumers) are affected by globalization and market distortions, too. The second section shifts the focus to industrialized-country agricultural policy, highlighting its adverse effects on developing countries. The current direction of farm policy reform in the United States and the European Union are examined, and their current approach to "decoupled" support is called into question. Although a weakening of the link between subsidies and production is welcome—and long overdue—large transfers to farmers continue to distort markets. The failure of WTO rules to adequately cover these transfers weakens the potential benefits of the multilateral trading system for the world's poor. The chapter concludes with some policy recommendations.

Impact of Agricultural Trade on the Rural Poor

Under certain conditions, agricultural trade has the potential to act as a powerful force for poverty reduction. Where production is widely dispersed and marketing arrangements protect smallholder farmers from monopolistic pricing, there is clear evidence that production for exports can enhance welfare. Because rural growth generates powerful multiplier effects, static trade gains can feed into dynamic longer-term benefits for poverty reduction (Delgado, Minot, and Wada 2001). The positive links between rice exports and poverty reduction in countries like Vietnam illustrate what can be achieved (Minot and Goletti 2000). However, individual success stories obscure some serious systemic problems. Agricultural trade cannot be considered in isolation from the wider structural forces that consign people to poverty. In particular, trade can serve to exacerbate inequality between those with access to capital, information, and political power and those without.

Some Elements of Continuity

The decade from 1994 to 2004 has witnessed a sustained expansion in world trade, with an average annual increase of 5.7 percent in the volume of merchandise trade, outpacing the growth of global GDP by almost 3 percentage points (UNCTAD 2005).

While some trade patterns are being transformed by the rise of intracompany trade, foreign investment, technology transfer, and the emergence of globalized production systems, others have remained constant, including the steady decline of agriculture in overall trade. Although it increased in real terms in the 1990s, agriculture now accounts for less than 6 percent of total trade, almost half of the 1980 level (FAO 2006; World Bank 2006). The very large group of low-income countries that continue to depend heavily on agricultural exports are operating in a segment of the world economy that represents a diminishing share of value-added. Real agricultural prices have been on a downward trend during several decades, with high volatility around the trend. This downward spiral is especially true for tropical beverages. Consider the case of coffee—a crop produced by 25 million farmers across the developing world. Taking inflation into account, the real price of coffee at the lowest point in 2001 was just around 25 percent of the level in 1960 (Oxfam International 2002a).[1] The slump in world prices resulted in deepening rural poverty, deteriorating indicators for health and nutrition, children being taken out of school, and rising rural unemployment from Ethiopia and Tanzania to Vietnam and southern Mexico. For example, in Nicaragua, where 20 percent of the rural labor force was employed in the coffee sector at some point during 2001, an estimated 35,000 permanent and 100,000 seasonal jobs were lost because of the fall in prices, and the poverty rate among coffee-producing households increased by 3 percentage points from 1998 to 2001 (Vakis, Kruger, and Mason 2004; Maluccio 2005). Macroeconomic and growth conditions in several countries deteriorated, as well as debt sustainability indicators in some countries— such as Uganda—benefiting from the Heavily Indebted Poor Countries (HIPC) program sponsored by the World Bank and the IMF. Since then, coffee prices (and that of other agricultural products) have been recovering slowly, but still remain lower than the prices throughout the 1980s (IMF 2006). On the other hand, for the giant coffee-roasting companies such as Nestlé and Kraft, lower world prices have translated into wider profit margins.

More generally, using the IMF's world price index, in early 2000 prices for 18 major commodities were lower in real terms than in 1980 (IMF 2001a). The past two decades have witnessed deep troughs in prices for many food and agricultural commodities. In each case, a price slump has translated into rising poverty.

Related to the downward and volatile trend in commodity prices, another element of continuity with the past has been a persistent decline in the terms of trade. Primary commodity exporters have to export more and more volume to retain a fixed import capacity. Although numbers vary according to the reference years and crops selected, it is difficult to find a good news story. According to the FAO, the real value of the export earnings (that is, the income terms of trade) of least-developed countries has fallen by half over the past 40 years (FAO 2004).

One other aspect of continuity in agricultural trade merits reference. Although developing countries have increased their share of world trade at a modest rate (their share of agricultural exports rose from 29.5 to 33.3 percent between 1990–94 and

2000–2003, mostly driven by an increase in trade among developing countries), the international agricultural trading system continues to be dominated by rich countries, which account for two-thirds of the total (FAO 2005). Such outcomes reflect the continued recourse of rich countries to extensive production and export subsidies—an issue returned to later.

Some Emerging Patterns . . .

Agricultural trade has not been immune to the broader changes emerging during globalization. These changes have important implications for smallholder farmers—and hence for poverty reduction efforts. One important development has been the emergence of high-value food products (HVFPs) as a growth point in the agricultural trading system (Delgado, Minot, and Wada 2001). This sector extends from fresh fruit and vegetables to dairy and livestock. Export growth rates for some product groups are rising by 14 percent a year, as witnessed by the proliferation of foodstuffs produced in poor countries and found on the supermarket shelves of rich ones.

The rapid rise of HVFPs has been associated with important changes in the supply chains linking industrialized-country consumers to developing-country producers. Traders, processors, and retailers are taking advantage of new opportunities provided by declining transport costs, improved communication systems, import liberalization, and more open foreign investment regimes. At the same time, mergers and acquisitions have reduced the numbers of multinational companies in global markets and increased the importance of intracompany trading.

Supermarket chains, together with large-scale food manufacturers, occupy an increasingly pivotal role (see also Chapter 6). The rise of large supermarket chains in industrialized countries is a dramatic example of concentration. In the United Kingdom, the top five supermarkets now account for 70 percent or more of all food sales (DFID 2004)—and 70–90 percent of fresh produce imported from Africa (Dolan and Humphrey 2001).

Less widely observed, but no less important, is the growing weight of supermarket chains in developing countries. In Latin America, supermarkets account for a population-weighted average of 60 percent in food retailing, with five chains accounting for almost half of supermarket sales in Brazil, more than 70 percent in Colombia and Argentina, and 80 percent in Mexico (Reardon and Berdegué 2002). Foreign multinationals—such as Wal-Mart, Carrefour, and Ahold—have entered local markets on an extensive scale through a process of mergers and acquisitions. Complex new sourcing and marketing systems are emerging. Carrefour uses its global sourcing network to contract melon producers in northeast Brazil to supply its 67 stores in that country and stores in 20 other countries. Major agro-exporters—such as Hortifruti in Chile—contract directly with national and global supermarket chains. In other cases, supermarkets contract farmers via large wholesale companies.

All these changes have important implications for farmers in developing countries. To an increasing extent, entry to export markets, and to local retail markets, is mediated through firms linked to or owned by major supermarket chains in industrialized countries. Once again, there is a marked trend toward concentration. In both Kenya and Zimbabwe, two of the largest suppliers of leguminous vegetables to the European Union and the top five exporters account for more than 75 percent of fresh vegetable exports.

. . . and Accompanying Problems

These changes also have important implications for the terms on which smallholder farmers enter world markets. For most producers, "the market" is rapidly becoming a small number of large-scale processors and traders or giant supermarket chains. One feature of the trend toward concentration in processing and retailing has been the emergence of buyer-driven supply chains, in which large numbers of producers interact with monopolistic marketing structures. These chains operate to transfer a large—and growing—share of value-added away from producers in developing countries to companies in industrialized countries.

The coffee supply chain, which is dominated by the "big four" roasters—Nestlé, Kraft, Proctor and Gamble, and Sara Lee—and supermarket chains, demonstrates the problem. In 1992 coffee-producing countries earned US$10 billion from a global market worth US$30 billion. In early 2000, they received less than US$6 billion in a market that has doubled in size—a decline from 30 percent to 10 percent (Oxfam International 2002a).

Across the food sector, supermarkets and large processors are increasing their domination of retail markets, which exercise further competitive pressures on small producers. In Brazil, the largest milk suppliers are Nestlé and Parmalat, both of which have links with global supermarket chains, such as Carrefour and Wal-Mart, that occupy a key place in the retail chain. Market domination has enabled the processors and supermarkets to exercise a downward pressure on prices paid to farmers, with many small farmers being forced out of the sector (Farina 2002).

Supermarket purchasing policies can create huge barriers to market entry. These include

- demands for product homogeneity and compliance with complex health and safety requirements;

- a need to maintain postharvest quality and prevent product deterioration, often including cold-storage facilities;

- short periods between picking and delivery of crops;

- high rates of product rejection;

- procurement practices, such as delays of up to 90 days in paying for products; and

- short-term contracts that provide no guarantee of future markets, thereby raising the risks of investment.

For reasons that are self-evident, poor farmers are not well placed to meet such requirements, especially when they are operating in rainfed areas that are distant from markets and served by a weak marketing infrastructure. For poor households operating on limited cash budgets, protracted delay between product delivery and payment is not an option. Similarly, high rates of product rejection and short-term contract arrangements expose poor farmers to levels of risk and adjustment costs that few can absorb. Supermarkets themselves have an in-built preference for dealing with large-scale operatives, because this practice lowers the costs of monitoring quality.

Such factors explain why the growth of the HVFP market and the growing presence of supermarket chains have tended to exclude poor farmers. In Kenya—often held up as a good example—the four largest exporters of vegetables sourced only 18 percent of their produce from smallholders, compared to 42 percent from large commercial farms and 40 percent from their own farms. In Zimbabwe, the smallholder share is less than 6 percent. The rapid growth of fruit and vegetable exports from Mexico has been similarly driven by U.S.-owned processors and distributors, overwhelmingly contracting with large-scale agribusiness firms (Appendini 1994).

Viewed in terms of the challenge of reducing rural poverty, the continuation of current trends poses grave risks. The obvious danger is that the rural poor will be excluded from the fastest-growing, highest-value-added markets, and that the lion's share of benefits from trade in this area will be captured by large-scale farms and global supermarket and processing chains. This exclusion will further erode the potential for trade to act as a force for poverty reduction, reinforcing the inequalities emerging during globalization.

Policy Challenges

The recurrence of severe crises in commodity markets makes the scale of the challenge self-evident. Industrialized-country governments remain wedded to a strongly non-interventionist stance, reciting the failures of the international commodity agreements in the 1970s. Yet whatever those failures, inaction would appear to be the worse case scenario in the face of a problem at the center of global inequality. John Maynard Keynes (1980, 123) once advised governments regarding the "long economic price," underlining that "this must not be taken to imply that basic prices should be fixed without regards to the requirements of a suitable standard of life for the majority of the producers concerned"; rather, "proper economic prices should be fixed not at the lowest possible level, but at a level sufficient to provide producers with proper nutritional and other standards." It is surely time to ask whether from a poverty reduction perspective, "second-best" options, such as supply management, may not be the better choice.

Regulation also has a role to play. Most industrialized countries have stringent antitrust rules that prevent the distortion of markets by concentrations of economic power. There are no such rules at a global level, notwithstanding the concentration of power among retailers and food processors. Looking beyond global markets, regulation at a national level could do much to enhance equity. There is an urgent need for effective international antitrust provisions to prevent collusion among the small groups of companies that now dominate most food markets.

To take one example, governments could do far more to promote good practice by supermarkets themselves. In the United States, supermarkets are required to pay suppliers within 30 days—and several developing countries are now enforcing this provision (Reardon and Berdedgué 2002). Supermarkets themselves could do more to set higher standards, including the provision of longer-term contracts, but ultimately it is up to the government to implement legislation that controls the requirements placed by supermarkets on farmers.

Public–private partnerships are also needed. In Brazil, the state of Paraná has developed a program aimed at enhancing the capacity of smallholder suppliers to meet production, processing, and packaging standards set by supermarkets, enabling them to capture a higher share of the value of their produce. On a smaller scale, NGOs have also developed expertise in this area. For instance, Oxfam is working in Guatemala with a local partner—the Organization for the Promotion of Trading and Research—which provides training and credit for small producers seeking to diversify production and enter export markets. Elsewhere—as in South Africa and the Philippines—farmer cooperatives have entered export markets, often working under contract for exporting firms or exporting directly.

There is now a growing body of research evidence on good practice. It is crucial that governments and donor agencies draw on that evidence to help small farmers and entrepreneurs undertake the investments in equipment, technology, and organizational development needed to redress the power imbalance with supermarkets.

Industrialized-Country Agricultural Policies as a Barrier to Equitable Globalization

The rural poor have highly diversified livelihoods (Bryceson 1999; Kydd et al. 2001). But most live and work in agriculture, often as smallholder farmers or agricultural laborers—or both. Integration through trade into international markets can have important implications because of its influence on prices in the product markets in which the poor operate.

The rural poor often figure prominently in the rhetoric of industrialized-country governments at trade negotiations. However, they are less visible on the radar screens of agricultural policymakers. Public policy in this sphere is dominated by powerful special interest groups representing large farmers and agro-industrial concerns, such as grain traders, and by complex rivalries between national governments (in the European Union) and state-level governments (in the United States; Thurston 2002). The end result is an essentially inward-looking system of pork-barrel politics and corporate welfare payments.

Yet industrialized-country agricultural policies have important implications for the rural poor in developing countries. The United States and the European Union dominate global markets for a wide range of commodities, including wheat and maize (the United States is the world's biggest exporter, and the European Union has a major presence in wheat), as well as sugar and dairy products (where the European Union is dominant). It follows that the terms on which rich countries produce and trade have important implications not just for exporters but for staple food producers facing competition from imports.

Levels of Support for Industrialized-Country Agriculture

The agricultural policies of both the United States and the European Union seek to achieve the twin goals of supporting farm income by driving a wedge between world and domestic prices while protecting world market shares. Income support is intimately related to output, creating incentives for production and the generation of export surpluses, which then must be disposed of on world markets, usually at prices that bear no relation to the costs of production. The upshot is that powerful agricultural exporting corporations are given access to surplus stocks financed by public subsidies.

Overall support for agriculture measured by the Producer Subsidy Estimate (PSE) of the Organisation for Economic Co-operation and Development (OECD) ran to US$273 billion in 2003–05: a figure equivalent to around one-third of the value of farm output. (The PSE is an indicator of the annual monetary value of gross transfers from consumers and taxpayers to agricultural producers arising from policy measures that support agriculture, regardless of their effects on production.) The bulk of this support is directed toward meat, dairy, sugar, and cereals. Between them, the United States and the European Union account for around one-half of the total PSE. The PSE is larger both in absolute terms and as a proportion of output in the European Union, but per capita subsidies to farmers are roughly equivalent.[2] Although the PSE for 2002–05 was slightly lower as a share of the value of output (30 percent versus 37 percent), it was more than US$30 billion higher in absolute terms than in 1986–88 (OECD 2006).

As has been widely observed, farm policies in the European Union and the United States have been singularly ineffective in achieving their stated public policy goals, which include the protection of poor farmers and rural communities, support for the environment, and consumer health. In the European Union, public opinion polls suggest that 80 percent of people are in favor of governments supporting small farmers. It is likely that a similar proportion would regard the current distribution of spending as unacceptable. Just 2 percent of farmers account for around half of all transfers. The French agriculture minister may extol the virtues of the Common Agricultural Policy (CAP) for "the rural way of life" in his country (Gaymard 2002), but only by turning a blind eye to the decline in the number of farmers involved in it by one-quarter since the mid-1980s.

On average, E.U. farms with the highest gross margins have the largest farm area and receive the greatest budget support (European Commission 2002a). This correlation is unsurprising, given that support levels are a function of output and land area. In the United States, the biggest 10 percent of subsidy recipients account for 66 percent of total transfers in 2005, whereas the bottom 80 percent of farms received only 17 percent of total transfers (EWG 2006). These figures reflect the close link between land area and output, on the one side, and subsidy transfers on the other. Current subsidy structures hurt small farmers in other ways. They are capitalized in rising land and land rental values, encouraging a high degree of concentration, and they increase levels of mechanization and inputs of pesticides and chemical fertilizers. Apart from promoting large-scale agriculture, these practices has been a source of environmental damage and consumer health fears.

Costs to Developing Countries—and the Problem with Modeling

Although the costs of current farm policies are increasingly visible to the public in rich countries, those transmitted to developing countries are less apparent. Yet it is among the rural poor in developing countries that the most serious consequences of rich-country profligacy are to be found. Various attempts have been made to capture the costs of rich-country farm policies for poor countries, usually through global modeling exercises using variable liberalization scenarios. For example, the IMF's 2002 *World Economic Outlook* used a general equilibrium model to estimate gains under a full liberalization for both industrialized and developing countries. Industrialized-country liberalization was found to generate a welfare gain equivalent to 0.13 percent of GDP for developing countries (IMF 2002). Using a partial equilibrium model, the World Bank has projected the effects of a 50 percent cut in tariffs for all countries, arriving at the conclusion that it will generate a welfare gain of US$0.56 per person for all developing countries and US\$0.12 for least-developed ones (Hoekman, Francis, and Olarreaga 2002). Other exercises have reached broadly similar quantitative conclusions (Anderson et al. 2001).

What do these exercises tell us? In short, not a great deal. Like all global models operating at high levels of aggregation, the results are highly sensitive to assumptions made, such as about supply and demand responses. To the extent that any consistent picture emerges, it is that sweeping liberalization by rich countries will produce outcomes for developing countries that, using any reasonable margin of error, are close to zero. The reasons for the small size of the overall effect are immediately apparent, given that agriculture is a small share of industrialized-country GDP, agricultural trade is a tiny share of world agricultural production, and price shifts produce countervailing effects between net importers and exporters. A particular determinant of those negligible results is the assumption of full employment utilized in many of those models (Díaz-Bonilla et al. 2002; Bouët 2006).[3]

In terms of the wider debate on agricultural trade and globalization, the political use of modeling exercises raises further concerns, as the simulations usually reach the conclusion that developing countries stand to gain most in welfare terms by liberalizing their own markets through tariff reductions, and thus provide a convenient rationale for the use by the IMF and the World Bank of loan conditions aimed at enforcing unilateral market liberalization (Oxfam International 2002d). But this policy prescription ignores the potentially damaging implications for smallholder farmers of premature trade liberalization, especially when import prices are artificially depressed through production subsidies. Although the damage inflicted by rich-country agricultural policies varies among countries, there are three important effects, as described in the remainder of this subsection.

Artificially depressed prices for staple food producers.   E.U. and U.S. agricultural policies give grain exporters access to cereals at prices far lower than those received by farmers (see below)—and often below the costs of production. In the United States, the target price received by farmers is around 30 percent higher than the intervention price at which grain traders can buy cereals for export. As the world market price-setter for wheat and maize, the United States occupies a particularly important role. For smallholder farmers in food-importing developing countries, the U.S. export price sets the terms of competition in local markets.

That competition is highly unequal. In Mexico, import liberalization under NAFTA has resulted in the United States capturing a growing share of the Mexican maize market, with exports in 2003–05 three times their average volume in 1990–93 (USDA/FAS 2006). Rising imports from the United States have restricted market outlets for Mexican maize farmers, including those in the poverty-belt states of the south, where more than 40 percent of maize farmers live below the poverty line

(UNDP 1997). The competition between Mexican and American maize farmers is highly unequal, given that the latter receive US$6–9 billion in support each year.

By denying domestic smallholders access to urban markets, subsidized exports undermine incentives for agricultural investment, restrict rural employment, encourage a transfer of food tastes to imported cereals, and promote import dependence. When Haiti liberalized its rice market under an IMF program in the mid-1990s, the country was promptly flooded with heavily subsidized U.S. rice, destroying livelihoods and leaving the country heavily dependent on imports. By the end of the 1990s, imported rice accounted for almost half of national consumption (IMF 2001b). In West Africa, local food staple producers have faced problems competing with imported rice and wheat, reinforcing other factors behind a long-run decline in per capita output (Reardon and Taylor 1996).

Set against the costs to producers, economists often point to the potential welfare gains for consumers from lower prices. Viewed in a broader poverty reduction context, however, there are two problems with the simplified consumer-welfare approach. First, imports can break the link between urban and rural economies, isolating rural centers from growth points and restricting the development of dynamic linkages. Second, for low-income countries in particular, dependence on food imports implies significant foreign exchange costs, with vulnerable populations exposed to the risks associated with world price volatility.

Import liberalization in developing countries has been widely associated with deteriorating balances in food trade. One FAO survey of 14 countries compared the food trade balance in 14 countries for 1990–94 with that in 1995–98. It found deterioration in each case, amounting to more than 80 percent for Senegal and Bangladesh and 50 percent for India (FAO 2000). Sub-Saharan Africa faces especially acute problems. In 2003, there were 16 countries in Sub-Saharan Africa where food imports represented more than one-quarter of export earnings (FAO 2005). Unless agricultural productivity can be increased, the region as a whole is unlikely to have the capacity to cover the gap between food needs and production through commercial imports. The central policy challenge is to develop the capacity to grow sufficient food in an environmentally sustainable fashion—not just to increase supply, but also to create income and employment.

Reduced and destabilized world prices for commodity exports. Subsidized overproduction and export dumping drive down international prices and close down market opportunities for developing countries. At the same time, government subsidies insulate producers and production decisions from world market trends, transmitting instability to world markets.

The European Union's sugar regime illustrates the problem.[4] Under the CAP, E.U. sugar farmers—most of them very large scale—receive high guaranteed prices for 12 million tons of sugar. The marginal return is sufficient to create incentives to produce a further 4.7 millions tons of nonquota sugar, which is dumped on world markets, making the European Union the world's largest sugar exporter.[5] One model suggests that the CAP sugar regime operates to lower world prices by 18–22 percent (Borrel and Hubbard 2000).

Apart from large-scale farmers, the sugar processing industry is a major beneficiary of subsidies. Just one company in Britain—British Sugar—is estimated to receive US$100 million annually (Oxfam International 2002b). The losers in this arrangement include lower-cost developing countries—such as Thailand, Cuba, and Mozambique—that lose markets and receive lower export prices.

Meanwhile, high tariffs exclude some of the world's poorest countries from the E.U. market. While that market has been liberalized under the Everything-But-Arms initiative of the E.U., the pace of liberalization in sugar has been tailored to the demands of the sugar lobby. One estimate is that Mozambique is currently losing around US$106 million annually as a result of lost export opportunities (Oxfam International 2002b). Because E.U. producers receive a fixed price regardless of world price, they can maintain output, forcing others to adjust.

Restricted market access. Under the right conditions, access to rich-country markets can provide producers in developing countries with important opportunities for poverty reduction. At the household level, production for exports can support the diversification of livelihoods and create incentives for investment. At the national level, improved market access can help diversify foreign exchange earnings and reduce the risk of dependence on a narrow range of commodities.

The problem facing developing countries is that tariff and nontariff barriers in agriculture are exceptionally high. Average tariffs range from 16 to 20 percent, with peaks in excess of 100 percent being not uncommon. These tariffs are some five to six times the average tariff applied by rich countries when they trade with one another in the manufacturing sector, suggesting that the rural poor enter world markets carrying a weighty handicap.

The Case of U.S. Cotton Subsidies
The plight of Africa's cotton farmers highlights in a stark way some of the real human consequences of current farm policies in rich countries. As the world's largest exporter and largest subsidizer, the United States has helped create, in the early 2000s, one of the deepest and most protracted crises in world cotton markets since the Great Depression, reinforcing African poverty in the process.[6]

Cotton is grown by an estimated 10–11 million households in West Africa. During the 1990s, production in the region had almost doubled, mainly as a result of increased acreage being brought into cultivation (Townsend 2001). Although there are serious social and environmental problems associated with cotton production, this expansion contributed to rural growth and poverty reduction. Because cotton is grown alongside food crops in intercropping systems, there is no evidence of displacement of food production. In addition to its importance at a household level, several countries in the region—including Burkina Faso, Mali, Chad, and Benin—depend heavily on cotton as a source of foreign exchange earnings.

Cotton yields in West Africa are low by international standards (at around one-quarter of the average), but the region is one of the world's most efficient producers. This superiority is largely because of the climate, the advantages of nonmechanized smallholder agriculture in managing plant developments, and the high-quality crop assured by handpicking. According to the IMF, producers in West Africa can operate profitably at world prices as low as US$0.50 per pound (IMF 2002). Few other exporters can rival this ability, even with far higher levels of productivity because of associated capital costs and lower-quality crops.

In the early 2000s, producers in Africa have had to adjust to the deepest and most protracted price depression in recent memory. Although nominal prices have increased somewhat in recent years to around US$0.55–0.58 per pound, this price is well below the long-run average of US$0.70 per pound (UNCTAD 2007). Several factors have been at play. These include new entrants to the market, rising productivity in China, and, in early 2000s, the effects of the global economic slowdown on world markets for garments and textiles. But the single biggest factor driving down prices has been the structure of farm subsidies in the United States.

Although a large number of countries grow cotton, just four—the United States, China, India, and Pakistan—account for about two-thirds of total production. The United States occupies a special position in this group not just as a major subsidizer, but also as an exporter of one-half of domestic production. These exports account for almost one-third of the world total. It follows that U. S. subsidies have powerful effects on world market prices.

Even by the generous standards of current U.S. farm policy, cotton producers occupy a special position. They receive the equivalent of US$230 per hectare in subsidies, compared with US$40–50 per hectare for wheat producers. Cotton is also the sector with the most concentrated distribution of benefits. In 2005, the largest 1 percent of cotton subsidy recipients account for nearly one-quarter of total transfers, and the top 10 percent for three-quarters. Ten individual farm corporations received payments in excess of US$26 million in 2005 (EWG 2006).

While these subsidies clearly confer significant benefits on a few very large farms, they generate significant costs elsewhere. Estimates by the International Cotton Advisory Committee (ICAC) suggest that cotton subsidies in the United States reduce world prices by 26 percent, or US$0.11 per pound. Ironically, this downward pressure

Table 5.1   Foreign exchange losses in selected Sub-Saharan African countries as a result of U.S. cotton subsidies (US$ millions)

Country	Actual export earnings in 2001/02	Export earnings with the withdrawal of U.S. subsidies	Value lost as a result of U.S. subsidies
Benin	124	157	33
Burkina Faso	105	133	28
Cameroon	81	102	21
Central African Republic	9	11	2
Chad	63	79	16
Congo	3	4	1
Côte d'Ivoire	121	153	32
Ethiopia	18	23	5
Ghana	7	9	2
Guinea	13	16	3
Kenya	5	6	1
Madagascar	10	13	3
Malawi	6	8	2
Mali	161	204	43
Mozambique	23	29	6
Nigeria	55	69	14
Somalia	2	3	1
South Africa	17	21	4
Sudan	65	82	17
Tanzania	79	100	21
Togo	61	77	16
Uganda	18	23	5
Zambia	29	37	8
Zimbabwe	69	87	18
Total	1,144	1,446	302

Source: Oxfam International (2002c).

on prices has been one of the factors driving up the costs of the subsidy program. In 2001–02, payments to cotton growers by the Commodity Credit Corporation amounted to US$3.6 billion. The world market value of the U.S. crop for the same year was US$3 billion. In other words, cotton was grown at a net cost to the American economy.

That cost pales into insignificance against the costs inflicted on Africa. Using the ICAC model, Oxfam estimates the total foreign exchange costs for the region of American cotton subsidy programs at US$301 million—equivalent to around one-quarter of all U.S. aid to Africa. Eight countries in West Africa account for two-thirds of this loss (Table 5.1). The small size of the economies involved and their high level of dependence on cotton produced extreme economic shocks. Burkina Faso, for instance, lost the equivalent of 1 percent of its GDP and 12 percent of export earnings, and Mali lost 1.7 percent of GDP and 8 percent of its export earnings.

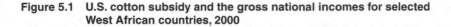

Figure 5.1   U.S. cotton subsidy and the gross national incomes for selected West African countries, 2000

US$ billion

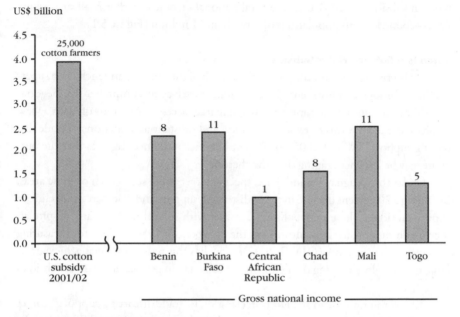

Sources: USDA/ERS (2002b); World Bank (2002).

Note: Numbers over bars for African countries represent national population in millions.

For a group of countries with some of the worst human development indicators in the world for rural poverty, child mortality, and illiteracy, economic losses on this scale clearly have grave consequences. If anything, the financial loss figures understate the effects, because household income in rural economies generates linkages and creates demand that spread growth more widely through a series of multiplier effects. Research carried out by IFPRI found that one additional dollar of farm income in Burkina Faso raised total income in the local economy by US$1.80 (Delgado et al. 1999). This finding would suggest that the real losses in income sustained as a result of U.S. cotton subsidies have been far higher than suggested by the static loss. In addition, governments in the region have spent an estimated US$60–80 million protecting their cotton sectors from world price trends, implying a significant fiscal burden and diversion of resources from spending in priority social areas.

U.S. policies on cotton subsidies raise far wider questions about tensions between development policy rhetoric and trade program realities. Some countries in West Africa—such as Burkina Faso and Benin—have lost more as a direct consequence of these subsidies than they have gained in HIPC Initiative debt relief. Others—such as Mali—have lost more than they get in American aid. The experience of Africa's cotton producers also provides an insight into the realities of the "level playing field" in world agriculture. Twenty-five thousand U.S. cotton farmers collectively received more in subsidies in 2001 than the total national income of either Mali or Burkina Faso—countries with populations of more than 11 million (Figure 5.1).

When Is a Subsidy Not a Subsidy?
The ministerial declaration adopted at the launch of the Doha round includes a superficially ambitious commitment: "We commit ourselves to comprehensive negotiations aimed at substantial improvements in market access; reductions of, with a view to phasing out, all forms of export subsidies; and substantial reductions in trade distorting support" (WTO 2005, 3). Recent historical evidence suggests that the outcome may be less encouraging than the rhetoric.

Under the Uruguay Round AoA, specific targets were set in each of these areas, including a 20 percent decline in trade-distorting support and a 36 percent decline in export subsidies. These targets have been met with something to spare, despite an increase in support for agriculture over the base period (1986–88) set for measuring progress under the AoA (OECD 2002). How has this reduction been achieved? In large measure, by changing the definition of subsidies in general and export subsidies in particular.

The relevant phrase in the Doha declaration is "trade distorting support." Under the AoA, which was the product of a compromise between the United States and the European Union, certain categories of support were deemed to be outside of WTO discipline. Direct payments of the type provided by the United States were categorized as Green Box, ostensibly on the grounds that they had minimal effects on production. Another discipline-free box—the Blue Box—was created for E.U. payments that included supply-control measures, such as a requirement that farmers take land out of cultivation. Both categories were given the status of "decoupled" payments on the grounds that they had minimal effects on production and trade.

This redefinition of subsidies helps to explain the widening gap between the PSE measure of support used by the OECD and the alternative measure—the Aggregate Measure of Support (AMS)—used for WTO purposes. In 1998, the AMS represented only one-third of the value of the PSE, reflecting a restructuring and reclassification of subsidies. In addition, the 1986–88 base period was one of exceptionally low world prices and commensurately high tariffs, support levels, and export subsidies. This circumstance left industrial countries with ample scope for meeting the AoA targets without having to make serious adjustments.

Both the European Union and—more ambiguously—the United States entered the Doha round bent on excluding decoupled payments from future WTO disciplines. This omission has important implications for developing countries. As an

Figure 5.2   Support to U.S. cotton farmers under the Farm Security and Rural Investment Act

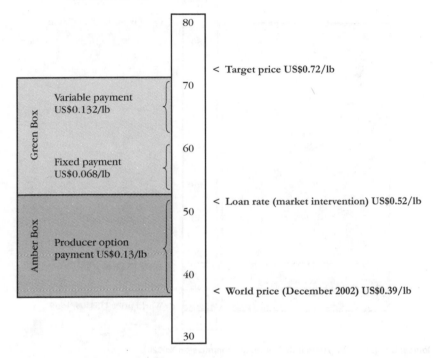

Source: Compiled using data from USDA/ERS (2002a,b).

approximation, these implications can be demonstrated by Figure 5.2, which captures the structure of support for American cotton farmers under current legislation. The figure shows that around two-thirds of total transfers to farmers will take the form of decoupled payments. The European Union operates a broadly analogous system in the cereals sector (Figure 5.3), with a similarly heavy dependence on "decoupled" payments during periods of low world prices. In early 2000s, these payments raised farm incomes some 60 percent above export price levels.

In the official view of the U.S. Department of Agriculture, the direct payments and countercyclical payments (which compensate farmers when world prices fall below specified levels) introduced under the 2002 Farm Security and Rural Investment Act (FSRI) retain all the features of decoupled payments. In theory, farmers can receive both transfers without planting any of their land at all, because payments are calculated on the basis of a formula using acreage and yield for a previous production period (known as the base period). When the farmer makes a planting decision,

Figure 5.3   Cereals sector support in the European Union, 1999/2000

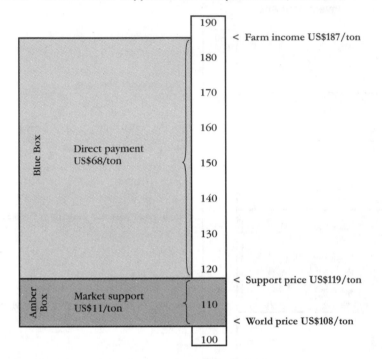

Source: Compiled using data from European Commission (2002b).

so the argument runs, there is no incentive provided by these payments to increase production at the margin, because the transfer is fixed in advance (USDA/ERS 2002b).

There are several problems with this argument that apply with equal force to the European Union's direct payments. First, decoupled payments provide farms with liquidity and can be used to finance investments that will raise future production. Second, the constant updating of the base period in the United States means that producers have an obvious interest in increasing crop acreage and yield, because it is what compensation rates are based on. Finally, production decisions today are clearly based on expectations about future support. To the extent that decoupled payments shield against risk, they can be expected to encourage investment and generate higher output during periods of low world prices.

In reality, it is virtually impossible to design subsidy programs that do not have some effect on production decisions and trade. Specific programs defined as decoupled have important effects in both areas (Josling 2000; OECD 2001). From the standpoint of an African farmer attempting to compete in world markets against U.S. cotton subsidies or in local markets against E.U. cereals, what matters is that the crop is being marketed at a price far below the income received by the producer in the exporting country. The net result is that they are competing against export dumping.

To the extent that direct payments facilitate levels of production that exceed domestic demand and the transfer of the resulting surpluses to world markets, they are production and export subsidies—and they should be treated as such for WTO purposes. The same applies to other interventions. For example, the European Union—one of the world's highest cost exporters of sugar—claims to maintain its domination of global markets without export subsidies. In fact, it achieves this remarkable outcome by financing exports through a small tax on the guaranteed price paid to farmers that is currently some three times higher than world market levels. This practice, too, is a transparent case of export subsidization by another name and should be treated as such.

The directions of current farm policies in the United States and the European Union give an added urgency to the challenge of addressing the problem of disguised export dumping. In the United States, the FSRI is expected to provide US$73 billion in additional support to agriculture over the next decade (OECD 2002). Moreover, by updating the base acreage for calculating direct and countercyclical payments, the new legislation has strengthened the link between government support and output.

In the European Union, the proposals of the "Agenda 2000" envisage continued movement toward decoupled support, combined with the consolidation of the European Union's global market position. In November 2002, political leaders adopted a budget that will keep CAP spending at current levels until 2013 (adjusted for inflation). Whatever the outcome of the clash between pro- and antireformers, there would appear to be little likelihood of CAP reform significantly reducing export surpluses in core product areas.

Three Principles for the Doha Round and Beyond

Reduced to its essentials, the central problem posed by agricultural policy in rich countries for the rural poor in developing countries is the built-in support that such policy provides for overproduction and export dumping. Corporate traders in rich countries are currently being given access to surpluses for export on heavily subsidized terms that are detrimental to the interests of developing countries. It follows that the central challenge for the Doha round is to address the dumping problem, at the same time providing a framework in which developing countries can achieve broader rural development objectives. Three measures suggest themselves:

- The phasing out of direct and indirect export subsidies. Industrialized countries should commit themselves to a schedule for phasing out export subsidies, including implicit subsidies and nominally decoupled support measures for production levels that exceed domestic demand.

- A review of decoupled payments. There is a pressing need for independent technical work to decompose decoupled support measures so that implicit export subsidy levels can be more effectively estimated.

- Recognition of the special status of developing countries. There are strong grounds for developing countries to protect their food systems—when necessary, through tariffs and quotas—for rural poverty reduction and food security. This necessity would remain even if world markets were not distorted by industrialized-country subsidies. One option that has been advocated by some developing countries during the Doha round is the inclusion in the WTO of a "development box" under which food security would take priority over any liberalization commitment. Another option is a special safeguards provision. This provision would be activated under predefined conditions, such as a surge in imports or a fall in import prices below a national average level.

Ultimately, success in the Doha round will depend on farm policy reform in rich countries. This process does not have to be a zero-sum game, in which poor farmers in rich countries lose as poor farmers in poor ones gain. There is ample scope for a redistribution of agricultural support in industrialized countries away from large farms and agribusiness companies toward rural livelihoods, small farmers, and wider public policy goals, such as environmental sustainability. The central challenge is to de-intensify production under a new, more sustainable system of production, under which support is geared toward lower levels of output.

It is readily apparent that agricultural exports are not a panacea for rural poverty in developing countries. The strength of the linkages between export activity and poverty reduction will depend critically on conditions in individual countries, including levels of inequality in access to productive assets and markets. However, the reform of rich-country farm policies and a new WTO regime could help create an enabling environment for pro-poor agricultural trade. The alternative approach of maintaining the current regimes will continue to marginalize the rural poor, further undermining the already strained credibility of the WTO in the process.

Some Wider Concerns

The previous sections discussed different problems and possible policy prescriptions mostly in terms of the operation of domestic and international markets for food and agricultural commodities. Making trade work for the rural poor will require new approaches to markets and rules. Ultimately, however, effective national strategies for poverty reduction are a requirement for unlocking the benefits of trade.

The starting point for identifying strategies aimed at achieving a more equitable distribution of benefits from agricultural trade has to be the recognition of the central problem: rural poverty itself. The rural poor typically lack access to land, assured supplies of water, and credit. Poor women farmers suffer particularly acute deprivation in each of these areas. As producers, they enjoy more restricted access to land, markets, and inputs, with adverse consequences for productivity and equity (Udry 1996; Mehra and Gammage 1999). Failure to overcome the exclusion of women producers will further marginalize poor countries, which suggests that gender equity should be one of the fundamental building blocks for any strategy to make globalization work for the poor.

Equally fundamental are the central role of rural development and the redistribution of opportunity in favor of poor producers and more marginal areas. Most of the poor live in areas characterized by a weak institutional structure, including poor-quality transport. High transport costs reduce the tradability of much agricultural output, partly explaining the high correlation between remoteness and poverty (IFAD 2001). The same factor raises the costs of essential inputs, such as fertilizers and seeds, and reduces farmgate prices for output. Sub-Saharan Africa faces especially acute problems in this area. The density of the region's total road network is only 12.5 meters per square kilometer, compared with more than 1,295 meters per square kilometer in India (World Bank 2006). The weakness of rural infrastructure not only reinforces the exclusion of smallholders from global markets, it also leaves them unable to compete against imports in urban markets (Killick 2001; UNDP 2005).

Addressing these problems requires fundamental changes in the distribution of public spending and, in countries where land ownership is highly unequal, the distribution of land and other assets. Yet there is little evidence of a commitment to redistributive strategies for rural growth on the parts of most governments, as witnessed by even the most cursory reading of their Poverty Reduction Strategy Papers. If governments and the multilateral institutions are serious about giving priority to reducing rural poverty, surely rural development should be accorded a far higher political priority.

In some areas, public policy has moved in a counterproductive direction. In the preglobalization era, input supply for smallholder farmers was often managed through parastatal market boards. The problems associated with these boards—such as the undue tax burden they placed on farmers and the fiscal burden imposed on the state— are well known. Less well documented, notably by the IMF and the World Bank, are the failures associated with their own privatization and liberalization programs. All too often, input supplies have collapsed—starving efficient producers of capital, seeds, fertilizers, and new technologies. The effects have been felt most severely in more remote areas that are less well served by private traders (Bryceson 1999).

In some cases, market liberalization with regulation has been clearly justified. For example, the cotton marketing boards of East Africa had largely destroyed the sector by the early 1980s. With varying degrees of success, private-sector investment has generated some recovery. In contrast, the cotton marketing boards of West Africa have achieved a fairly strong track record at several levels. Production and exports have both expanded, the input supply system has improved, and farmers are capturing a growing share of income. Despite this achievement, the IMF and the World Bank have in the past advised rapid liberalization of state marketing systems, citing as evidence the fact that farmers in the region still receive a lower share of world prices than farmers operating in liberalized systems (IMF 2002). What they do not acknowledge is that lower producer prices are in part a product of repayment for inputs that farmers in many other African countries without marketing agencies now lack. Ideologically driven liberalization threatens to exclude poor farmers from global market opportunities. Without denying the case for market reforms, it can be concluded that the market liberalization policies of the 1990s have generally not been helpful to smallholders (Kydd, Dorward, and Poulton 2001). There is a strong case to be made for a positive reappraisal of the role of the state in developing rural institutions, especially with respect to input supplies.

Concluding Thoughts

There is nothing automatic about the outcomes associated with globalization. Integration into international trade has always created winners and losers. What is different about today's globalization is the speed of change and the scale of the gap between winners and losers. More equitable rules of the game in the WTO, coupled with concerted national strategies for poverty reduction, provide the key to closing that gap.

Notes

1. Coffee prices have since recovered: From 2001 to 2006, the International Coffee Organization's composite indicator price for coffee increased from US$0.4560 per pound to US$0.9575 per pound (the price in 1979 was US$0.1917 per pound; UNCTAD 2007).

2. The European Union's PSE represented 40 percent of the value of farm output in 2005 compared with 18 percent in the United States, or US$98 billion and US$43 billion, respectively.

3. See also Chapter 2 for more details on some of the shortcomings of global modeling exercises. Chapter 2 also reviews empirical studies that use a combination of global computable general equilibrium and micro models to estimate effects on poverty.

4. The regime has subsequently undergone relatively minor reforms, which leave the European Union as the world's second-largest exporter of sugar.

5. The European Union also imports, at domestic guaranteed prices, 1.6 million tons of sugar from African, Caribbean, and Pacific countries. An equivalent amount is then re-exported at prices currently approximating one-third of the domestic level.

6. This section is based on Oxfam International (2002c).

References

Anderson, K., B. Dimaranan, J. Francois, T. Hertel, B. Hoekman, and W. Martin. 2001. The costs of rich (and poor) country protection to developing countries. *Journal of African Economies* 10 (3): 227–257.

Appendini, K. A. 1994. Agriculture and farmers with NAFTA. In *Mexico and the North American Free Trade Agreement: Who will benefit?* ed. V. Bulmer-Thomas, N. Craske, and M. Serrano. London: Macmillian in association with the Institute for Latin American Studies, University of London.

Borrel, B., and L. Hubbard. 2000. Global economic effects of the EU Common Agricultural Policy. *Economic Affairs* 20 (2): 18–26.

Bouët, A. 2006. *What can the poor expect from trade liberalization? Opening the "Black Box" of trade modeling.* Markets, Trade, and Institutions Division Discussion Paper 93. Washington, D.C.: International Food Policy Research Institute.

Bryceson, D. F. 1999. African rural labor, income diversification, and livelihood approaches: A long-term development perspective. *Review of African Political Economy* 26 (80): 171–189.

Delgado, C., N. Minot, and N. Wada. 2001. High value agriculture. In *Shaping globalization for poverty alleviation and food security.* 2020 Focus 8. Washington, D.C.: International Food Policy Research Institute.

Delgado, C., J. Hopkins, and V. Kelly, with P. Hazell, A. A. McKenna, P. Gruhn, B. Hojjati, J. Sil, and C. Courbois. 1999. *Agricultural growth linkages in Sub-Saharan Africa.* Research Report 107. Washington, D.C.: International Food Policy Research Institute.

DFID (U.K. Department for International Development). 2004. *Concentration in food supply and retail chains.* London.

Díaz-Bonilla, E., S. Robinson, M. Thomas, and Y. Yanoma. 2002. *WTO, agriculture and developing countries: A survey of issues.* Trade and Macroeconomics Division Discussion Paper 81. Washington, D.C.: International Food Policy Research Institute.

Dolan, C., and J. Humphrey. 2001. Governance and trade in fresh vegetables: The impact of UK super-markets on the African horticulture industry. In *Globalisation and trade: Implications for exports from marginalised economies,* ed. O. Morrissey and I. Filatotchev. Oxford: Routledge.

European Commission. 2002a. *Indicative figures on the distribution of direct farm aid.* Memo 0/02/198. Brussels.

———. 2002b. EUROSTAT. Brussels.

EWG (Environment Working Group). 2006. EWG Farm subsidy database. Washington, D.C.

FAO (Food and Agriculture Organization of the United Nations). 2000. *Agriculture trade and food security issues and options in the WTO negotiations from the perspective of developing countries: Country case studies.* Vol. II. Rome.

———. 2004. *The state of agricultural commodity markets (SOCO).* Rome.

———. 2005. FAOSTAT. Rome.

———. 2006. *FAO statistical yearbook 2005–2006.* Rome.

Farina, E. 2002. Consolidation, multinationalization, and competition in Brazil: Impacts on horticulture and dairy product systems. *Development Policy Review* 20 (4): 441–457.

Gaymard, H. 2002. CAP is something we can be proud of. Letter to the *Financial Times,* September 23.

Hoekman, B., N. Francis, and M. Olarreaga. 2002. *Reducing agriculture trade tariffs versus domestic support: What's more important for developing countries.* Policy Research Working Paper 2918. Washington, D.C.: World Bank.

IFAD (International Fund for Agricultural Development). 2001. *Rural poverty report: The challenge of ending rural poverty.* Oxford: Oxford University Press.

IMF (International Monetary Fund). 2001a. *International financial statistics (IFS).* Washington, D.C.

———. 2001b. *Haiti 2001: Article IV consultation.* Washington, D.C.

———. 2002. *World economic outlook.* Washington, D.C.

———. 2006. *World economic outlook.* Washington, D.C.

Josling, T. 2000. New farm programs in North America and their treatment in the WTO: Discussion. *American Journal of Agricultural Economics* 82 (3): 775–777.

Keynes, J. M. 1980. The international control of raw material prices. In *The collected writings of John Maynard Keynes,* vol. 27, ed. J. M. Keynes. London: Macmillan.

Killick, T. 2001. Globalization and the rural poor. *Development Policy Review* 19 (2): 155–180.

Kydd, J., A. Dorward, and C. Poulton. 2001. New institutional economics, agricultural parastatals and marketing policy. In *Renewing development in Sub-Saharan Africa: Policy, performance, and prospects,* ed. I. Livingstone and B. Deryke. London: Routledge.

Kydd, J., A. Dorward, J. Morrison, and G. Cadisch. 2001. The role of agriculture in pro-poor economic growth in Sub-Saharan Africa. Background paper prepared for Department of International Development, Imperial College of Science, Technology and Medicine at Wye. Mimeo.

Maluccio, J. A. 2005. *Coping with the "Coffee Crisis" in Central America: The role of the Nicaraguan Red de Protección Social*. FCND Discussion Paper 188. Washington, D.C.: International Food Policy Research Institute.

Mehra, R., and S. Gammage. 1999. Trends, countertrends, and gaps in women's employment. *World Development* 27 (3): 533–550.

Minot, N., and F. Goletti. 2000. *Rice market liberalization and poverty in Vietnam*. Research Report 114. Washington, D.C.: International Food Policy Research Institute.

OECD (Organisation for Economic Co-operation and Development). 2001. *The Uruguay Round Agreement on Agriculture: An evaluation of its implementation in OECD countries*. Paris.

———. 2002. *Agricultural policies in OECD countries: Monitoring and evaluation*. Paris.

———. 2004. *Agricultural policies in OECD countries: At a glance—2004 edition*. Paris.

———. 2006. *Producer and consumer support estimates, OECD database 1986–2005*. Paris.

Oxfam International. 2002a. *Mugged: Poverty in your coffee cup*. Oxford.

———. 2002b. The great EU sugar scam. Oxfam Briefing Paper 27. Oxford.

———. 2002c. *Cultivating poverty: The impact of US cotton subsidies on Africa*. Oxford.

———. 2002d. *Rigged rules and double standards: Trade globalization and the fight against poverty*. Oxford.

Reardon, T., and J. E. Taylor. 1996. Agroclimatic shock, income inequality, and poverty: Evidence from Burkina Faso. *World Development* 24 (901): 14.

Reardon, T., and J. A. Berdegué. 2002. The rapid rise of supermarkets in Latin America: Challenges and opportunities for development. *Development Policy Review* 20 (4): 371–388.

Thurston, J. 2002. How to reform the Common Agricultural Policy. European Rural Communities Paper 1. London: Foreign Policy Center.

Townsend, T. P. 2001. *New developments in non-US cotton production and consumption*. Washington, D.C.: International Cotton Advisory Committee.

Udry, C. 1996. Gender, agricultural production, and the theory of the household. *Journal of Political Economy* 104 (5): 1010–1046.

UNCTAD (United Nations Conference on Trade and Development). 2005. *Handbook of statistics*. Geneva.

———. 2007. *Commodity price statistics database*. Geneva.

UNDP (United Nations Development Programme). 1997. *Human development report 1997: Human development to eradicate poverty*. New York: Oxford University Press for UNDP.

———. 2005. *Human development report 2005: International cooperation at crossroads*. New York: Oxford University Press for UNDP.

USDA/ERS (U.S. Department of Agriculture/Economic Research Service). 2002a. *Agricultural outlook*. Washington, D.C.

———. 2002b. *The 2002 Farm Bill: Side by side comparison with 1996–2001 farm legislation*. Washington, D.C.

USDA/FAS (Foreign Agriculture Service). 2006. Production, supply, and distribution database. Available at http://www.fas.usda.gov/psdonline/psdDownload.aspx.

Vakis, R., D. Kruger, and A. D. Mason. 2004. Shocks and coffee: Lessons from Nicaragua. Social Protection Unit Discussion Paper. Washington, D.C.: World Bank.

World Bank. 2002. *Global economic prospects: Making trade work for the world's poor*. Washington, D.C.

———. 2006. *World development indicators 2006*. Washington, D.C.

WTO (World Trade Organization). 2005. *The road to Doha and beyond: A road map for successfully concluding the Doha Development Agenda*. Geneva.

Agriculture and Market Power

Sophia Murphy

The topic of globalization effects on the rural poor is vast. To assess the influence of something as vaguely defined as globalization on a population as large and varied as the people living in poverty today is perhaps impossible. There are so many questions, so many conflicting analyses, so many variables to take into account. What is globalization? Is it a process we can control? How can we consider its effects over time? How does it affect different cultures? How does it work when filtered through different national policies? Yet we must think these questions through: we live alongside some 1.1 billion people who live in extreme poverty, in a world that has never had such opportunity to end this outrage.

Many of the organizations I work with—farm groups, social justice advocates, environmentalists, among many others—point to globalization as the process that is leading us away from the solutions we need. They want to be heard, and they want to see more passion injected into the search for answers. Thus, those who believe that globalization will be the solution to poverty have a lot of convincing to do. Many of those closest to the communities living in poverty do not agree.

Let me be the first to admit that some of my claims here are sweeping. Anyone who knows anything about globalization and agriculture will be able to fault some part of my argument. However, my goal is to present an overview and offer a perspective that is too often ignored. With this caveat in mind, I focus this essay on two topics. First, I share some reflections on globalization as a political and economic experiment. Second, I describe some observations from my work on the effects of global trade rules on agriculture and some recommendations from the quest for better rules to govern agricultural trade.

Globalization

This topic itself has two components, which are too often conflated in the debate on globalization's effects:

- Globalization describes a series of technological breakthroughs that have transformed both the capacity to store and manage data and the ability to communicate. This technological development has brought radical economic, social, and cultural shifts around the world.

- Globalization is also used to describe a series of economic policy choices that have piggybacked on these technological breakthroughs. Although dressed in the guise of inevitability, these policies are choices—choices that are undermining the basis of liberal democracy as we defined it, and in some countries lived it, for much of the twentieth century.

It is on these choices that I want to focus. They reflect a political and economic standpoint that I can characterize as

- deeply averse to government;

- deeply averse to regulation, even where market failure has been proved;

- deeply averse to taxation;

- convinced that development must be funded solely from private sources and international trade revenues;

- privileging capital over labor, such that capital movements are freed while labor remains fixed, and returns on capital are maximized while the gains made by organized labor to secure decent livelihoods are eroded;

- convinced that people do not value what they do not pay for;

- obsessed with economic efficiency coupled with a disdain for notions of equity; and

- indifferent to widening income gaps and the political, social, and economic damage such gaps create.

This philosophy has nothing to do with globalization, of course, in the sense of the technology changes described first above. There is no necessary connection between the Internet and the conviction that all state-managed trade is bad. However, the companies that benefit most from this political and economic project have been very adroit at linking the concepts, making tariff reduction seem as necessary as digitalizing information storage systems.

Clearly, many people would agree that—put in these stark terms—these are not premises that can foster a system that will eradicate poverty. However, they are an amazingly resilient part of much that passes for globalization.

The Uruguay Round AoA

Let me turn to my second area of reflection: multilateral agricultural trade rules. In my view, we should judge these rules by their results. To be useful, multilateral trade rules must further some very fundamental objectives:

- the realization of the right to food,

- the creation of decent livelihoods for those who work in the agricultural sector, and

- the protection of agricultural production systems that ensure genetic diversity and ecological sustainability.

If 70 percent of the world's poor depend on rural economies for their survival, and if the key to rural economic health is agriculture, then ensuring decent prices for agricultural production has to be one of the fundamental policy objectives in fighting poverty.

How does the Uruguay Round AoA fare against this standard? Many people believe there are only two things wrong with the AoA: the lack of political will to implement the agreement and the capacity of rich countries to create exceptions to the rules for themselves. Both observations reflect abuses of power by industrialized countries and must be addressed. They are not, however, the only problems.

Even if the European Union ended all export restitution payments; the United States, Japan, and the European Union ceased all payments to farmers; and all countries established duty-free market access for all agricultural products, agricultural market distortions would still remain. There would be no guaranteed food security or decent livelihoods for those dependent on agriculture. These reforms alone would not ensure the most efficient use of limited natural and genetic resources. Perhaps most concretely, market distortions would continue to disrupt agriculture in industrial and developing countries and to limit the benefits of increased agricultural trade.

The AoA does not just fail to discipline industrialized countries' expenditures on agriculture or their selective use of very high tariffs. More fundamentally, the AoA framework ignores:

- The universal human right to food. Food is a fundamental human right; it must be accessible to all, not only those with purchasing power in the market.

- The relatively inelastic nature of supply in agriculture. Supply responses to shortfalls are slow, which means that physical stocks must be maintained to protect against shortfalls related to weather, conflicts, and other crises. However, private companies are interested in profits, and stocks are expensive to maintain. It falls to the public sector to ensure that food reserves are available.

- The political and economic weaknesses of most farmers. Farmers do not set prices, which are determined by the companies to which farmers sell their products. Yet government interventions in the agricultural sector falsely assume farmers will respond to price signals and change their production levels accordingly. In fact, the response is asymmetrical: investment in infrastructure and production rises when prices are high. The problem is that production remains high even when prices fall.

- The horizontal and vertical integration of the agricultural system. A handful of companies dominate each part of the food chain. A growing number of chemical companies (now dominant players in the seed business) are signing contracts with grain traders and food processors. These same companies buy, ship, and mill grain, then feed it to livestock or turn it into cereal, often crossing several national borders in the process. The system is oligopolistic, not competitive.

- The fact that countries do not trade and farmers do not trade. In fact, the transnational agribusinesses do much of the actual trading.

The models used by governments to predict the outcome of the Uruguay Round AoA did not provide accurate results. They were wrong about the direction prices would take, wrong about who would get the increased exports, and wrong about how industrialized-country farmers would respond to changes in support programs. They failed to predict such phenomena as increased export volumes coupled with diminishing export values (Murphy 1999). This failure is in part because the assumptions underpinning the models ignored vital aspects of the imperfect markets that characterize world agricultural trade. By ignoring the oligopolistic nature of global agricultural markets, globalization exacerbates the market inefficiencies in agricultural production and distribution. In fact, the same companies that want to protect their oligopoly are writing the rules that we call "globalization." They are the result of deliberate, and reversible, policy choices.

I have asserted that poverty eradication will depend on strong agricultural growth. This growth requires that governments look after farmers' interests. Farmers have two primary concerns: access to resources and market power. The first—access to land, credit, seed, breeding stock, and water—is key. And so is the second: the prices that farmers can command for their production. It is here I want to focus for a moment, before offering some final thoughts on ways forward.

Market Power

It is a given of agricultural markets that producers outnumber buyers, usually by thousands to one. This fact gives buyers the advantage in setting prices and has been one of the market failures that public policy in agriculture has traditionally tried to countervail. Existing multilateral rules, however, have made some of the tools that were used illegal. Price floors for commodities, for example, are now judged to be a subsidy.

The dominance of a few firms in multiple agricultural markets obviously affects the economics of the sector. To increase profits, the farmer needs to increase the selling price over her costs of production. Grain buyers and processors, on the other hand, make their profits in other ways. The volume of sales is key to company profits, because grain companies own shipping, rail, and barge companies, which need to be kept full and on the move to be profitable. Large commodity traders prefer price volatility, because they speculate on the commodity exchanges and because uncertainty increases the potential profits. As the companies acquire interests in milling, crushing, and livestock operations, the grain becomes a cost for their business. The company's overriding interest is then to keep grain prices down. Neither volatile nor low prices serve the farmer. In fact, both the farmer and the consumer share a strong overall interest in price stability.

Policymakers and the interested parties must understand what behavior is rational for these dominant firms. It should change the assumptions that shape policy recommendations because these are the actors whose behavior must be modified. The incentives and restrictions are not the same as those that would be useful to change farmers' behavior. Policies designed with only producers, consumers, and government actors in mind miss the real power in the agricultural economy, whether local or global.

As for whether trade and investment flows are helping fight poverty, consider this: according to some estimates, between 1975 and 1993, producers of seven basic commodities worldwide were underpaid as much as US$96 billion (Redfern 2002). In 1992, the world coffee economy was worth US$30 billion, of which producers received US$10 billion. Ten years later, it was worth more than US$60 billion, yet producers received less than US$6 billion of that total (Oxfam International 2002). If globalization is to eradicate poverty, it cannot be premised on policies that drive overproduction of commodities and allow an oligopolistic market to set prices at starvation levels.

Vertical integration in the food and agricultural sector of the United States and the European Union deserves international attention, because it undermines the assumptions that have persuaded governments to embrace trade agreements and change their agricultural policies to increase food imports. To date, few corporate mergers or joint ventures have received governmental, much less intergovernmental, scrutiny outside the country in which they are headquartered. However, such corporate behavior is an area that must get more regulatory attention because of effects in third-country markets and the effects of vertical integration on the price and availability of food in the world market.

Recommendations

The anticipated benefits of creating a specific AoA at the WTO have not materialized. The hope was that open markets, seen as the best way to ensure broadly based development, would gradually replace the inefficiencies of what has traditionally been a government-controlled sector in most countries.

However, after a decade of lowering floor prices, production levels remain high. They are high in countries that subsidize and high in countries that do not, such as Canada and Brazil. This finding should not be surprising: producers cannot affect prices by withholding production and so have no reason to leave land fallow when prices fall. They maximize production even as prices collapse, to offset at least their fixed costs (see, for example, Ray 2001). For instance, Darrin Qualman, executive secretary of the National Farmers Union of Canada, argued that Canadian farmers had seen an impressive expansion in their export markets, but their incomes were the lowest they have been since the Great Depression. The amount of land in production, however, did not change (Qualman 2005).

State involvement in agriculture has often been a disaster. However, there are also examples of sound government intervention. Canada masterminded cheap systems to administer agriculture that were legal under the General Agreement on Tariffs and Trade and provided consumers with a good product at a fair price while ensuring their producers a good return. State-trading enterprises can provide an interesting mix of economic return with due regard for distribution—a key element missing in agricultural systems entirely dependent on transnational agribusiness.

As the Doha round negotiations continue and the WTO AoA undergoes revision, I offer the following ideas for consideration to improve multilateral rules for agriculture:

- Document the operations of transnational agribusinesses, to better understand their global market reach. At the WTO, this effort could mirror the questionnaire required by countries that operate state-trading enterprises. Governments should document private-sector activity that is at or above a given level of market control.

- Evaluate the sources of market distortion, whether public or private. Beyond export subsidies alone, trade negotiators should look at dumping more broadly, comparing the cost of production (with a reasonable profit) in the country of origin to the price offered in the international market. The persistent dumping that currently characterizes commodity trade could be remedied through import tariffs, or through export taxes imposed in the country of origin (for details, see Ritchie, Wisniewsky, and Murphy 2000).

- Create a multilateral working group to discuss competition issues specifically related to international agricultural trade.

- Revisit commodity agreements and ways to manage supply that prevent chronic overproduction.

It is up to the international community to devise political and economic policies that realize these objectives. I think globalization has been used to justify wholly unacceptable policy. It is time to harness the new technologies and apply some longstanding wisdom about the importance of strong agricultural development if poverty is to be eradicated. There is a long way to go to make globalization an instrument to end poverty. It is time to begin.

References

Murphy, S. 1999. *Trade and food security: An assessment of the Uruguay Round Agreement on Agriculture*. London: Catholic Institute for International Relations.

Oxfam International. 2002. *Mugged: Poverty in your coffee cup*. Oxford.

Qualman, D. 2005. The farm crisis: Its causes and solutions. The National Farmers Union's submission to the Ministers of Agriculture Meeting, Kananaskis, Alberta, July 5.

Ray, D. E. 2001. Crop agriculture faces long-term price and income problems. Testimony before the U.S. House Committee on Agriculture, February 14. Available online at http://apacweb.ag.utk.edu/farmbill.html.

Redfern, A. 2002. Third World perspective. Article in proceedings of a meeting of the British Society of Animal Science and the Scottish Centre for Animal Welfare Sciences, York, April 7–8. Available at http://www.bsas.org.uk/downloads/chpfdww.pdf.

Ritchie, M., S. Wisniewski, and S. Murphy. 2000. *Dumping as a structural feature of U.S. agriculture: Can WTO rules solve the problem?* Minneapolis, Minn., U.S.A.: Institute for Agriculture and Trade Policy.

Chapter 6

The Rise of Supermarkets in the Global Food System

Thomas Reardon and C. Peter Timmer

Supermarkets are traditionally viewed by development economists, policymakers, and practitioners as the rich world's place to shop.[1] But supermarkets are no longer just niche players for rich consumers in the capital cities of developing countries. The rapid rise of supermarkets in these countries in the past 5–10 years has transformed agrifood markets, albeit at different rates and depths across regions and countries.

This chapter describes the transformation of agrifood systems in Africa, Asia (excluding Japan), and Latin America. We focus on the determinants of and patterns in the diffusion of supermarkets and then discuss the evolution of their procurement systems. It is these systems that are having the most notable consequences for agrifood systems and hence for output markets.

Determinants of Supermarket Diffusion in Developing Countries

The determinants of the diffusion of supermarkets in developing regions can be conceptualized as a system of demand by consumers for supermarket services and supply of those services—hence investments by supermarket entrepreneurs. Both functions have incentives and capacity variables.

This chapter is derived from Reardon and Timmer (2007).

On the demand side, several forces drive the observed increase in demand for supermarket services (and are similar to those observed in Europe and the United States in the twentieth century). One demand incentive is that urbanization, with the entry of women into the workforce outside the home, increased the opportunity cost of women's time and their incentive to seek shopping convenience and processed foods to save home preparation time. A second is that supermarkets, often in combination with large-scale food manufacturers, reduced the prices of processed products.

On the demand capacity side, several variables were key. Real per capita income growth in many countries of the regions during the 1990s, along with the rapid rise of the middle class, increased demand for processed foods, which is the entry point for supermarkets, as they can offer a greater variety of these products and lower prices than traditional retailers because of economies of scale in procurement. In addition, rapid growth in the 1990s in ownership of refrigerators meant an increased ability to shift from daily shopping in traditional retail shops to weekly or monthly shopping. Growing access to cars and public transport reinforced this trend.

The supply of supermarket services was driven by several forces, only a subset of which overlap with the drivers of initial supermarket diffusion in Europe and the United States. On the supply incentives side, as discussed later, the development of supermarkets was very slow before (roughly) the early mid-1990s, as only local capital was involved. In the 1990s and thereafter, FDI was crucial to the takeoff of super-markets. European, U.S., and Japanese chains, as well as chains in richer countries in the regions under study (such as in Hong Kong, South Africa, and Costa Rica) had an incentive to invest because of saturation and intense competition in home markets and the much higher margins to be made by investing in developing markets. For example, Carrefour earned three times higher margins on average in its Argentine operations than its French ones in the 1990s (Gutman 2002). Moreover, initial competition in the receiving regions was weak, generally with little fight put up by traditional retailers and domestic-capital supermarkets. And there are distinct advantages to early entry, and hence occupation of key retail locations.

On the supply capacity side, there was a deluge of FDI in the retail sector that was induced by the policy of full or partial liberalization of retail-sector FDI undertaken in many countries in the three regions in the 1990s and subsequently.[2] Overall FDI grew rapidly in the 1990s in these regions. In addition, retail procurement logistics technology and inventory management were revolutionized in the 1990s, such as with the introduction of Efficient Consumer Response.[3] This movement was led by global chains and is diffusing now into developing regions through knowledge transfer and imitation and through innovation by domestic supermarket chains.

These changes were in turn key to the ability to centralize procurement and consolidate distribution (these, along with other improvements in organization and institutions of procurement, are discussed in more detail later) to "drive costs out of the system," a phrase used widely in the retail industry. Substantial savings were thus possible through efficiency gains, economies of scale, and reductions in coordination costs. These efficiency gains fuel profits for investment in new stores and, through intense competition, reduce prices to consumers of essential food products.

Patterns of Supermarket Diffusion in Developing Countries

Although there is significant variation in trends over countries in a given area, such as South America (contrasting, for example, Brazil and Bolivia), within individual countries over zones, and between rural and urban areas, several broad patterns are clearly observed. From earliest to latest adopter of supermarkets in emerging markets, there have been three waves of diffusion.

Experiencing supermarket-sector takeoff in the early to mid-1990s, the first-wave countries include much of South America and East Asia outside China (and Japan), northern Central Europe, and South Africa—areas where the average share of supermarkets in food retail went from roughly only 10–20 percent in about 1990 to 50–60 percent on average by the early 2000s (Reardon and Berdegué 2002; Reardon et al. 2003). Compare that to the 70–80 percent share that supermarkets have in food retail in 2005 in the United States, United Kingdom, or France, and one sees a process of convergence. Examples include frontrunners, where the supermarket takeoff started in the early 1990s, such as Argentina with a 60 percent supermarket share in food retail in 2002 (Gutman 2002), Brazil with 75 percent (Farina 2002), Taiwan with 55 percent in 2003 (Chang 2005), and the Czech Republic with 55 percent (Dries, Reardon, and Swinnen 2004).

Although a small number of supermarkets existed in most countries during and before the 1980s, they were primarily local firms using domestic capital,[4] and they tended to exist in major cities and wealthier neighborhoods. That is, they were essentially a niche retail market serving 5–10 percent of national food retail sales in 1990 (for at-home consumption that is not bought at restaurant-retail for consumption away from home). By 2000, however, supermarkets occupied 50–60 percent of national food retail among these frontrunners, almost approaching the 70–80 percent share for the United States or France. South America and parts of developing East Asia and transition Europe had thus seen in a single decade the same development of supermarkets that the United States experienced over five decades.

There is another set of countries perched at the tail end of the first wave and near the start of the second wave (although we classify them as first-wave countries), with their supermarket takeoff in the mid-1990s. These countries include Costa Rica and Chile, now with about 50 percent shares (Reardon and Berdegué 2002), South Korea with 50 percent in 2003 (Lee and Reardon 2005), the Philippines and Thailand with approximately 50 percent each (Thailand Development Research Institute 2002; Manalili 2005), and South Africa with 55 percent (Weatherspoon and Reardon 2003).

The second-wave countries include parts of Southeast Asia and Central America and Mexico, and southern Central Europe, where the share of supermarkets in food retail went from about 5–10 percent in 1990 to 30–50 percent by the early 2000s, and the takeoff occurring in the mid- to late 1990s. Examples of these include Mexico (50 percent share; Reardon et al. 2007), Colombia (47 percent share; de Hernandez 2004), Guatemala (36 percent in 2002; Orellana and Vasquez 2004), Indonesia (30 percent; Rangkuti 2003), and Bulgaria (25 percent; Dries, Reardon, and Swinnen 2004).

The third-wave countries include those where the supermarket revolution take-off started only in the late 1990s or early 2000s, reaching about 10–20 percent of national food retail by around 2003; they include some of Africa and some countries in Central and South America (such as Nicaragua [Balsevich 2006], Peru, and Bolivia), Southeast Asia (such as Vietnam; Tam 2004), China, India, and Russia. The latter three are the foremost destinations for retail FDI in the world (Burt 2004), and each presents a fascinating third-wave case that will influence the development of agrifood markets in developing regions in the twenty-first century.

China, for example, had no supermarkets in 1989, and food retail was nearly completely controlled by the government. The sector began in 1990, and by 2003 it had climbed meteorically to a 13 percent share in national food retail, US$71 billion of sales, and 30 percent of urban food retail; it was the fastest growing sector in the world, at 30–40 percent per year (Hu et al. 2004). Many of the driving forces for supermarketization were in place (such as rising incomes and urbanization). It merely took a progressive privatization of the retail market and, even more important, a progressive liberalization of retail FDI that started in 1992 and culminated in 2004 to drive immense competition, even a full-out race, in investment among foreign chains and between foreign chains and domestic chains. This process is not only in full swing today, but it greatly accelerated in 2005 with the full liberalization of FDI as a condition to China's accession to the WTO.

Russia is a similar case, with a late start because of policy factors, despite propitious socioeconomic conditions, and then a very rapid takeoff spurred by the immense competition in investments that is under way now (Dries and Reardon 2005).

India is an interesting case, with its substantial middle class as a springboard for the spread of supermarkets; it is already considered to be among the top three retail FDI candidates in the world and is poised at the edge of a supermarketization take-off, although the share in food retail is still only 5 percent. At present, FDI is far from fully liberalized, and regulations concerning joint ventures in retail still dam what observers think is an imminent flood of foreign investment. In May 2005, Wal-Mart announced that it intends to enter the retail market in India (CIES 2005). The Indian government immediately responded that it was highly likely that retail FDI would be liberalized by mid-2005 or soon thereafter, which will facilitate the entry of Wal-Mart (M&M Planet Retail 2005). South Africa's Shoprite and Hong Kong's Dairy Farm chains also entered in 2004 and 2005, as did Germany's Metro. It seems likely that, with a policy change regarding retail FDI, there will be a similar competitive race in investment in the sector from chains from around the world and throughout India.

Sub-Saharan Africa presents a very diverse picture, with only South Africa firmly in the first wave of supermarket penetration, but the rest either in the early phase of the third-wave takeoff—or in what may be a pending but not yet started takeoff of supermarket diffusion. Kenya, Zambia, and Zimbabwe, for example, are in the early phase of the third wave and have substantial numbers of supermarkets, initiated by both domestic investment and FDI from South Africa. This investment was attracted by a middle-class base and high urbanization rates, but supermarket penetration is still approximately at the stage of that in South America in the early 1980s. The share of supermarkets in urban food retail is about 10–20 percent in the large and medium-sized cities, and the share of produce hovers around 5 percent (see, for example, Neven and Reardon 2004 for Kenya). Even with mainly domestic investment and some South African retail capital and technology, there is still considerable uncertainty about the rate at which the supermarket sector in these countries will grow.

The great majority of Africa, however, can be classified as not yet experiencing a substantial takeoff of supermarket diffusion. At the upper end of this group are a score or so of supermarkets in such countries as Mozambique, Tanzania, Uganda, and Angola—places where South African retail FDI is just starting (see Weatherspoon and Reardon 2003 for evidence on investments by the South African chain Shoprite). Perhaps a decade or two from now this process will be recognized as a "fourth wave." Supermarkets in these countries show signs of early growth and are surrounded by a more general trend of the growth of self-service in large semi-traditional stores in urban areas.

At the lower end of this group are the very poor countries of Africa, such as Ethiopia, Sudan, Burkina Faso, and Mali. It is unlikely that such countries will see supermarket growth for several decades. Even then, it will depend on higher urbanization rates, better investment climates, lower transaction costs, improved infrastructure, much more rapid income growth, and political stability. It will take significant improvements in most of these areas to stimulate FDI by global supermarket chains. We have shown that supermarkets, even in places like South Africa and Kenya, spread beyond the middle class into the food markets of the urban working poor. But the supermarket sector usually requires a critical mass of middle-class urban consumers to build the initial base before expanding into the rest of the urban market.

Note that the growth rates of supermarket food sales as well as retail FDI are inversely correlated with the three waves, so that the fastest growth is occurring in the supermarket sector in China versus only 5–10 percent in the more mature, relatively saturated supermarket sectors, such as those in Brazil and Taiwan.

In general, these three waves of diffusion are correlated with socioeconomic characteristics of the areas that are related to consumers' demand for supermarket services and product diversity and quality: income and urbanization. These characteristics are in turn correlated with the opportunity cost of time, in particular that of women, and reduction in transaction costs through improvements in roads and transport and increased ownership of refrigerators. These demand-side factors are necessary, but not sufficient, to explain the very rapid spread of supermarkets in the 1990s and 2000s in these countries, most of which had at least a very small supermarket sector before 1990. That is, supply-side factors were also of extreme importance, especially the influx of retail FDI as countries liberalized investment rules and improved procurement systems (discussed later in this chapter).

As is predictable from the diffusion model outlined above, the interspatial and socioeconomic-group patterns of diffusion have differed over large and small cities and towns, and over rich, middle, and poor consumer segments. In general, there has been a trend from supermarkets occupying only a small niche in capital cities serving only the rich and middle classes to their spread well beyond the middle class and deep penetration into the food markets of the poor.

Supermarkets have also spread from big cities to intermediate towns and, in some countries, to small towns in rural areas. About 40 percent of Chile's smaller towns now have supermarkets, for instance, as do many small or medium-sized towns even in such low-income countries as Kenya. And supermarkets are now spreading rapidly beyond the top 60 cities of China in the coastal areas and are moving to smaller cities and the poorer and more remote interior. As large stores have spread, there has also been a diversification to meet market segments, with a trend toward larger formats, such as hypermarkets and discount stores.

Thus, in most of the first-wave regions supermarkets have by now penetrated into the lower-income consumer markets and small towns—and the second-wave countries are fast approaching the same situation. This scenario is in sharp contrast to the conventional and now-outmoded vision of the supermarkets as being a luxury niche in output markets. The ability of supermarket chains to spread to smaller towns and to the food markets of the urban poor was driven by competition in the higher-income market segments and was facilitated by the cost (and thus price) reductions made possible by rapid transformation of supermarket procurement systems, as discussed further later.

In addition to the varying spatial pattern of supermarket diffusion just described, there is substantial variation in the speed of retail market change over product categories. The takeover of food retailing in these regions has occurred much more rapidly in processed, dry, and packaged foods, such as noodles, milk products, and grains, for which supermarkets have an advantage over mom-and-pop stores because of economies of scale. The supermarkets' progress in gaining control of fresh food markets has been slower, and there is greater variation across countries because of local habits and responses by wetmarkets and local shops. Usually the first fresh-food categories in which the supermarkets gain a majority share include such "commodities" as potatoes and the sectors experiencing consolidation in first-stage processing and production: often chicken, beef and pork, and fish.

A rough rule of thumb emerging from empirical studies is that the share of the supermarkets in fresh-produce retail is lower than its share in overall food retail, and this gap closes as the latter rises. For instance, the share of supermarkets in Guatemala of fresh-produce retail is about 10 percent, whereas their share in overall food retail is about 35 percent; hence, the market penetration for produce is one-third of overall food market penetration. By contrast, the shares are 50 percent versus 75 percent (produce market penetration and overall food market penetration rate by supermarkets, respectively), or two-thirds, in Brazil. The latter figure is the same as in France.

Hence, at earlier stages of supermarket development, the freshness, convenience (proximity to consumer residences), and lower cost of small produce shops and wetmarkets easily dominate the retail produce sector. As the supermarket sector expands and gains market share, the competition between supermarkets and wetmarkets becomes increasingly stiff and is based on shopping experience, price, quality, freshness, and variety. In the big cities of Mexico or China, the differences in prices between supermarkets and wetmarkets for commodity produce items is narrowing and is often equal for key items. In a recent study of 15,000 consumers in the Asia-Pacific region by A. C. Nielsen, it was found that supermarkets are eroding the share of the wetmarkets in retail by attempting to replicate the experience of the traditional wetmarket while reducing prices to compete directly (M&M Planet Retail 2004). Supermarkets in the emerging market regions have been making significant inroads into these categories only in the past 5 years or so, and usually only after making changes in their procurement systems to cut costs and increase quality.

Despite the slower growth in supermarket share in domestic fresh produce, it is revealing to calculate the absolute market share that supermarkets now represent, even in produce, thus indicating how deeply and quickly these stores have penetrated. For example, Reardon and Berdegué (2002) calculate that supermarkets in Latin

America buy 2.5 times more fruits and vegetables from local producers than is exported as produce from Latin America to the rest of the world. That ratio is already 2:1 in China (Hu et al. 2004). The dominance of domestic procurement should be contrasted with the nearly exclusive focus on produce exports in government and donor programs to spur growth in agricultural diversification and access to dynamic markets.

The final important pattern to note is that the supermarket sector in these regions is increasingly and in most cases overwhelmingly multinationalized (foreign-owned) and consolidated. The multinationalization of the sector is illustrated in Latin America, where global multinationals constitute roughly 70–80 percent of the top five chains in most countries. This element of being FDI-driven differentiates supermarket diffusion in these regions from that in the United States and Europe. The tidal wave of FDI in retail was mainly due to the global retail multinationals Ahold, Carrefour, and Wal-Mart; smaller global chains, such as Casino, Metro, and Makro; and regional multinationals, such as Dairy Farm International (Hong Kong) and Shoprite (South Africa).

In some larger countries, domestic chains, sometimes in joint ventures with global multinationals, have taken the lead. For example, the top chain in Brazil is Companhia Brasileira de Distribuição (in a partial joint venture with Casino of France since 1999, and an equal-shares joint venture by 2005), and the top chain in China is the giant national chain Lianhua (based in Shanghai, in partial joint venture with Carrefour), with some 3,500 stores by 2004. The extent of multinationalization is correlated in general with the wave stage (with the least multinationalization of the supermarket sector in the third-wave countries), but there is a tendency toward convergence.

The rapid consolidation of the sector in those regions mirrors what is occurring in the United States and Europe. For example, in Latin America the top five chains per country have 65 percent of the supermarket sector (versus 50 percent in the United States [Kinsey 2004] and 72 percent in France). The consolidation takes place mainly via foreign acquisition of local chains and secondarily by larger domestic chains absorbing smaller chains and independents. These takeovers are done using large amounts of FDI: in the first 8 months of 2002, for instance, six global retailers— British Tesco; French Carrefour and Casino; Dutch Ahold and Makro; and Belgian Food Lion—spent 6 billion bhat or US$120 million in Thailand (Jitpleechep 2002). In 2002, Wal-Mart spent US$660 million in Mexico building new stores. As noted earlier, supermarket-sector consolidation is correlated with the wave stage, again with a tendency toward convergence.

These trends of multinationalization and consolidation fit the supply function of our supermarket diffusion model. Global and retail multinationals have access to investment funds from their own liquidity and to international credit that is much cheaper than the credit accessible by their domestic rivals. The multinationals also have access to best practices in retail and logistics management, some of which they developed as proprietary innovations. Global retailers adopt retailing and procurement technology generated by their own firms or, increasingly, through joint ventures with global logistics multinationals—as Carrefour does with Penske Logistics of the United States in Brazil. Where domestic firms have competed, they have had to make similar investments; these firms either had to enter joint ventures with global multinationals or obtain low-cost loans from their governments (as the Shanghai-based national chain did) or national bank loans.

Evolution of Supermarket Procurement Systems

Technology change in the procurement systems of supermarkets in developing regions is a key determinant of change in the markets facing farmers. Diffusion of technology—defined broadly as physical production practices and management techniques—in procurement systems in developing countries can also be conceptualized as a system of demand and supply for new technology. Here we focus on technology for retail product–procurement systems, as these choices most strongly affect suppliers.

Demand for technology change in the procurement practices of food retailers is generally driven by the overall competitive strategy of the supermarket chain. However, specific choices are usually made by procurement officers, such as those in the produce procurement division. Hence, it is crucial to understand the objectives of these officers in supermarkets in developing countries. We present a tentative hypothesis based on numerous interviews with such individuals.

Decisions on what products go on retail shelves rest with the procurement officers in supermarket chains. Whether in the United States, Europe, Nicaragua, Chile, or China, they experience several common "pressures" from supermarket managers, operating under intense competition and low profit margins on average. They are caught between the low-cost informal traditional retailers selling fresh local products, on one side, and efficient global chain competitors, such as Wal-Mart, on the other. The procurement officers respond to this pressure by reducing purchase and transaction costs and raising product quality. Reflecting the varied demand of consumers, these individuals seek to maintain diversity, year-round availability, and products with assured quality and safety levels.

Based on those objectives, we outline a rough model for demand (by procurement officers) for and supply (by the supermarket chain to the procurement divisions) of changes in procurement systems (technology, organization, and institutions). The demand function incentives and capacity variables are discussed first. There are several incentives:

- the ability of the traditional wholesale system to meet the procurement officer's objectives without the chain having to resort to costly investments in an alternative system;[5]

- the need to reduce costs of procurement by saving on inputs (in this case purchased-product costs and transaction costs with suppliers); and

- the need to increase procurement of products that can be sold at higher margins, and hence diversify the product line into "products" rather than mere commodities (bulk items).

The capacity variables include

- the consumer segment served by the chain (crucial, because higher-value products cannot be marketed to poorer consumers, for whom cost considerations are paramount); and

- the resources of the procurement office (including the number of staff available to manage procurement, which determines the ability to make organizational and institutional changes in procurement systems, such as operating a large distribution center).

One variable that reflects both incentive and capacity is the size of the chain and thus product throughput in the procurement system. Usually retailers have a "step level" or threshold throughput, in which they go from store-based to centralized procurement as economies of scale permit.

The supply of procurement technology by the overall chain to individual product-procurement offices (such as those for fresh foods) is an investment and is a function of several variables. Incentive variables include

- the importance of the product category to the chain's profits and marketing strategy;[6]

- the need for assurance of various product attributes to meet customers' demands (such as expansion of product choice, attribute consistency over transactions, and year-round availability, quality, and safety); and

- the costs of the technology (such as transport, construction, and logistics services).

   The capacity variables include

- the size of the chain or its access to financial capital to make the investments; and

- the capacity of the chain to manage complex and centralized procurement systems.

   The incentive and capacity determinants of demand for and supply of changes in procurement system technology vary markedly over the three regions and countries, as they do over chains and zones within countries. There is substantial variation within the supermarket sector in a given country, with the four to five leading chains (the majority of the market) tending to be the early adopters of changes in procurement system technology. These can be characterized as the change agents in the retail sector and, by extension, in the output markets in the country. The second- and third-tier chains usually tend to be late adopters, but adopt they must, to compete with the leaders on costs. That they often lag substantially in the adoption of the technologies leads to their lower competitiveness and hence the consolidation processes observed. It is thus crucial to understand the broad patterns observed in the procurement technologies that result. These patterns can be described as the four pillars of change in the organization and institutions of procurement systems (Reardon et al. 2003).

   The first pillar is a trend toward centralization of procurement (per chain). As the number of stores in a given supermarket chain grows, there is a tendency to shift from a per-store procurement system to a distribution center serving several stores in a given zone, district, country, or region (which may cover several countries). This change is accompanied by fewer procurement officers and increased use of centralized warehouses.

   The second pillar is the adoption of organizational innovations—shifting from reliance on spot markets (in particular, traditional wholesale markets and brokers) to greater use of specialized and dedicated wholesalers. They are specialized in a product category and dedicated to the supermarket sector as their main clients. The changes in supplier logistics have moved supermarket chains toward new intermediaries, sidestepping or transforming the traditional wholesale system. These specialized wholesalers cut transaction and search costs, and they enforce private standards and contracts on behalf of the supermarkets.

The third pillar is the adoption by leading supermarket chains of the institutional innovation of contracts with their suppliers—in particular by means of their dedicated, specialized wholesalers managing a preferred supplier system for them. Such contracts are part of what the industrial organization literature terms "vertical restrictions" that fall short of full vertical integration (generally avoided by both supermarket chains and food processors) but that approximate in certain ways the outcomes from vertical merger (Carlton and Perloff 2000).

The fourth pillar of procurement system change is the rise of private quality and safety standards implemented by supermarket chains and large-scale processors. Food retailing in these regions previously operated in the informal market, with little use of certifications and standards, but the emerging trend indicates a rapid rise in the implementation of private standards in the supermarket sector and other modern food industry sectors, such as medium- to large-scale food manufacturers and food service chains. The rise of private standards for quality and safety of food products and the increasing importance of the enforcement of otherwise virtually unenforced public standards are crucial aspects of the imposition of product requirements in procurement systems. In general, these standards function as instruments of coordination of supply chains by standardizing product requirements over suppliers, who may cover many regions or countries. Standards specify and harmonize the product and delivery attributes, thereby enhancing efficiency and lowering transaction costs.

Who Wins and Who Loses in the Retail-Driven Transformation of Agrifood Product Markets during Globalization?

The rise of supermarkets has been controversial everywhere, but their rise to dominance in rich countries over decades instead of years allowed farmers, processors, wholesalers, and traditional small-scale retailers to adjust gradually to the new ways of doing business. These adjustments meant learning cultivation techniques for new crops with standards of product and process quality that were simply not relevant to commodity production. They meant finding new sources of employment as small retail shops and neighborhood markets closed. Consumers tended to shift rapidly from traditional retailers to supermarkets, pulled by convenience, sometimes better prices, and often, greater diversity and quality of products. But this switch has also meant that consumers needed to make adjustments, such as going longer distances to the market and making less frequent, but larger, purchases.

These adjustments tended to be difficult in financial and personal terms, but they were manageable when spread across generations. The adjustment pressures from the rapid emergence of supermarkets (and large-scale processors) in developing countries are far more severe because the change is so fast. The parallels to the overall structural transformation of an economy and the pressures it puts on agriculture are obvious. During the structural transformation, entire societies undergo the wrenching changes associated with agricultural modernization, migration of labor from rural to urban areas, and the emergence of urban industrial centers. The structural transformation has taken as long as three centuries in England and the United States (and is still continuing), and as little as a century in Japan.

Distribution of Net Benefits from the Transformation of Output Markets

Multinational corporations, including global retailers and food manufacturers, are increasingly dominant in this global food supply chain—and are among the key players in the supermarket revolution in developing countries. Not surprisingly, profits in the global food supply chain tend to accrue to the relatively scarce resource in the system, and to whoever controls those resources, because scarcity has value. In the global food retail system, there are three basic possibilities for what resource is scarcest in the food system: farm output, marketing technology, or consumers.

First, there have been longstanding concerns that population growth will outstrip growth in food supplies. If so, the scarce resource in this system is the food commodity itself—the rice, potato, Belgian endive, bell peppers, fresh fish, or chuck steak. Because supermarket quality and safety standards are so high and rigid, the ability to supply the raw commodities that meet these standards might command a price premium and additional profits for the farmers. Supporting commodity supply, of course, is the land and labor (and knowledge and technology) required to grow the commodities. Thus, ultimately, if commodities themselves are the scarce resource, capable of earning excess profits, these profits will accrue to land, labor, or both (or to the management that harnesses the knowledge, technology, and finance, although for small farmers this function tends to be in the same hands as the land and labor).

But historical evidence does not support the view that agricultural commodities will be the ultimate source of scarcity in the food system. Modern agricultural technology is land-saving, there is abundant rural labor (again, on a global level), rural finance is readily available when there is a profit to be made in lending it, and water is becoming scarce only because it is provided free in most cases. What might be scarce at the farm level is the management ability to meet high quality standards and deliver reliably a safe product that meets environmental requirements and is fully traceable to its point of production. There are likely to be significant economies of scale to this management ability, even if there are few scale economies in the physical production of most agricultural commodities.

A second possible scarce resource is access to or control of (through IPR) the technology, organization, or institutions that lower transactions costs throughout the entire food supply chain and improve coordination. However, the technology for managing supply chains—in the food system and elsewhere—is changing rapidly, even in the United States (Kinsey 2004). The technologies, organizations, or institutions discussed in this chapter give supermarket managers exquisite control over procurement, inventory levels, and knowledge of consumer checkout profiles.

For example, information technology is a key component of the vector of technologies used by the chains. It provides a powerful competitive advantage in cost control, quality maintenance, and product tracking in case of defects or safety problems. When this technology is applied globally to the food supply chain of a transnational supermarket, transactions costs will be pushed out of the system all the way from the food aisle, through global marketing functions, to individual farmers. In general, these technologies drive down transactions costs throughout the supply chain. In addition, by reducing the need to hold large inventories, these marketing and logistics technologies reduce capital costs and risks. Because inventory is basically a form of "dead capital," improved logistics and inventory management (such as in Efficient Consumer Response) generate real capital savings as well as lower transactions costs. And both contribute to higher productivity and faster economic growth.

The important question is whether access to this technology is sufficiently restricted that it is "scarce"—that is, can excess profits be earned by controlling it? The evidence suggests that it is easily duplicated as computer power becomes cheaper and local managers learn to imitate the market leaders. IPR seems not to be a serious impediment to this imitation, despite the efforts of supermarket chains to establish proprietary control. It is the knowledge that such techniques are feasible and available that is important, not the specific code written for a particular supermarket's computers. The parallel to the "technological treadmill" (Cochrane 1993) so familiar to American farmers is striking: first adopters of a new technology have a temporary cost advantage and thus above-average profits, but competition leads all market players to adopt it quickly, reducing the advantage of the innovator and stimulating the innovator to adopt an even newer technology to regain cost and profit advantages. This story seems to hold for marketing technology as well.

The third possibility for the resource that is most scarce in this system is access to consumers themselves, and especially to knowledge of how consumers behave—what they want and, therefore, how best to serve them. As concentration in food retailing rises, there seems to be an opportunity for the leading firms—Carrefour, Wal-Mart, Metro, Tesco, Ahold, and others—to control this access and thus to earn higher marketing margins and profits. This possibility has been a longstanding worry in the United States, at least since the 1940s.

The evidence so far, in rich and poor countries alike, is that access to consumers has been highly competitive. Market power is used to drive down costs, and these lower costs are then passed along to consumers as lower prices. Why? Because supermarkets need to increase market share to achieve the economies of scale that permit their costs to be pushed even lower. So far, this whole system has been highly contestable. Economists know that contestable markets pass nearly all the benefits of the marketplace (the sum of producer and consumer surplus) through to consumers.[7]

Basic competitive forces will place most monopoly profits or rents in the hands of the owners of the scarcest resource. The evidence so far is that access to affluent consumers and to powerful information technology and the ability to implement organizational and institutional changes in supply chains are scarcer than the ability to produce high-quality commodities, especially when individual producers are forced to compete on a global playing field. But this result does not mean that multinational and regional supermarket chains are earning monopoly profits, because they have access to or even control over those scarce resources. The cost of information technology is dropping according to Moore's Law,[8] and access to affluent consumers has turned out to be highly contestable, thus generating competitive results despite the industry structure.

Surprisingly, the picture so far is one of intense competition and low profit rates. Consumers are the main winners in the supermarket revolution. For example, a recent study in Chile (LatinPanel study for 2004, reported in Camara Nacional de Comercio 2005) showed that supermarkets, by charging lower prices for food compared with traditional retailers, reduced the cost of the food consumption basket of the lower- and middle-income consumers in Chile.

However, the continuous competitive pressure to lower costs, raise quality, and thus to differentiate products for the consumers induces supermarket chains to require continuous investments by their suppliers to increase quality and reduce costs at the production level. Those investments are challenging for a subset of farmers and processing firms, creating a mixed picture of the benefits of the retail transformation for the farm sector, as discussed in the next section.

Emerging Evidence of Effects on Small Processors and Farmers

A mix of opportunities and challenges faced farmers in the deeply transformed agrifood markets of the 1990s and 2000s. In particular, there is evidence that small farmers are particularly challenged to meet the volume, cost, quality, and consistency requirements of the increasingly dominant supermarket chains and large-scale agroprocessors. That they are challenged does not necessarily mean that there is widespread exclusion and thus upstream consolidation in the food system driven by transformation of the output market. The picture is mixed, and the emerging effects are conditioned by several factors. The results are merely preliminary, because the research is just beginning on the influence of the recent transformation of food markets upstream on farmers and processors.

First, a fairly unambiguous picture is emerging of relatively rapid exclusion of small processing and food manufacturing firms in supermarket procurement systems in developing countries. Although there are very few studies on this process, the forces at work all seem to lead to exclusion. For example, Hu et al. (2004) note that although supermarket chains in Beijing tend to diversify their offerings of processed products, there is a strong tendency toward selection of a few medium-to-large firms capable of delivering products of consistent quality in large volumes. This practice assures "one-stop shopping" for the chains—that is, a given firm is able to supply a diversity of product lines, which reduces transaction costs for the chain. The chains reap economies of scale from large volumes of processed products moving through their distribution centers, and they seek to work with larger firms that can ship to their centers or have their own distribution centers that they can use to distribute to stores. Hu et al. (2004) give an example of a Beijing chain that consolidated the number of its processed food suppliers from 1,000 to 300 in 1 year, once the chain had established its distribution center. Dries and Reardon (2005) note a similar tendency in Russia for dairy products, and Balsevich, Berdegué, and Reardon (2006) found the same for meat products in Costa Rica and Nicaragua. Moreover, the effects on the majority of growers are felt indirectly, through the choice by supermarkets of larger processors, as processed food constitutes half to two-thirds of the food sales of a typical supermarket or hypermarket in developing regions.

With respect to effects of processing-firm procurement practices on farmers, the literature has been most rich in the "first wave" areas, as expected. For example, Schejtman (1998) and Key and Runsten (1999) examined the participation of small farmers in contract farming schemes of agroprocessors in Latin America in the 1980s and 1990s. They found a mixed picture with specific conditions under which these firms use contract farming (rather than full vertical integration) and, when doing contract farming, contract with small farmers. Recent work in Central and Eastern Europe by Swinnen and Dries of the University of Leuven and colleagues (for example, Swinnen 2003; Dries and Swinnen 2004; Dries and Reardon 2005) also shows a mixed picture, with substantial involvement of small milk producers in Poland but very low participation of small producers in Russia, Slovakia, and the Czech Republic. In the latter three countries, the exclusion of small farmers is widespread, as it is in much of South America, such as in Brazil (Farina 2002), Argentina (Gutman 2002), and Chile (Dirven 2001). Swinnen and Dries and their colleagues find that large-scale processors tend to rely on small farmers in particular when there is incentive (insufficient supply from larger firms) and capacity (sufficiently low transaction costs because of effective associations). When the capacity is insufficient but the incentive is high, large firms often try to resolve idiosyncratic market failures facing small growers by providing technical assistance and input credit, similar to actions undertaken by supermarkets, as discussed earlier.

Second,[9] however, changes in supermarket procurement systems also affect growers directly in the case of fresh fruit and vegetables. Thus, the processing sector does not mediate the link between farmers and supermarkets or the wholesalers that serve them, which is why most recent studies of the direct effects of supermarkets on producers have been in this category. Supermarkets in developing countries source from a mix of (1) from farmers directly, (2) from specialized and/or dedicated wholesalers, and (3) from the traditional wholesale market. The effect of supermarkets on farmers is mainly manifest where (1) and (2) have significantly emerged as sourcing strategies of supermarkets, as the supermarket is able to transmit through these channels their quality and other attribute requirements. Selection among farmers (directly by supermarkets or through the specialized wholesalers) aims at maximizing quality and minimizing costs of products. There is thus the potential for exclusion of farmers who do not "make the grade."

Supermarket chain buying agents prefer first to source from large- or medium-scale farmers if they can, such as in the case of bananas in Central America (Berdegué et al. 2005), tomatoes, kale, and bananas in Kenya (Neven et al. 2006), tomatoes in Mexico (Reardon et al. 2007), and potatoes in Indonesia (Natawidjaja et al. 2007). In all of these cases, where medium and large farmers suffice, small growers are simply not included in the supermarkets' procurement system.

For example, in Kenya, Neven et al. (2006) show that for kale (similar results hold for tomatoes and bananas), those farmers included in the supermarket channel relative to those who were not (1) had farms that were 10 times larger (14 cultivated hectares, hence medium-sized farms, versus 1.3 hectares), (2) had twice the education, (3) had 4 times greater share of their land irrigated, (4) were thrice more likely to have a cell phone and 10 times more likely to have a truck and packing shed, and (5) hired 10 times more permanent labor and 5 times more casual labor (thus, considering their larger farms, were more capital-intensive than small farms). Hence, Kenya illustrates a situation in which medium-sized farms are available to supply domestic supermarkets and thus constituted the main suppliers of modern retailing of produce.

What happens when medium-sized and large growers are not available (as is common for most horticultural products in most developing countries, regardless of region) or do not produce enough to meet the year-round needs of supermarkets? This situation is by far the most common in domestic markets of Asia, Latin America, and much of Africa, with only a few exceptions in terms of products and places. The relevant studies available (with the exception of one on China) tend to confirm that asset-poor small farmers are almost universally excluded from supplying supermarket chains. As a rule of thumb, only the top tercile of asset-rich small farmers tend to participate. We cite two studies whose findings are typical.

For Guatemala, Flores, Reardon, and Hernandez (2006) show that the lettuce farmers included in the supermarket channel, relative to those not included (1) had twice the farm size (2 versus 1 hectare), (2) were twice as specialized in lettuce (58 versus 23 percent of cropping) and in horticulture (91 versus 79 percent in horticulture instead of basic grains), (3) had 40 percent more education, (4) were twice as close to paved roads, (5) were nearly twice as likely to have irrigation (51 versus 37 percent), (6) were four times as likely to have a truck, and (7) were twice as likely to be in an organization for small farmers (focused on marketing and production; 79 versus 42 percent). Finally, as included farmers use far more labor-intensive practices to meet supermarket requirements (for field practices, sorting, and packing) and are four times more likely to double-crop over the year, they hire 2.5 times more labor (typically from local asset-poor households) than do farmers not included in the channel. If, for example, 50 lettuce farmers shift from the traditional to the supermarket channel, the data show that they hire 20 additional full-time workers for the two seasons. There is thus a significant exclusion effect on the producer side, and an inclusion effect on the farm hired-laborer side.

Similarly, for Indonesia, Natawidjaja et al. (2007) show that tomato growers included in the supermarket channel, relative to those not included (1) had 17 percent more education, (2) were 26 percent more specialized in tomatoes, (3) had 38 percent larger farms (but still less than 1 hectare per household of cultivated land), (4) were 20 percent more likely to crop thrice over the year (possible because of irrigation), (5) had 10 percent more irrigation before entering the supermarket channel, and (7) had 58 percent higher per-hectare profit rates, but (8) hired 30 percent less labor because of greater capital intensity (such as greater use of plastic covers for the fields, which reduces the need to weed).

As illustrated above for the relations between produce growers and supermarkets, several key points can be noted, based on the cited studies:

- In all regions, small farmers are not excluded on the basis of size of their land-holding or land tenure, except when these factors affect the capacity to implement certain technologies that, in turn, have an impact on quality, productivity, costs, or the ability to plant and/or harvest at the needed times during the year. (The sole exception is the Kenya study.)

- Other assets appear to play a much bigger role than does land. In particular, those included in the supermarket channel have more education; more access to transport and roads; have greater prior holdings of irrigation, and other relevant physical assets, such as wells, cold chain, greenhouses, and good quality irrigation water. If they are selling to a specialized wholesaler, they do not usually have the asset of a rural producers organization. In the very rare instances when small farmers sell directly to the supermarket, they have a very good rural producers organization. The mass of excluded farmers, such as most of the traditional tomato farmers in West Java (Natawidjaja et al. 2007), lack these assets.

- There are two exceptions to the "exclusion of the asset-poor" rule. The first is where procurement modernization is as yet insignificant, there is a cap on farm size, and assets are relatively evenly distributed. In our set of seven studies, only the China case (Wang et al. 2006) meets these criteria. The second is where NGOs have assisted (implicitly or explicitly subsidized) the participation of the asset-poor small farmers (in fact by alleviating that asset poverty). Only those Nicaraguan tomato farmers dealing with the lead chain exemplifies this case (Balsevich, Berdegué, and Reardon. 2006), at a cost of US$800 a year of assistance per farm, about 10 times the public budget for farm extension and assistance!

- Farmers in the supermarket channel tend to earn substantially (from 10 to 100 percent) more in net terms, so the payoff to making the threshold investment is substantial. The effects, in the early stages of supermarket penetration, on exclusion of asset-poor small farmers growing fresh produce should be placed in the context that typically only 10–30 percent of all farmers are selling through the modern channels. That number will continue to grow (from being nearly zero only a decade ago), which will create a relentlessly increasing market challenge for the asset-poor.

Third, an even less well-researched but equally intriguing subject is the indirect effect of the food industry transformation on producers for the traditional food industry, which now competes with the modern food industry. Traditional firms alter their procurement practices, at least to some extent, to cut costs and raise quality to compete with those of the modern food industry and thus stem the loss of customers to supermarkets. As far as we know, this process has not been researched systematically in any country, but "ripple effects" of technology and organization appear to be emerging from the epicenter of the supermarket revolution to other segments of the market. These ripples imply that producers may well be affected both in the most dynamic demand segments (the urban market progressively dominated by supermarkets) and at the traditional retail and wholesale segments that compete with supermarkets.

Implications
The supermarket revolution has come to developing countries, and is spreading fast, in waves of diffusion. This revolution tends to have unambiguous effects on rich and

poor consumers alike, first in processed and semi-processed foods (such as flour, oil, rice, dairy, and meat) and then gradually in fresh produce and fish, by offering a wider range at a lower price than traditional retailers offer.

The leading chains are modernizing their procurement systems, which has effects upstream on processors and farmers. The effects on processors are generally un-ambiguous: the retail transformation favors large or medium-scale processors. The indirect effect on farmers is mixed, however, and the evidence ranges from large processors favoring medium-sized or large farmers, the elite of small (asset-endowed) farmers, or in the absence of these two, small asset-poor farmers whom the processors (where they find it necessary) work to upgrade. The effects on fresh-produce farmers follow a similar mixed pattern to that found among large processors, for similar reasons. In the early stages, the effects of market expansion of the supermarkets on the processors and the farmers means that those asset-poor farmers and small processors who are not selected by supermarkets and large processors as suppliers are not hurt, but merely forego the income gains to be had from the new dynamic market channels. It is only in the more advanced stages, when supermarkets dominate, that a supplier's having insufficient capacity to meet the quality and cost requirements of the super-markets can spell exclusion.

As the supermarket revolution introduces competition on costs and quality into the local market, the distinction between the local and the global—between the domestic and the export market—becomes blurred. Development agencies and NGOs have emphasized targeting either local markets, which they presumed to be nearly hermetically sealed from the global market, or export markets as a way to break local demand constraints. But the presence and even the dominance of supermarkets in local food markets mean that nearly all suppliers are faced increasingly with a mix of challenges and opportunities of both. Helping small farmers gear up to that chal-lenge is crucial.

Undertaking market-oriented development assistance programs now means dealing with a handful of big companies. Reorienting development programs and researchers to this fundamentally different reality is urgent but not easy, because each locale has unique characteristics. The export market is a logical target for develop-ment assistance, but in many cases the domestic market in supermarkets is already more important and is growing much more rapidly than the export market. Super-markets in Latin America and China already buy from local producers twice as much produce as either of those areas export to the rest of the world. So development pro-grams need to align their marketing programs to focus on supermarkets.

Finally, it is clear from this discussion that public policy is only half the story in understanding the transformation of markets in developing countries. Policy was indeed crucial in the initial stages of liberalization, but public policy is now forced to share power with the emerging force of private institutional change. While public attention is focused on public standards and market policies, such as those represented by the WTO, there has been a rapid rise in private standards that have reshaped markets in developing countries. Policymakers and other shareholders need to understand that change and build it into the design of development assistance programs.

The private standards imposed by large firms in developing countries are dovetailing with global private standards imposed by powerful players in food retail and food manufacturing. Such private standards, developed in the context of the strategic goals of the large firms, will shape food markets in the years to come. In 2003, for example, Comité International d'Entreprises à Succursales—the association of large supermarkets and food manufacturers based in Paris and consisting of the top 250 supermarket chains and 250 food manufacturers—launched its new worldwide harmonization initiative on food safety standards, which were private standards to be imposed on their suppliers over the next 2 years. The combined annual sales of these companies reach US$2.8 trillion, a sum that dwarfs development assistance or even international trade. Market-led development is now supermarket-led development.

Notes

1. We use the term "supermarkets" as shorthand for large-format modern retail stores, such as supermarkets, hypermarkets, and discount stores. Our discussion focuses on large format, because convenience stores tend to have only a small share (about 5–10 percent) of modern retail sales.

2. For example, partial liberalization of retail trade occurred in China in 1992, with full liberalization of the sector by the end of 2004; in Brazil, Mexico, and Argentina in 1994; in various African countries through South African investment after apartheid ended in the mid-1990s; and in Indonesia in 1998. Partial liberalization occurred in India in 2000.

3. Efficient Consumer Response is a retail-industry voluntary "self-examination and self-improvement" movement started in the United States in 1993 that aimed to improve supply chain efficiency. It has several elements: "(1) Efficient Store Assortment—addresses how many items to carry in a category, what type of items and in what sizes/flavors/packages, and how much space to give to each item. This is closely linked to category management. (2) Efficient Replenishment—focuses on shortening and eliminating costs in the order cycle, starting with accurate point-of-sale data. Includes efficiencies to be gained by using continuous replenishment programs, EDI [Electronic Data Interchange], cross docking, computer assisted ordering and new receiving techniques. (3) Efficient Promotion—addresses inefficient promotional practices that tend to inflate inventories and practices, whose effects may not be fully passed through to consumers to influence their purchase decisions. (4) Efficient New Product Introduction—addresses improving the entire process of introducing new products, which is subject to high failure rates, thereby bringing extra costs into the system" (available at http://www.fmi.org/media/bg/ecr1.htm; accessed June 2007).

4. The existence of these early supermarket chains serving a tiny niche market in some developing areas (for example, in Puerto Rico) was noted as early as 1953 by Holden (1953) in the Holden-Galbraith study.

5. Usually procurement officers find this ability to be low, as Boselie (2002) shows in the case of Ahold for fresh produce in Thailand. Compared to the North American or European market, produce marketing in these regions is characterized by poor institutional and public physical infrastructure support. Private infrastructure, such as packing houses, cold chains, and shipping equipment among suppliers and distributors, is usually inadequate. Risks and uncertainties, both in output and in suppliers' responsiveness to incentives, are high. The risks may arise from various output and input market failures, such as inadequacies in credit, third-party certification, and market information.

6. For example, we observed a small chain in an intermediate city in China that invested in building a distribution center for processed and/or packaged foods but continues to buy fresh foods from the spot market (traditional wholesalers). At the same time, a national chain also invested in a large distribution center for packaged and/or processed foods and recently built a large center for fresh foods as well. As throughput has reached critical mass, these products have attained a threshold importance in profits and chain marketing strategy.

7. Even at this late stage in the supermarket revolution in the United States, adoption of state-of-the-art marketing technology generates annual benefits equal to half the size of the entire farm economy. This staggering result is driven by the calculation that Wal-Mart alone, the leader in the marketing-technology revolution, lowers the annual inflation rate by roughly 1 percent a year (Greenhouse 2004).

8. Moore observed an exponential growth in the number of transistors per integrated circuit and predicted that this trend would continue (Moore 1965; see also http://www.intel.com). Moore's Law is often used generically to indicate the rapid pace of change in information technology.

9. This discussion of effects on horticultural farmers is drawn from Reardon and Berdegué (2007).

References

Balsevich, F. 2006. Essays on producers' participation, access, and response to the changing nature of dynamic markets in Nicaragua and Costa Rica. Ph.D. dissertation, Michigan State University, East Lansing, Michigan, U.S.A.

Balsevich, F., J. Berdegué, and T. Reardon. 2006. Supermarkets, new-generation wholesalers, tomato farmers and NGOs in Nicaragua. Department of Agricultural Economics Staff Paper 3. East Lansing, Mich., U.S.A.: Michigan State University.

Berdegué, J. A., F. Balsevich, L. Flores, and T. Reardon. 2005. Central American supermarkets' private standards of quality and safety in procurement of fresh fruits and vegetables. *Food Policy* 30 (3): 254–269.

Boselie, D. 2002. Business case description: TOPS Supply Chain Project, Thailand. Agrichain Competence Center Working Paper. Den Bosch, the Netherlands: Ketennetwerkem, Clusters en ICT International Agri Supply Chain Development Program.

Burt, T. 2004. Global retailers expand markets. *Financial Times,* June 22.

Camara Nacional de Comercio. 2005. Cae consumo de sectores medios y bajos. *Noticias CNC.* Available at http://www.cnc.cl. Accessed May 2005.

Carlton, D. W., and J. M. Perloff, eds. 2000. *Modern industrial organization,* 3rd ed. Reading, Mass., U.S.A.: Addison-Wesley.

Chang, C. C. 2005. The role of retail sector in agro-food system, Chinese Taipei. Presentation at the Pacific Economic Cooperation Council's Pacific Food System Outlook 2005–06 annual meeting, May 11–13, Kun Ming, China.

CIES (International Committee of Food Retail Chains). 2005. Wal-Mart Q1 results, interest in India. *CIES Food Business Forum,* May 13.

Cochrane, W. W. 1993. *The development of American agriculture: A historical analysis.* Minneapolis, Minn., U.S.A.: University of Minnesota Press.

De Hernandez, L. 2004. *Colombia retail food sector annual, 2004.* GAIN Report CO4011. Washington, D.C.: U.S. Department of Agriculture, Foreign Agricultural Service.

Dirven, M. 2001. Dairy sector clusters in Latin America. *International Food and Agribusiness Management Review* 2 (3): 301–313.

Dries, L., and T. Reardon. 2005. *Central and Eastern Europe: Impact of food retail investments on the food chain.* European Bank for Reconstruction and Development Cooperation Program Report 6. London: Investment Center, Food and Agriculture Organization of the United Nations.

Dries, L., and J. Swinnen. 2004. Foreign direct investment, vertical integration and local suppliers: Evidence from the Polish dairy sector. *World Development* 32 (9): 1525–1544.

Dries, L., T. Reardon, and J. Swinnen. 2004. The rapid rise of supermarkets in Central and Eastern Europe: Implications for the agrifood sector and rural development. *Development Policy Review* 22 (5): 525–556.

Farina, E. 2002. Consolidation, multinationalization, and competition in Brazil: Impacts on horticulture and dairy product systems. *Development Policy Review* 20 (4): 441–457.

Flores, L., T. Reardon, and R. Hernandez. 2006. Supermarkets, new-generation wholesalers, farmers organizations, contract farming, and lettuce in Guatemala: Participation by and effects on small farmers. Department of Agricultural Economics Staff Paper 7. East Lansing, Mich., U.S.A.: Michigan State University.

Greenhouse, S. 2004. Wal-Mart, a nation unto itself. *New York Times,* April 17.

Gutman, G. 2002. Impact of the rapid rise of supermarkets on dairy products systems in Argentina. *Development Policy Review* 20 (4): 409–427.

Holden, R. H. 1953. Marketing structure and economic development. *Quarterly Journal of Economics* 67 (August): 344–361.

Hu, D., T. Reardon, S. Rozelle, P. Timmer, and H. Wang. 2004. The emergence of supermarkets with Chinese characteristics: Challenges and opportunities for China's agricultural development. *Development Policy Review* 22 (4): 557–586.

Jitpleechep S. 2002. Who is who. *Bangkok Post* article. Available at http://www.siamfuture.com. Posted August 28.

Katjiuongua, H. B. 2004. *Fresh fruit and vegetable marketing: The case of supermarket procurement from tomato producers in Zambia*. Report to the U. S. Agency for International Development. East Lansing, Mich., U.S.A.: Michigan State University.

Key, N., and D. Runsten. 1999. Contract farming, smallholders, and rural development in Latin America: The organization of agroprocessing firms and the scale of outgrower production. *World Development* 27 (February): 381–401.

Kinsey, J. 2004. Supply chain innovations in the U.S. retail sector. Presentation at the International Conference on Supermarkets and Agricultural Development in China: Opportunities and Challenges, May 24–25, Shanghai.

Lee, J.-H., and T. Reardon. 2005. *Forward integration of an agricultural cooperative into the supermarket sector: The case of Hanaro Club in Korea*. Joint Working Paper, Department of Industrial Economics, Chung-Ang University, Seoul, Korea, and Department of Agricultural Economics, Michigan State University, East Lansing, Mich., U.S.A.

M&M Planet Retail. 2004. Consumers forsake wet markets in Asia. *Daily News by M&M Planet Retail*, June 7.

———. 2005. Wal-Mart hopes for India boosted. *Daily News by M&M Planet Retail*, May 31.

Manalili, N. M. 2005. The changing map of the Philippine retail food sector: The impact on trade and the structure of agriculture and the policy response. Presentation at the Pacific Economic Cooperation Council's Pacific Food System Outlook 2005–06 annual meeting, May 11–13, Kun Ming, China.

Moore, G. E. 1965. Cramming more components onto an integrated circuit. *Electronics* 38 (8): 1–4.

Natawidjaja, R. S., T. Reardon, S. Shetty, with T. Perdana, E. Rasmikayati, T. Insan, S. Bahri, and R. Hernandez. 2007. *The effects of retail and wholesale transformation on horticulture supply chains in Indonesia: With tomato illustration from West Java*. Report for the World Bank by the Center for Agricultural Policy and Agribusiness Studies (CAPAS) Padjadjaran University, Bandung, and Michigan State University, East Lansing, Mich., U.S.A.

Neven, D., and T. Reardon. 2004. The rise of Kenyan supermarkets and evolution of their horticulture product procurement systems. *Development Policy Review* 22 (6): 669–699.

Neven, D., M. Odera, T. Reardon, and H. Wang. 2006. Horticulture farmers and domestic supermarkets in Kenya. Staff Paper 2006-06. Department of Agricultural Economics, Michigan State University, East Lansing, Mich., U.S.A.

Orellana, D., and E. Vasquez. 2004. *Guatemala retail food sector annual, 2004*. Global Agriculture Information Network Report GT4018. Washington, D.C.: U.S. Department of Agriculture, Foreign Agricultural Service.

Rangkuti, F. 2003. *Indonesia food retail sector report 2003*. Global Agriculture Information Network Report ID3028. Washington, D.C.: U.S. Department of Agriculture, Foreign Agricultural Service.

Reardon, T., and J. A. Berdegué. 2002. The rapid rise of supermarkets in Latin America: Challenges and opportunities for development. *Development Policy Review* 20 (4, September): 317–334.

————. 2007. The retail-led transformation of agrifood systems and its implications for development policies. A background paper prepared for the World Bank's World Development Report 2008: Agriculture for Development. Centro Latinoamericano para el Desarrollo Rural, Santiago, Chile, and Michigan State University, East Lansing, Mich., U.S.A.

Reardon, T., and C. P. Timmer. 2007. Transformation of markets for agricultural output in developing countries since 1950: How has thinking changed? In *Handbook of agricultural economics*, Vol. 3, *Agricultural development: Farmers, farm production, and farm markets,* ed. R. E. Evenson and P. Pingali, 2807–2855. Amsterdam: North-Holland.

Reardon, T., C. P. Timmer, C. B. Barrett, and J. A. Berdegué. 2003. The rise of supermarkets in Africa, Asia, and Latin America. *American Journal of Agricultural Economics* 85 (5): 1140–1146.

Reardon, T., J. A. Berdegué, F. Echanove, R. Cook, and N. Tucker. 2007. The rise of supermarkets and the evolution of their procurement systems in Mexico: Focus on horticulture products. Working Paper. Michigan State University, East Lansing, Mich., U.S.A.

Schejtman, A. 1998. Agroindustria y pequeña agricultura: Experiencias y opciones de transformación. In *Agroindustria y pequeña agricultura: vínculos, potencialidades y oportunidades comerciales,* No. de venta 5.98.11.6.4 46 (LC/G.2007-P). Santiago, Chile: Naciones Unidas (United Nations) Comisión Económica para América Latina y el Caribe (CEPAL).

Swinnen, J. 2003. Vertical integration, interlinking markets, and growth in transition agriculture. Paper presented at the 80th European Association of Agricultural Economics Seminar on the Role of Institutions in Rural Policies and Agricultural Markets, September 24–26, Ghent, Belgium.

Tam, P. T. G. 2004. *Regoverning markets: Securing small producer participation in restructured national and regional agri-food systems: The case of Vietnam*. Report to the Regoverning Markets Project. Ho Chi Minh City, Vietnam: Nong Lam University.

Thailand Development Research Institute. 2002. *The retail business in Thailand: Impact of the large scale multinational corporation retailers*. Bangkok: Thailand Development Research Institute.

Wang, H., X. Dong, S. Rozelle, J. Huang, and T. Reardon. 2006. Producing and procuring horticultural crops with Chinese characteristics: A case study in the greater Beijing area. Staff Paper 2006-05. Department of Agricultural Economics, Michigan State University, East Lansing, Mich., U.S.A.

Weatherspoon, D. D., and T. Reardon. 2003. The rise of supermarkets in Africa: Implications for agrifood systems and the rural poor. *Development Policy Review* 21 (3): 333–355.

Chapter 7

Globalization of Agrifood Systems and the Nutrition Transition

Corinna Hawkes

In a fundamental shift termed the "nutrition transition," the consumption of foods high in fats and sweeteners is increasing throughout the developing world, while the share of cereals is declining and the intake of fruits and vegetables remains inadequate. These poor-quality diets are associated with rising rates of overweight, obesity, and diet-related chronic diseases, such as heart disease, diabetes, and some cancers. More people now die of heart disease in developing countries than in industrialized ones.

The dietary transitions taking place are deeply rooted in the processes of globalization, which lead to changing incomes and lifestyles. By radically altering the nature of agrifood systems, globalization is also altering the quantity, type, cost, and desirability of foods available for consumption. As the FAO explains, "globalization is having a major impact on food systems around the world . . . [which] affect availability and access to food through changes to food production, procurement, and distribution . . . in turn bringing about a gradual shift in food culture, with consequent changes in dietary consumption patterns and nutritional status that vary with the socioeconomic strata" (Kennedy, Nantel, and Shetty 2004, 1).

The links between globalization and diet are generally underresearched, though analysts have suggested the following mechanisms are central to the globalization–diet nexus:[1]

- food trade and global sourcing (see Chapter 5);

- FDI;

- global food advertising and promotions;

- retail restructuring (notably the development of supermarkets; see Chapter 6);

- emergence of global agribusiness and transnational food companies (see Chapter 5);

- development of global rules and institutions that govern the production, trade, distribution, and marketing of food (see Chapter 6);

- urbanization; and

- cultural change and influence.

Yet determining the precise relationship between these mechanisms and changing diets is a challenge, as is determining their comparative importance to the nutrition transition. Such challenges are a reflection of the complex and multidimensional interactions between global economics and health (see Kickbusch and de Leeuw 1999; Woodward et al. 2001; Lee, Buse, and Fustukian 2002; Harris and Seid 2004; Labonte 2004; Huynen, Martens, and Hilderink 2005). Different perspectives give rise to an often polarized debate about the relative merits and demerits of globalization in terms of health (Lee et al. 2002): some say it is mainly good for health (Dollar 2001; Feacham 2001); others, that it is inherently problematic (Berlinguer 1999; Baum 2003). The reality, as for any policy choice, is that globalization is likely to bring threats and opportunities, improving health in some circumstances and damaging it in others (Yach and Bettcher 1998; Cornia 2001; Labonte 2004).

The complexity of the interactions and the potential for gains and losses is particularly pertinent to nutrition, given that nutritional problems lie along a spectrum from under- to overnutrition. Processes of globalization operating throughout the food supply chain have different effects on different parts of the spectrum. Such processes may introduce opportunities to address undernutrition by raising incomes and cheapening food, but in doing so they introduce risks for overnutrition. Alternatively, they may benefit both under- and overnutrition by increasing the diversity of food available for consumption. Or they may damage both by generating inequality and exclusion, making an adequate and healthy supply of food accessible only to the rich.

Comprehending these scenarios and trade-offs is a central challenge for policymakers in a globalizing world. What will be gained and lost? And who will be the winners and losers? As Labonte (2004, 52) points out, "Tracing the impacts of globalization on health to answer such questions can be a daunting task." To do so, Labonte

(2004) stresses the need to understand the mechanisms central to globalization. Equally, he notes it is necessary to examine the global, national, community, and household contexts in which these mechanisms are operating. This approach is important, because even though the mechanisms are operating globally, their effects are context dependent: homogenizing processes can have very heterogeneous effects. So the same globalization processes will have different outcomes for people at risk from undernutrition relative to those at risk from overnutrition, for urban compared to rural populations, and for the poor relative to the rich.

Globalization is thus a dynamic process of both mass global change and local differentiation. In dietary terms, these trends can be articulated as "dietary convergence" and "dietary adaptation"; each, in a seemingly contradictory unity, is part and parcel of the nutrition transition (Kennedy, Nantel, and Shetty 2004). According to Kennedy, Nantel, and Shetty (2004, 9), dietary convergence is "increased reliance on a narrow base of staple grains, increased consumption of meat and meat products, dairy products, edible oil, salt and sugar, and a lower intake of dietary fibre," whereas dietary adaptation is "increased consumption of brand-name processed and store-bought food, an increased number of meals eaten outside the home and consumer behaviors driven by the appeal of new foods available." Convergence, the authors argue, is driven mainly by income and price. Adaptation, in contrast, is driven by demands on time, increased exposure to advertising, availability of new foods, and the emergence of new food retail outlets.

In this chapter, I argue that the globalization of agrifood systems sheds light on the coexistence of the apparently contradictory processes of dietary convergence and adaptation. Focusing on the dynamics of the nutrition transition in middle-income countries, I explore how one of the central mechanisms of globalization, the integration of the global marketplace, is leading to both convergence and adaptation in dietary habits. I highlight the importance of three major processes of market integration: the production and exchange of goods within agriculture, the flow of investment across borders in the form of FDI in food processing and retailing, and the global communication of information in the form of the advertising and promotion of food. I focus on the negative aspects of dietary change, using case studies to exemplify the implications of specific policy changes for the consumption of foods associated with the nutrition transition. I suggest that although the links between global economic change and diet are never direct or obvious, there are, over the long-term, grounds for concern about the effects of market integration on food consumption patterns, including among the poor. I conclude that more structural responses to deal with the policies and processes of the global marketplace are needed to address the negative health trends associated with the nutrition transition.

Role of Agricultural Production and Trade in Changing Diet Quality

Global market integration is characterized by the combination of formerly separated markets into a single market. Agriculture is central to this aspect of globalization and the theory of comparative advantage that lies behind it: creating efficiency by locating the production of agricultural goods where there is a comparative advantage in producing them. In a globally integrated agricultural market, the idea is that nations specialize in producing foods consistent with their resource endowment and then trade those foods with other countries. The desired result is greater economic efficiency, a more consistent food supply, lower costs of production, and—in theory—cheaper food.

Prior to the era of modern economic globalization, countries tended to favor the protection of domestic agricultural markets, a tendency clearly inconsistent with the economic efficiency envisioned by the theory of comparative advantage. Increasing the market orientation (that is, the degree of liberalization) of the production and exchange of agricultural goods within and between nations has thus become a critical component of globalization. During the 1970s and 1980s, many low- and middle-income countries underwent "structural adjustment," which included implementing more market-oriented agricultural policies.

The pace of reform accelerated in the 1990s as many countries liberalized their agricultural markets internally and internationally. Regional trade agreements, signed at a steady but slow pace through the 1970s and 1980s, soared to a rate of 15 per year in the 1990s (FAO 2004b). And in 1994, agriculture was included in global trade rules for the first time: the Uruguay Round of the General Agreement on Tariffs and Trade (GATT)'s AoA pledged countries to reduce tariffs, export subsidies, and domestic agricultural support. Food and agricultural trade were also affected by bilateral agreements and new rules on technical barriers to trade. This range of policy shifts over the past 20–30 years has led to a more liberal global agricultural marketplace, although it cannot yet be described as "open," because high levels of protection still exist in various forms.

This more liberal agricultural market has enabled more and different food trade, more foreign investment, and the enlargement of transnational food companies (TFCs). In developing countries, food import bills as a share of GDP more than doubled between 1974 and 2004, and the amount of trade made up of processed agricultural products rose much faster than primary agricultural products (FAO 2004b). More open trade and investment have made the purchase of companies, products, and services easier across national borders, creating incentives for TFCs to grow through global vertical integration and sourcing (Heffernan et al. 1994).

Global vertical integration—when a company brings together the entire process of producing, distributing, and selling a particular food under its control by buying and contracting other companies and services worldwide—reduces the

Table 7.1   World oilcrops primary production (thousand tons)

	1980	1990	1995	2000	2004
World production	49,298	75,411	91,857	110,043	132,727

Source: Based on data from FAO (2005).

transaction costs associated with having different suppliers and creates economies of scale (Martinez 2002). Global outsourcing—when a company searches for inputs, production sites, and outputs where costs are lower and where regulatory, political, and social regimes are favorable—enables TFCs to cut costs and helps safeguard against the uncertainty of commodity production and product sales (Heffernan et al. 1994).

These changes in the global agrifood system have altered the supply of foods associated with the nutrition transition. Vegetable oils are a case in point. Oilcrops have been one of the most dynamic agricultural sectors in recent decades; production grew at a rate of 4.1 percent a year between 1979 to 1999, relative to 2.1 percent for agriculture as a whole (Bruinsma 2003). World oilcrop production increased by more than 70 percent between 1990 and 2004 (Table 7.1), with growth driven by the top three oils: soybean, palm, and canola/rapeseed.

Growth has been concentrated in Asia and Latin America, not the traditional production zones of North America and Western Europe. Between 1994 and 2004, edible oil production in China increased nearly twofold, soybean oil production grew by half in Brazil and by twofold in Argentina, and palm oil production rose by two-thirds in Malaysia (Beckman 2005). Similar trends are seen for consumption. During this time frame, vegetable oil consumption in the United States and Western Europe increased by just one-quarter, whereas it doubled in China and increased by half in India.

Overall, between 1982–84 and 2000–02, vegetable oils contributed more than any other food group to the increase of caloric availability worldwide by 70 kilocalories per person per day (calculated from FAO 2005). Vegetable oils can thus clearly be implicated in rising dietary fat intakes worldwide (Drewnowski and Popkin 1997). Increased consumption can be explained in part by rising demand but also by supply-side policies, as illustrated by a case study of the three largest emerging economies (Brazil, China, and India) and the world's most abundant oil (soybean).

Brazil is the world's second-largest soybean producer and exporter (the United States is the largest producer and Argentina the largest exporter). Through the 1960s and 1970s, government policies explicitly promoted production, export, and domestic consumption of soybean oil (Schnepf, Dohlman, and Bolling 2001). In the 1990s, in line with the globalization agenda, the government opened up its soybean market

Table 7.2   Brazil: Soybean and soybean oil production, exports, and consumption

Measure	1989–91	2002–04
Soybean production (tons)	19,629,093	48,079,460
Soybean oil production (tons)	2,679,413	8,735,573
Soybean oil exports (tons)	732,659	2,312,539
Calories available from soybean oil per person per day	326	251.2[a]
Urban household consumption of soybean oil (percent of total daily caloric consumption)	11.4	10.1[b]

Source: Based on data from FAO (2006). Household consumption statistics from IBGE (2004).
Notes: The numbers represent 3-year averages around 1990 and 2003. FAO data suggest a clear decline in calories available for consumption of soybean oil, whereas household consumption statistics show a very slight decline in percentage consumed. It is not clear whether the urban bias of the household consumption statistics can explain this discrepancy. Household statistics also do not account for food consumed away from home.
[a]Data for 2003.
[b]Data for 2000–02.

and reduced government intervention. New policies reduced restrictions on foreign investment (to encourage the entry of more foreign capital into the soybean market), restructured farm income taxes (to encourage greater investment in soybean production), lowered import tariffs on fertilizers and pesticides (to facilitate higher soybean yields), and eliminated the soybean export tax (to promote greater exports; Schnepf, Dohlman, and Bolling 2001). The government also devalued the Brazilian real, causing the cost of Brazilian beans on the world market to fall.

These policy changes spurred, as intended, the acceleration of production and exports. Production costs fell and returns to producers rose, encouraging them to bring more (low-cost) land into production (USDA 2004). And in light of lower production and transportation costs, vertically integrated TFCs, such as U.S.-based Cargill (the largest soybean exporter in Brazil) and Bunge (the largest soybean processor), increased their investments in the Brazilian crushing industry (Schnepf, Dohlman, and Bolling 2001).

The result of these policy shifts was a more than doubling of soybean oil production between 1990 and 2003, a more than tripling of exports, and one of the lowest soybean oil prices worldwide (Beckman 2005; Table 7.2). But somewhat ironically, the massive investment and growth in soybean oil production in the 1990s was not actually associated with increased consumption in Brazil: although the data are difficult to interpret, caloric consumption per person (already relatively high) appeared to decline or at least stabilize during the 1990s. Rather, production was set for the global market, facilitating dietary changes across the globe in such countries as China and India that were also liberalizing their markets in line with the globalization agenda.

Table 7.3   China: Soybean product imports and consumption
of soybean oil

Measure	1989–91	2002–04
Imports of soybeans (tons)	1,961,944	21,835,050
Imports of soybean oil (tons)	435,735	1,799,324
Calories available from soybean oil per person per day	27	125.95[a]

Source: Based on data from FAO (2006).
Note: The numbers represent 3-year averages around 1990 and 2003.
[a]Data for 2003.

China implemented new tax and import regulations to encourage soybean oil imports and greater domestic production in the 1990s (Beckman 2005). Brazil, able to produce at low prices, became a major source for China of soybeans (for crushing) and soybean oil (Hsu and Gale 2001). Between 2002 and 2004, Brazil remained a crucial supplier of soy to China when greater trade openness led to a doubling of agricultural imports, of which soy formed a large proportion (Gale 2005). Consequently, the amount of soybean oil available for consumption in China has soared (Table 7.3). Although these increases probably brought some benefits to underconsuming populations, consumption of vegetable oils in urban and some rural areas now exceeds recommended levels, a trend the Chinese government has identified as a source of concern, given the rapidly rising rates of obesity and chronic diseases in the country (Ma 2004; State Council Information Office 2004).

Recent trade policies will likely increase the ready availability of soybean oil: China's accession to the WTO has further reduced import tariffs and quantitative restrictions, which is predicted to significantly raise soybean oil imports, lower prices, and increase demand (Hsu and Gale 2001; Diao, Fan, and Zhang 2002; Fang and Beghin 2002; Fuller et al. 2003). Moreover, China continues to view Brazil as a good source of cheap soybeans: the government is planning to invest US$5 billion in Brazilian transportation systems to help that country continue to produce soybean oil at competitive prices (U.S. Commercial Service Brazil 2005).

India, although it is the world's fifth-largest producer of soybean oil, likewise imports Brazilian soybeans and oil. In the mid-1990s, India was a relatively small importer of vegetable oils; by 1998 the country had become the world's leading importer (Dohlman, Persaud, and Langes 2003). This rapid change can be directly related to market liberalization. In 1994–95, as part of unilateral efforts to liberalize trade and the need to follow international rules negotiated under the GATT (which culminated in the signing of the AoA and the founding of the WTO), India eliminated the state monopoly on vegetable oil imports (Dohlman,

Table 7.4   India: Soybean product imports and
consumption of soybean oil

Measure	1989–91	2002–04
Imports of soybeans (tons)	102	5,857
Imports of soybean oil (tons)	25,944	1,079,359
Calories available from soybean oil per person per day	10.73	40.94[a]

Source: Based on data from FAO (2006).
Note: The numbers represent 3-year averages around 1990 and 2003.
[a]Data for 2003.

Persaud, and Langes 2003). Facing low domestic production, imports poured in, especially of the cheapest oils: palm and soybean oil (Table 7.4).

Brazilian (and Argentinean) soybeans and oil were favored owing to their lower price and transportation costs relative to those of the United States. Brazil also had the advantage of a growing season and thus cheaper beans during the seasons of low production in India. The result was lower prices for vegetable oils, increased consumption, and increased share of consumption of imported oils: by the end of the 1990s, soybean oil accounted for 21 percent of consumption (and palm oil 38 percent) in India (Dohlman, Persaud, and Langes 2003). These numbers stand in stark contrast to the complete dominance of consumption of peanut, rapeseed, and cottonseed oil in the 1970s, a reflection of domestic production (Dohlman, Persaud, and Langes 2003). Today, prices of edible oils in India are more affected by soybean output in Brazil, Argentina, and the United States than by domestic production (Prasad 2004). Estimates of demand suggest that Indian consumers are sensitive to the prices of vegetable oils. According to Meenakshi and Ray (1999), the own price elasticity[2] for vegetable oils among urban consumers is −1.187.

This complex web of economic internationalization illustrates how a series of policy reforms in three different countries had the effect of integrating the global soybean oil market and, in so doing, facilitated the dietary convergence of soybean oil consumption worldwide. Convergence has occurred in the use of soybean oil not only in cooking but also in hydrogenated form in processed foods. Hydrogenation leads to the creation of *trans* fats, which increase the risk of coronary heart disease (FDA 2003). Governments in Brazil, the other countries of Mercosur,[3] Canada, and the United States have ruled accordingly that *trans* fats must be labeled on packaged foods (Hawkes 2004b). Yet dietary convergence of soybean oil consumption is likely to continue: the WTO is expected to reach an agreement in the next few years to further liberalize the vegetable oils market (Beckman 2005).

It is important to note, though, that the increasingly integrated nature of the soybean oil market is equally likely to facilitate dietary adaptation. The increased sup-

Table 7.5   Price and income elasticities for vegetable oils in China, northeast region (urban)

Commodity	Price elasticity	Income elasticity
Soybean oil	−0.8672	0.1722
Other vegetable oil	−1.3191	0.3178

Source: Fang and Beghin (2002).

Note: Price elasticities are income compensated.

ply of soybean oil on the world market is leading to greater competition with alternative oils, thereby providing a bottom-line incentive for increased differentiation and the development of oils to cater to higher-value market niches (Beckman 2005). The process is already in evidence. In China, for example, consumer demand for soybean oil in the northeast region (where soybean is the staple oil) is less affected by price than are nonstaple and condiment oils. The elasticities shown on Table 7.5 suggest that as their incomes increase, consumers are more likely to diversify their oil consumption (Fang and Beghin 2002).

TFCs are already beginning to adapt soybean oil to appeal to higher-value market niches—in this case, the wealthy "health-conscious consumer" aware of the detrimental health effects of *trans* fats. In September 2004, Monsanto, in partnership with Cargill, announced the development of the "Vistive™" soybean (Monsanto 2004). The bean has a low linolenic acid content, thus reducing the need for partial hydrogenation and, therefore, the *trans* fat content. Cargill intends to pay producers a premium for the beans, which will be passed onto food processors and eventually, as a component in processed foods, onto consumers willing to pay more for a *trans* fat–free product. In October 2004, competitor DuPont, in partnership with Bunge, also introduced a soybean with similar properties, "Nutrium™" (Bunge 2004).

In years to come, it is possible that leading companies will compete as much on high-priced oils for the health-conscious market as on low prices for the mass market; the former will encourage dietary adaptation whereas the latter its convergence. Thus, the same processes driving the global market integration of vegetable oils may well have very different outcomes for low- and higher-income consumers.

Role of FDI in Food Processing and Retailing in Changing Diet Quality

Like trade, investing across borders plays a fundamental role in integrating the global marketplace. It allows companies to buy, sell, and invest in other companies in other countries. FDI is one of the most important types of investment. FDI can be defined as a long-term investment by an individual, government, or enterprise from one country in an enterprise based in another, in which the foreign enterprise becomes a foreign affiliate of the parent (transnational) company. It is one of the processes through which vertical integration can take place and TFCs can grow. FDI in developing countries grew more than sixfold between 1990 and 2000, faster than either GDP or trade, and it is now the largest source of external financial input into these countries (UNCTAD 2000; Mody 2004).

The global regulatory environment around FDI has become significantly more liberal in past decades: between 1991 and 1999, there were 1,035 changes in regulations governing FDI worldwide—94 percent of these facilitated FDI by decreasing disincentives or increasing incentives for investment (UNCTAD 2000). Many of the new regulations were forged in trade agreements and investment treaties: the number of bilateral investment treaties rose from 181 at the end of 1980 to 1,856 at the end of 1999 (UNCTAD 2000).

As with trade, fewer barriers and more incentives to investment enable transnational companies to cut costs, gain market power, and obtain efficiencies in marketing and distribution. This process has brought huge changes in the global agrifood system, as already described in the case study of vegetable oils. Back in the 1970s, the first major phase of FDI in the food supply chain focused on producing raw commodities for export, as such TFCs as Cargill and Bunge invested abroad in oilcrops and cereals for export. In the 1980s, as liberalization accelerated, FDI began to shift away from raw materials for export to processed foods for the host market, as TFCs such as PepsiCo and Nestlé invested in foreign manufacturing facilities for such foods as sodas, confectionaries, baked goods, and snacks.

Food processing is now the most important recipient of FDI relative to other parts of the food system, and FDI is more important than trade in the global processed foods market. U.S. FDI in food processing companies grew from US$9 billion in 1980 to US$36 billion in 2000, with sales increasing from US$39.2 in 1982 to US$150 billion in 2000 (Bolling and Somwaru 2001). Trade, by contrast, generated a relatively small US$30 billion in processed food sales in 2000.

Investments in outlets selling processed foods have also soared, especially since 1990. FDI from U.S.-based supermarket chains grew to nearly US$13 billion in 1999, up from around US$4 billion in 1990 (Bolling and Somwaru 2001). In 1998, U.S.-based TFCs, such as McDonald's and KFC, invested US$5.7 billion in eating and drinking places overseas (Harris et al. 2002). Although a large proportion of this investment is still targeted at high-income countries, an increasing share is entering developing markets, notably in Latin America, Asia, and Central and Eastern Europe (Hawkes 2005).

FDI is thus playing a role in the nutrition transition by shaping the processed foods market and making more processed foods available to more people (Hawkes

2005). As detailed in Hawkes (2005), FDI has made it possible to lower prices, open up new purchasing channels, optimize the effectiveness of marketing and advertising, and, ultimately, increase sales. The result has been a dual process of dietary convergence toward processed foods consumption (albeit not among the lowest-income consumers) and dietary adaptation to a wider range of processed foods targeted at different niche markets, as illustrated well by the case of Mexico.

The globalization of the Mexican food economy is profoundly linked with its neighbor, the United States. Market integration between the two countries began in earnest in the 1980s and was greatly accelerated by NAFTA, signed by the United States, Mexico, and Canada in 1994. The agreement contained important provisions designed to facilitate foreign investment, including equal treatment of domestic and foreign investors, prohibition of applying certain performance requirements to foreign investors (such as minimum amount of domestic content in production), increased rights for foreign investors to retain profits and returns from initial investments, and the prohibition of new laws that would change the status of foreign investments once established (Zahniser and Link 2002; Zahniser 2005).

One consequence of NAFTA was a rapid acceleration of U.S. FDI in Mexican food processing and retailing. TFCs were attracted to Mexico because of its increasing purchasing power (a large, young, and growing population, including a middle class), close proximity, and rising urbanization. In 1999, U.S. companies invested US$5.3 billion in Mexico's food processing industry, a 25-fold increase from US$210 million in 1987 and more than double the US$2.3 billion in the year before NAFTA (Bolling, Elizalde, and Handy 1999; Zahniser and Link 2002). In 1998, sales from U.S. food industry affiliates in Mexico exceeded US$12 billion, easily surpassing the value of U.S. processed foods exports (US$2.8 billion; Zahniser and Link 2002). Nearly three-quarters of FDI was in highly processed foods, such as snacks, confectionaries, pasta, soft drinks, and mayonnaise.

NAFTA also stimulated huge investments from U.S.-based retailers, such as Wal-Mart and 7-Eleven (a joint U.S.-Mexican company), in supermarkets, discount stores, and convenience stores (Chavez 2002). The result was an explosive growth of such stores in Mexico, from fewer than 700 to 3,850 in 1997 and 5,729 in 2004 (Skully 1998; Snipes 2004). Walmex is now the nation's leading retailer, with 710 supermarkets and discount stores in 79 cities, serving 663 million customers and employing more people (109,075) than any other company in Mexico (Wal-Mart de Mexico 2004, 2005). Sales have grown rapidly over the past decade, increasing by 11 percent in 2004 to reach a record high of US$12.4 billion (Wal-Mart de Mexico 2004). The chain continues to grow, investing US$625 million in 2005 to open a further 77 stores (Snipes 2004). Walmex's success has left its three main Mexican rivals scrambling, crushing even the French supermarket giant Carrefour, which withdrew in 2005.

More dynamic than the supermarkets, though, are the convenience stores—sales from such stores rose by 17 percent in 2004 (Condesa Consulting 2005; Guthrie 2005). 7-Eleven doubled the number of its stores between 1999 and 2004 to 500 and plans to double in size again in the next few years (BMI 2005; Condesa Consulting 2005). The market leader, OXXO (owned by Coca-Cola subsidiary Femsa), tripled its stores to 3,500 between 1999 and 2004 and also plans further growth. In a little more than a decade, supermarkets, discounters, and convenience stores grew to account for 55 percent of all food retail in Mexico by 2004 (BMI 2005).

Modern retailers are ideally placed to facilitate the expansion of the processed foods market. The market for processed foods tends to grow through segmentation, which involves the development of new products targeting different market niches to activate and reactivate demand in a changing consumption environment (Wilkinson 2002). Supermarkets are ideally placed to deliver the adaptive tendencies of this market dynamic. (See also Chapter 6.) Through sheer size, they are able to make available a far wider range of processed foods than the traditional family-owned Mexican *tienda*. With a firm base of capital investment, they are able to take the risks inherent in introducing new foods. Supermarkets are equally able to deliver on price, being well placed to sell processed foods at lower costs stemming from economies of scale in storage, distribution, and marketing (Reardon et al. 2003).

A major reason for Wal-Mart's success is, in fact, its use of streamlined purchasing systems and advanced distribution logistics, which enable it to decrease prices while increasing profits. Reflecting its aggressive stance on low prices, Walmex's tagline is "low prices everyday." Convenience stores are also part of the processed foods revolution. They may not have the variety available at supermarkets, but they are far greater in number, more easily accessible, and open 24 hours a day (Condesa Consulting 2005). They tend to stock only processed foods high in fats, sweeteners, and salt—typically hot and cold processed snacks, soft drinks, doughnuts, and ice cream.

Despite the critical role played by supermarkets and convenience stores in the processed foods market, the role of thousands of traditional *tiendas* should not be forgotten. *Tiendas* (along with open markets) account for 45 percent of food retail in Mexico. Whereas modern retailers dominate the more affluent large and medium-sized cities, *tiendas* dominate in poorer, small towns and rural areas and cater to mainly low-income populations. In 2003, *tiendas* accounted for more than 90 percent of food purchases in small towns, compared with less than 30 percent in towns with populations of more than 250,000 (Condesa Consulting 2005). They have been critical in making soft drinks, snacks, and confectionary available in poorer neighborhoods and rural areas.

Coca-Cola has a formidable system of distribution to thousands of *tiendas* all over the country, actively encouraging owners to stock its drinks by providing such incentives as point-of-sale materials and refrigerators in return for an exclusivity agreement. By way of illustration, Coca-Cola Femsa sells around 70 percent of its products from small retailers in the Valley of Mexico, compared with a little more than 7 percent in supermarkets (Coca-Cola Femsa 2001). Yet the amount of food purchased from *tiendas* is declining yearly, and they are closing in the face of competition from modern retailers, particularly convenience stores: according to the Mexican Chamber of Commerce, for every convenience store that opens, five *tiendas* close (Condesa Consulting 2005).

FDI has fostered much of the growth of processed foods and modern retailing in Mexico, either directly by increasing the size of the market or indirectly by stimulating competition with domestic firms. Although companies from other countries have also invested, the United States still dominates FDI: approximately two-thirds of the US$6.4 billion FDI in Mexican agricultural and food industries between 1999 and 2004 was from the United States (Zahniser 2005). This investment has made more processed foods available to more people in more places and at more times and thus facilitated dietary convergence toward consumption.

The processed food sector expanded by 5–10 percent a year between 1995 and 2003, with recent sales growth being concentrated in snacks (12 percent increase between January and June 2004), baked goods (55.4 percent growth between 2000 and 2003), and dairy products (48.1 percent growth between 2000 and 2003; Condesa Consulting 2001; Snipes 2004). Between 1984 and 1998, purchases of refined carbohydrates increased by 37.2 percent and those of soda by 6.2 percent, while fruits and vegetables fell by nearly 30 percent (Rivera et al. 2004). Soft drink consumption is notoriously high: consumption of Coca-Cola drinks (mainly Coke™) rose from 275 8-ounce servings per person per year in 1992 to 487 in 2002, more than the 436 servings in the United States (Coca-Cola Company 1993; Leith 2003). Consumption of *comidas chatarras* ("junk food") is very high among children in parts of the country (Jimenez-Cruz, Bacardi Gascon, and Jones 2002b). Even in rural areas, it is typical for children to buy soft drinks and snacks every day at school breaks (Leatherman and Goodman 2005). Food demand studies suggest that consumers are sensitive to the prices of soft drinks, meaning that price declines will have stimulated consumption relative to other foods. Table 7.6 shows that Mexican consumers are more sensitive to the price of soft drinks (and other nonalcoholic beverages) than to that of any other food group.

Increased consumption of energy-dense, high-fat, high-sugar processed foods appears to be associated with increased intake of dietary fats and sugars in Mexico (Filozof et al. 2001; Bermudez and Tucker 2003; Jacoby 2004; Rivera et al. 2004). Calories from soda increased from 44 to 61 kilocalories per capita per day between 1992 and 2004 (Arroyo, Loria, and Mendez 2004). Between 1988 and 1999, the per-

Table 7.6 Price elasticities (Marshallian) for food groups, Mexico

Food	Price elasticity
Beef	−0.63
Pork	−0.13
Poultry	−0.82
Processed meat	−0.77
Seafood	−0.63
Vegetables	−0.81
Fruit	−0.71
Grains	−0.58
Beans	−0.43
Cheese	−0.72
Milk	−0.96
Nonalcoholic beverages	−1.14

Source: Dong, Gould, and Kaiser (2004).

centage of total energy intake from fat increased from 23.5 percent to 30.3 percent (Rivera et al. 2004). Although total fat intake is highest in wealthier regions, the greatest increases were seen in the poorer, southern regions.

At the same time, obesity and diabetes are reaching epidemic proportions in Mexico. Nearly 60 percent of adults in Mexico are overweight or obese, a 78-percent increase from 33 percent in 1988 (Rivera et al. 2004). The greatest relative changes have occurred in the poorest regions, and obesity is now quite high in some poor rural communities (Sánchez-Castillo et al. 2001). And obesity is not associated with high-quality diets: people who are underweight, normal weight, or overweight/obese are equally likely to suffer from anemia (Eckhardt et al. 2005). Obesity is also giving rise to an epidemic of diabetes that is growing fastest in the poor regions (Jimenez-Cruz, Bacardi Gascon, and Jones 2002a). More than 8 percent of Mexicans now have diabetes, which WHO estimates costs the country US$15 billion a year (Barcelo et al. 2003; Martorell 2005).

Market integration with the United States can be clearly associated with dietary convergence to processed foods in Mexico. But as the process of market segmentation continues, integration is also facilitating adaptation to a wider variety of processed foods. In the face of increasing concerns about obesity and diabetes, one of these adaptations is to "health." A high-value niche market for diet foods is now developing. Sales of diet foods rose by 20 percent in 2003, a rate that is expected to continue (*Latin America News Digest* 2004). Wal-Mart stocks more than 250 diet products, including low-carb chocolate and sugar-free candy, and reports that consumer spending on such products is increasing (Kelly 2005). In 2005, Coca-Cola introduced 20 new health drinks, which market analysts say is a response to fears that public concern about diabetes could lead to lower consumption of carbonated soft drinks (Aspin 2005). Diet foods are sold at much higher prices, targeting more affluent, health-conscious consumers (*Latin America News Digest* 2004; Kelly 2005).

In the meantime, supermarkets are developing another type of niche market. To attract low-income consumers, they are increasing their stock of lower-priced, private-label goods (such as cheaper, B-brand sodas) and introducing smaller pack sizes, which although more expensive per unit are more affordable because of their lower prices (BMI 2005). The integration of the processed foods market in Mexico is therefore likely to continue to have divergent outcomes between different income groups.

Role of Food Advertising and Promotion in Changing Diet Quality

Advertising and other forms of promotional marketing, such as trade and investment, are fundamental to the process of global market integration. Advertising provides a means to speed the flow of product spread by trade and FDI in the global marketplace, and it adds value to these products by improving their perceived value and desirability. In so doing, it provides an incentive for producers to produce more and for consumers to consume more. As put by Leslie (1995, 402), "located in a pivotal position between production and consumption, the advertising industry plays a key role in constituting geographic boundaries of markets in the internationalization of consumer culture."

Marketing has thus grown as both a process and a product of globalization, as a facilitator as well as an outcome. Globalization brought with it an increased incentive to advertise. In a larger, more dynamic marketplace, there is a need to turn over products quickly, and advertising can help speed up that process. It also provides a way to attract attention to new products and to create perceived differences between similar products.

Globalization brought with it more places to advertise. Television ownership spread rapidly through the developing world during the last decades of the twentieth century, accompanied in the 1990s by the market liberalization of public television and subsequent increase in commercial programming (James 2000). Technological development further broadened global communication networks, notably through the Internet and phone networks.

Globalization also brought to the developing world advertising agencies with the most expertise in designing marketing campaigns. As part of domestic reform and trade agreements, the market for advertising services became more liberal, with typically fewer restrictions on foreign ownership of agencies. These were thus able to "transnationalize" in the 1980s and 1990s through FDI, mergers, and acquisitions, growing—like the TFCs that commission their services and the media networks they use—into huge, vertically integrated corporations (Leslie 1995). From 1980 to 2004, global advertising expenditure rose from US$216 billion to US$512 billion (Worldwatch Institute 2004).

Owing to its visibility, promotional marketing has become one of the hallmarks of globalization. Food is a classic example—Coca-Cola signs are ubiquitous in countries around the world in what is often termed "Coca-Colonization." There can be no doubt that advertising and promotions have played a role in the nutrition transition—and in a way more obvious than trade and FDI. Marketing explicitly involves designing strategies and implementing activities to influence consumption habits and create demand. Companies use a multitude of highly sophisticated techniques to encourage more people to consume the product, more frequent consumption among people already familiar with the product, and consumption of more of the product at one time (Hawkes 2002). Products most frequently promoted tend to be the highly processed food introduced though FDI. The evidence shows that such advertising influences dietary habits among children (Hastings et al. 2003; McGinnis, Gootman, and Kraak 2006). Though this evidence comes mainly from the United States, studies also suggest that children in developing countries like food advertising and are interested in trying advertised foods, often buying products tied to special promotions (Hastings et al. 2007). In fact, there are reasons to believe that children in developing countries may be more influenced by marketing than those in developed countries. Children in developing countries are less likely to have a sophisticated understanding of modern marketing techniques, and, in general, marketing theory states that promotion has a greater effect on *category* consumption in "unsaturated" markets where there is still unrealized potential.

Although it appears homogeneous, global marketing is in fact a highly adaptive process. It involves not simply placing the same marketing campaigns around the world, but tailoring the medium and the message to multiple and diverse audiences (Keegan 1999). This strategy of "think global act local" or "glocal" is based on the observation that, as put by the Coca-Cola chief executive officer, "the forces that are making the world more connected and homogeneous are simultaneously triggering a powerful desire for local autonomy and preservation of unique cultural identity" (Daft 2000).

TFCs aim for greater global consumption, but they do it by recognizing the differences between markets: in new markets, campaigns focus on creating consumer awareness of the brand through introductory advertising; in emerging markets, the focus is on expanding consumer perception of possible consumption occasions; and in developed markets, there is a greater emphasis on public relations (Hawkes 2002).

Within these general categories, market research plays an important role in helping to design highly targeted marketing campaigns. Marketing thus has a homogeneous aim but operates heterogeneously, as illustrated well by the dynamic advertising market in Thailand.

The advertising industry in Thailand is among the most developed, dynamic, and creative in the region (Prystay 2004). Advertising revenues have grown at double-digit figures in recent years, and in 2004 stood at approximately 85 billion baht (US$2 billion; *Nation [Thailand]* 2004).[4] The country has a tradition of openness to foreign trade and investment, and advertising is not subject to any regulations on foreign participation (USTR 2005). Advertising in Thailand has been stimulated by the creation of a more competitive marketplace through the influx of foreign brands in the wake of trade agreements.

Soft drinks, snacks, and fast food are heavily advertised in Thailand: a 2004 survey found a total of 67 different snack products advertised to children between 7:00 a.m. and 10:30 a.m. on weekends (Mulchand 2004). Coca-Cola, Pepsi, KFC, and McDonald's are all major market players and advertise aggressively to their main target audience: teenagers. To appeal to teens, sports, music, and movies have become major promotional vehicles (Hawkes 2002; Coca-Cola 2003). Soccer is sponsored because the sport is the "top passion" for teens and young people, while music is sponsored to target those youth not interested in sports (*Nation [Thailand]* 2000). The aim of these techniques is to encourage food consumption habits that teens will carry into adulthood.

Another commonly used technique in Thailand is giveaways, something extremely popular with young people. McDonald's, for example, ran a campaign in 1998 giving away every day for 28 days a free "Snoopy" dressed in a different "cultural costume" with the purchase of an Extra Value Meal. The campaign sold 2.5 million meals, boosting revenues by more than 80 million baht (US$1.95 million; Hawkes 2002). The technique specifically aims to encourage a daily consumption habit.

To attract different market segments, KFC also regularly introduces new menus, such as the "Yum Dance Menu" introduced in 2003 designed to attract more women aged 15–39 into the restaurants (BMI 2003). Teenagers make up 40 percent of KFC's customer base (*Nation [Thailand]* 2003) and are the largest consumer segment in the US$5.2-million soft-drinks market. Young people aged 5–24 spend 160 million baht annually on snacks (US$3.9 million; Mulchand 2004). The dynamism of promotional marketing in Thailand has led to concerns that it is encouraging poor-quality diets in young people. The prevalence of overweight and obesity among children and adolescents has increased significantly in recent decades, rising from 7.7 percent to 13.2 percent between 1991 and 1996 among men and from 15.7 percent to 25.0 percent among women (Kosulwat 2002). It is also high among children, reaching almost 11 percent in parts of the poorer northeast of the country (Langendijk et al. 2003).

Health advocacy groups in Thailand are now calling for restrictions on food advertising (Hawkes 2007). The government has already restricted advertising of alcohol, and in 2004 it met with advertising representatives and NGOs to discuss banning TV food advertisements that target children through "prize draws, freebies, and discounts" for children aged 5–16 (Hawkes 2004a; *Knight Ridder Tribune Business News* 2004; Mulchand 2004). Health concerns are also affecting the soft drinks and fast food markets. According to a 2004 survey conducted by an advertising agency, the majority of middle- and high-income earners in Bangkok are starting to shun foods with high fat levels, including fast food; 67 percent of respondents in all age groups said they ate in fast food restaurants less than once a week (*Thai Press Reports* 2004).

The case of Thailand exemplifies the role of advertising in market integration. Advertising and promotions spread information about products to speed up their flow through the marketplace, and they increase the market competitiveness for similar products. Global marketing is facilitating the spread of global brands, but it is also stimulating local competition and affecting prices. In so doing, it is helping to expand sales of not just food brands but food categories. Yet, ironically, one reason for its success is that it caters to the adaptive nature of a dynamic marketplace. Its message and medium—and the products it advertises—are constantly redefined, following as well as creating market trends.

An important question here is whether advertising and other forms of promotion have a disproportionate influence on groups of lower socioeconomic status. Somewhat surprisingly, there is a paucity of studies on the subject, so no clear conclusions can be drawn (McGinnis, Gootman, and Kraak 2006). But as long as the fundamental and structural forces driving global market integration need advertising, advertising will continue to seek new targets. As the wealthy turn away from fast food, it is likely that advertising will increasingly target lower-income consumers, whose desire for such food has already been stimulated by their earlier popularity among wealthier groups.

Conclusion: Toward More Structural, Institutional Policies in Diet-Related Prevention of Chronic Diseases

Implications of the Globalization of Agrifood Systems for the Diets of the Poor

Globalization is often viewed as "Coca-Colonization"—a homogeneous process with homogeneous outcomes. This chapter has attempted to show that globalization practices produce different outcomes—they produce, in other words, convergence and differentiation. Just as the increased global consumption of oils, meats, and sweeteners is a hallmark of globalization, so is the creation of niche markets. Both dietary convergence and adaptation stem from simultaneous processes of increasing concentration and dynamism in the global food market. Thus, the creation of similarity and difference is simply following the logic of the global marketplace.

The chapter has similarly attempted to show that the combination of dietary convergence and adaptation arising from globalization is an important dynamic in changing diets worldwide. Others have argued that the increased differentiation brought by globalization in fact promotes better diets through greater diversity (Regmi, Ballenger, and Putnam 2004). It is also often pointed out that income-induced changes in demand is the key driver, rather than changes on the supply side. Indeed, increasing national income is associated with increasing rates of obesity and chronic diseases (Ezzati et al. 2005; Strong et al. 2005). In practice, it is difficult to disentangle the effects of income changes from globalization as a whole: although income changes provide the conditions that permit transitions to take place, the nature and direction of the transition is affected by changes in supply and demand. Pingali and Khwaja (2004) attempt to take both into account by conceptualizing the nutrition transition as occurring in two stages: first, "income-induced diet diversification," when consumers move away from inferior goods to superior foods (for example, substituting traditional staples for meat); and second, "diet globalization," when the influences of globalization become more marked, with increased consumption of proteins, sugars, and fats.

This chapter has focused on the more negative elements of the nutrition transition stemming from changes in the food supply. It has also tried to grapple with the implications of the combination of convergence and differentiation for the diets of the poor. The three case studies discussed raise serious concerns that the duality of processes will lead to poor-quality, obesogenic diets among low-income groups, as in the industrialized world. Market integration increases the incentive to sell cheap (low-quality) food around the world, while simultaneously increasing the incentive to create market niches. "Sound" business practices, fostered by national and global market liberalization policies, could thus be facilitating the uneven development of dietary habits.

An important dynamic here is not just market integration itself but the context of existing social bifurcation in which it is operating (as proposed by Labonte 2004). People with more money, information, and education are more likely to demand higher-value products and less likely to be influenced by advertising. Conversely, poorer people are less flexible and more likely to be influenced by the mass production trends of the global marketplace—the economic and cultural convergence toward low diet quality, cheap vegetable oils, *trans* fats, "B-brand" processed foods,

and advertised products whose desirability has been stimulated by their earlier popularity among wealthier groups. Higher-income groups are more likely to move on and
adapt the more expensive, health-market niches—*trans* fat–free vegetable oils and
highly processed diet foods.

In other words, what originally started as differentiation to a more privileged
Western-style diet will become readily available as cheap (and profitable) food for the
developing poor. Such dynamics already appear to be driving increased obesity and
diabetes rates among the poor. A recent review found that obesity can no longer be
considered a problem limited to groups of high socioeconomic status in developing
countries, and that the burden of obesity moves toward the poor as GNP increases
(Monteiro et al. 2004).

To better understand these dynamics, more must be done to grapple with how
economic and commercial practices within the global marketplace are unevenly
affecting diets, and how precisely these practices are spurring changes in the consumption habits of poor, more vulnerable people in developing countries. Although there
is a generally good understanding of the homogeneous characteristics of the nutrition
transition—increased consumption of high-fat, high-sugar, energy-dense foods—
relatively little information exists on its heterogeneous effects on communities and
households. More research is needed on how diets in poor households are changing,
what foods people are eating, and how all these dietary considerations might be linked
to structural and institutional factors prevalent in the global economy. This important research gap needs to be addressed urgently.

Policy Implications

Governments have tended to respond, if at all, to these powerful global forces with
relatively "soft," consumer-oriented policy options, such as education and nutrition
labeling. Dietary adaptation shows clearly that consumers do have real clout in the
modern food system—and that labeling can be a powerful incentive for changing
behavior in the food industry. But the consumers most able to adapt and respond to
information tend to be those already educated and knowledgeable about nutrition
(Hawkes 2004b). The current conflicts between supply-side economics and
demand-side dietary concerns, and the possibility that dietary convergence will
have negative implications for the poor, thus demands a response on both sides.
Tougher, more highly structural responses are needed to address problems with
structural roots.

Developing more highly structural policies to address the spread of poor-quality
diets and diet-related chronic diseases is, however, a significant challenge—and not
least because it means confronting the forces of the global marketplace. It is a double-
edged challenge, because global economic development of a certain type is associated
with better health—higher GDPs are associated with higher life expectancies, which

is good for the poor. And if economic development lifts people out of poverty, they will be more able to demand and consume higher-quality foods.

What is needed, therefore, is better economic development through upstream changes in the global marketplace, aiming at large population-level effects to improve diet quality. This need invariably requires looking beyond the health sector as narrowly defined, and enters into debates and policy arenas dealt with by other sectors and disciplines. The need for a cross-sectoral response has been recognized in the most important global policy instrument developed to address diet-related chronic diseases—WHO's Strategy on Diet, Physical Activity, and Health (WHO 2004).

Restricting food marketing to children is an example of a structural response to the problem, because it provides a strong incentive for companies to create and promote healthier products. Such approaches are being more widely implemented, although the powerful incentives created by FDI and trade to achieve in the global marketplace make restrictions prone to being undermined (Hawkes 2004a, 2007).

Two areas that could be more fundamental entry points for change in the global marketplace are FDI and agriculture. Many of the decisions made about diet quality are in fact decisions about FDI made by transnational food companies and investors. FDI represents a single entry point to many of the dynamics influencing the production, sale, and advertising of energy-dense, nutrient-poor foods in the global marketplace and thus could be an effective lever for change (Hawkes 2005). Because the amount of FDI will always outweigh any funding for chronic-disease prevention, there is a real need to harness and rechannel FDI. To accomplish this redirection, a policy framework is needed for FDI that balances the needs of industry and investors with public health.

Agriculture is another upstream entry point for change. Agriculture plays a fundamental role in food production, and there are mutual benefits arising for both the agricultural and health sectors in promoting healthier diets. Both these sectors would benefit from understanding the effect on diet quality *and* rural livelihoods of economic policies regarding industry-driven food systems, as well as from understanding the nature of consumer demand for healthy foods.

The benefits of these approaches are that they influence markets, not just the products sold in markets. And at the global scale, even relatively small changes can have big effects. It is also a long-term approach that could help build international capacity and political capital and could reinforce national action. Perhaps most important, it is the approach that is most likely to benefit the poor.

Notes

1. See Lang (1997, 1999); McMurray and Smith (2001); Babinard and Pinstrup-Andersen (2001); Evans et al. (2001); Gehlhar and Coyle (2001); Caballero and Popkin (2002); WHO

(2002); Beaglehole and Yach (2003); Chopra and Darnton-Hill (2004); FAO (2004a); Regmi, Ballenger, and Putnam (2004); UN SCN (2004); Hawkes (2005); Yach, Beaglehole, and Hawkes (2005).

2. The percentage change in quantity demanded of a food item that occurs in response to a percentage change in the price of the same food item.

3. The Southern Common Market between Argentina, Brazil, Paraguay, and Uruguay.

4. All currency equivalents use December 2005 exchange rates and are therefore not a precise representation of changes over time.

References

Arroyo, P., A. Loria, and O. Mendez. 2004. Changes in the household calorie supply during the 1994 economic crisis in Mexico and its implications for the obesity epidemic. *Nutrition Reviews* 62 (7): S163–S168.

Aspin, C. 2005. Coke Mexico in health push amid spiraling diabetes, *Reuters,* August 30.

Babinard, J., and P. Pinstrup-Andersen. 2001. Globalization and nutrition. In *The unfinished agenda: Perspectives on overcoming hunger, poverty, and environmental degradation,* ed. P. Pinstrup-Andersen and R. Pandya-Lorch. Washington, D.C.: International Food Policy Research Institute.

Barcelo, A., C. Aedo, S. Rajpathak, and S. Robles. 2003. The cost of diabetes in Latin America and the Caribbean. *Bulletin of the WHO* 81: 19–27.

Baum, F., ed. 2003. *The new public health,* 2nd ed. Oxford: Oxford University Press.

Beaglehole, R., and D. Yach. 2003. Globalisation and the prevention and control of non-communicable disease: The neglected chronic diseases of adults. *Lancet (U.K. edition)* 362 (9387): 903–908.

Beckman, C. 2005. *Vegetable oils: Competition in a global market.* Bi-weekly Bulletin 18. Ottawa: Agriculture and Agri-Food Canada.

Berlinguer, G. 1999. Globalization and global health. *International Journal of Health Services* 29 (3): 579–595.

Bermudez, O. I., and K. L. Tucker. 2003. Trends in dietary patterns of Latin American populations. *Cadernos de Saúde Pública* 19 (Suppl. 1): S87–S99.

BMI (Business Monitor International). 2003. FDI alert—KFC spreads its wings in Thailand. *Business Monitor International FDI Alert,* July 11. London.

———. 2005. *Mexico food and drink report Q3 2005.* London.

Bolling, C., and A. Somwaru. 2001. U.S. food companies access foreign markets though direct investment. *Food Review* 24 (3): 23–28.

Bolling, C., J. C. Elizalde, and C. Handy. 1999. U.S. firms invest in Mexico's processed food industry. *Food Review* 22 (2): 26–30.

Bruinsma, J. 2003. *World agriculture: Towards 2015/2030—An FAO perspective*. London: Earthscan.

Bunge. 2004. DuPont, Bunge introduce new soybean oil that eliminates *trans* fats in foods. Press release. White Plains, N.Y.

Caballero, B., and B. M. Popkin, eds. 2002. *The nutrition transition: Diet and disease in the developing world*. London: Academic Press.

Chavez, M. 2002. The transformation of Mexican retailing with NAFTA. *Development Policy Review* 20 (4): 503–513.

Chopra, M., and I. Darnton-Hill. 2004. Tobacco and obesity epidemics: Not so different after all? *British Medical Journal (Clinical Research edition)* 328 (7455): 1558–1560.

Coca-Cola Company. 2003. Thailand—First in Asia to launch Fanta blueberry splash. Coca-Cola press release. February 26.

———. 1993. *Annual report 1993*. Atlanta, Ga.

———. 2001. *Annual report 2001*. Monterrey, Mexico.

Condesa Consulting. 2001. *Mexico product brief: The Mexican market for processed foods 2001*. GAIN (Global Agriculture Information Network) Report MX1099. Washington, D.C.: U.S. Department of Agriculture, Foreign Agricultural Service.

———. 2005. *Mexico's retail food sector 2005*. GAIN Report MX5303. Washington, D.C.: U.S. Department of Agriculture, Foreign Agricultural Service.

Cornia, G. A. 2001. Globalization and health: Results and options. *Bulletin of the World Health Organization* 79 (9): 834–841.

Daft, D. 2000. Comment and analysis—Back to classic Coke: Coca-Cola went astray by becoming over-centralised, slow, and insensitive. *Financial Times (London)*, March 27.

Diao, X., S. Fan, and X. Zhang. 2002. *How China's WTO accession affects rural economy in the less-developed regions: A multi-region general equilibrium analysis*. Washington, D.C.: International Food Policy Research Institute.

Dohlman, E., S. Persaud, and R. Langes. 2003. *India's edible oil sector: Import's fill rising demand*. Electronic Output Report OCS-0903-01. Washington, D.C.: U.S. Department of Agriculture, Economic Research Service.

Dollar, D. 2001. Is globalization good for your health? *Bulletin of the World Health Organization* 79 (9): 827–833.

Dong, D., B. W. Gould, and H. M. Kaiser. 2004. Food demand in Mexico: An application of the Amemiya-Tobin approach to the estimation of a censored food system. *American Journal of Agricultural Economics* 86 (4): 1094–1107.

Drewnowski, A., and B. M. Popkin. 1997. The nutrition transition: New trends in the global diet. *Nutrition Reviews* 55 (2): 31–43.

Eckhardt, C. L., L. E. Torheim, E. Monterrubio, S. Barquera, and M. Ruel. 2005. Overweight women remain at risk for anemia in countries undergoing the nutrition transition. Presentation at the 18th International Nutrition Congress, September 19–22, Durban, South Africa.

Evans, M., R. C. Sinclair, C. Fusimalohi, and V. Liava'a. 2001. Globalization, diet, and health: An example from Tonga. *Bulletin of the World Health Organization* 79 (9): 856–862.

Ezzati, M., S. Vander Hoorn, C. M. M. Lawes, R. Leach, W. P. T. James, A. D. Lopez, A. Rodgers, and C. J. L. Murray. 2005. Rethinking the "diseases of affluence" paradigm: Global patterns of nutritional risks in relation to economic development. *PLoS Medicine* 2 (5): 404–412.

Fang, C., and J. C. Beghin. 2002. Urban demand for edible oils and fats in China: Evidence from households survey data. *Journal of Comparative Economics* 30 (4): 732–753.

FAO (Food and Agriculture Organization of the United Nations). 2004a. *Globalization of food systems in developing countries: Impact on food security and nutrition.* Rome.

———. 2004b. *The state of agricultural commodity markets 2004.* Rome.

———. 2005. FAOSTAT. Rome.

———. 2006. FAOSTAT. Rome.

FDA (U.S. Food and Drug Administration). 2003. Federal register final rule: *Trans* fatty acids in nutrition labeling, nutrient content claims, and health claims. *Federal Register* 68 (133): 41433–41506.

Feacham, R. G. A. 2001. Globalisation is good for your health, mostly. *British Medical Journal* 323 (7311): 504–506.

Filozof, C., C. Gonzalez, M. Sereday, C. Maza, and J. Braguinsky. 2001. Obesity prevalence and trends in Latin-American countries. *Obesity Reviews* 2 (2): 99–106.

Fuller, F., J. Beghin, S. De Cara, J. Fabiosa, C. Fang, and H. Matthey. 2003. China's accession to the WTO: What is at stake for agricultural markets? *Review of Agricultural Economics* 25 (2): 399–414.

Gale, F. 2005. *China's agricultural imports boomed during 2003–04.* Washington, D.C.: U.S. Department of Agriculture.

Gehlhar, M., and W. Coyle. 2001. Global food consumption and impacts on trade patterns. In *Changing structure of global food consumption and trade,* ed. A. Regmi. Washington, D.C.: U.S. Department of Agriculture, Economic Research Service.

Guthrie, A. 2005. Snack-food stores in Mexico grab double-digit annual sales gains. *Wall Street Journal,* February 2.

Harris, J. M., P. R. Kaufman, S. W. Martinez, and C. Price. 2002. *The U.S. food marketing system, 2002.* Washington, D.C.: U.S. Department of Agriculture.

Harris, R. L., and M. J. Seid. 2004. Globalization and health in the new millennium. *Perspectives on Global Development and Technology* 3 (1/2): 1–46.

Hastings, G., M. Stead, L. McDermott, A. Forsyth, A. M. MacKintosh, M. Rayner, C. Godfrey, M. Caraher, and K. Angus. 2003. *Does food promotion influence children? A systematic review of the evidence.* London: Food Standards Agency.

Hastings, G., L. McDermott, K. Angus, M. Stead, and S. Thomson. 2007. The extent, nature, and effects of food promotion to children: A review of the evidence. Technical paper prepared for the World Health Organization. Geneva: World Health Organization.

Hawkes, C. 2002. Marketing activities of global soft drink and fast food companies in emerging markets: A review. In *Globalization, diets and noncommunicable diseases.* Geneva: World Health Organization.

———. 2004a. *Marketing food to children: The global regulatory environment.* Geneva: World Health Organization.

———. 2004b. *Nutrition labels and health claims: The global regulatory environment.* Geneva: World Health Organization.

———. 2005. The role of foreign direct investment in the nutrition transition. *Public Health Nutrition* 8 (4): 357–365.

———. 2007. Regulating food marketing to young people worldwide. *American Journal of Public Health* 97 (11): 1962–1973.

Heffernan, W. D., D. H. Constance, L. Gouveia, and E. Mingione. 1994. Transnational corporations and the globalization of the food system. In *From Columbus to Conagra: The globalization of agriculture and food,* ed. A. Bonanno, L. Busch, and W. H. Friedland. Lawrence, Kans., U.S.A.: University Press of Kansas.

Hsu, H.-H., and F. Gale. 2001. *China: Agriculture in transition.* Washington, D.C.: U.S. Department of Agriculture.

Huynen, M. T. E., P. Martens, and H. B. M. Hilderink. 2005. The health impacts of globalisation: A conceptual framework. *Globalization and Health* 1 (14). Available at http://www.globalization andhealth.com/content/1/1/14.

IBGE (Instituto Brasileiro de Geografi a e Estatística). 2004. *Pesquisa de orçamentos familiares 2002–2003: Análise da disponibilidade domiciliar de alimentos e do estado nutricional no Brasil.* Rio de Janeiro.

Jacoby, E. 2004. The obesity epidemic in the Americas: Making healthy choices the easiest choices. *Revista Panamericana de Salud Publica* 15 (4): 278–284.

James, J. 2000. Do consumers in developing countries gain or lose from globalization? *Journal of Economic Issues* 34 (3): 537–551.

Jimenez-Cruz, A., M. Bacardi Gascon, and E. Jones. 2002a. The fattening burden of type-2 diabetes on Mexicans. *Diabetes Care* 27 (5): 1213–1215.

———. 2002b. Fruit, vegetable, soft drink, and high-fat containing snack consumption among Mexican children. *Archives of Medical Research* 33 (1): 74–80.

Keegan, W. J. 1999. *Global marketing management*. Englewood Cliffs, , N.J., U.S.A.: Prentice-Hall.

Kelly, J. T. 2005. Slimming down. *Business Mexico* 14 (10): 8–11.

Kennedy, G., G. Nantel, and P. Shetty. 2004. Globalization of food systems in developing countries: A synthesis of country case studies. Food and Nutrition Paper 83. Rome: Food and Agriculture Organization of the United Nations.

Kickbusch, I., and E. de Leeuw. 1999. Global public health: Revisiting healthy public policy at the global level. *Health Promotion International* 14 (4): 285–288.

Knight Ridder Tribune Business News. 2004. Thailand may ban snack-food TV ads that lure children with freebies, March 30.

Kosulwat, V. 2002. The nutrition and health transition in Thailand. *Public Health Nutrition* 5 (1A): 183–189.

Labonte, R. 2004. Globalization, health, and the free trade regime: Assessing the links. *Perspectives on Global Development and Technology* 3 (1/2): 47–72.

Lang, T. 1997. The public health impact of globalization of food trade. In *Diet, nutrition and chronic disease: Lessons from contrasting worlds,* ed. P. Shetty and K. McPherson. Chichester, U.K.: John Wiley and Sons.

———. 1999. Diet, health and globalization: Five key questions. *Proceedings of the Nutrition Society* 58 (2): 335–343.

Langendijk, G., S. Wellings, M. van Wyk, S. J. Thompson, J. McComb, and K. Chusilp. 2003. The prevalence of childhood obesity in primary school children in urban Khon Kaen, Northeast Thailand. *Asia Pacific Journal of Clinical Nutrition* 12 (1): 66–72.

Latin America News Digest. 2004. Diet products consumption in Mexico up 20 Pct Y/Y 2003, April 14.

Leatherman, T. L., and A. Goodman. 2005. Coca-Colonization of diets in the Yucatan. *Social Science and Medicine* 61 (44): 833–846.

Lee, K., K. Buse, and S. Fustukian. 2002. *Health policy in a globalising world.* Cambridge: Cambridge University Press.

Lee, K., A. J. McMichael, C. Butler, M. Ahern, and D. Bradley. 2002. Global change and health—The good, the bad, and the evidence. *Global Change and Human Health* 3 (1): 16–19.

Leith, S. 2003. Coca-Cola still dominates lucrative Mexican soft drink market. *Atlanta Journal and Constitution,* September 7.

Leslie, D. 1995. Global scan: The globalization of advertising agencies, concepts, and campaigns. *Economic Geography* 71 (4): 402–426.

Ma, J. 2004. Blame for health crisis placed on poor knowledge; Leading official says more needs to be done to teach public about healthy diets. *South China Morning Post,* October 13.

Martinez, S. W. 2002. *Vertical coordination of marketing systems: Lessons from poultry, egg, and pork industries.* Washington, D.C.: U.S. Department of Agriculture.

Martorell, R. 2005. Diabetes and Mexicans: Why the two are linked. *Preventing Chronic Disease* 2 (1): 1–5.

McGinnis, J. M., J. A. Gootman, and V. I. Kraak. 2006. *Food marketing to children and youth: Threat or opportunity?* Washington, D.C.: National Academies Press.

McMurray, C., and R. Smith. 2001. Diseases of globalization: Socioeconomic transition and health. London: Earthscan.

Meenakshi, J., and R. Ray. 1999. Regional differences in India's expenditure pattern: A complete demand systems approach. *Journal of International Development* 11 (6): 47–74.

Mody, A. 2004. Is FDI integrating the world economy? *World Economy* 27 (8): 1195–1222.

Monsanto. 2004. Monsanto launches VISTIVE™ soybeans: Will provide a trans fats solution for the food industry. News release, Monsanto, St. Louis, Mo., U.S.A.

Monteiro, C., E. C. Moura, W. L. Conde, and B. M. Popkin. 2004. Socioeconomic status and obesity in adult populations of developing countries: A review. *Bulletin of the World Health Organization* 82 (12): 940–946.

Mulchand, S. 2004. Thai clamp-down on snack food ads looms. *Media (Hong Kong),* April 9.

Nation (Thailand). 2000. Passion for sports fuels cola war, December 18.

———. 2003. KFC does a "Yum Dance" for teens, July 11.

———. 2004. Ad revenues set to rise by 20%, June 28.

Pingali, P., and Y. Khwaja. 2004. Globalization of Indian diets and the transformation of food supply systems. ESA Working Paper 04-05, Agricultural and Development Economics Division. Rome: Food and Agriculture Organization of the United Nations.

Prasad, M. 2004. E-oil market in India linked to Brazil, Argentina, and U.S. soya moods. *Asia Africa Intelligence Wire,* February 27.

Prystay, C. 2004. Tickled in Thailand by ads with attitude. *Far Eastern Economic Review,* May 13.

Reardon, T., C. P. Timmer, C. B. Barrett, and J. Berdegué. 2003. The rise of supermarkets in Africa, Asia, and Latin America. *American Journal of Agricultural Economics* 85 (5): 1140–1146.

Regmi, A., N. Ballenger, and J. Putnam. 2004. Globalisation and income growth promote the Mediterranean diet. *Public Health Nutrition* 7 (7): 977–983.

Rivera, J. A., S. Barquera, T. Gonzalez-Cossyo, G. Olaiz, and J. Sepulveda. 2004. Nutrition transition in Mexico and in other Latin American countries. *Nutrition Reviews* 62 (7): S149–S157.

Sánchez-Castillo, C. P., J. J. Lara, A. R. Villa, M. Escobar, H. Gutierrez, A. Chavez, and W. P. T. James. 2001. Unusually high prevalence rates of obesity in four Mexican rural communities. *European Journal of Clinical Nutrition* 55 (10): 833–840.

Schnepf, R. D., E. Dohlman, and C. Bolling. 2001. *Agriculture in Brazil and Argentina: Developments and prospects for major field crops.* Washington, D.C.: U.S. Department of Agriculture.

Skully, D. 1998. Mexican supermarkets spur new produce distribution system. *Agricultural Outlook* (August): 14–16.

Snipes, K. 2004. *Mexico exporter guide: Annual 2004.* GAIN Report MX 4313. Washington, D.C.: U.S. Department of Agriculture, Foreign Agricultural Service.

State Council Information Office. 2004. Material for the press conference of the State Council Information office: The nutrition and health status of the Chinese people. Mimeo.

Strong, K., C. Mathers, S. Leeder, and R. Beaglehole. 2005. Preventing chronic diseases: How many lives can we save? *Lancet* 366 (9496): 1578–1582.

Thai Press Reports. 2004. Bangkok consumers starting to avoid fatty food, December 31.

UNCTAD (United Nations Conference on Trade and Development). 2000. *World investment report 2000.* Geneva.

UN/SCN (United Nations System Standing Committee on Nutrition). 2004. *Fifth report on the world nutrition situation: Nutrition for improved development outcomes.* Geneva.

U.S. Commercial Service Brazil. 2005. *U.S. country commercial guide: Brazil.* São Paulo.

USDA (U.S. Department of Agriculture). 2004. *Brazil: Soybean expansion expected to continue in 2004/05.* Washington, D.C.

USTR (U.S. Trade Representative). 2005. *2005 national trade estimate report on foreign trade barriers.* Washington, D.C.

Wal-Mart de Mexico. 2004. *Annual report 2004.* Delegación Miguel Hidalgo, Mexico: Wal-Mart de Mexico.

———. 2005. About us. Available at http://www.walmartmexico.com.mx/acercai.html?id=75.69443742506317. Accessed August 2005.

WHO (World Health Organization). 2002. *Globalization, diets, and noncommunicable diseases.* Geneva.

———. 2004. *Global strategy on diet, physical activity, and health.* Geneva.

Wilkinson, J. 2002. The final foods industry and the changing face of the global agro-food system. *Sociologia Ruralis* 42 (4): 329–346.

Woodward, D., N. Drager, R. Beaglehole, and D. Lipson. 2001. Globalization and health: A framework for analysis and action. *Bulletin of the World Health Organization* 79 (9): 875–881.

Worldwatch Institute. 2004. World and U.S. advertising expenditure 1950–2004. Available at http://www.worldwatch.org/globaltrends. Accessed September 2004.

Yach, D., and D. Bettcher. 1998. The globalization of public health, I: Threats and opportunities. *American Journal of Public Health* 88 (5): 735–738.

Yach, D., R. Beaglehole, and C. Hawkes. 2005. Globalisation and noncommunicable diseases. In *Promoting health: Global perspectives,* ed. A. Scriven and G. S. Basingstoke. New York: Palgrave Macmillan.

Zahniser, S. 2005. *NAFTA at 11: The growing integration of North American agriculture.* Washington, D.C.: U.S. Department of Agriculture.

Zahniser, S., and J. Link. 2002. *Effects of North American Free Trade Agreement on agriculture and the rural economy.* Washington, D.C.: U.S. Department of Agriculture.

Economic Policies in Developing Countries to Make Globalization Work for the Poor

Isher Judge Ahluwalia

This essay focuses on what policymakers in developing countries can do to make globalization work for the poor in their own countries. I will use my comparative advantage as an economist to stress what can be done in economic policy to improve the lot of the poor, both through national policymaking and through international negotiations to mould the international economic environment.

Globalization offers new opportunities but also poses new challenges. Developing countries need to pursue economic policies that enable them to exploit these opportunities while overcoming the challenges that arise in the process of globalization and that stand in the way of pro-poor growth. By opening their markets to foreign trade and negotiating with other trading partners to open their markets, developing countries can participate in the process of globalization, which allows for greater opportunities of trade in goods and services among nations, making it possible for these countries to attain higher growth and less poverty.

However, to translate the potential benefit of greater exports into actual gains, policymakers in these countries have to prepare their economies to compete in the global marketplace by cutting costs and improving the quality of their goods and services. This effort often requires economic policy changes in the direction of market-oriented reforms, as well as sound macroeconomic policies. The process of adjusting to market-oriented policy reforms in the course of globalization also requires that the policymakers build social safety nets for those who are adversely affected, particularly the poor.

Growth: A Necessary, but Not Sufficient, Condition

Sustained medium-to-high economic growth rates at low inflation rates are necessary but by no means sufficient to reduce poverty in developing countries. In Essay 1, M. S. Swaminathan rightly observes that trickle down takes time, and that the poor must be helped to move out of poverty. I would only add that direct programs for poverty alleviation need to focus on creating capabilities and assets for the poor, so that they can join the ranks of the nonpoor in a growing economy.

A realistic pursuit of pro-poor growth in most developing countries requires a larger role for the private sector and a redefined role for the public sector. A common problem facing most developing countries today is that governments do not have resources to accelerate significantly the pace of public investment, while pressures to increase government subsidies grow. The governments are also not enacting enough policy reforms to create conditions in which private investment can replace public investment in many areas in which, previously, only public investment could do the job.

Similarly, most of these countries are faced with poor productivity performance, particularly in the public sector, where commercial and economic considerations are often dominated by political considerations in matters of economic management. In such situations, it is important to evolve a strategy in which the public sector focuses on improvements in economic and political governance, resource mobilization, human capital accumulation, empowerment of the poor, and creation of an investment climate in which the private sector can help generate higher growth. Reforms in the infrastructure and financial sectors are especially important in building a healthy investment climate for growth. Policies and institutions must also be reformed to encourage R&D in the context of the new IPR regime.

It is now widely recognized that efforts at resource mobilization need to be directed toward realistic tax rates and better tax administration. On government expenditures, the emphasis has to be on quality. Thus, government consumption in the form of unproductive and wasteful expenditure needs to be cut, while government expenditures on health, education, and poverty alleviation must be scaled up, ensuring, at the same time, better delivery of public goods and services, and an environment of governance in which the private sector can function effectively.

Policies with respect to agriculture, industry, and foreign trade must be reformed with a view to improving productivity through creating incentives for the private sector. At the same time, macroeconomic policies must ensure that the gains in competitiveness attained through these policy reforms are not eroded by high inflation rates. Although growth is necessary, it is not sufficient for sustainable improvement in the economic and social conditions of the poor. Policies have to be vigilantly implemented to ensure that poverty measured in terms of income, as well as poverty manifested by indicators of human well-being such as nutrition and health, is reduced in the course of development.

Importance of Keeping Trade Open

For far too long the developing countries have focused their energies on foreign aid flows. In Essay 4, S. Aziz rightly draws attention to the declining official flows of capital to developing countries. I agree that we should ask for more aid, but more trade enables developing countries to exploit the opportunities offered by globalization, provided they make their economies competitive. The international economic environment must open its doors to more trade in areas of importance to developing countries, such as agriculture and textiles.

The increasing proliferation of bilateral free trade agreements and regional agreements has further undermined the multilateral efforts for trade liberalization. Such agreements distract attention from the principal task of lowering the trade barriers through multilateral negotiations at the WTO, which is an important aspect of globalization.

It is very important for developing countries to press for greater trade liberalization within a multilateral framework. Industrialized countries' removal of tariff and nontariff barriers, and also of the more recent nontariff barriers in the form of labor standards and environmental standards, is essential for developing countries to partake of globalization in generating the higher growth that forms the basis of poverty reduction. This argument is not to deny the importance of labor and environmental standards for these countries, which are being pursued at the insistence of civil society and other multilateral institutions, such as the International Labour Organization. But there is no basis for linking these to trade policy and enforcing the linkage through the WTO, so as to deny market access to developing countries.

Similarly, use of antidumping duties for contingent protection is now practiced not only by industrialized countries but also increasingly by developing ones. India has the second-largest number of antidumping cases in the world, next to only those in the United States. Such practices are economically inefficient and favor producers at the expense of consumers.

The distorting features of the WTO AoA, including its negative implications for food security in developing countries, have been amply documented. This is a very important area of concern for developing countries. Agricultural subsidies in OECD member countries are very high, and the developing countries have to work toward getting these subsidies lowered. Sometimes a misguided case is made for increasing the subsidies to agriculture in developing countries on the grounds that industrialized countries provide very high agricultural subsidies. Not only can developing countries not afford these subsidies, given their resource constraints, but such a course of action also reduces their effectiveness in getting the OECD countries to lower their own subsidies, which distort agricultural trade patterns and have significant adverse effects on market access for the agricultural produce of developing countries.

If bilateral and regional free trade agreements, textile quotas, and agricultural subsidies are examples of how the process of globalization has been limited to suit selected countries and hurt developing countries in general, there are other dimensions in which hasty globalization has the potential of adversely affecting the poor in the developing countries. A clear case in point is the opening of capital accounts. The rapid liberalization of private capital flows across national borders and the resultant vulnerabilities and financial crises are all too well known recently. Some of the affected economies are still struggling to recover. In hindsight, it is clear that developing countries need to find a delicate balance between reforming their financial sectors and opening their capital accounts. Although globalization in the form of an open capital account allows the possibility of attracting private capital flows that can be used to break critical infrastructure and other bottlenecks to faster growth, it is important to ensure that the financial sector is strong enough to absorb the shocks that are an inevitable part of a process that is driven by relative economic returns in different countries.

Another significant aspect of globalization with grave potential for adverse effects on developing countries is that relating to IPR protection through the TRIPS agreement in the WTO. In discussing the effects of globalization on the poor, it is important to consider the implications of that agreement in the context of farmers' rights, seeds, and biodiversity. But the effects of TRIPS on affordable access to drugs for the poor must also be assessed. Certainly, developing countries need more time from the WTO to set up the legal infrastructure needed to implement the patents regime.

There is also a need to ratify and implement properly the additional flexibility agreed to by WTO members in August 2003 and December 2005 that allows generic versions of patented medicines to be made under compulsory licenses for export to countries that cannot manufacture the medicines themselves. Under the original TRIPS, if a developing country faced a public health emergency, it could use compulsory licensing to produce a patented drug within its borders. But if the country in question did not have domestic capacity or capability to produce the drug, it was not able to grant compulsory licensing only to a producer in another developing country to produce and export the drug to the country in question at much lower prices than the patented drugs. Fortunately, there was recognition of this problem in the Doha Round, largely owing to major efforts of civil society groups, research institutions, and the Commission on Macroeconomics and Health set up by WHO. The August 2003 and December 2005 decisions at WTO tried to address that issue. More generally, it is necessary to take into account the humanitarian issues that have been raised with respect to affordable access to drugs, especially for the poor, and to monitor the application of certain provisions of TRIPS to ensure that developing countries have the flexibility to cope with public health emergencies.

Conclusion

Globalization offers unprecedented opportunities coupled with significant challenges for developing countries, particularly in their struggle for poverty alleviation. Increasingly, different countries are pushing for globalization along different dimensions to suit their own national or regional interests. It is very important, therefore, for developing countries as a group to strengthen multilateral institutions and actively participate in multilateral discussions and negotiations, at the same time preparing their economies for global competitiveness. Such an approach needs to be combined with domestic policies that make growth pro-poor, many of which are discussed in this volume.

Chapter 8

Globalization, Governance, and Agriculture

Eugenio Díaz-Bonilla

A current debate related to globalization is whether the "policy space" (or more generally, sovereignty) of developing countries has been reduced by that phenomenon. These discussions are not new. After World War II, with many developing countries emerging as independent states, there were heated arguments about the costs and benefits for developing countries of the process of integration into world markets. More negative evaluations came from those who saw political and economic dependency embedded in the productive structure of developing countries. The literature on colonialism and neocolonialism (see, for instance, Nkrumah 1965) emphasized the negative effects of direct colonial control that led to the extraction of the value of primary products on the periphery of empires. Similarly, the theory of dependency (Dos Santos 1970; Cardoso and Faletto 1979) criticized the economically imbalanced and socially unequal structures created by "dependent capitalism" in developing countries. In general the concern was the pattern of integration into the world economy (that was variously characterized as colonial, asymmetric, dependent, and subordinated), and the constraints that such a system imposed on the development opportunities and policies of the developing countries. Mainstream development economics, on the other hand, emphasized the importance of greater participation in the world economy, particularly through financial and trade flows, to improve welfare in developing countries (Little, Scitovsky, and Scott 1970).

A separate debate during the 1970s focused on multinational corporations, both in developing and developed countries, with very different interpretations about the welfare implications for and constraints on the functioning of the states with the emergence and expansion of big international firms (Servan-Schreiber

1968; Vernon 1971). Most of these arguments are being echoed in current discussions on globalization.

During the late 1970s the notion of interdependence across nations, focusing mostly on industrialized countries, highlighted the limits of national autonomy and power to define outcomes in nontraditional areas of diplomacy, such as environmental and monetary issues (Keohane and Nye 1977; Cooper 1980). Since the 1980s and 1990s, as the strong trend toward greater world integration became obvious, the debate broadened to the more general influence of globalization on the economic, political, and social structure and processes in both industrialized and developing countries, with some arguing that globalization is helping accelerate growth and reduce poverty, while others are convinced that the opposite is taking place.

Part of that discussion is whether these trends result from the actions of governments or from forces that governments cannot control or even moderate through public policies and institutions (Díaz-Bonilla 2001b). This perspective of a more general debate is pursued in this chapter: the interaction between globalization and the operation of governments, including the issue of whether nation-states are losing relevance as policy and institutional centers for the advancement of the welfare of their citizens in the context of an increasingly integrated world. In particular, the discussion highlights the implications for agriculture of the links between globalization and governance in developing countries.

The chapter is organized as follows. The first section, where the general links between globalization and governance are briefly presented, serves as background to the analysis. Additionally, the notion of governance as utilized here is explained. The second and third sections review some of the discussions related to how globalization may be shaping the way governments design and implement policies, and the possible effects on the agricultural sector and the poor, looking at the government's responsiveness (second section) and effectiveness (third section). Finally, some conclusions are presented.

Framework

Globalization and Governance

The answer to what the effects of globalization are on governance, agriculture, and poverty depends on how broadly the term "globalization" is defined and the possible channels linking globalization and domestic outcomes (Díaz-Bonilla and Robinson 2001; Figure 8.1).[1] The different dimensions of globalization (such as increased trade, capital flows, labor migrations, and so on at the top of Figure 8.1) affect the functioning of the government, civil society, markets, and the environment in developing

Figure 8.1   Globalization dynamics

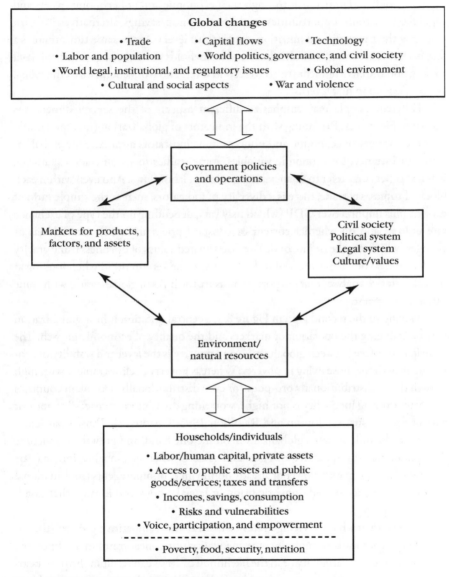

Source: Adapted from Díaz-Bonilla and Robinson (2001).

countries (second level in the figure). In turn, these changes have different influences on households and individuals through their economic and noneconomic assets and capabilities, income opportunities, and consumption/savings alternatives, in turn changing their poverty and nutrition status (third level). At the same time, there is a feedback mechanism from individuals and households to markets, government, civil society, and the environment (third to second level) and from countries to the global system (second to first level).

Different people may emphasize different aspects of the several dimensions shown in Figure 8.1. Beginning with the indicators of globalization (first level), analysts use a variety of economic and noneconomic indicators as proxies for globalization. For instance, for economic variables, some studies focus on trade expansion, whereas others may refer to financial integration or labor flows. And even within each block of topics, say trade, there is a diversity of indicators, such as the simple ratio of exports plus imports over GDP (which may vary, depending on the type of exchange rate utilized and on whether current or constant prices are used), tariffs levels or changes (which may be de jure or de facto), estimated values of openness using gravity models, and so on. This variety of indicators has to be kept in mind when looking at the quantitative analyses that purport to measure the links of globalization with some variable of interest.

Moving to the second level in Figure 8.1, a central question is how globalization may be changing the operation of markets and the quality of economic growth. The principal interface between globalization and poverty is the level and stability of economic growth for those living in poverty. Whereas poverty declines rapidly with high growth that is distributionally pro-poor (or even distributionally neutral, in countries where preexisting inequality is not high), worsening distribution may easily wipe out part of those gains (see Lipton and Ravallion 1995; Chapter 2). Thus, a particular concern is the link between globalization, on the one hand, and growth and income distribution on the other hand. A related issue is whether globalization may be strengthening the market power of already dominant economic agents (multinational corporations, concentrated domestic firms, or large landowners) in ways that disadvantage the poor.

But even with higher average rates of neutral and competitive growth (that is, one that neither leads to more income inequality nor concentrates market power), increases in income variability or in the likelihood of crises can result in the poor bearing significant additional downside risks. Vulnerable populations may suffer long-lasting damage to their already low levels of human and physical capital if more-frequent crises increase the possibility of illness or force poor families to sell productive assets or take their children out of school (Lipton and Ravallion 1995). Another key question is then whether globalization may have increased the variability of growth, and, more worryingly, the recurrence of crises.

Globalization may affect not only markets but the operation of governments themselves, with consequences for their capacity to design and implement policies. As a result, the level and distribution of public goods and services may be influenced, with diverse effects on poor households and individuals. Some observers see important constraints on the policies that governments can use in the presence of increased globalization, whereas others consider that the state still retains significant autonomy. These issues are the main focus of this chapter.

Globalization can also influence civil society and the political process, having an effect on such variables as political participation and the ability of civil society to monitor and control government operations. Figure 8.1 emphasizes the importance of noneconomic assets and capabilities, such as social capital (contacts, networks, and institutions of the civil society), and political assets and capabilities, leading to participation and empowerment for the poor. Important issues in this regard include the protection of life and personal security, the construction of democratic institutions, and the rule of law.

Finally, there are also links between globalization and the environment and natural resources. Globalization may influence the rate of growth and the development pattern—with implications for the intensification of agricultural production systems, the process of industrialization, and the increased utilization of energy sources, which in turn have consequences for air, water, and soil pollution; for hazardous wastes and noise; and for climate change and global warming.

In summary, the main points to highlight here are, first, the different dimensions of globalization and the variety of indicators utilized as proxies to quantify it. Second, there are direct channels between globalization and the operation of governments, but globalization may also have indirect effects on governments through its effects on markets, civil society, or the environment and their cross linkages.

Defining Governance in the Context of Globalization

Governance has been defined as "the traditions and institutions by which authority in a country is exercised," which includes "(1) the process by which governments are selected, monitored and replaced, (2) the capacity of the government to effectively formulate and implement sound policies, and (3) the respect of citizens and the state for the institutions that govern economic and social interactions among them" (Kaufmann, Kraay, and Zoido-Lobatón 1999, 1).[2]

As shown in Figure 8.1, globalization may affect civil society and the political process, which would lead to changes in the first and third components of governance, influencing such variables as political participation and the ability of civil society to monitor and control government operations. The first and third components can be grouped under the general notion of the degree of responsiveness of a government to society.

Second, globalization can also affect the functioning of government itself, with consequences for its capacity to design and implement policies (the second component). Some of these issues are discussed later under the heading of the influence of globalization on the effectiveness of governments. An issue is whether the rules or institutions associated with globalization (such as WTO, IMF, and World Bank) limit the "policy space" of developing countries. Another angle to the notion of effectiveness, which goes beyond whether some set of policies and interventions are available to developing countries, is whether globalization has also affected markets and the natural environment in ways that limit the resources available to implement policies, diminish the positive effects of available policies, and/or overwhelm the response capabilities of developing countries (perhaps because of the frequency and severity of crises—from macroeconomic to health or environmental crises—which force governments to allocate scarce resources to respond to those disruptive events).

In what follows, some of the linkages between globalization and governance will be explored in terms of governments' responsiveness and effectiveness in the design and implementation of policies and programs, particularly those in support of rural and agricultural development.

Globalization and Responsive Government

For the poor—and in particular the rural poor, who tend to be more isolated—it matters whether they have access to political assets and capabilities leading to voice, participation, and empowerment within the political system. Globalization can affect legal, political, and civil society institutions and practices in ways that may help or hurt the poor in general and those in rural areas in particular.

Democracy, Good Governance, and Welfare

It seems clear that during the past decades there has been an advance of democratic rule in the world. A detailed study by Marshall and Gurr (2005) shows the changes since the 1950s, when there were 78 independent states but only 23 ruled by democratic regimes (the rest divided about equally between 28 autocratic regimes and an intermediate category of 27 states they call "anocratic regimes"); by 2005, 88 countries were democracies, only 29 were considered autocracies, and there were 44 anocracies. The dramatic shift toward democracy and away from autocratic regimes began in the late 1980s and continued through the 1990s and 2000s.

Does the advance of democracy matter for social welfare and the poor? Although some studies yield inconclusive results (Moore et al. 1999), other analyses argue that there is a positive relation between democracy and good governance on one hand and improved social welfare on the other hand. Sen has emphasized the fact that no substantial famine has ever occurred in any independent and democratic country with a relatively free press (see, for instance, Sen 1984). Other research documents the positive effects of democracy on the decline of child malnutrition, among other variables (Smith and Haddad 2000).

On the other hand, bad governance appears to negatively affect overall growth and income distribution. It may also have a negative influence on the poor through different channels (Thomas et al. 2000), such as the misallocation of budgets to big investment projects (where there are more opportunities for graft) instead of much-needed operational and maintenance expenditures. To the extent that these big investments (such as modern, well-equipped hospitals) can be justified more easily in urban centers, the neglect of rural areas, where the majority of the poor live, is further increased. Access to public services may also be distorted by payment of bribes, and, in consequence, the distribution of those services across the population would mimic a market allocation based on capacity to pay. Another example is corruption in government procurement of supplies and equipment, which leads to inflated prices or poor-quality products, thus substantially diminishing the welfare-enhancing effect of a given budget allocation.

Globalization and Democracy

Admitting that democracy and good governance may help increase growth and reduce poverty, the question of the link between globalization and political and institutional quality remains unanswered. Lipset (1960) and others have argued that economic development is, over time, associated with the expansion of democracy. More recently, advocates of globalization have argued that free trade and capital flows lead to greater growth and productivity, which expands the middle class and, with it, the demand for expanded political rights, democracy, and good governance. During the 1970s and 1980s, different studies looked at the relationship between the degree of economic openness and rent-seeking activities. It was argued that economically closed countries, where the state holds substantial power over the fate of firms, fortunes, and people, tend to be captured by elites and vested interests, undermining political institutions and the rule of law and leading to corruption and waste of resources (Krueger 1974; Bhagwati 1982; Hirschman 1982). In addition, more recent empirical studies seem to show that there is an inverse relationship between trade and financial openness on one hand and corruption on the other (see, for example, Wei 2000). In particular, Dreher and Siemers (2005) found that corruption and capital account restrictions are related (although they point out that the empirical relationship is not completely robust).

However, others have argued that globalization may be undermining democracy by exacerbating poverty and skewing income distribution, generating crises, and/or empowering some actors (or weakening others) in ways inimical to the proper functioning of democratic institutions. In particular, critics of globalization argue (echoing the early work of Servan-Schreiber 1968 and Vernon 1971) that opening economies increases the power of multinational corporations, to the detriment of democratic governance (for the opposite view that greater economic openness increases the level of competition, reducing the market power of concentrated firms, see Hallward-Driemeier 2001). In any case, liberalization and privatization associated with increased integration also creates opportunities for the capture of rents by well-positioned private actors, mostly of local origin, with potentially negative implications for the institutional quality of those countries (Schamis 1999; Hellman, Jones, and Kaufmann 2000).

The more general debate on whether globalization, through accelerated growth, is contributing to the creation of a middle class (that eventually demands political rights, thus helping to strengthen democracy) or is generating stagnation and worsening income distribution (to the detriment of stable democratic institutions) is complicated by inconclusive evidence on the links among globalization, growth, volatility, poverty, and income distribution. This evidence depends on the indicators used to proxy globalization, the variables of interest, periods considered, and several other factors (see Díaz Bonilla 2001b; Harrison 2006; Chapter 2). Therefore, different studies have skipped the intermediate variables (growth, volatility, and income distribution) and tried to analyze directly the link between globalization and democracy.

Empirical analyses present different views on whether globalization strengthens democracy. Hamilton (2002) finds positive (simple pairwise) correlations between a democracy indicator and both the lowering of tariffs and increases in the share of trade over GDP. Li and Reuveny (2003) obtain more mixed results. They look at the effects of four components of globalization—trade openness measured as exports and imports over GDP, foreign direct investment inflows, portfolio investment inflows, and the spread of democratic ideas across countries—and find that trade openness and portfolio investment inflows are negatively associated with democracy, whereas foreign direct investment inflows and, not surprisingly, the spread of democratic ideas are positively correlated to democracy.

The result that the measure of trade openness utilized in the study may be negatively correlated with democracy is not so unexpected, once it is considered that many developing countries that are natural-resource exporters (some poor, such as those in Sub-Saharan Africa; others not so poor, such as several oil exporters) all have large trade/GDP ratios, and many of them have nondemocratic governments. In fact, concentrated natural resources (minerals, oil), particularly when in the hands of the state, seem to be correlated with low quality of governance and high levels of social strife (Collier and Hoeffer 1998). For instance, López-Cordova and Meissner

(2005), after controlling for commodity exports (including oil) and other factors, find that trade openness (defined by a gravity model to avoid the potential endogeneity of trade and democracy) is positively correlated to democracy in general, and that, at the same time, the control variables for exporters of commodities show a negative correlation with democracy.[3] They argue that their results suggest that openness raises competition for the election of the executive, and generates more checks and balances. In another study, however, Rigobon and Rodrik (2004) find that trade openness may not be good for democracy but seems to improve the rule of law. This paradox of the asymmetric effect of trade (which the authors label as one of their most striking results) needs more analysis. It must also be noted that they use a trade/ GDP variable without controlling for commodity exporters. Giavazzi and Tabellini (2005), using a difference in differences methodology to try to control for the possible endogenous determination of the variables of interest, find no effects of trade openness on democracy. Finally, Eichengreen and Leblang (2006) tackle directly the issue of endogeneity and study the two-way connections between globalization and democracy using data on trade, capital controls, democracy, and several instruments annually for the period 1870–2000 (with the number of countries varying with time). They interpret their results as providing support for a positive two-way relationship between globalization and democracy, both for the trade and the financial components, although with some exceptions (one being countries with labor scarce economies, which can be also seen as consistent with the result of the negative effects of resource abundance).

So far the discussion has focused on economic indicators of globalization and democracy. Moving away from the economic analyses, it has been argued that the spread of democracy has been strongly influenced by the globalization of communications (Giddens 1999). The information monopoly on which authoritarian political systems are based has been eroded by an open framework of global communications. This observation is in line with one of the indicators (the spread of democratic ideas) used in Li and Reuveny (2003). Authoritarian governments do not have the flexibility and dynamism necessary to operate in the global electronic economy (Giddens 1999). According to this line of argument, the same advances in the technology of communications that allowed corporations to operate more effectively at the world level are increasing the links across societies, as well as changing the dynamics of the interaction among markets, the state, and civil societies within each country and internationally. Different political and social alliances are formed across countries to confront global concerns—from the violation of human rights to environmental problems and access to affordable drugs. In fact, López (2005) has argued that globalization may help (or force) governments to invest more in public goods in rural areas. Globalization communications limit the ability of governments to repress the political mobilization of the poor in protests against the economic elites who divert public resources toward private goods, mostly harmful subsidies to the rich that have detrimental effects for rural development and the environment.

Improved communications and information sharing have also begun to expose abuses of power and cases of corruption that may have previously gone unnoticed. Although this exposure may induce some cynicism because of the (perhaps false) perception that corruption has increased, the communications revolution offers the means to better control corruption. The Internet increases communication between public institutions and the general public as much as among different groups in civil society (see also Chapter 2).

Summary

All in all, it seems that globalization—at least in the form of increased information and communications—is fostering democracy. In turn, the expectation is that the trends toward the expansion of democracy may increasingly put limits on cronyism and corruption, empowering civil society to control governments and insist on the rule of law. All these trends, it is argued, should over time be good for the poor, particularly the rural poor, to the extent that they constitute a majority in many developing countries.

However, although some aspects of globalization, particularly the political and informational aspects, may be helping democracy, it has been argued that others (especially some economic factors) could be working in the opposite direction, by limiting the possibility of governments in developing countries to respond to the needs of their citizens. If the pressing needs of the majority of the population expressed in the political arena are not satisfied, then periods of instability and even reversion to authoritarian rule may occur. Therefore, it is important to determine whether globalization may be limiting the effectiveness of governments to respond to the people. This issue is discussed next.

Globalization and Effective Governments

The argument that economic globalization may be weakening governments and, as a result, impeding them from answering democratic demands, has several components. First, it is said that international legal frameworks and institutions (such as the WTO agreements, the IMF, or the World Bank) may be constraining the set of available economic policies, particularly for developing countries, thus compromising national sovereignty and affecting growth and efforts to alleviate poverty. Second, even if there were no legal constraints, some argue that countries are forced to cut welfare expenditures to reduce costs and maintain a globally competitive economy. This process is sometimes called the "disciplining or efficiency effect" of globalization. However, it has also been noted, mainly in the context of developed countries, that globalization may lead to additional expenditures to shelter those affected by it (the compensation effect). Which effect dominates is an empirical question to which we turn below. Third, the needed additional resources to confront change and crises may not be available if, as some suggest, globalization is negatively affecting government revenues and placing limits on some policies. Finally, economic globalization may leave countries more vulnerable to international economic factors, including fluctuations in world prices and capital flows. If globalization is increasing the frequency and severity of crises, then governments have more problems to deal with. Even if not leading to more crises, globalization, because of amplified external competition, may accelerate domestic economic change, which increases the need for government resources to help affected populations. Also, capital flows may impose limits on monetary and exchange rate policies in ways that may harm overall growth, agricultural and rural development, and poverty alleviation.

This section looks at some of the arguments related to legal and institutional constraints (policy space), availability of resources, and crises by focusing on three issues of the many involved: WTO agreements in relation to agriculture; fiscal aspects and their relation to public agricultural expenditures; and monetary conditions, with their impact mainly on exchange rates and agricultural credit.

Are Developing Countries Legally Constrained to Implement Agricultural Policies?

Developing countries seem to have sufficient legal room ("policy space") under the WTO AoA to implement policies in support of their agricultural sectors and rural development:

- Green Box measures of Annex 2 of the AoA, which includes government services from agricultural research and extension to pest controls and infrastructure, plus a variety of other interventions;[4]

- Blue Box measures (Article 6, paragraph 5), which allow direct payments under production-limiting programs, based on fixed area and yields or number of heads, with payments made on 85 percent or less of the base level of production;

- the "de minimis" exemption (Article 6, paragraph 4), which allows countries to exclude from prohibited subsidies up to 10 percent of the total value of production of a basic agricultural product during the relevant year and similar values for nonproduct-specific support; and

- the special and differential provisions of Article 6, paragraph 2, which exempts these countries from reduction commitments on "measures of assistance, whether direct or indirect, to encourage agricultural and rural development (which "are an integral part of the development programs of developing countries"), on "investment subsidies generally available to agriculture," on "agricultural input subsidies to low-income or resource-poor producers," and "on support to eradicate illicit narcotic crops through diversification."[5]

Furthermore, different proposals being considered in the Doha Round would allow developing countries to maintain current instruments and may add some new ones, such as extended policies under Article 6.2 and a special safeguard for food security and livelihood security. Therefore, legally, developing countries do not seem constrained in the implementation of most, if not all, of the range of possible policies in support of agriculture (including some whose efficiency and equity may be disputed).[6] However, the existence of policy space is different from having the financial and other resources needed to implement those policies. Additionally, the AoA does not seem to constrain industrialized countries much either, but rich countries have the money and human and institutional resources to implement these policies, with important negative effects on agriculture in developing countries (see, for example, Diao, Díaz-Bonilla, and Robinson 2003). Therefore, criticisms of the imbalances allowed by the AoA (see Chapter 5 and Essays 2, 3, and 4) can go in parallel with the recognition that there is policy space to pursue agricultural and rural development strategies based on investments, technology, credit, and safety nets for the poor.[7]

Moreover, Pardey, Wright, and Nottenburg (2002) note that patents and other forms of intellectual property are not currently greatly constraining the freedom to operate for agricultural researchers working on staple food crops in developing countries (see also Chapter 3). They consider that a greater constraint is the failure to invest in fostering the domestic expertise needed to evaluate, access, and regulate the new technologies. Still, the implementation of some WTO agreements may impose excessive costs in terms of financial and administrative resources (Finger and Shuler 1999). The case of IPR related to health issues is different, in that the built-in flexibility in TRIPS for health issues (Correa 2000), ratified at the WTO ministerial meeting at Doha in November 2001, and the recent agreement on drug licensing (see Essay 3) must be carefully monitored to determine whether the policy space for developing countries to confront health problems is preserved. In addition, there is the problem that industrialized countries have been pressuring developing nations into accepting further obligations beyond what the WTO legal texts require, particularly in the context of bilateral trade agreements.

More generally, a major problem for developing countries (besides the large policy space allowed by the AoA for rich countries, which use it to the detriment of poor ones) is not so much the issue of constraints in the WTO framework, but the lack of financial and human resources to implement sustained programs of investment in rural development, poverty alleviation, and food security. These financial constraints may result from other characteristics of globalization, as discussed next.

Is Globalization Eroding Fiscal Revenues?

Fiscal trends.   Since the mid- to late 1980s there has been a polarized debate on whether IMF stabilization programs and World Bank structural adjustment programs constrain developing-country policies (mainly fiscal, monetary, and exchange rates) in ways that are harmful to economic development and the poor (Stiglitz 2002). This debate will not be analyzed here (see, for instance, Dorosh and Sahn 2000; Kheralla et al. 2000).[8] Rather than constraints from the international financial institutions for the implementation of certain policies, a different issue, which is the focus of this section, is whether developing countries may lack the financial resources to carry out those policies because of globalization. For instance, there is the question of tax erosion and loss of public resources in the context of globalization. This process may happen both directly (for example, because of tax competition at the world level reducing the sources of revenues or the international mobility of capital and high-income individuals who do not want to be taxed) and indirectly (through the influence of globalization on the rate and quality of growth and, therefore, on tax collection). In turn, the level of government revenues affects the possibility of implementing transfer policies (such as food subsidies or other poverty-oriented programs) and of financing public services and investments in health, education, and related areas.

Particularly, trade liberalization may reduce government revenues from trade taxes, although the net result depends on the form of liberalization and the reaction from trade flows: if trade liberalization represents a move from quantitative barriers to tariffs (or from prohibitive tariffs with no trade to lower tariffs that allow some trade), revenues may increase. Trade taxes (both imports and exports) as percentages of current revenues seem to have declined in most developing countries.[9] According to the World Development Indicators database (World Bank 2006a) the share of trade taxes in revenues fell in East Asia and Pacific from 12.8 percent in the 1990s to 6.1 percent in the first half of the 2000s; comparable figures for Latin America and the Caribbean are from 11.7 to 6.2 percent; for South Asia, from 22.6 to 16.2 percent; for lower–middle income groups, from 13.1 to 7.5 percent; and for upper–middle income groups, from 8.3 to 3.3 percent (both income categories include developing countries). Data are not available for low-income countries (the bottom tier of developing countries), including those in Sub-Saharan Africa.

Table 8.1   General government consumption expenditure (percent of GDP)

Country category	1960s	1970s	1980s	1990s	Early 2000s
East Asia and Pacific	8.2	9.6	13.0	11.4	11.0
Latin America and the Caribbean	9.6	10.5	10.3	13.2	14.9
South Asia	8.9	9.6	10.7	10.9	10.8
Sub-Saharan Africa	11.3	14.1	16.2	16.4	16.8
Developing countries	9.5	11.0	12.2	13.4	13.8
High-income OECD countries	15.2	16.7	17.8	17.2	17.4

Source: World Bank (2006a).

Notes: Consumption expenditure is calculated as total spending minus spending on public investments. GDP, gross domestic product; OECD, Organisation for Economic Co-operation and Development.

But this trend may simply reflect the movement of tax structure toward less-distorting taxes. Indeed, some trade taxes include export taxes, with their disincentive effects, and import taxes have well-known negative effects on welfare. A more relevant approach would be to determine whether taxes in general (not only trade taxes) have declined. Again, data are scarce, but from the 55 developing countries that have data available over the past two decades, average tax revenues as percentage of GDP were about the same in the 1990s and the first half of the 2000s at 14.6 and 14.5 percent, respectively (the medians were 13.9 and 13.2 percent and the modes 12 and 15.5 percent, respectively). This stability contrasts with the upward trend in taxes in countries that are members of OECD (World Bank 2006a).

Moving to the spending side, a related argument, already referred to, is that globalization forces cuts in government expenditures to maintain competitiveness (the disciplining effect of globalization). Table 8.1 shows the size of the central governments in the economy (not counting local governments), measured by public consumption (that is, the data do not include public investments). As in high-income countries, public consumption has been increasing in general for all developing regions since the 1960s. Public consumption in Sub-Saharan Africa and Latin America and the Caribbean is relatively greater than in the developing regions of Asia (between 3 and 6 percentage points higher).

Although it is difficult to generalize from these figures, taxes seem to have been stable as a percentage of GDP, while government consumption appears to have increased somewhat. However, there is no consistent data on other sources of incomes (such as income from assets, government activities, or grants) and other possible outlays (such as public investments). If the trend toward more consumption with stable taxes were true, then there may be a gap that will have to be filled with other sources of income: cuts in nonconsumption expenditures, money financing (that is, seigniorage tax), or increases in debt.

Table 8.2   Public and publicly guaranteed debt service
(percent of gross national income)

Country category	1970s	1980s	1990s	2000–04
East Asia and Pacific	n.a.	2.6	2.8	1.9
Latin America and the Caribbean	2.2	4.4	3.2	4.1
Middle East and North Africa	2.1	3.7	6.5	3.8
South Asia	0.9	1.2	2.5	2.2
Sub-Saharan Africa	1.6	n.a.	3.1	2.6
Low- and middle-income countries	1.8	3.5	3.2	3.0

Source: Based on data from World Bank (2006a).
Note: n.a., not available.

Debt service of public and publicly guaranteed debt was lower in the 1970s for all developing regions than in subsequent decades (Table 8.2). Debt service peaked in the 1980s for both Sub-Saharan Africa and Latin America and the Caribbean and subsequently declined in the 1990s. For Latin America and the Caribbean, however, it increased again in the early 2000s to close to the levels experienced in the 1980s (and double the levels of debt servicing in Asian countries). These increases appear to be linked to the surge in capital flows to developing countries associated with financial globalization (see below).

Looking at the overall fiscal position of developing (and industrial) countries, data suggest a deterioration mostly during the 1980s, but an improvement since then: the average government fiscal deficit was 6 percent of GDP among developing countries in the first half of the 1980s, but it has declined to around 2 percent by the end of the 1990s (with a similar decline in industrialized countries; see Tytell and Wei 2004).

The general picture from these figures is that the fiscal position in the past decades became tighter in the 1980s and 1990s, and the fiscal margin may have improved somewhat during the 2000s (probably helped by the previous fiscal adjustment, the resumption of growth after the crises of the 1980s and 1990s, and a decline in world interest rates).

Deteriorating public-sector finances, along with the decline in world agricultural prices in the mid-1980s, led to fiscal adjustments and pressures to reduce support for agriculture in many countries. For instance, at the beginning of the 1980s several countries in South America, such as Brazil and Chile, embarked on accelerated programs to expand wheat production (and other cereals) because of concerns about shortages heightened by high prices in the second half of the 1970s. When prices collapsed in the mid-1980s, these programs represented a high cost for the government, and support for those crops was substantially diminished (Díaz-Bonilla 1999). More generally, van Blarcom, Knudsen, and Nash (1993) find that during the period of structural adjustment programs in the 1980s, agricultural expenditures declined as share of total spending. The discussions surrounding the U.S. farm bills in the 1980s and 1990s, the adjustments in the E.U. CAP in the 1990s, and the structural adjustment programs that unilaterally (or as a condition of loans) reduced support for agriculture in many developing countries during the 1980s and 1990s can all be seen as part of the same effort to confront deteriorating fiscal positions in the context of weak world commodity markets (Díaz-Bonilla 2001a).

The estimates by Fan and Pardey (1998) of public-sector agricultural expenditures in Asia (measured in PPP values)[10] show that, although growing on average at 4.6 percent annually in 1972–93, the pattern was a declining one: during the 1970s they grew at 9.5 percent, they slowed down to 3.5 percent during the 1980s, and had a negligible increase of less than 0.5 percent in 1990–93. Kheralla et al. (2000) also report diminished expenditures in subsidies and public-sector enterprises in Sub-Saharan Africa. In Latin America and the Caribbean , data from FAO show that agricultural expenditures in constant currency and in per capita terms for an unweighted average of 18 countries[11] declined from the mid-1980s to the mid-1990s, but then recovered to about the values at the beginning of the series (Figure 8.2). If instead of the average, the unweighted median is utilized, there seems to have been an increase above historical values in the early 2000s. Allcott, Lederman, and López (2006) divide public agricultural expenditures in Latin America and the Caribbean into nonsocial subsidies, or private goods (export subsidies, internal commercialization, forestry subsidies, targeted rural production subsidies, and an estimated share of other categories) and public goods (such as investment in R&D, plant and animal disease control, and environmental protection). These researchers document the decline in the share of expenditures devoted to nonsocial subsidies over the period, from 40–45 percent in the late 1980s to 30 percent in 2001, while the average rural public expenditures per person (as shown in Figure 8.2) increased over the period.

Taxes on agriculture include (1) direct taxes on income, persons, and personal wealth or property and (2) indirect taxes, such as sales taxes, excises, stamp taxes, and import and export taxes.[12] Khan (2001) notes that there are serious data problems that impede determining the level of explicit direct and indirect taxes paid by farmers in developing countries, because, among other things, national tax data are not classified by source or sector and include taxes collected by state and local governments. Nevertheless, Khan points out some facts and trends on agricultural taxation in recent years. First, taxes on land and income are not major contributors to agricultural tax revenues (generally not exceeding 20 percent of the total). Instead, the bulk of agricultural tax revenue comes from taxes and duties on marketed agricultural products in domestic and foreign markets (but usually food items are exempted from sales taxes).

Figure 8.2   Agricultural expenditure in Latin America and the Caribbean

Constant local currency (1995 = 1)

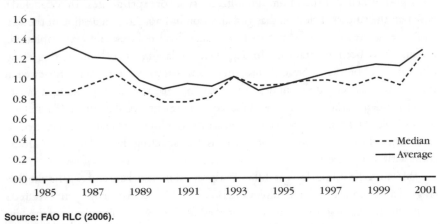

Source: FAO RLC (2006).

Second, the explicit tax burden on farmers has been lower than for other groups. Third, taxes on exported and imported products have traditionally been a major source of government revenue in many poor developing countries, but the contribution of export taxes in most developing countries has fallen significantly since the mid-1980s, particularly in Latin America and Asia. However, they are still high in several countries in Sub-Saharan Africa. Fourth, the explicit tax burden on agriculture has fallen significantly in the past 20 years, mostly from reductions in indirect taxes (such as export taxes), but also from declines in direct taxes on income and land (Kahn 2001).

But what are the links of these trends with globalization? This is discussed next.

Globalization and constraints on government taxes and expenditures.   As mentioned, there are two competing theories related to the effect of globalization on fiscal issues: the discipline or efficiency hypothesis, according to which globalization leads to lower government taxes and expenditures, and the compensation hypothesis, according to which greater integration in world markets requires more and not less expenditure to compensate those affected. It should be noted that efficiency may also require more spending (that must be financed somehow) of the type that increase productivity and competitiveness. Therefore, the efficiency hypothesis, at least when considering expenditures, may not necessarily lead to smaller government, but only to a different pattern of spending (in the case of taxes, however, the efficiency view points clearly to less government). Which effect prevails is therefore an empirical matter.

Since the late 1990s there has been an active literature on the topic, which focused initially on industrialized countries and expanded later to developing ones.

Schulze and Ursprung (1999) summarize much of the earlier literature, which focused on industrialized countries, dividing the analyses into three groups of studies: on taxes, government consumption, and different types of expenditures. They conclude, based on the studies reviewed, that globalization has not led to a decline of the welfare state or the ability of countries to conduct fiscal policies, and even capital tax revenues have been maintained (although taxes on labor increased, suggesting a relative shifting of burdens). Nevertheless, they warn that the various studies reviewed in their analysis use very different dependent variables for taxes and spending, a variety of independent variables that were supposed to represent globalization, different control variables, and a diversity of econometric methodologies. Thus, they conclude that statements of the type "globalization is, or is not, affecting the welfare state" always come with many caveats.

More recent studies look at different aspects of fiscal debate and expand the coverage of developing countries. Adserà and Boix (2002) find that trade openness affects positively the size of government (measured as the ratio of current receipts of the general government to GDP) in democratic governments: as trade expands, the public sector grows in democratic regimes. Therefore, the compensation effect dominates. Aizenman and Jinjarak (2006) define globalization as a process that induces countries to embrace greater trade and financial integration and macro stabilization. These researchers look at taxes, using the hypothesis that globalization should limit the ability of governments to collect what they call "easy-to-collect" taxes (such as those on trade and on money holdings [seigniorage]) and shift the tax burden to "hard-to-collect" taxes (value-added tax, income tax, and related taxes). Utilizing as dependent variables the annual revenue collection via value-added tax, seigniorage, and tariff revenues as a percentage of GDP on a sample of 86 developing countries, they find that trade openness and financial integration have a positive relationship with hard-to-collect taxes and negative one with the easy-to-collect taxes. In another study, Tytell and Wei (2004) use an indicator of financial integration that controls for the endogeneity of capital flows and macroeconomic policies, and annual data for 62 countries (40 of which are developing countries) over the period 1975–99. They do not find evidence that financial globalization reduces fiscal deficits (that is, they do not find the so-called discipline effect of globalization, at least regarding the fiscal variable considered; the results may be different for monetary policy, as discussed below).

Dreher, Sturm, and Ursprung (2006) recognize that, in general, aggregate analyses have not found a robust effect of globalization on aggregate government expenditures. Instead, they look at the structure of government spending (that is, the shares of different types of expenditures). They use data from 108 countries during 1970–2001, classify expenditures according to four categories (capital expenditures, expenditures for goods and services, interest payments, and subsidies and other current transfers), and apply a different indicator of globalization (the KOF Index of Globalization, which tries to capture the economic, political, and social dimensions of globalization).[13] This index allows the authors to use the overall index and three subindexes, as well as other, more conventional, proxies of globalization in their estimations. Yet the measures of globalization did not have a significant influence on aggregate spending or on the structure of spending for any of the specifications. Dreher, Sturm, and Ursprung (2006, 17) conclude that there may be "three explanations for this result. First, the efficiency and compensation effects might neutralize each other. Second, the effects of globalization might be blurred by potential indirect effects between different expenditure categories. And third, the effects of globalization might be exaggerated in the popular discussion and might simply not exist." In summary, globalization (as operationalized by the indicators used in these studies) do not seem to have affected the size of the government, on the tax or expenditure side, although it may have changed, in some cases, the composition on both sides of the ledger.

There is not much analysis on the effect of globalization on agricultural expenditures. An exception is Allcott, Lederman, and López (2006), who examine the effects of the size and composition of rural expenditures on agricultural GDP in 15 Latin American countries during 1985–2001. As mentioned, they divide government expenditures into nonsocial subsidies (or private goods) and public goods. Their more general result is the positive (negative) impact of the public (private) goods on agricultural GDP per person. In the context of this chapter, however, the main point is that in their estimations, trade openness leads to more agricultural spending in general (but the coefficient is not statistically significant), and of that spending, the share of private goods increases (which is significant). Greater openness to trade seems to be compensated for by increased subsidies (which reduces agricultural GDP per person), but as all expenditure also appears to increase with more trade, the overall effect of openness on agricultural GDP is not clear (it is positive in some of their regressions and negative in others).

An overall conclusion of this fiscal review is that developing countries suffered some fiscal retrenchment in the 1980s and 1990s, which seems to have affected agricultural expenditures during those years. The fiscal position appears to have improved somewhat in the 2000s, and (at least for those countries in Latin America and the Caribbean for which more complete data were available) agricultural expenditures have recovered. At the same time, the share of government expenditures on public goods in this sector seems to have increased.

On the tax side there seems to be less explicit taxation of agriculture, at least in the form of export taxes. Although it is difficult to assess in general terms whether expenditure and taxation levels related to agriculture in developing countries are adequate, it seems that at least the composition of both components of the fiscal equation has been moving toward somewhat more welfare-enhancing configurations. The connection, positive or negative, between globalization and these trends (at least regarding the proxies utilized in the different empirical studies) is not obvious.

Perhaps rather than looking at fiscal variables per se, it would be better to focus on another channel influencing fiscal policy in developing countries: the operation of capital markets that, in the context of the opening of capital accounts, may limit the range of some macroeconomic policies, which is reviewed in the next section.

Is Globalization Constraining Monetary, Exchange Rate, and Credit Policies?

Integration in international capital markets and domestic monetary conditions in developing countries have also changed during the past decades. Capital flows to developing countries has gone through two cycles, peaking twice, first in the early 1980s and again in the mid-1990s (Figure 8.3).

As shown in Figure 8.3, aggregate net resource flows (which include public and private debt, FDI, portfolio flow, and grants) more than doubled from about 1.5 percent of GDP in the early 1970s to about 3.5 percent in early 1980s, subsequently declining during the debt crisis of the 1980s to around 2 percent. They increased again significantly during the 1990s, peaking at around 5.5 percent of GDP in 1998, followed by a decline (to about 3 percent of GDP) after a sequence of developing-country crises in the late 1990s and early 2000s, only to begin increasing thereafter. Aggregate net transfers (the lower curve in Figure 8.3, which subtracts from the aggregate net resource flows—shown by the upper curve—both interest payments on long-term loans and FDI profits) show similar cycles, but highlights more clearly the lack of aggregate financial flows during the debt crises of the 1980s and late 1990s/early 2000s. Those crises have been accompanied by new debates about globalization and the integration of developing countries in the international economy. Other indicators of globalization, such as the degree of capital control, interest rate differentials, and the co-movement between domestic savings and investments, also show increased financial integration. The question is whether globalization is affecting the economy in general—and monetary, exchange rate, and related policies in particular—in ways that could hurt agricultural and rural development.

Economic growth and volatility. The behavior of capital flows has several implications for the economy in general and the agricultural sector in particular. Capital flows can accelerate growth and help finance additional investments, but they also tend to expand domestic money supply and increase the price of nontradables, as well as appreciating the domestic currency. Consequently, there may be a positive growth and investment effect on agriculture in general from capital inflows, including particularly such products as livestock and dairy, which in many countries are more tightly linked to the evolution of income and demand in the domestic market. On the

Figure 8.3   Aggregate net resource flows as a percentage of GDP

Percent gross domestic product

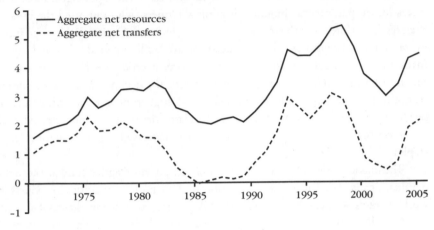

Source: World Bank (2006b).

other hand, the overvaluation of the domestic currency will hurt tradable sectors, including agricultural exportable products and those that compete with imports. In addition, capital flows can experience sudden reversals (as in the 1980s debt crisis and during the sequence of financial crises of the 1990s; Figure 8.3), which may lead to forced depreciation of the domestic currency, banking and fiscal crises (when there is widespread domestic private and public debt denominated in dollars), and sharp declines in growth (see Calvo, Izquierdo, and Mejia 2004, who analyze this phenomenon, which they call "sudden stops"). Although the devaluation associated with capital outflows improves relative prices for tradable agriculture, growth declines affect products that depend on domestic market incomes, and the banking and fiscal crises can negatively affect the supply side of a variety of products (through credit constraints and cuts in public expenditures supporting the agricultural sector). Also, production may be affected by increases in prices of imported inputs.

For instance, capital outflows and devaluations during the 1980s debt crises in Latin America and the Caribbean, and the correlated strong decline in overall growth during what has been called the "lost decade," affected production of livestock and dairy products and of raw materials for nonfood manufacturing products, while food crop production (which tends to be more tradable) fared relatively better during the period, but below the performance of the sector in the 1960s and 1970s. For the subsequent crises during the 1990s, Shane and Liefert (2000) show that for many (but not all) of the agricultural producers in crisis countries, currency depreciation improved their terms of trade; for some, however, they worsened, especially those who imported a large share of inputs for production and whose prices rose more than prices for output, such as Indonesian poultry farmers (who imported the bulk of their feed) or Koreans in the soybean-processing industry. Capital flight raised interest rates in crisis countries, which reduced the availability of credit, lowered capital investment in agriculture, and raised input costs if producers had to borrow to finance input purchases. Besides the price effects, the decline of incomes resulting from the crisis negatively affected products with higher income elasticities, such as beef or fresh fruits. Other products with less elastic demand were not affected, and, in some cases, the income decline appears to have increased the demand for inferior staples.

The financial crises also had important effects on world agricultural markets: the devaluations in Asia led to the contraction of demand for agricultural products in world markets, whereas those in Brazil and Argentina expanded world supplies, leading to the decline of world agricultural prices at the end of the 1990s and beginning of the 2000s (IMF 1999; see also Langley 2000).

Beyond the simple narrative of the facts, the question again is: what are the links between those events and globalization, variously defined? An IMF study concludes that, although there are good theoretical reasons why financial globalization should increase growth and reduce volatility in consumption, the empirical evidence is mixed regarding the links to growth, and several middle-income countries better integrated into world financial markets may have suffered from greater volatility as a result of that integration (Prasad et al. 2003).

In a follow-up study, the same authors present a more positive view of financial globalization (Kose et al. 2006): although they still did not find an obvious direct link between financial globalization and growth, they argued that the latter generated several indirect effects (such as financial market development, institutional development, better governance, and macroeconomic discipline) that contributed to growth. They argue that crises were not necessarily related to reduction of capital controls and further financial integration, but to fixed exchange rates that proved unsustainable (more on this issue below). In the same vein, some more recent studies suggest that economies that are more open and integrated into the world economy, both financially and through trade, have less volatility and appear to weather crises with less disruption; in particular greater trade integration appears to reduce the likelihood of financial crises associated with sudden stops in capital flows and current account reversals.[14] However, these views are not without their dissenters. For instance, Easterly, Islam, and Stiglitz (2000) find that trade openness (measured by exports and imports over GDP) increases growth volatility. This correlation may be simply because, as noted, some of

Table 8.3   Inflation rates in developing countries

Developing region	1960s	1970s	1980s	1990s	2000–05
Africa	5.1	12.6	17.2	25.9	8.3
Asia	3.6	10.3	9.0	8.1	2.7
Latin America and the Caribbean	6.6	31.5	91.1	130.5	7.9
Middle East	3.7	10.6	18.7	11.9	5.7
All developing countries	4.3	15.7	35.5	33.3	6.0

Source: World Bank (2006a).

the countries with larger trade/GDP ratios are also producers of primary commodities, and in several cases, only a few of them suffered from the volatility in the prices of those goods.

Globalization and inflation.   Inflation in developing countries also followed a cycle of increases and declines in most regions (Table 8.3). Inflation peaked during the early 1990s in Africa (about 32 percent annual rate in 1992) and in Latin America and the Caribbean (460 percent in 1990), but in Asia the highest inflation was in 1974 (about 30 percent). There are clear differences across regions, with Latin America and the Caribbean showing the highest inflationary pressures, followed by Africa. Asia experienced only mild increases, more in line with inflation in the industrialized world and converging in the 2000s to annual rates less than 3 percent. In all developing regions, as in the industrialized world, inflationary pressures have abated since mid- to late 1990s.

There is now a lively debate about the links between globalization and lower inflation. Rogoff (2003), Romer (1993), and Frankel (2006) have argued that globalization has reduced inflation through different channels, including more competition by low-cost economies. Also, Tytell and Wei (2004), for instance, find that their measure of financial integration (in which they try to isolate the component of capital flows that is external to the countries) appears to be associated with the decline in inflation and conclude that financial globalization may have induced countries to pursue low-inflation monetary policies. Also they find that increases in trade openness are associated with lower inflation rates.

In general, lower inflation rates are associated with less price volatility. And if, as has been argued very early by Johnson (1947) and Schultz (1954), price volatility is more important than average prices in explaining agricultural supply (see also Timmer 1991, among others), then agriculture may benefit from the currently more stable inflationary environment. Stable inflation does not force excess adjustments on the agricultural prices (which tend to be more flexible than other goods and services and therefore absorb larger adjustments).[15]

Globalization, exchange rates, and credit. One of the characteristics of the state of development during the 1960s and 1970s in many developing countries was the granting of preferential loans through sectorally specialized institutions (industrial as well as agricultural and rural banks). In Brazil during the second half of the 1970s, for instance, agricultural credit represented about 100 percent of agricultural GDP, with interest subsidies that in some years amounted to some 5 percent of GDP (World Bank 1986). The expansion of credit was commonly financed through rediscounts from the country's central bank or similar institutions. In the context of closed capital accounts, the creation of excess liquidity added to inflationary pressures or fueled trade deficits, but developing countries retained some level of independence in the conduct of their monetary policies. During the 1980s, and then more markedly in the 1990s, many developing countries began to open up their capital accounts, which has important implications for the trade-offs among different exchange rate regimes and the conduct of monetary policies.

The exchange rate is one of the most important macro prices, with implications for both real and nominal variables. The importance of the real exchange rate and exchange rate policies for the performance of the agricultural sector, particularly the tradable sector, both in developed and developing countries, has been long recognized (Schuh 1974, 1976).

The opening of the capital account, generating greater integration with world financial markets, has led to what has been called the "impossible trinity" of macroeconomic policymaking: a country cannot have a fixed exchange rate, an open capital account, and an independent monetary policy simultaneously; it can use only two out of these three policy instruments. Countries can better handle international capital flows if they either have a more flexible exchange rate regime or have an extremely hard peg, such as dollarization. In general, most developing countries have moved from rigid pegs (Rogoff et al. 2003) and have devalued their real exchange rates compared to the 1960s and 1970s (Wood 1988; Cashin, Cespedes, and Sahay 2002). This policy in principle should have helped the agricultural sector, which is considered mostly a tradable sector, both with exportables and import substitutes.

But even with nominally floating exchange rates, the tendency in developing countries to try to maintain stable exchange rates (what has been called "fear of floating"; see Calvo and Reinhart 2002), combined with an open capital account, has probably resulted in more constrained monetary and credit policies (more on this topic below).

A related new development in monetary, financial, and fiscal conditions, particularly since the 1980s, has been the increase in dollarization[16] of developing countries (using various definitions of this term; Reinhart and Rogoff 2003), with countries abandoning their own currency (such as Panama a long time ago, and more recently

Table 8.4   Supply of money (percent of GDP)

Country category	1960s	1970s	1980s	1990s	2000–02
East Asia and Pacific	n.a.	25.2	41.7	81.6	129.5
Latin America and the Caribbean	15.8	17.5	19.1	24.3	26.7
South Asia	22.2	25.7	35.4	41.0	52.2
Sub-Saharan Africa	29.0	29.3	32.8	33.9	35.7
Low- and middle-income countries	19.4	22.6	32.8	43.7	62.6
High-income OECD countries	61.7	60.3	67.0	71.0	80.6
World	53.3	52.8	60.4	68.8	78.1

Source: World Bank (2006a).

Note: Supply of money is measured as a broader monetary aggregate that includes transaction balances. GDP, gross domestic product; n.a., not available; OECD, Organisation for Economic Co-operation and Development.

Ecuador and El Salvador) to different degrees of currency substitution, domestic asset and liability dollarization, and external indebtedness in dollars. Although the reasons for dollarization originally appeared to be linked to high inflation in these countries, the phenomenon has persisted and even intensified, despite declines in inflation.[17] The main conclusions from recent empirical studies are that in dollarized economies, monetary policy may be affected by a more unstable demand; those economies also show lower and more volatile growth; and the policy appears to have heightened the possibility of banking crises (Levy Yeyati 2005).

However, this changed monetary context is not equally present in all developing countries: large countries, such as India and China, maintain controls on capital account and do not show significant levels of dollarization. Asia in general is less dollarized than is Latin America and the Caribbean or Sub-Saharan Africa. In addition, Latin American countries also have very open capital accounts. Therefore, the possibility of resorting to direct agricultural credit financed by money creation is very different among those countries.

But at the same time, the financial deepening of developing countries' economies measured different monetary aggregates over GDP (Table 8.4) has increased over time, particularly in East Asia. High-inflation economies, such as those of Latin America and the Caribbean and, to a lesser degree, Sub-Saharan Africa, although also showing greater monetization of their economies, are clearly below the average for developing countries and the world. This monetization has increased while financial integration in world markets has advanced, although it is not clear what the links may be between financial globalization and greater domestic financial deepening (but see Kose et al. 2006, for a more positive view). In any case, a consequence of expanding monetary aggregates has been more credit availability.

The specific question here is whether the different monetary conditions led to restrictions in overall credit for the agricultural sector. In general, the approach in many developing countries of directed credit to agriculture—subsidizing interest rates and the use of certain inputs—began to find operational limits, and not necessarily because of the overall monetary conditions. Adams et al. (1984) found that directed agricultural credit programs benefited mostly large farmers and undermined the banking system through low collection rates or unsustainable subsidies. Moreover, such policies did not allow for proper mobilization of rural savings, did not ensure that funds were not diverted to other uses, and did not have a clear effect on a sustained expansion of new agricultural technologies. Consequently, interest in agricultural credit programs declined among donors: for instance, the World Bank's volume of agricultural lending in the 1990s was only one-third as large as in the 1980s (FAO/GTZ 1998). In addition, the IMF, the World Bank, and other international organizations—as part of the structural adjustment and stabilization programs of the mid-1980s and 1990s—supported financial sector reforms, including agricultural banks and parastatal companies that, among other things, provided credit to farmers (FAO/GTZ 1998; Kherallah et al. 2000). The problems with the agricultural financial system may have led to declines in agricultural credit through this channel.

Wenner and Proenza (1999) consider the percentage of agricultural credit over total credit and agricultural credit as a percentage of agricultural GDP for a number of Latin American and Caribbean countries (Bolivia, Brazil, Costa Rica, El Salvador, Guatemala, Honduras, Jamaica, Mexico, Peru, and Dominican Republic) for three periods: 1984–86, 1990–92, and 1994–96. They show that the unweighted average ratio of agricultural credit over total credit declined over these periods (17.8, 15.7, and 11.3 percent, respectively); the same is true for the percentage of agricultural credit over agricultural GDP (38.8, 33.4, and, 27.5 percent, respectively). Of the 10 countries, 9 showed lower ratios in the last period compared to the first for the first indicator and 7 for the second. Another study suggests that there have been declines in the supply of rural credit in China in the second part of the 1990s, with negative consequences also for nonfarm rural enterprises (Cheng and Xu 2004). However, in such regions as East Asia, where monetization and total credit as percentage of GDP have increased significantly more than in Latin America and the Caribbean, it should be expected that agriculture may have received increased lending.

At the same time, real interest rates showed important increases in the 1990s, particularly in Sub-Saharan Africa and Latin America and the Caribbean, where the real rates appear very high (Table 8.5).[18] Honohan (2000) found that as financial liberalization progressed, the general level of real interest rates increased more in developing countries than in industrialized ones, and the volatility of interest rates also increased in most liberalizing countries. In industrialized countries it has been recognized that

Table 8.5   Real interest rates (percent)

Country category	1970s	1980s	1990s	2000s
East Asia and Pacific	2.3	4.4	5.8	5.4
Latin America and the Caribbean	n.a.	5.2	8.5	10.4
South Asia	5.0	3.6	6.4	7.1
Sub-Saharan Africa	−0.7	4.8	9.7	12.5
Low- and middle-income countries	1.2	4.2	7.4	9.5

Source: Based on data from World Bank (2006a).
Notes: Values are the median across a sample of countries in each region. n.a., not available.

interest rates affect agriculture, which tends to be more capital-intensive than other sectors. However, the literature on the links between interest rates and agriculture in developing countries tends to be far more limited. In general, studies focus on the need to have interest rates high enough to ensure the viability of rural financial institutions, to help mobilize local savings and allocate credit to the more efficient uses (Adam, Graham, and von Pischke 1984), but interest rates that are too high will reduce the use of fertilizers and other inputs and adversely affect agricultural productivity.

Changes in monetary and financial conditions raise a series of questions regarding the conditions for agricultural institutions and agricultural credit going forward. The past approach of financing agriculture by resorting to generous rediscounts from central banks to be channeled through specialized institutions seemed restricted both by the general monetary conditions in countries with open capital accounts and the failures of those intermediaries in the past. On the other hand, the decline in inflation and increased monetization or financial deepening of the economies, as in East Asia, may lead to increases in agricultural credit as part of the general expansion in overall credit. However, if prevalent market conditions discriminate against agricultural credit or some types of farmers (for risk conditions or other reasons), then specialized institutions may be required. But they will require better management and incentives than in the past and must be coordinated with a sustainable monetary program that does not lead to inflation or exchange rate crises.

Increased financial globalization appears to have been accompanied by some negative developments, such as higher interest rates and an increased likelihood of bank crises, but, on the positive side, it may have led to lower and less volatile inflation and greater monetarization of the economy, and the exchange rate regimes in many developing countries may have moved away (with the exception of the dollarizers) from rigid pegs. Therefore, the influence of globalization on the agricultural sector of developing countries may vary, depending on the specific configuration of the different factors.

Conclusion

In general, it seems that globalization has been associated with more open and democratic societies, making governments at least potentially more responsive to the needs of the society, with positive implications for the rural population and the poor, who are a majority in many developing countries. At the same time, however, globalization is changing—and may be constraining, in some cases—the way in which governments can answer the demands of the electorate. Although there are no major constraints on developing countries' agricultural policies emanating from the WTO legal framework, deeper integration in world financial markets may pose limits to the type of fiscal and monetary policies pursued. Investments and credit for agriculture must be embedded in macroeconomic policies that are sustainable and do not lead to recurrent economic crises.

The recent era of globalization appears to be associated with some important changes in domestic macroeconomic policies in developing countries. Exchange rates have been unified in many countries, regimes appear to have moved toward managed floats, and there is a tendency toward less appreciated real exchanges rates (all of which may imply fewer exchange rate crises, after the spate of traumatic episodes of the mid- to late 1990s). Regarding fiscal policies, which were constrained during the debt crises of the 1980s and 1990s, governments seem to have recovered some room for maneuver. Still, the levels of agricultural expenditures may be less than what is needed to develop a dynamic agricultural sector, although it seems that the composition of expenditures in agriculture appear to have become somewhat more efficient, with a greater focus on public goods. Distorting trade taxes on agriculture also appear to have been reduced. Economies are operating in a less inflationary environment, and monetization or financial deepening of the economies (as in East Asia) seems to be increasing, which may lead to further expansion of agricultural credit as part of the general expansion in private credit. However, monetary policies appear constrained by the opening of capital accounts and the spreading of dollarization in some developing countries. Interest rates have also been high in real terms in many developing countries, at least until recently. In any case, the past approach of financing agriculture by resorting to generous rediscounts from central banks to be channeled through specialized institutions seemed restricted both by the general monetary conditions and the failures of those intermediaries in the past. Developing countries have been reducing overall trade protection, which—combined with adjustments in exchange rates and other macro policies—appears to have eliminated or at least reduced the "policy bias" against agriculture, if it ever existed.

Agriculture in developing countries should benefit, in general, from this improved setting for domestic policy. Perhaps that is the reason why, as documented in Chapter 1, agricultural growth, total and per person, appears to have been faster in the past two decades or so, compared to the 1960s and 1970s.

Establishing with certainty the links between these changes and globalization is more difficult. Part of the reason for that uncertainty is the use in the quantitative studies of many different proxies for globalization, even within the same dimension or variable (for instance, trade over GDP, tariffs, indicators from gravitational models, capital flows over GDP, price and interest rate differentials, and different measures of capital market liberalization, many of which can be measured in nominal, constant, or purchasing-power-corrected exchange rates, and which, furthermore, can be considered in levels or in changes). The aspect that is supposed to be affected by globalization (the dependent variable) also takes many different forms in the studies reviewed (in the case of fiscal variables alone, the studies surveyed utilized tax rates, tax collection or expenditures as percentage of GDP, and changes in the shares over time, all with different exchange rate valuations). Additionally, when analyzing the impact of globalization, many studies do not properly distinguish three levels that must be considered separately: (1) the degree of integration in the world system (globalization), (2) the conditions that prevail at the world level, and (3) the relevant domestic conditions. Discussing the impact of globalization without considering all three levels would be like opening a window and trying to evaluate the results of that action without taking into account the weather conditions outside and the health of the people inside can help to illustrate the point (Díaz-Bonilla, 2001b).

In any case, developing countries will not be able to address the challenges of globalization within a purely national setting. Even though they may implement the best policies, there are some issues that are global in nature and cannot be resolved until industrialized countries adopt a posture more committed to building a truly pro-development and pro-poor world economy.

Take for instance, agricultural policies. Current negotiations in the Doha Round must eliminate the combination of agricultural protectionism and high subsidies in industrialized countries that has limited agricultural growth in the developing world and weakened food security in vulnerable countries by competing with their domestic production. Also, WTO-related rules should consider the development needs of poor member countries and should not impose inefficient and unfair policy constraints and disproportionate administrative burdens (see also Chapter 5 and Essays 2–4).

Regarding financial and monetary conditions, the past 20 years have witnessed serious international financial crises, several of which stemmed from policy changes in industrialized countries that affected their exchange rates, interest rates, and capital flows, with destabilizing effects on the world economy and weaker countries. For example, both the debt crisis of the 1980s and the sequence of financial crises since the mid-1990s are related to important increases in the value of the dollar and strong upward adjustments in real interest rates. Although developing countries must reduce their vulnerability through better macroeconomic and financial policies, these may not be enough, if the major industrialized countries do not foster world financial stability with adequate macroeconomic policies and do not help establish a more equitable international system to cope with financial crises when they occur.

Although those issues may be more important for middle-income developing countries, the poorest countries—lacking access to international capital markets—need expanded aid flows to generate the resources necessary to reach the U.N. Millennium Development Goals by 2015. In particular, international financial institutions should increase funding for rural and agricultural development, poverty alleviation, and interventions in health, nutrition, and education.

Global issues—including preserving peace, fostering world macroeconomic stability, sustaining an open trade system, investing in technology for the poor, and improving environmental conditions—require global approaches and institutions. In the future, with a more stable world and domestic macroeconomic environment, and if the important policy-induced imbalances in world agricultural markets are diminished, it could be argued that the evolution of agriculture in developing countries will come back to being determined more by the internal dynamics of the sector, defined by increasingly market-oriented sectoral policies and the traditional interplay of technology, population, weather, and natural resources. Then, the main question will be for how long the cycle of technological change spurred by the Green Revolution can continue if more investments are not allocated to that end.

Notes

1. This section is based on Díaz-Bonilla and Robinson (2001).

2. Within dimension 1, Kaufmann, Kraay, and Zoido-Lobatón (1999) consider such issues as voice and accountability, civil and political rights, freedom of media, and political instability and violence. In dimension 2, the authors include commitment to policies, capacity of civil service, independence of civil service, quality of public service provision, and regulatory burden. Finally, in dimension 3, the elements considered are the rule of law and control of graft and corruption.

3. This work covers from 1870 to 2000, and the authors note that the relationship between international trade and democracy is positive, but the coefficient tends to become less statistically significant over time. They use an aggregate measure of democracy, which includes three components: (1) competitiveness and openness of executive recruitment, (2) constraints on the chief executive, and (3) competitiveness and regulation of political participation. They look at the relation of trade openness and the aggregate measure, but then examine each component separately, finding again that openness is positively associated with all of the components of the polity score, although the statistical significance drops in recent years.

4. The whole list includes public stockholding for food security purposes; domestic food aid; direct payments to producers, as decoupled income support; government financial participation in income insurance and income safety-net programs; payments made either directly or by way of government financial participation in crop insurance schemes or for relief from natural disasters; structural adjustment assistance provided through producer retirement programs; structural adjustment assistance provided through resource retirement programs; structural adjustment assistance provided through investment aids; payments under environmental programs; and payments under regional assistance programs. (Note that neither "boxes" nor "colors" are mentioned in the AoA.)

5. Also, most developing countries have set their tariffs at levels higher than the applied tariffs, allowing for possible changes in the effective levels of protection.

6. Developing countries also retain access to different policies to promote their industries as part of the promotion of science and technology. Amsden and Hikino (2000) argue that the constraints on policies that developing countries face are related less to legal aspects than to the political pressures from industrialized countries in favor of radical market opening and to the lack of answers from developing countries when confronted with such pressures.

7. Some observers have criticized the AoA for not having enough instruments to protect the agricultural sector of developing countries. Trade protection of crops is generally not equivalent to protection of the livelihoods of poor people. First, there are important differences in the rural and urban configurations of poverty in developing countries (Díaz-Bonilla, Thomas, and Robinson 2004). Second, the implicit tax on food also has negative consequences for the poor. Díaz-Bonilla, Diao, and Robinson (2004) simulate a situation in which the tax revenues of the implicit and mostly privatized tax are obtained through a less distorting tax instrument and invested in agricultural technology (Green Box measures), with more positive effects on overall income, employment, agricultural production, and food security.

8. The main issue here is determining the proper counterfactual. Usually these programs are implemented when countries face economic crises, and therefore, a before-and-after analysis is inadequate. The adequate comparison would be with what would have happened without the program. On one hand, these programs provide financial resources that countries do not have, and therefore, this component should help smooth the crises. On the other hand, critics argue that the policy conditionality attached to the resources may have aggravated the crisis, or that the program at least could have been better designed to help growth and poverty alleviation.

9. Fiscal data used here come from the World Development Indicators of the World Bank. However, there are important changes between the 2004 version, which included more fiscal data, and the latest version, in which most fiscal data for previous decades seem to have been eliminated.

10. The countries included in the study are Bangladesh, China, India, Indonesia, Republic of Korea, Malaysia, Myanmar, Nepal, Pakistan, Philippines, Sri Lanka, and Thailand.

11. The countries are Argentina, Bolivia, Brazil, Chile, Colombia, Costa Rica, Dominican Republic, Ecuador, Guatemala, Honduras, Jamaica, Mexico, Nicaragua, Panama, Paraguay, Peru, Uruguay, and Venezuela.

12. Those taxes are explicit. Krueger, Schiff, and Valdés (1990) argue that implicit taxes, such as overvalued exchange rates, nontariff barriers, import tariffs, and procurement programs (monopoly marketing) affecting output prices, have been more important in defining the level of taxation of agriculture.

13. The KOF Index, constructed by Konjunkturforschungsstelle (KOF), the Swiss Institute for Business Cycle Research, uses a variety of indicators combined to form six groups: actual flows of trade and investment, restrictions of international transactions, variables measuring the degree of political

integration, variables quantifying the extent of personal contacts with people living in foreign countries, variables measuring transborder flows of information, and a proxy for cultural integration. These six groups are combined to form the three subindexes for economic, political, and social aspects, and then further combined into an overall index of globalization.

14. See Glick, Guo, and Hutchison (2004) on the openness of capital accounts and the probability of currency crises; Calvo, Izquierdo, and Mejia (2004) on trade openness and crises generated by sudden stops; and Kose, Prasad, and Terrones (2005) on economies more open to trade and financial flows being able to absorb higher levels of volatility without having adverse effects on growth.

15. Lower inflation may also benefit the poor. Easterly and Fischer (2000), using household data for 38 countries find that both in their perception (the poor are more likely to mention inflation as a concern) and in reality (several measures of welfare of the poor are negatively correlated with inflation in general, and high inflation lowers the share of the bottom quintile and the real minimum wage and increases poverty), inflation is a real problem for the poor.

16. The term "dollarization" is a simplified way to refer to the increased use of a foreign currency—usually (but not always) the U.S. dollar—to perform one or several of the monetary functions of medium of exchange, store of value, and unit of account.

17. Causes for that persistence may include volatility of domestic inflation vis-à-vis volatility of the real exchange rate. Such volatility is possibly linked to a lack of a credible monetary policy and imperfections in financial markets and regulations that offered implicit advantages to holdings of dollars (such as the perceived implicit guarantee of government intervention to bail out banks in case of a large devaluation).

18. The countries included are Bangladesh, India, Nepal, and Sri Lanka in South Asia; China, Indonesia, Malaysia, Myanmar, Philippines, and Thailand in East Asia and the Pacific; Bolivia, Chile, Colombia, Costa Rica, Ecuador, El Salvador, Guatemala, Guyana, Honduras, Jamaica, Nicaragua, Panama, Peru, Trinidad and Tobago, Uruguay, and Venezuela in Latin America and the Caribbean; and Burundi, Cameroon, Central African Republic, Chad, Congo, Gabon, The Gambia, Kenya, Nigeria, Sierra Leone, South Africa, Swaziland, Zambia, and Zimbabwe in Sub-Saharan Africa. The low- and middle-income category includes additional countries from North Africa, the Middle East, and transition economies.

References

Adams, D. W., D. H. Graham, and J. von Pischke, eds. 1984. *Undermining rural development with cheap credit*. Boulder, Colo., U.S.A.: Westview Press.

Adserà, A., and C. Boix. 2002. Trade, democracy, and the size of the public sector: The political underpinnings of openness. *International Organization* 56 (2): 229–262.

Aizenman, J., and Y. Jinjarak. 2006. Globalization and developing countries—A shrinking tax base? NBER Working Paper 11933. Cambridge, Mass., U.S.A.: National Bureau of Economic Research.

Allcott, H., D. Lederman, and R. López. 2006. Political institutions, inequality, and agricultural growth: The public expenditure connection. World Bank Policy Research Working Paper 3902. Washington, D.C.: World Bank.

Amsden, A. H., and T. Hikino. 2000. The bark is worse than the bite: New WTO law and late industrialization. *Annals of the American Academy of Political and Social Science* 570 (1): 104–114.

Bhagwati, J. N. 1982. Directly unproductive profit seeking (DUP) activities. *Journal of Political Economy* 90 (5): 988–1002.

Calvo, G. A., and C. M. Reinhart. 2002. Fear of floating. *Quarterly Journal of Economics* 117 (2): 379–408.

Calvo, G. A., A. Izquierdo, and L.-F. Mejia. 2004. On the empirics of sudden stops: The relevance of balance-sheet effects. NBER Working Paper 10520. Cambridge, Mass., U.S.A: National Bureau of Economic Research.

Cardoso, F. H., and E. Faletto. 1979. *Dependency and development in Latin America.* M. Mattingly Urquidi, translator. Berkeley, Calif., U.S.A.: University of California Press.

Cashin, P., L. Cespedes, and R. Sahay. 2002. Keynes, cocoa, and copper: In search of commodity currencies. IMF Working Paper 02/223. Washington, D.C.: International Monetary Fund.

Cheng, E., and Z. Xu. 2004. Rates of interest, credit supply and China's rural development. *Savings and Development* 28 (2): 131–156.

Collier, P., and A. E. Hoeffer. 1998. On the economic causes of civil war. *Oxford Economic Papers* 50 (4): 563–573.

Cooper, R. 1980. *The economics of interdependence.* Council on Foreign Relations Series. New York: Columbia University Press.

Correa, C. M. 2000. *Intellectual property rights, the WTO, and developing countries: The TRIPS Agreement and policy options.* Penang, Malaysia: Third World Network.

Diao, X., E. Díaz-Bonilla, and S. Robinson. 2003. *How much does it hurt? The impact of agricultural trade policies on developing countries.* Issue Brief. Washington, D.C.: International Food Policy Research Institute.

Díaz-Bonilla, E. 1999. South American wheat markets and MERCOSUR. In *The economics of world wheat markets,* ed. J. M. Antle and V. Smith. Cambridge, Mass., U.S.A.: CAB International.

———. 2001a. Globalization and agriculture: Some facts, interpretations, and policy issue. In *Globalization and rural development,* ed. O. Solbrig, R. Paarlberg, and F. Di Castri. Cambridge, Mass., U.S.A.: Harvard University Press.

———. 2001b. Globalization, poverty, and food security. In *Sustainable food security for all by 2020: Proceedings of the 2020 Conference,* September 4–6, Bonn, Germany. Available at http://www .ifpri.org/2020conference/PDF/summary_diaz-bonilla.pdf.

Díaz-Bonilla, E., and S. Robinson. 2001. *Shaping globalization for poverty alleviation and food security.* 2020 Vision Focus 8. Washington, D.C.: International Food Policy Research Institute.

284 GLOBALIZATION OF FOOD AND AGRICULTURE AND THE POOR

Díaz-Bonilla, E., X. Diao, and S. Robinson. 2004. Thinking inside the boxes: Alternative policies in the development and food security boxes. In *Agricultural policy reform and the WTO: Where are we heading?* ed. G. Anania, M. E. Bohman, C. A. Carter, and A. F. McCalla. London: Edward Elgar.

Díaz-Bonilla, E., M. Thomas, and S. Robinson. 2004. Food security and the World Trade Organization: A typology of countries. In *Agricultural Trade Liberalization: Policies and Implications for Latin America,* ed. M. S. Jank. Baltimore: The Johns Hopkins University Press for the Inter-American Development Bank.

Dorosh, P. A., and D. E. Sahn. 2000. A general equilibrium analysis of the effect of macroeconomic adjustment on poverty in Africa. *Journal of Policy Modeling* 22 (6): 753–776.

Dos Santos, T. 1970. The structure of dependence. *American Economic Review* 60 (2): 231–236.

Dreher, A., and L. Siemers 2005. The intriguing nexus between corruption and capital account restrictions. Swiss Institute for Business Cycle Research (KOF) Working Paper 05-113. Zurich: Swiss Federal Institute of Technology Zurich. Available at http://www.kof.ch/pdf/wp_113.pdf.

Dreher, A., J. E. Sturm, and H. W. Ursprung. 2006. The impact of globalization on the composition of government expenditures: Evidence from panel data. CESIFO Working Paper 1755. Munich: Center for Economic Studies and Ifo Institute for Economic Research.

Easterly, W., and S. Fischer. 2000. Inflation and the poor. World Bank Policy Research Working Paper 2335. Washington, D.C.: World Bank.

Easterly, W., R. Islam, and J. Stiglitz. 2000. Shaken and stirred: Explaining growth volatility. *Proceedings of the Annual World Bank Conference on Development Economics 2000,* ed. B. Pleskovič and Nicholas Stern. Washington, D.C.: World Bank.

Eichengreen, B., and D. Leblang. 2006. Democracy and globalization. NBER Working Paper 12450. Cambridge, Mass., U.S.A.: National Bureau of Economic Research. Available at http://www.nber.org/papers/w12450.

Fan, S., and P. Pardey. 1998. Government spending on Asian agriculture: Trends and production consequences. In *Agricultural public finance policy in Asia.* Tokyo: Asian Productivity Organization.

FAO/GTZ (Food and Agriculture Organization of the United Nations/German Agency for Technical Cooperation). 1998. *Agricultural finance revisited: Why?* FAO/GTZ Africa 1. Rome.

FAO RLC (Regional Office for Latin America and the Caribbean of the Food and Agriculture Organization of the United Nations). 2006. *GPR: Base de datos de estadísticas e indicadores de gasto publico agrícola y rural.* Santiago, Chile.

Finger, J. M., and P. Shuler. 1999. Implementation of the Uruguay Round commitments: The development challenge. Presented at the World Bank Conference on Agriculture and the New Trade Agenda: Interests and Options in the WTO 2000 Negotiations, October 1–2, Geneva.

Frankel, J. 2006. What do economists mean by globalization? Implications for inflation and monetary policy. Written for academic consultants meeting, Board of Governors of the Federal Reserve System, September 28, Washington, D.C. Available at http://ksghome.harvard.edu/~jfrankel/FRB-Globalzn&InflOct4.pdf.

Giavazzi, F., and G. Tabellini. 2005. Economic and political liberalizations. *Journal of Monetary Economics* 52 (7): 1297–1330.

Giddens, A. 1999. Reith lecture on democracy. BBC World Service—Online Network. Available at http://www.bbc.co.uk/radio4/reith1999/lecturer.shtml.

Glick, R., X. Guo, and M. Hutchison. 2004. Currency crises, capital account liberalization, and selection bias. Santa Cruz Center for International Economics Working Paper 1037. Santa Cruz, Calif., U.S.A.: Center for International Economics, University of California at Santa Cruz. Available at http://repositories.cdlib.org/cgi/viewcontent.cgi?article=1037&context=sccie.

Hallward-Driemeier, M. 2001. Openness, firms, and competition. Washington, D.C.: World Bank. Available at http://rru.worldbank.org/Documents/PapersLinks/1248.pdf.

Hamilton, C. 2002. Globalization and democracy. Discussion Paper 3653. London: Center for Economic Policy Research.

Harrison, A. 2006. Globalization and poverty. NBER Working Paper 12347. Cambridge, Mass., U.S.A.: National Bureau of Economic Research.

Hellman, J. S., G. Jones, and D. Kaufmann. 2000. Seize the state, seize the day: State capture, corruption, and influence in transition. Policy Research Working Paper 2444. Washington, D.C.: World Bank.

Hirschman, A. 1982. The rise and decline of development economics. In *The theory and experience of economic development,* ed. M. Gersowitz, C. Díaz-Alejandro, G. Ranis, and M. Rosenzweig. London: George Allen and Unwin.

Honohan, P. 2000. How interest rates changed under financial liberalization: A cross-country review. Working Paper 2313. Washington, D.C.: World Bank.

IMF (International Monetary Fund). 1999. *World economic outlook (WEO): International financial contagion.* Washington, D.C.

———. 2006. International Financial Statistics (IFS) database. Washington, D.C.

Johnson, D. G. 1947. *Forward prices for agriculture.* Chicago: University of Chicago Press.

Kaufmann, D., A. Kraay, and P. Zoido-Lobatón. 1999. Governance matters. Policy Research Working Paper 2196. Washington, D.C.: World Bank.

Keohane, R., and J. Nye. 1977. *Power and interdependence: World politics in transition.* Boston: Scott Foresman.

Khan, M. H. 2001. Agricultural taxation in developing countries: A survey of issues and policy. *Agricultural Economics* 24 (2001): 315–328.

Kherallah, M., C. Delgado, E. Gabre-Madhin, N. Minot, and M. Johnson. 2000. *Agricultural market reforms in Sub-Saharan Africa: A synthesis of research findings.* Washington, D.C.: International Food Policy Research Institute.

Kose, M. A., E. S. Prasad, and M. E. Terrones. 2005. Growth and volatility in an era of globalization. *IMF Staff Papers* 52 (Special Issue): 31–63. Washington, D.C.: International Monetary Fund.

Kose, M. A., E. S. Prasad, K. S. Rogoff, and S.-J. Wei. 2006. Financial globalization: A Reappraisal. NBER Working Paper 12484. Cambridge, Mass., U.S.A.: National Bureau of Economic Research.

Krueger, A. O. 1974. The political economy of the rent-seeking society. *American Economic Review* 64 (3): 291–303.

Krueger, A. O., M. W. Schiff, and A. Valdés. 1990. *Economía política de las intervenciones de precios agrícolas en América Latina.* San Francisco: Banco Mundial, Centro Internacional para el Desarrollo Económico, afiliado al Instituto de Estudios Contemporáneos.

Langley, S. V., ed. 2000. *International agriculture and trade reports: International financial crises and agriculture.* Washington, D.C.: U.S. Department of Agriculture, Economic Research Services.

Levy Yeyati, E. 2005. Financial dollarisation: Evaluating the consequences. Business School Working Papers 03/2005. Buenos Aires: Universidad Torcuato Di Tella. Available at http://www.utdt .edu/Upload/CIF_wp/wpcif-032005.pdf.

Li, Q., and R. Reuveny. 2003. Economic globalization and democracy: An empirical analysis. *British Journal of Political Science* 33 (1): 29–54.

Lipset, S. M. 1960. *Political man. The social bases of politics.* Garden City, N.Y., U.S.A.: Anchor Books.

Lipton, M., and M. Ravallion. 1995. Poverty and policy. In *Handbook of development economics,* vol. 3, ed. J. Behrman and T. N. Srinivasan. Amsterdam: North-Holland.

Little, I., T. Scitovsky, and M. Scott. 1970. *Industry and trade in some developing countries.* London: Oxford University Press for the Development Center of the Organisation for Economic Cooperation and Development.

López, R. 2005. Under-investing in public goods: Evidence, causes, and consequences for agricultural development, equity, and the environment. *Agricultural Economics* 32 (1): 211–224.

López-Cordova, J. E., and C. M. Meissner. 2005. Globalization and democracy 1870–2000. NBER Working Paper 11117. Cambridge, Mass., U.S.A.: National Bureau of Economic Research.

Marshall, M., and T. R. Gurr (with contributions by V. Asal, B. Harff, D. Khosla, and A. Pate). 2005. *Peace and conflict 2005: A global survey of armed conflicts, self-determination movements, and democracy.* College Park, Md., U.S.A.: Center for International Development and Conflict Management, University of Maryland. Available at http://www.cidcm.umd.edu/inscr/PC05 print.pdf.

Moore, M., J. Leavy, P. Houtzager, and H. White. 1999. Polity qualities: How governance affects poverty. Working Paper 99. Brighton, U.K.: Institute for Development Studies, University of Sussex.

Nkrumah, K. 1965. *Neo-colonialism—The last stage of imperialism.* London: Thomas Nelson & Sons.

Pardey, P., B. D. Wright, and C. Nottenburg. 2002. *Are intellectual property rights stifling agricultural biotechnology in developing countries? The 2000–2001 Annual Report.* Washington, D.C.: International Food Policy Research Institute.

Prasad, E., K. Rogoff, S.-J. Wei, and M. A. Kose. 2003. Effects of financial globalization on developing countries: Some empirical evidence. IMF Occasional Paper 220. Washington, D.C.: International Monetary Fund.

Reinhart, C. M., and K. Rogoff. 2003. The modern history of exchange rate arrangements: A reinterpretation. *Quarterly Journal of Economics* 119 (1): 1–48.

Reinhart, C. M., K. Rogoff, and M. Savastano. 2003. Addicted to dollars. NBER Working Paper W10015. Cambridge, Mass., U.S.A.: National Bureau of Economic Research.

Rigobon, R., and D. Rodrik. 2004. Rule of law, democracy, openness and income: Estimating the interrelationships. NBER Working Paper 10750. Cambridge, Mass., U.S.A.: National Bureau of Economic Research.

Rogoff, K. 2003. Globalization and global disinflation. Paper prepared for the symposium Monetary Policy and Uncertainty: Adapting to a Changing Economy, sponsored by the Federal Reserve Bank of Kansas, August 28–30, Jackson Hole, Wyo., U.S.A.

Rogoff, K., A. Husain, A. Mody, R. Brooks, and N. Oomes. 2003. Evolution and performance of exchange rate regimes. IMF Working Paper 03/243. Washington, D.C.: International Monetary Fund.

Romer, D. 1993. Openness and inflation: Theory and evidence. *Quarterly Journal of Economics* 108 (4): 869–903.

Schamis, H. 1999. Distributional coalitions and the politics of economic reform in Latin America. *World Politics* 51 (January): 236–268.

Schuh, G. E. 1974. The exchange rate and U.S. agriculture. *American Journal of Agricultural Economics* 56 (1): 1–13.

———. 1976. The new macroeconomics of agriculture. *American Journal of Agricultural Economics* 58 (5): 802–811.

Schultz, T. W. 1954. The instability of farm prices reconsidered. *Journal of Farm Economics* 36 (5): 777–786.

Schulze, G., and H. W. Ursprung. 1999. Globalisation of the economy and the nation state. *World Economy* 22 (3): 295–352.

Sen, A. 1984. *Resources, values, and development.* Cambridge, Mass., U.S.A.: Harvard University Press.

Servan-Schreiber, J. J. 1968. *The American challenge*. New York: Atheneum.

Shane, M., and W. Liefert. 2000. The international financial crisis: Macroeconomic linkages to agriculture. *American Journal of Agricultural Economics* 82 (3): 682–687.

Smith, L. C., and L. Haddad. 2000. *Explaining child malnutrition in developing countries: A cross-country analysis*. Research Report 111. Washington, D.C.: International Food Policy Research Institute.

Stiglitz, J. 2002. *Globalization and its discontents*. New York: W. W. Norton.

Thomas, V., M. Dailami, A. Dhareshwar, D. Kaufmann, N. Kishor, R. López, and Y. Wang. 2000. *The quality of growth*. Oxford and Washington, D.C.: Oxford University Press and World Bank.

Timmer, Peter. 1991. Food price stabilization: Rationale, design, and implementation. In *Reforming economic systems,* ed. D. H. Perkins and M. Roemer. Cambridge, Mass., U.S.A.: Harvard Institute for International Development, Harvard University.

Tytell, I., and S. J. Wei. 2004. Does financial globalization induce better macroeconomic policies? IMF Working Paper WP/04/84. Washington, D.C.: International Monetary Fund.

Van Blarcom, B., O. Knudsen, and J. Nash. 1993. The reform of public expenditures for agriculture. World Bank Discussion Paper 216. Washington, D.C.: World Bank.

Vernon, R. 1971. *Sovereignty at bay: The multinational spread of U.S. enterprises*. New York: Basic Books.

Wei, S.-J. 2000. Natural openness and good government. NBER Working Paper 7765. Cambridge, Mass., U.S.A.: National Bureau of Economic Research.

Wenner, M. D., and F. Proenza. 1999. Rural finance in Latin America and the Caribbean: Challenges and opportunities. Sustainable Development Department, Microenterprise Unit Working Paper. Washington, D.C.: Inter-American Development Bank.

Wood, A. 1988. Global trends in real exchange rates: 1960–84. World Bank Discussion Paper 35. Washington, D.C.: World Bank.

World Bank. 1986. *World development report 1986*. New York: Oxford University Press.

———. 2006a. *World development indicators 2006*. Washington, D.C.

———. 2006b. Global Development Finance database. Washington, D.C.

Changing Paradigms during Globalization

Sartaj Aziz

Globalization is a powerful and irreversible phenomenon that is offering new opportunities to countries at the upper end of the competitive ladder but is also creating enormous difficulties for many low-income countries, because they are unable to face competition in an unequal world.

The basic concepts that propel globalization are sound, but, like all good ideas, they have their limitations and pitfalls. The preconditions under which these concepts can be practiced and implemented are also not readily forthcoming in all developing countries. Globalization has indeed helped millions of people to improve their living standards, particularly in high- and middle-income countries, by liberalizing the economy to allow freer movement of capital and technology. The unprecedented communication revolution and the spread of information technology have not only facilitated greater integration of the world economy but have also promoted the spread of democracy and a vibrant civil society.

But globalization has not worked for about half the world population that is living on less than US$2 per person a day. Even worse is the case of the 1.1 billion people, or one-fifth of humankind, who are chronically poor and barely survive on less than US$1 a day (World Bank 2006). The poverty situation in the least-developed countries is much worse than in the rest of the developing world: about 760 million people, 19 percent of the total population, were seriously undernourished in 2002–04 (FAO 2006).

The past years have witnessed an unprecedented public uproar about the effects of globalization on the poor. The media showed thousands of young people, mostly from western countries, protesting at many major international meetings during the early 2000s. But, apart from some progress on the debt issue, there are as yet no signs that the major changes that are needed in global governance, in the policies of international economic institutions, and in the theology of the free market are being seriously considered.

Unless these drastic changes are made fairly quickly and decisively, the present global system will further impoverish the already poor, pushing them to desperation and even terrorism. The Millennium Summit goal of halving poverty by 2015, adopted by heads of state and government in September 2000, is not just a pious wish but a critical threshold that the rich members of the global community must cross if they want to see a more stable and orderly world in the future.

A great deal has been already written about globalization—its various meanings, philosophical foundation, and positive and negative effects on different countries and regions. But there is as yet no coherent framework of policies and actions on the basis of which globalization can be made to work for the poor. This commentary attempts to identify some of the main elements of such a framework.

Conceptual Issues

The conceptual framework of globalization has to be modified to make it more balanced and consistent with ground realities. The Bretton Woods institutions (the IMF and World Bank) were created in 1945 to implement Keynesian economic policies, including policies to stimulate economic growth and expand employment through higher government spending. But in the early 1980s, in the wake of the Latin American economic crisis, the philosophy of these institutions changed to focus on free market systems without a floor. As a result, even poor countries are being asked to open their markets prematurely. Most of these low-income countries primarily depend on agricultural exports, but their share in global agricultural trade has been falling, because they cannot compete with the heavily subsidized agricultural exports from industrialized countries. These subsidies, estimated at US$260–280 billion in 2003–05, provide about 30 percent additional income to farmers in countries that belong to the OECD. That is why U.S. farmers can export wheat at prices below their cost of production: there is always a subsidy available that covers the difference. On the other hand, Pakistan is an efficient producer of wheat and can export wheat without subsidies, but in the distorted current markets it is not allowed by the IMF conditionalities to subsidize its wheat exports even by a far smaller amount than does the United States or other developed countries.

Thus, industrialized countries themselves do not practice what they preach. And yet they encourage the international financial institutions to put pressure on developing countries to eliminate their meager agricultural subsidies. The far larger subsidies of the industrialized countries also weaken incentives for agricultural production in developing countries because of competition from cheaper imports.

The poverty reduction strategies being adopted by developing countries under the guidance of the World Bank and the IMF primarily focus on stabilization policies in the expectation that lower budget deficits and low inflation will automatically lead to higher investment and growth. There is some icing on the cake in the form of social safety nets or targeted interventions to counter any negative fallout of these strategies on the poor. But when fiscal space is squeezed by the adjustment process and the pattern of growth promotes inequality and poverty, then a separate poverty reduction program, which creates only limited employment opportunities, can hardly reverse the overall trend.

Another major flaw in the present conceptual framework of globalization concerns the role of government. Even if the superiority of the market system in determining resource allocation and prices is accepted, there is no denying the important role that the state must play in protecting the rights of the weak and poor segments of the population and in meeting their basic needs. The inherent inadequacies of the market are, in fact, fully understood in the more advanced societies. That is why they have created laws and institutions against monopolies to protect the consumer and small businesses, and they have developed an elaborate system of taxation and social security to protect the weak and assist the poor. But at the global level, they refuse to recognize the effects of inappropriate globalization policies on the poor and develop similar compensating mechanisms and policies.

Policy Framework for Poverty Reduction

Once these fundamental flaws are recognized in the present conceptual framework of globalization, the task of evolving an alternative policy framework that goes beyond liberalization—that acknowledges the limitations of free market ideology and can lay the foundation of sustainable and equitable growth—would be relatively straightforward. An alternative policy framework that would make globalization work for the poor has to include policies and actions at global, national, and local levels.

Global Policies

At the global level, the present trading and financial systems do not provide a level playing field for developing countries and poor people; aid flows are not only inadequate but also not targeted at problems caused by poverty, and the policy prescriptions being imposed in the name of globalization are generally inappropriate. In fulfillment of the pledge to reduce the proportion of poor people by half by 2015, five specific actions at the international level are urgently called for.

The first step would be to implement as speedily as possible the commitments made at WTO ministerial meeting in Doha, in November 2001, to reduce agricultural subsidies. Because this effort will take time, it is equally necessary to explore innovative measures under which, as long as these subsidies continue, they do not depress agricultural markets. Correspondingly, developing countries should not be pressured, in the meantime, to reduce their food or agricultural subsidies. A fundamental change in present trade policies for agriculture and simple manufactures, which are based on double standards, will be the acid test of sincerity in dealing with the issue of global poverty.

The second major step would be to implement in letter and spirit the Monterrey Consensus adopted in Mexico in 2002 as an effective response to the events of September 11. The proposal put forward at that time by then U.K. Finance Minister Gordon Brown (2002) to launch a Marshall Plan by setting up a US$50-billion-a-year investment fund "that will help build the capacity of the poorest countries for sustainable development" continues to be discussed and promoted in the G8 fora. A sharp increase in the flow of official development assistance (ODA) to low-income countries remains an urgent priority. There are hopeful indications that the United States and other donor countries are expanding their aid budgets, but it is equally important that the bulk of this increased ODA is in the form of grants or very soft loans and is provided for sectors that directly benefit the poor and improve their capacities through education and health services. There is also an urgent need for more flexible forms of lending for poverty reduction. If structural adjustment loans can be given for changes in macro policies, such as exchange rate adjustment and deficit reduction, why not give similar nonproject loans and grants for policy and institutional changes to reduce poverty? Similarly, grants and soft loans with a grant element of at least 70 percent for poverty reduction and human development should be factored in when calculating the fiscal deficit.

The third area for speedy action is that of debt relief. In June 2005 the Multilateral Debt Relief Initiative followed the enhanced Initiative for HIPC. The Multilateral Debt Relief Initiative will cancel 100 percent of the debt claims by the IMF, the International Development Association of the World Bank, and the African Development Fund on countries that have reached (or will eventually reach), the completion point under the enhanced HIPC Initiative. However, implementation needs to be accelerated and the resulting net flows to the poor countries included must be monitored to ensure that they receive the resources needed to attain the Millennium Development Goals. The debt relief initiative has to go further, also considering substantial relief for other low-income countries. Without such relief, the majority of developing countries will not have the resources to accelerate their rates of economic growth, which is one of the most important prerequisites for poverty reduction.

Fourth, perhaps the time has arrived to give concrete shape to many ideas for new and innovative sources of financing development, which have been under discussion for a long time. With budgetary problems and domestic concerns facing most donor countries, the required increase in ODA and debt relief would be difficult to achieve in the coming years without some form of autonomous funding that is no longer dependent on national budgets. The proposal for a carbon tax on petroleum consumption has received some support in Europe recently. Similarly, there may be some scope for the Tobin tax, a tax on global currency movements. The idea of generating revenues from global commons like seabed mineral and fishing rights for providing global public goods has been gaining ground. Public support for such initiatives can be expanded if these are exclusively linked to debt relief, poverty reduction, and sustainable development initiatives and if the contribution of each country can be counted against its ODA.

Finally, international economic institutions must be allowed to modify their free market philosophies, which thrust upon developing countries a standard adjustment policy to achieve macroeconomic stability by reducing government spending, raising utility charges, and eliminating all subsidies. They also bring about a degree of economic liberalization in trade and financial sectors that is not in line with the institutional structures and regulatory mechanisms of the countries concerned, thereby imposing heavy economic and social costs, as experienced during the Asian economic crisis of 1997. In the process, the growth rate slows down, unemployment goes up, poverty increases, and the fiscal squeeze makes it increasingly difficult for most governments to stimulate the economy or provide essential social services. In developing countries in which the fiscal deficit is, say, higher than 6 percent of GDP, the current account deficit is more than 4 percent, and the rate of inflation is relatively high, the stabilization agenda should receive priority under the guidance of the IMF. But where the macroeconomic situation is relatively stable, the focus should shift to investment, growth, and poverty reduction, and the responsibility for the preparation and implementation of Poverty Reduction Strategy Papers should shift from the IMF to the World Bank, in cooperation with the regional development banks and the United Nations Development Programme.

National Policies

At the national level, developing countries have to assume primary responsibility for poverty reduction and show real political commitment to policies and programs that are required for moving toward this objective. In the past years, a large number of developing countries have prepared Poverty Reduction Strategy Papers to qualify for loans from IMF's Poverty Reduction and Growth Facility, but these documents have not influenced national policies and priorities in any meaningful manner. Nor does the involvement of a few middle-level civil servants in preparing these "home-grown" papers really indicate any strong commitment or involvement at the political level. In fact, as already mentioned, the main thrust of these IMF-sponsored strategies is so heavily tilted toward stabilization policies and conditionalities that impose additional burdens on the poor that political leadership would generally find it difficult to identify with and implement such a strategy.

A determined attack on poverty and hunger will require renewed commitment on the part of political leaders and a series of actions flowing from this commitment. First, a National Poverty Reduction Strategy rather than a Poverty Reduction Strategy Paper could be formulated as a major component of a 5-year plan or as an independent strategy. If the country is negotiating an arrangement with the IMF, a Poverty Reduction Strategy Paper can be a subsidiary part of the national strategy after a careful consistency check to ensure that the macroeconomic targets and policies in the paper provide enough fiscal space for poverty reduction and social spending.

These National Poverty Reduction Strategies will have to be based on a new development paradigm, which recognizes the role of the state not just in preventing failures in the market system but also in ensuring social justice for the poor. It will also start from the premise that social and human development is an essential prerequisite for sustainable development and cannot be treated as a marginal objective to be financed from residual financial resources that the adjustment process may have to spare or through trickle-down effects of other programs.

Third, these strategies will have to go beyond social safety nets or targeted interventions to a pro-poor growth strategy that focuses directly on improving the incomes of the poor through mainstream interventions in the process of growth and through pro-poor policies that benefit the poor substantially rather than marginally. The traditional growth strategy, which tried to reduce inequalities through limited redistribution policies, is not sustainable. A rapid growth strategy is needed that automatically improves the lives of the poor by focusing on sectors where the poor earn their livelihoods, such as agriculture, small-scale irrigation, and livestock, and that relies on factors of production the poor possess—namely, labor or skills.

Fourth, a principal cause of poverty is the social gap, reflected in the low level of human development, the lack of social protection, and a persistent neglect of rural areas. An effective National Poverty Reduction Strategy must therefore ensure universal access to education, enforcement of the rule of law in all parts of the country, favorable terms of trade for agriculture, major expansion of rural infrastructure, and improved delivery and quality of social services.

Social Mobilization at the Local Level

Although basic changes in the global economic system are required to provide a level playing field and a strong political commitment to poverty reduction is necessary at the national level, social mobilization at the local level will be absolutely vital to ensure people's participation and empowerment.

There have been many successful examples of social mobilization and microcredit programs through which community organizations have been able to market their produce, undertake small infrastructure projects, and improve the delivery of social services in their areas. But it has not been easy to scale up such pilot projects, partly because of local political or ethnic rivalries and partly due to apprehensions that political empowerment of the poor, if it grows, will get out of hand.

The National Poverty Reduction Strategy in each country has to face these issues squarely in the light of its own circumstances and promote affirmative action to decentralize administrative authority and financial powers, strengthen the role of civil society through community organizations, improve governance through proper enforcement of property rights and a better judicial system, and ensure that the resources being provided for the benefit of the poor are not hijacked by the local elite. These are very sensitive political subjects and cannot be dealt with adequately in a Poverty Reduction Strategy Paper, which is prepared under the supervision of such donors as the IMF or World Bank. Only a strategy based on strong political commitment from top leadership can deal with these issues more effectively and comprehensively.

Conclusion

It is important to emphasize that poverty is a complex phenomenon in which inherent causes are compounded by human biases and discriminatory policies that are accentuated by the tyranny of the present global economic system. At the national level, overcoming poverty requires a major process of social transformation that goes beyond the traditional patterns of growth and in which the governments and civil society work together to develop human resources, empower poor people, and build their networks to bring about decisive change in favor of the poor. But these efforts, even if launched, would not go very far if agricultural subsidies in OECD countries continue to destroy incentives for agriculture in low-income countries, the flow of ODA keeps falling in real terms and is accompanied by harmful conditionalities, and the debt burden continues to cripple the economic capacity of low-income countries. The Millennium Development Goal of halving poverty by 2015 can be met only if there is vigorous and simultaneous action at the global, national, and local levels in favor of the poor.

References

Brown, G. 2002. How to win the peace. In *Democratic Leadership Council (DLC) Blueprint Magazine—The W Economy,* March/April. Available at http://www.ndol.org/ndol_ci.cfm?contentid=250311&kaid=124&subid=158.

FAO (Food and Agriculture Organization of the United Nations). 2006. FAOSTAT. Rome.

World Bank. 2006. *World development indicators 2006.* Washington, D.C.

Chapter 9

Conflict, Food Insecurity, and Globalization

Ellen Messer and Marc J. Cohen

Thishis chapter explores how globalization, broadly conceived to include international human rights norms, humanitarianism, and alternative trade, might influence peaceful and food-secure outlooks and outcomes. For more than two centuries, proponents and critics of an open global economy have debated whether free flows of goods, services, and capital make the world more or less peaceful and food-secure. Proponents argue that as nations expand the commercial, financial, communications, and cultural ties that bind them, they are less likely to go to war (see Schneider, Barbieri, and Gleditsch 2003 for a summary of these positions). Critics counter that as global economic liberalization worsens socioeconomic inequalities within and among nations, conflict frequently follows (see, for example, Danaher 1994; Lappé, Collins, and Rosset 1998; Shiva 1999; Araghi 2000; Bello 2001; on the ills of financial globalization, see Stewart 1993; Smith 1994; Addison 2005).

Not surprisingly, the two sides disagree over whether more liberalized trade in agricultural commodities will provide a way out of poverty for developing-country farmers and economies or will exacerbate their poverty problems; so much depends on contexts. What is not in dispute is that trade in primary commodities is associated with most wars of the 1980s, 1990s, and 2000s, either as cause or source of conflict or as means of payment for arms and armies (P. Collier 2003). Because the contexts of

The authors thank María Soledad Bos, Mary Ashby Brown, Maina Muthee, Ella Yadao, and IFPRI's Spatial Analysis Group for their help in developing this chapter. They are also grateful to Joachim von Braun, James Garrett, and Rajul Pandya-Lorch of IFPRI and Professor Indra de Soysa of the Norwegian University of Science and Technology for their helpful comments and suggestions.

conflicts are integrally linked to food insecurity (Messer, Cohen, and D'Costa 1998; FAO 2000), the connections between global trade and conflict are a concern for food and nutrition policymakers, who are especially interested in agricultural commodities, which have been left out of most globalization-conflict models (see, for example, P. Collier 2003).

As our previous studies have demonstrated (Messer 1994, 1996a; Messer, Cohen, and D'Costa 1998; Messer and Cohen 2001; Messer, Cohen, and Marchione 2001), most wars of the late twentieth and early twenty-first century have been "food wars," meaning that food is used as a weapon, food systems are destroyed in the course of conflict, and food insecurity persists as a legacy of conflict. We have shown that food insecurity—used here to denote food shortage, lack of access to food, malnutrition, or some combination of these—can also be a source of conflict. Our concern here is to demonstrate how globalization (including trade in primary agricultural commodities but also global norms and institutions promoting humanitarianism, human rights, and alternative development and trade) is connected to conflict and food insecurity. Our entry point to explore these connections is to examine cases of food wars for a single year, to see whether and how the country-level attributes of conflict, food security, and trade in agricultural and other primary commodities support globalization-and-peace, globalization-and-war, or neither hypothesis.

Because no previous studies explicitly attempt to explore the links among all three factors, a second way to consider the relationships is to summarize and integrate the analytical frameworks and findings of the many previous studies that have dealt with any two of the three factors: conflict and food insecurity, conflict and globalization, and globalization and food insecurity. This literature review fills gaps and critiques certain conclusions of the existing conflict-transformation literature, which emphasizes conflict typologies and historical trends.

A third approach is to sketch particular country-level, historical contexts where widely grown and traded agricultural commodities, such as sugarcane, coffee, and cotton, appear to have contributed to conflict, to see what lessons these cases suggest for agricultural policy. A fourth and final perspective is to consider where globalization, widened in concept to include humanitarian operations, human rights norms, and alternative trade organizations, appears to have contributed to more peaceful and food-secure outlooks and outcomes. We conclude by suggesting how greater scrutiny of the local and country-level conditions of agricultural production and trade, along with this broader globalization concept, might be useful for formulating more comprehensive agricultural, globalization, and conflict models for research and policymaking.

Conflicts, Food Insecurity, Globalization, and Their Consequences

A first, and the simplest, way to gauge the connection of globalization to food insecurity and conflict is to identify, classify, and count conflict countries and then, for each one, ascertain and describe the food-security status, openness to trade, and how these relate to conflict. If the simplified pro-trade position ("globalization/more liberalized trade is peace-promoting") is correct, we would expect conflict countries not to be heavily involved in trade, which is supposed to create peace-promoting ties, but instead to be relatively isolated. An aggregate picture of the resulting conflict–food insecurity–globalization scenarios also offers a snapshot in time of how globalization is proceeding, whether promoting peace or conflict, in the initial years of the twenty-first century.

The results of this exercise, which we undertook in 2003 using 2002–03 as our year of record, describe 44 countries, 25 active-conflict, 17 postconflict, and 2 conflict-refugee recipient countries where war-related violence, economic and public-welfare disruptions, and refugee flows contributed to food insecurity.[1] It is worth noting that four years later, in 2006, conflict persisted in 18 of the 25 countries (72 percent), and seven new conflicts had erupted even as cease-fires took hold in seven of the previous battle zones. Significantly, some of these "new" conflicts involved the renewal of old hostilities, such as fighting in Chad, Lebanon, Nigeria, and Thailand (Center for Systemic Peace 2007; UCDP 2007).[2] Thus there is a rather stable set of developing and transition countries in conflict in the decade of the 2000s.

Map 9.1 shows conflict countries and aggregate percentages of food-insecure people; Map 9.2 displays conflict countries and estimated needs for humanitarian assistance. Tables 9.1 and 9.2 characterize these countries, using standard world data sets, to show

- conflict status (Eriksson, Wallensteen, and Sollenberg 2003; Marshall and Gurr 2003; SIPRI 2003a),

- the food-insecure portion of the populace (FAO 2003b),

- the population considered in need of humanitarian assistance by the U.N. system (OCHA 2003),

- major exports (CIA 2003), and

- openness to trade (defined by the U.S. government's State Failure Taskforce and the World Bank as imports and exports as a share of GDP; Esty et al. 1995; World Bank 2003).

The figures and tables indicate, not surprisingly, that conflict and postconflict countries tend to be food insecure, with greater than 20 percent of the population—

Figure 9.1   Countries in conflict and percentage of food-insecure people, 2002–03

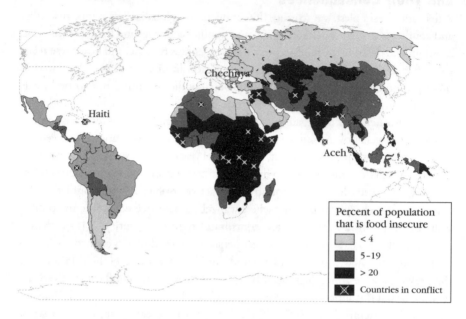

Figure 9.2   Countries in conflict and estimated need for humanitarian assistance, 2002–03

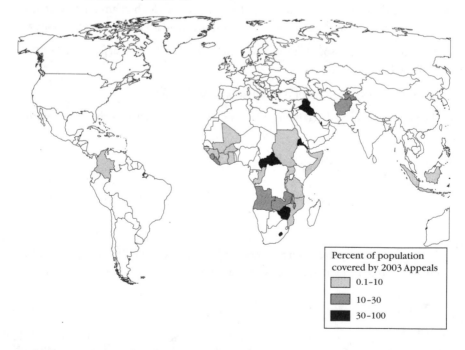

and in many cases far more—lacking access to adequate food, although not all highly food-insecure populations are in conflict countries.

A comparison of columns 1 and 2 in Tables 9.1 and 9.2 shows that the food-insecure share of the populace usually far exceeds the percentage of the population judged to be in need of humanitarian assistance. The wide ranges in these numbers also suggest that judgments of food insecurity and humanitarian need may require additional country-by-country scrutiny in a careful comparison. Furthermore, a number of active conflicts did not generate U.N. appeals for humanitarian assistance, although the conflict countries in question (Nepal, Sri Lanka, and the Philippines) had a substantial incidence of food insecurity overall, and the actual conflict situations constituted food wars.[3] It is also true that some countries have very high levels of food insecurity and no conflict (Niger, for example). For the sake of comparison over time, we note that the United Nations appealed for nearly half a billion U.S. dollars worth of food and other humanitarian assistance for 31 million people in conflict-affected countries in 2006 (OCHA 2007).

Regarding the assertions that globalization promotes peace, or that openness to trade lowers conflict potential, we observe that a simple measure of "openness to trade" at one point in time appears not to be a good indicator of conflict potential or food-security status. These wide-ranging numbers do not support the proposition that openness to trade promotes peace.[4]

The evidence presented in the tables also appears to refute the notion that, after 10 or more years of globalization, the first decade of the twenty-first century is becoming more peaceful than the 1990s were, as some analysts assert (Gleditsch et al. 2002, 616; Marshall and Gurr 2003, 1; Human Security Centre 2005). What they classify as "interstate" wars of the 1980s and 1990s may be fewer and less intense, but internal conflicts multiplied during the 1990s, elevating the total numbers of wars at least to prior levels (Smith 1997). And significant interstate (really, transnational) wars erupted in the 2000s in Afghanistan and Iraq as many of the civil wars of the previous decade wound down.[5] Also, continuing food insecurity in former war zones potentiates renewed conflict.[6]

Taxonomies of conflict, moreover, do little to elucidate the influence of the fighting on food security and other livelihood considerations. There is, for example, considerable debate over whether women and children account for a disproportionate share of those affected.[7] Nor do the taxonomies shed much light on the role of globalization in fomenting or resolving conflict. In the countries we have characterized as post-conflict—Cambodia, El Salvador, Mozambique, and Nicaragua, for instance—the consequences of previous wars continue to exact a toll on food security and economic development. These countries still suffer the consequences of food wars, which deliberately destroyed agricultural production capacity, markets, and health infrastructure

(Text continues on page 309)

Table 9.1 Countries in conflict and food insecurity, 2002–03

Region/country	Population that is food insecure (percent of total population)[a]	Population in need of humanitarian assistance (percent of total population)		Major exports	Imports + exports/ GDP (percent)	Notes
Sub-Saharan Africa	33	16,636,000	(2.8)		57	
Burundi	70	416,000	(6.8)	Coffee, tea, sugar, cotton	29	Active, high-intensity
Republic of the Congo	30	174,000	(4.7)	Oil, coffee, cocoa, sugar, timber, diamonds	105	Sporadic fighting; active, medium-intensity
Democratic Republic of the Congo	75	2,600,000	(4.6)	Diamonds, oil, coffee, copper, cobalt	15	"African World War"; 16 million food-insecure people in country; active, low-intensity
Côte d'Ivoire	15	3,000,000	(9.2)	Cotton, coffee, cocoa, oil	76	
Ethiopia	42	4,200,000	(6.7)	Coffee, qat, bauxite, alumina, gold, diamonds, fish	n.a.	Ethnic rebellions ongoing in drought-affected regions; internal displacement from past wars; active, low-intensity
Guinea	28	400,000	(6.4)	Bauxite, alumina, gold, diamonds, coffee, fish, agricultural products	40	Refugees
Liberia	42	1,000,000	(23.6)	Rubber, timber, iron, diamonds, cocoa, coffee	n.a.	Active, low-intensity
Rwanda	41	40,000	(0.5)	Coffee, tea, hides, tin ore	15	Low-intensity conflict continues
Somalia	71	750,000	(9.4)	Livestock, bananas, hides, fish, charcoal, scrap metal	n.a.	Active, low-intensity
Sudan	25	2,800,000	(7.3)	Oil, cotton, sugar, gum Arabic, livestock, sesame, peanuts	29	Active, high-intensity
Tanzania	43	506,000	(1.4)	Gold, coffee, cashew nuts, manufactures, cotton	24	Refugees
Uganda	19	750,000	(3)	Coffee, fish, tea, cotton, gold, flowers	33	Active, high-intensity

Asia	16[b]	7,100,000		East Asia: 66 South Asia: 24	
Afghanistan	70	4,100,000 (14.3)	Opium poppies, heroin, cotton, carpets, gems	n.a.	Active, medium-intensity
Myanmar (Burma)	7		Heroin, wood products, rice, pulses, beans, fish	—	Rebellions in Shan and Karen states; active, multiple medium-intensity conflicts
India	21		Textile goods, gems and jewelry, engineering goods, chemicals, leather manufactures	20	Border conflict with Pakistan over Kashmir (productive farming territory); localized rebellions; active, multiple conflicts of intensities ranging from low to high (Kashmir)
Indonesia	6	3,000,000 (1.4)	Oil and gas, electrical appliances, plywood, textiles, rubber	62	Separatist rebellion in Aceh, with 15 percent of Indonesia's oil and gas production at stake; active, medium-intensity
Nepal	17		Carpets, clothing, leather goods, jute goods, grain	43	Active, high-intensity
Philippines	22		Electronic equipment, machinery and transport equipment, garments, coconut products, chemicals	98	Communist and Muslim insurgencies, military mutiny; active, multiple medium-intensity conflicts
Sri Lanka	25		Clothing, tea, diamonds, coconut products, petroleum products	73	Ceasefire holding in most conflict zones; active, low-intensity
Europe	**n.a.**	**1,200,000**		**Europe and Central Asia: 66; Europe EMU: 56**	
Russia	4	1,200,000 (0.8)	Petroleum and petroleum products, natural gas, wood and wood products, metals, chemicals, civilian and military manufactures	60	Separatist rebellion in oil-rich Chechnya; active, medium-intensity
Latin America	**10**	**3,000,000 (0.6)**		**30**	
Colombia	13	3,000,000 (6.6)	Cocaine, coffee, cut flowers, coal, clothing	30	Active, high-intensity
Haiti	49		Manufactures, coffee, oils, cocoa	46	
Peru	11		Fish and fish products, gold, copper, zinc, crude petroleum and by-products, lead, coffee, sugar, cotton	33	

(continued)

Table 9.1 (continued)

Region/country	Population that is food insecure (percent of total population)[a]	Population in need of humanitarian assistance (percent of total population)		Major exports	Imports + exports/ GDP (percent)	Notes
Near East / North Africa						
Algeria	10	28,500,000	(7.3)	Oil	52	Active, medium-intensity
Iraq	27	27,000,000	(100)	Oil	n.a.	Active, high- to medium-intensity; United Nations appealing for food aid for entire populace
Israel-Palestine	n.a.	1,500,000		Fruit, vegetables, limestone (West Bank and Gaza)	63	Active, medium-intensity
Turkey	3			Apparel, foodstuffs, textiles, metal manufactures, transport equipment	65	Active, medium-intensity
Total countries in conflict		56,436,000				

Sources: SIPRI (2000); USCR (2000); CIA (2003); Eriksson, Wallensteen, and Sollenberg (2003); FAO (2003b); Marshall and Gurr (2003); OCHA (2003); World Bank (2003).

Note: EMU, Economic and Monetary Union; GDP, gross domestic product; n.a., not available.

[a] According to the definition of food insecure in FAO (2003b).

[b] Excluding Afghanistan and Tajikistan.

Table 9.2 Postconflict countries and food insecurity, 2002–03

Region/country	Population that is food insecure (percent of total population)[a]	Population in need of humanitarian assistance (percent of total population)	Major exports	Imports + exports/ GDP (percent)	Notes
Sub-Saharan Africa	**33**	**10,090,000**		**57**	
Angola	49	3,700,000 (28.2)	Crude oil, diamonds, refined petroleum products, gas, coffee, sisal, fish and fish products, timber, cotton	127	Returnees in need of assistance
Central African Republic	44	2,200,000 (59.5)	Diamonds, timber, cotton, coffee, tobacco	29	
Eritrea	61	2,300,000 (52.3)	Livestock, sorghum, textiles, food	97	IDPs, returnees in need of assistance
Mozambique	53	590,000 (3.4)	Aluminum, prawns, cashews, cotton, sugar, citrus, timber, bulk electricity	66	Land mines; damage to human and physical capital
Sierra Leone	50	1,300,000 (22.8)	Diamonds, cocoa, coffee	25	Returnees, refugees in need of assistance
South Africa			Gold, diamonds, platinum, other metals and minerals, machinery and equipment	53	
Togo	25		Re-exports, cotton, phosphates, coffee, cocoa	82	
Asia	**16**[b]	**1,000,000**		**East Asia: 66 South Asia: 24**	
Cambodia			Timber, garments, rubber, rice, fish	115	Land mines
Tajikistan	71	1,000,000 (15.2)	Cotton, textiles, electricity	147	Large population remains internally displaced
Europe					
Armenia	51		Diamonds, mineral products, foodstuffs, energy	72	
Azerbaijan	21		Oil and gas, machinery, cotton, foodstuffs	81	
Bosnia	8		Metals, clothing, wood products	85 (in 2000)	
Georgia	26		Scrap metal, machinery, chemicals; fuel re-exports; citrus fruits, tea, wine	60	
Serbia	9		Manufactured goods, food and live animals, raw materials	n.a.	

Table 9.2 (continued)

Region/country	Population that is food insecure (percent of total population)[a]	Population in need of humanitarian assistance (percent of total population)[a]	Major exports	Imports + exports/ GDP (percent)	Notes
Latin America	**10**	**403,000**		**37**	
El Salvador	14	143,000	Coffee, sugar, textiles, electricity, light manufactures	59	
Guatemala	25	260,000	Coffee, sugar, bananas, other fruits, vegetables, meat, electricity, oil, clothing	39	Land mines remain a problem in Central America.
Nicaragua	29		Coffee, shrimp and lobster, cotton, tobacco, bananas, beef, sugar, gold	n.a.	
Total countries post conflict		**11,493,000**			

Sources: SIPRI (2000); USCR (2000); CIA (2003); Eriksson, Wallensteen, and Sollenberg (2003); FAO (2003b); Marshall and Gurr (2003); OCHA (2003); World Bank (2003).

Note: EMU, Economic and Monetary Union; GDP, gross domestic product; IDP, internally displaced person; n.a., not available.

[a]According to the definition of food insecure in FAO (2003b).

[b]Excluding Afghanistan and Tajikistan.

Table 9.3   Contending schools of thought on conflict, globalization, and food security

Analyst	Main cause(s) of conflict	Role of globalization	Role of food insecurity
State Failure Task Force	Nondemocratic governance	Lack of openness to trade contributes to conflict	High infant mortality contributes to conflict
Environmental security	Intergroup competition over scarce resources	None specified	Food insecurity is a manifestation of resource scarcity
Ethnic conflict	Intergroup competition over wealth and power	None	None
U.N. University	Poverty, inequality, slow growth, militarism	None	Slow growth in food production contributes to conflict
International Development Organization	None specified	Humanitarian assistance can fuel conflict	Sustainable livelihoods critical to peace
World Bank	Poverty, economic decline, dependence on primary product exports	Dependence on primary product exports a key factor in conflict	Poverty, inequality, declining incomes per person all contribute to conflict
International Peace Research Institute, Oslo (PRIO)	Economic, political, and social factors, not environmental scarcities	Openness to trade has indirect pacifying effects, but reliance on primary product exports contributes to conflict	None specified

Sources: State Failure Task Force: Esty et al. (1995, 1998), Goldstone et al. (2003), Marshall and Gurr (2003); Environmental security: Homer-Dixon (1999); Ethnic conflict: Gurr and Harff (2000), Paarlberg (2000), Marshall and Gurr (2003); U.N. University: Nafziger and Auvinen (2000); International Development Organization: Schafer (2002); World Bank: P. Collier (2003); PRIO: de Soysa (2000, 2002), Hegre, Gissinger, and Gleditsch (2003).

(see Simler et al. 2003 on Mozambique, for example), while land mines and unexploded ordnance continue to kill or maim people and make farming hazardous.

In sum, we agree with Marshall and Gurr (2003, 2), who note, "the globalization of the economy, of communications, and of governance by their very nature creates new threats and challenges, as well as opportunities." Conflict scenarios, which usually involve food insecurity, also involve international flows of arms and other commodities as aspects of globalization. It is therefore necessary to probe the steps by which globalization contributes to conflict or peaceful outcomes in particular cases.

Conflict Scenarios

Over the past decade, analysts have proposed a number of scenarios and correlations connecting globalization, conflict, and, less consistently, food insecurity. We summarize the views of the key analysts in Table 9.3 and provide a more detailed discussion of their findings in this section.

Conflict Causes Food Insecurity:
Reducing Availability, Access, and Utilization

Food-(in)security studies, including our own, document an unsurprising overlap between conflict and food insecurity. Elsewhere we have quantified the effects of conflict on food availability: cumulative declines in mean food production and growth rates of food production in 13 of 14 African conflict countries during 1970–94 (Messer, Cohen, and D'Costa 1998; Messer, Cohen, and Marchione 2001).[8] Using the same methodology and extending the analysis through 1997 and across regions, FAO found that, during 1970–97, the developing world experienced conflict-induced losses of agricultural output of US$121 billion in real terms. In Sub-Saharan Africa, the losses in the 1980s and 1990s accounted for more than 50 percent of all aid received and far exceeded foreign investment inflows (FAO 2000).

In almost all affected countries, where the majority of the workforce depended on agricultural livelihoods (World Bank 2003), civil war lowered GDP per person by an estimated 2.2 percentage points per year (World Bank 2000, 57). UNICEF statistics furthermore demonstrated little improvement in child malnutrition and mortality rates in conflict countries, which were and are unlikely to design and implement plans for child survival even when they have ratified the Convention on the Rights of the Child (Mason, Csete, and Jonsson 1996). In national budgets, military spending far exceeded peaceful social and economic expenditures for agriculture and rural development, including health, primary education, and food and nutrition programs (Sivard 1996; SIPRI 2003b). Although this disparity is largely true across countries, in the late 1990s and early 2000s low- and middle-income countries devoted nearly 13 percent of government budgets to defense (World Bank 2003). In sum, to borrow the entitlement language of Amartya Sen (1981, 1999), conflict causes food insecurity by reducing food production, entitlements to produce or gain access to food, and human welfare and capabilities through the destruction of the environment, health and health care, education, and other social infrastructure.

Food Insecurity as a Cause or Correlate of Conflict

Studies of the political economy of war seldom look directly at food insecurity as either a cause or a consequence of conflict, because of the complexity of the evidence of causation and the changing conceptualization of conflict. During the Cold War, scholars and politicians focused on the struggles for land and access to subsistence underlying the peasant wars of the twentieth century (Wolf 1969). U.S. food aid helped friendly governments maintain food security and political power (Wallerstein 1980; Cohen 1984). Agricultural modernization efforts, notably the Green Revolution in parts of Asia and the U.S. government's Alliance for Progress in Latin America, were framed and presented as alternatives to the "Red Revolution" of peasant uprisings (Wallerstein 1980).

After the Cold War, concern shifted from "war studies" to "peace studies," which analyze the causes of conflict and its prevention, management, and transformation. Some focused on perceived environmental scarcities and their consequences, including food insecurity, as either underlying or trigger causes (Homer-Dixon 1999), whereas others stressed political-cultural identities (Rupesinghe 1996; Gurr and Harff 2000; Paarlberg 2000). Still others tried to put resource scarcity, population pressure, and ethnic and religious strife together in the same model (for example, Kahl 2006).

In yet another reframing, modelers associated with the World Bank's project on the Economics of Civil Wars, Crimes, and Violence (P. Collier and Hoeffler 1998, 2000; P. Collier 1999, 2000, 2001, 2003) considered the economic motivations for war, arguing that conflict was precipitated in some cases by "greed" (the desire to control resources) and in others by "grievance" (the perception of unfairness by those receiving the short end of contested resources). They concluded that in most cases of active conflict, greed trumps grievance (P. Collier 2000). Their studies looked at contexts that take into account levels and sources of national and household income, ethnolinguistic fractionalization, natural resource endowments, and population size. But they did not focus on these economic correlates—extreme poverty, inequality, declining per capita incomes—as root causes of conflicts, only on how warring parties pay for them (P. Collier 2003) and, perhaps by default, why the military as an occupation in situations of abject penury might be so attractive.

Scholars at the International Peace Research Institute in Oslo (PRIO), like the World Bank team, found that natural resource abundance tends to fuel civil war. They did not find a link between resource scarcity and internal conflict (de Soysa 2000, 2002). None of these authors, however, put multiple factors and frameworks together, to see where food insecurity and globalization, taken together, affect conflict potential.

Additional political studies of the economic correlates of war, as a principal finding, have also found conflict associated with high infant mortality (Esty et al. 1995, 1998) or intergroup competition over land and water (Markakis 1998; Homer-Dixon 1999)—both sets of factors closely related to food insecurity. But like Collier's studies for the World Bank, these do not deal with food insecurity or agricultural trade as a direct causative or correlative factor in conflict.

A partial exception is the work of Nafziger and Auvinen (2000), which found that between 1980 and 1995, poverty, low growth in incomes and food production, high inequality, and inflation—combined with high military spending and a tradition of military conflict—heightened countries' vulnerability to humanitarian emergencies. But this study did not specify the precise pathways through which these factors might combine and lead to conflict. Similarly, Ohlsson (2000) recognized that conflict potential is especially high when inequalities or environmental degradation lead to extreme marginalization of large segments of populations, who suffer loss of livelihoods and face the prospect that new generations will never be able to sustain themselves.

More recent political-economic narrative country-level case studies, which have tried to trace the causal pathways, still mostly leave out food security as a goal or food insecurity as a motivation for armed uprisings or for joining military operations (Arnson and Zartman 2005; Kahl 2006). At their best, these case studies do consider (1) where the misery of hunger caused by corrupt leadership that appropriates natural resources, and also hoards and sells food, leads to discontent and violence (for example, chapters on Peru and Sierra Leone in Arnson and Zartman 2005); (2) where profits from cash crops, such as coffee, have provided the economic foundations for continuing inequality and violence (the chapter on Colombia in Arnson and Zartman 2005); and (3) where lack of food among combatants who have taken refuge in remote and undersupplied locations may spell the end of a longstanding rebellion (the chapter on Angola in Arson and Zartman 2005). But food insecurity and a sense of outrage at injustice as root causes of conflict are the exception rather than the rule in these efforts to test Collier's propositions about greed and grievance with real data (Esty et al. 1995, 1998; Homer-Dixon 1999; Nafziger and Auvinen 2000; P. Collier 2003).

Our own review of country case studies indicates that both greed and grievance are implicated in intergroup competitions over resources, including access to cash crops and resources to produce and profit from them, but also development and emergency aid (Messer, Cohen, and Marchione 2001). The trigger conditions for violence may be

- natural, such as a prolonged drought (as in Ethiopia in 1973–74; see Shepherd 1975);

- economic, such as a change in price of the principal food (rice in Indonesia; see Fuller and Falcon 1999) or cash crop (coffee in Rwanda; see Uvin 1996), which deprives the affected population of its perceived just standard of living; or

- political, such as the denial of access to land or social welfare programs in Chiapas, Mexico (G. Collier and Quaratiello 1999).

Historically, as Wolf (1969) has shown, most individuals, households, communities, and peoples denied access to resources adequate to feed themselves and to live their lives with dignity have failed to rebel because they are insufficiently organized and are terrorized and repressed. But such conditions of unchanneled frustration and hopelessness can lead to violence and conflict once political leadership emerges that can successfully mobilize this discontent in ways that serve a leader's or group's particular political ends, usually articulated as a struggle for social justice or political identity.[9]

Based on Wolf's framework, we can hypothesize about the connections of globalization and particular export commodities to food insecurity and conflict. Twentieth-century peasant revolutions stemmed from peasant perceptions of subsistence crises, precipitated by landlord greed and peasant grievance connected to competition between cash crops and food crops for land, labor, water, and other resources (Wolf 1969). Such crises have also been linked to more general patterns of government failure to implement effective land or other agrarian reforms, as well as to failures of government or local elites to respond adequately to natural disasters, more liberalized trade, or sudden changes in commodity prices that threaten anticipated livelihoods and standards of living. As we show in our discussion of case studies below, all these factors in particular cases have led individually or in combination to a breaking point, where local farmers felt that they had nothing more to lose, and so rose up in armed conflict to protest and try to reverse the ultimate threat to their subsistence or basic human dignity.

Two possible reasons why we do not see more of these subsistence crises framed as peasant (or urban) revolutions is (1) they have been hijacked by leaders who push other greed and/or grievance agendas into armed violence that is not self-limiting the way one expects peasant revolutions should be (P. Collier 2003; P. Collier and Hoeffler 2004; Arnson and Zartman 2005). Instead, those who lead the violence have a vested interest in keeping conflict going because they profit from war; or (2) international agents intervene to feed people, try to find ways to limit suffering and deliver development assistance, or help them organize more effectively to solve their crises at the local level without violence, as in the case of the Negros region in the Philippines (see below), or as seen in the efforts of humanitarian aid workers to help populations rehabilitate livelihoods in Sudan and Ethiopia and other former theaters of war (see, for example, Barrett and Maxwell 2005; Young and Osman 2006).

Trade as a Cause or Correlate of Conflict

Studies of the possible relationship between globalization and conflict have similarly underplayed the food factor, along with the steps through which trade and either war or peace are related. The U.S. government-funded State Failure Task Force found "openness to trade" (that is, the share of imports and exports in GDP) to be a weak correlate of civil war avoidance (Esty et al. 1995, 1998).[10] But the methodology they used was not designed to describe the underlying peace-protecting mechanisms, so it does not offer much guidance to policymakers.

The World Bank's study on civil wars came to a rather contrary conclusion, finding a high risk of internal conflict in contexts combining low per capita income, economic decline, high inequality, and dependence on primary commodity exports, which can fund war economies (P. Collier 2003). But their examples of high-value "blood" commodities (gems, minerals, timber, drugs, and petroleum) generally did not include such cash crops as coffee (P. Collier and Hoeffler 1998; P. Collier 2000, however, makes passing reference to coffee).

PRIO scholars bridged the gap between these two studies, determining that the empirical evidence supports both the view that, in general, trade openness considerably reduces the likelihood of civil war (de Soysa 2002) and the view that natural resource abundance tends to fuel civil war (de Soysa 2000), particularly where primary products are the only exports (Hegre, Gissinger, and Gleditsch 2003). Thus, trade can contribute to peace, albeit indirectly, by contributing to growth. Across Sub-Saharan Africa, however, where cash-crop production tends to increase inequalities, civil war is a more likely outcome, although poverty, poor governance, and violence may also result from "too little globalization rather than too much" (Hegre, Gissinger, and Gleditsch 2003, 272).

Consistent with these ambiguous findings, Tables 9.1 and 9.2 indicate no clear pattern of trade openness among the conflict and postconflict countries. For some, the trade openness score exceeds the 2001 global average of 40 percent, the low- and middle-income-country average of 49 percent, and the high-income-country average of 38 percent (World Bank 2003). But quite a few war-prone nations have much lower scores. The ambiguous results contribute to the strong disagreement in the literature over the relationship between global economic links and conflict. They may also indicate that not enough attention has been paid to financial factors in globalization. Addison (2005), for example, citing the cases of Afghanistan, Angola, and Sierra Leone, demonstrates that international and national financial policies and farmer-unfriendly terms of trade, particularly for key cash crops, can precipitate or fuel conflict in new or postconflict situations.

Arms and "Blood Commodities" Foster War, Not Peace

Clearly, the nature of the commodities and the terms on which they are traded have considerable bearing on whether global trade promotes peace or war. Globalization's integration of markets includes a US$17 billion (in 1990 dollars) market in arms, which conflict-prone governments buy with income from minerals, drugs, petroleum, and other licit and illicit commodities. Between 1998 and 2002, legal arms suppliers sold US$5.1 billion worth of weapons to Africa. Globally, the black market in small arms is valued at US$2–10 billion, and it supports lesser crime, corruption, and thuggery at multiple social levels, as well as full-scale war (O'Grady 1999; Mtonga 2003; Shah 2003; SIPRI 2003b).[11]

In Africa, military purchases are often financed through international transfers, including private sales of, and concessionary access to, primary commodities. Petroleum and natural gas resources and their control figure prominently in many of the late-twentieth-century conflicts and in geopolitics generally—from Azerbaijan to

Sudan (see Tables 9.1 and 9.2). Trade in gems, minerals, and timber finances arms and mercenaries for many current African and Asian hostilities. Sales of diamonds support hostilities in West Africa and the Democratic Republic of the Congo (DRC), which also concedes cobalt, coltan, gold, copper, and timber to its military supporters. Countries that trade in these primary commodities show higher rates of poverty and child mortality than nations that do not, and they also have a higher propensity to conflict (Kaldor 1999; SIPRI 2000; Ross 2001; P. Collier 2003). It remains a question whether cane, cotton, coffee, and cocoa—all high-value commodities traded on international markets—also sometimes function as blood commodities, which have been used to fund war, not peaceful development.

On the opposite track, globalization also includes efforts to stem trade in illicit conflict-funding commodities. The Kimberly process, which certifies diamonds as not financing hostilities in Africa, and a timber certification process intended to restrict funds to the military in Myanmar are two examples of such efforts. Going beyond such monitoring and regulation, agricultural fair-trade certifications and child-labor protocols also address problems of extreme poverty and other correlates of conflict at the local level. In such situations, export crops, such as "peace" coffee, can have a positive influence on peace promotion and food security.

Agricultural Trade, Conflict, and Food Insecurity: Evidence from Case Studies

Cash cropping can raise household incomes, enhance household productive capacities, and raise state revenues that can be used to improve food security and build additional infrastructure that serves economic development. But the peace dividend depends on the types of commodities, the scale and breadth of trade, the structural conditions of production and distribution of benefits, the financial terms of trade, and a particular leader's calculation about the costs of warfare versus benefits of peace, assuming her or his side will win (Dorussen 2002).

Research suggests that trade reduces conflict incentives only when other internal political stressors are absent and when trading-partner countries enjoy relatively symmetric economic and military relations (Schneider, Barbieri, and Gleditsch 2003). Otherwise, the revenues from food or cash crop production may qualify as one of the sources of greed or grievance in the inception, transformation, and postwar prevention of conflict. Given all these qualifications, it is probably more instructive to examine particular case studies of cash crops, food insecurity, and conflict under particular political-economic conditions.

For example, small farmers have succeeded in entering markets for high-value-added fruit and vegetable exports in such countries as Vietnam and Uganda, where an increase in staples output accompanied the growth in small farmers' export production. Case studies also show that export cropping contributes to poverty reduction and food security where policies, practices, and institutions ensure that small farmers, especially women, have access to land, capital, information, education, and health infrastructure (von Braun and Kennedy 1994; Kherallah et al. 2002; Watkins and von Braun 2003). But international marketing of cash crops, such as French beans, grown for export in Burkina Faso and Zambia, involves multiple layers of brokers and many cultural, health, and environmental considerations for both growers and consumers. As a result, market conditions can shift very rapidly, reducing cash crop incomes relative to food crops (Freidberg 2004). Power relations are not symmetrical, and the playing field is bumpy, not level.

The social relations of production also exert considerable influence over the relationship between legal export crop production and conflict. Transnational corporations (TNCs), such as United Fruit Company, invested heavily in tropical agriculture and produce fruits, coffee, and chocolate, which have large markets in temperate zones where they cannot be produced. Historically, these TNCs have allied with national elites to control land, dominate markets and transportation, limit wages, and create tariff conditions favorable to their accumulation of wealth, sometimes at the expense of land-poor or landless workers. They also lobby governments and international trade organizations to protect their investments through favorable financial and economic policies and sometimes through military assistance and intervention (Schlesinger and Kinzer 1999; Lafeber 2002).[12]

Whether market shifts and income reversals push farming populations toward conflict also depends on what other crops and sources of incomes are possible substitutes, how farmers understand and respond to structural conditions of production and commerce, and what additional political forces drive them toward arms. Although in 2003 U.S. Agency for International Development Administrator Andrew Natsios envisioned peaceful farmers in Afghanistan producing fruits, nuts, and other agricultural commodities, such as cotton, for international markets, contraband opium poppies proved to be a more lucrative and underpoliced scenario, and their sales helped fuel continuing armed violence in that country (Constable 2003). In Colombia, a sharp decline in the price of coffee in 2002 pushed farmers into coca production, dominated by cartels and intimately linked to the country's continuing political violence (EIU 2003).

Perhaps the most important way in which trade in some primary agricultural commodities has destabilized incomes and contributed to food insecurity and conflict, however, is through rapid changes in global markets and prices. In the case of sugarcane, for example, global demand dipped suddenly, based on unprecedented competition from artificial sweeteners and high-fructose syrups, in addition to U.S. and European market quotas. In the cases of coffee and cotton, production over-expanded, leading to gluts in supply and price declines, which were exacerbated by selective barriers to trade. These fluctuations jeopardize livelihoods and living standards of people who depend on income from the particular cash crops. And in the absence of opportunities for rapid crop substitutions or possibilities of other livelihood diversification, they can contribute to violence of various kinds (Revathi 1998; Oxfam International 2002). For example, loss of livelihoods caused by the plunge in coffee prices contributed to social and political instability and, ultimately, to genocidal violence in Rwanda in 1994 (Uvin 1996).

But other structural and cultural factors are also involved—not all affected farmers rebel, after all, and some continue to produce the commodity while seeking and finding alternative sources of income. In El Salvador in the late 1990s, the combination of the global coffee price collapse and the devastation of Hurricane Mitch, which also unearthed deadly land mines from the prior civil war, left poor coffee farmers destitute (Equal Exchange 1998). They held out, however, for promised land reforms and also benefited from emigrant remittances; they did not renew conflict. As far as we know, Vietnam, whose soaring production of coffee has contributed to the world glut, has not experienced politically destabilizing effects (Oxfam International 2002); inequality is relatively low in the country (Minot, Baulch, and Epprecht 2003). In Brazil, falling coffee revenues were one of many factors behind growing discontent in the early part of the 2000s. But Brazilians achieved political change through the ballot box in 2002, electing a president who campaigned on a platform of freedom from hunger (Jones 2003).

Historically, conflict potential is also tied to demands for secure access to land and water. The original and the 1990s' Mexican Zapatista rebellions, for instance, involved demands for land—and subsistence over and against sugarcane and cattle interests, both domestic and trade commodities. Twentieth-century revolutions in El Salvador and Nicaragua were struggles for land and justice, subsistence, and control over coffee holdings and income, not just or mainly ideological conflicts. Solutions feature "peace" (fair-trade) coffee, not just peace agreements.

Sugarcane, cotton, and coffee, which account for a substantial share of export earnings (Tables 9.4 and 9.5), provide possible sources of both greed and grievance in countries involved in food wars. Reports also indicate that locals fight over access to land and water to grow the crops and then over the crops themselves. Revenues from these crops provide a major proportion of foreign exchange for governments and their opponents, who can use them to buy arms. In 2000, coffee alone generated more than 50 percent of Ethiopia's foreign exchange earnings. In Burundi, the figure exceeds 60 percent. Sugar and cotton, both important cash crops for domestic and international markets, are also important crops in many of the conflict countries considered here, although their position in international trade is weakened by crop sub-

Table 9.4   Countries in conflict and coffee, cotton, and sugar export values
(percent of total export value)

Region/country	Coffee	Cotton	Sugar
Sub-Saharan Africa			
Burundi	61.9	n.a.	4.1
Republic of Congo	n.a.	n.a.	0.6
Democratic Republic of Congo	5.1	n.a.	n.a.
Côte d'Ivoire	6.5	3.8	0.64
Ethiopia	50.7	1.1	2.0
Guinea	0.9	0.9	n.a.
Liberia	n.a.	n.a.	n.a.
Rwanda	32.8	n.a.	n.a.
Somalia	n.a.	n.a.	n.a.
Sudan	n.a.	1.4	1.1
Tanzania	10.9	6.8	1.4
Uganda	27.2	4.9	n.a.
Asia			
Afghanistan	n.a.	n.a.	n.a.
Burma	n.a.	n.a.	n.a.
India	n.a.	n.a.	n.a.
Indonesia	n.a.	n.a.	n.a.
Nepal	n.a.	n.a.	n.a.
Philippines	n.a.	n.a.	n.a.
Sri Lanka	n.a.	n.a.	n.a.
Europe			
Russia	n.a.	n.a.	n.a.
Latin America			
Colombia	8.2	n.a.	1.5
Haiti	5.9	n.a.	n.a.
Peru	3.2	0.2	0.2
Near East / North Africa	n.a.	n.a.	n.a.
Algeria	n.a.	n.a.	n.a.
Iraq	n.a.	n.a.	n.a.
Israel-Palestine	n.a.	n.a.	n.a.
Turkey	n.a.	n.a.	n.a.

Sources: Data compiled using FAO (2000, 2002, 2003a).
Note: n.a., no data or not applicable.

sidy policies and import quota limits in the United States, the European Union, and elsewhere.

Historically, sugarcane is the crop most immediately associated with peasant revolution and demands for land reform, as in the Mexican Revolution of 1910, and it is also widely associated with immiserating labor conditions, especially in the Caribbean and the Philippines. Periodically, falling prices have led to sometimes violent

Table 9.5   Postconflict countries and coffee, cotton, and sugar export
values (percent of total export value)

Region/country	Coffee	Cotton	Sugar
Sub-Saharan Africa			
Angola	0.05	n.a.	n.a.
Central African Republic	2.75	6.2	0.03
Eritrea	n.a.	n.a.	n.a.
Mozambique	n.a.	3.2	9.29
Sierra Leone	n.a.	n.a.	n.a.
South Africa	n.a.	n.a.	n.a.
Togo	3	12	0.22
Asia			
Cambodia	n.a.	n.a.	n.a.
Tajikistan	n.a.	n.a.	n.a.
Europe			
Armenia	n.a.	n.a.	n.a.
Azerbaijan	n.a.	n.a.	n.a.
Bosnia	n.a.	n.a.	n.a.
Georgia	n.a.	n.a.	n.a.
Serbia	n.a.	n.a.	n.a.
Latin America			
El Salvador	11.5	n.a.	1.5
Guatemala	21.3	n.a.	7.1
Nicaragua	27.0	n.a.	5.7

Sources: Data compiled using FAO (2002, 2003a).
Note: n.a., no data or not applicable.

struggles over land, as landowners have sought to prevent workers from taking over idle parcels (Karnow 1989; Bale 1998). More recently, owners of Philippine sugar estates in the province of Negros refused to redistribute land for cultivation of food crops, as workers had demanded. But rather than engage in armed rebellion, former sugarcane workers have collaborated with NGOs to develop other sources of income and attracted international attention by mobilizing around the right to food (FIAN 2002).

There is also an incipient organic and fair-trade market in cane sugar (World Shops 2003; Equal Exchange 2005). This market is an example of how "alternative globalization" attempts to fill food-security gaps and offer new markets, averting hopelessness and violence of underemployment when sugarcane, as a principal cash crop, fails.

Cotton economies historically have also been associated with immiserating labor conditions and violent conflict (Moore 1966) and with disastrous income fluctuations for small farmers. World prices for cotton, like those of other agricultural export commodities, are subject to sharp fluctuations, and in recent years cotton prices have fallen precipitously, at least in the short term, because of U.S., Chinese, and other producer-country export subsidies totaling US$5.8 billion annually (Watkins and von Braun 2003).

Because cotton is a thirsty crop, some analysts anticipate there will be an increase in interpersonal and intergroup violence as farmers and, in some cases, (former) pastoralists struggle over access to water and improved irrigated land to grow cotton, which some call "white gold." Such conflict has been reported among Afar pastoralists, fighting with government farm managers in the Awash Valley in Ethiopia (Nicol 2000), although, again, structural conditions present additional motivations for conflict. In 2003, livelihood-security experts observed fields that were uncultivated, unsown, and in ruins, although production of irrigated forage crops might revive mixed pastoralism in the region (Lautze et al. 2003). Anticipated income from irrigated cotton may be an added factor in long-standing struggles between pastoralists and farmers for control over land and water, further complicated by the state's attempt to impose its will and determine land use. Which crops receive priority is a large part of the land value–income–conflict equation, along with social and political conditions governing outcomes in land holding, access to water, and labor conditions.

In Chad, where cotton has been the principal export since independence, revenues have played an important financial role in the country's frequent bouts of civil war. In the past decade, violence has flared as northern herders have shot southern farmers who object to animals grazing in their cotton fields (Azam and Djimtoingar 2002).

In Central Asia, where cotton export promotion has long undermined local natural resources and productive capacity around the Aral Sea, some observers fear cotton could also prompt conflict. Downstream republics of Kazakhstan, Turkmenistan, and Uzbekistan want water to grow cotton, while the upstream nations of Kyrgyzstan and Tajikistan (a bloody civil war zone in the 1990s) want more water for food crops and electricity (Postel 1999; Babu and Tashmatov 2000).

Even where cotton production is not a source of conflict over land, water, or control of the crop, cotton promoters, including many African leaders, likely exaggerate its potential contributions to peace, prosperity, and sustainable development (see Tefft 2000; Toumani Toure and Compaore 2003).[13] Cotton in 2003 accounted for up to 40 percent of export revenues and 10 percent of GDP in Benin and Chad (Watkins and von Braun 2003). West African leaders frequently protest that the subsidies of other producer nations contribute to worldwide overproduction, falling prices, and income losses for millions of small-scale African cotton farmers. But if all producer countries scale up production in response to a freer market, other developing-country producers might well produce another market glut, with West Africa remaining at a disadvantage. This scenario would be comparable to the coffee-price crash experienced in the 1980s and 1990s after Vietnam rapidly expanded production (Oxfam International 2002). Nor would a liberalized global cotton market solve conflict-potentiating competition for water and land; indeed, it might exacerbate the tensions.

It is unclear whether the benefits from a liberalized global cotton market will really trickle down to poor African farmers, as African leaders (Toumani Toure and Compaore 2003), economists (Tefft 2000), and some NGOs (see Oxfam America 2004; IATP 2005) assert. Unfortunately, their scenarios leave out critical factors, such as worldwide production, exchange rates, relative crop and factor prices, and farmer landholding and marketing arrangements that together determine how much crop income actually reaches the farmer, the value of this income relative to the price of basic foods, and whether the farmer's land tenure and agricultural investment are secure and stable or subject to competition or violent seizure by competing individuals or groups. The history of coffee production, as a contrary case in point, suggests that all these latter factors are very important: in the absence (and sometimes even the presence) of commodity trade groups, agreements, and regulations (such as the International Coffee Agreement), commodity production can soar, glut the market, and drive prices down, engendering sharp income losses at both national and household levels.

Coffee is the agricultural commodity that has the closest recent interconnections with violent conflict. In 2000, it was the developing world's second-largest earner of export revenues after petroleum. Huge price fluctuations surrounding the "bitter brew" are part of the complex forces of causation that contributed to the 1994 genocide in Rwanda, periodic regional and community violence in Mexico and Colombia, the unstable legacies of civil strife in Central America, and conflict potential elsewhere (Paige 1998; Oxfam International 2002). The influence of the falling price of coffee on war dynamics and narco-cropping in Colombia has received substantial attention in the past few years (P. Collier 2003; EIU 2003). Coffee incomes can also influence development outlooks and conflict dynamics when prices are high, as when farmers identified with different ethnic groups or class interests compete for access to coffee lands, bushes, technical and marketing assistance, and product, as in Central America (Paige 1998). Independent of prices, coffee profits historically underwrote military force in Idi Amin's bloody dictatorship in Uganda (Melady 2003),[14] a brutal rebel army in Sierra Leone (Kamara n.d.), and Ethiopia's changing spectrum of political leadership (Ofcansky and Berry 1991; U.S. Department of State 2005).

In addition to price, other factors—land tenure patterns, labor relationships, control of processing, transport, the commercial system governing coffee from cultivation

to consumption, and the country's financial system—all influence whether coffee cultivation is more likely to contribute to prosperity and peace or to inequity and violence.

Central American national political economies historically provide the backdrop
for either labor oppression and underdevelopment, as in Guatemala and El Salvador,
or rising standards of living based on smallholder production and expansive social
welfare policies, as in Costa Rica (Paige 1998). In El Salvador, expansion of coffee
production, and also of cotton and sugar for export, drove smallholders off the land
and into peonage. Mechanization after World War II then reduced employment,
forcing excess labor into urban areas, where jobs were scarce. These socioeconomic
conditions, but especially coffee, polarized class relations and were the root causes of
civil war (Paige 1998, 105). During the 1980s, the government used scorched-earth
tactics against the rebels, guaranteeing hunger and starvation for affected civilian
populations (North 1985, especially p. 112). Subsequently, the 1990s peace process
promised land reform, but progress in its implementation has been very slow
(Creelman 2000; Power 2004).

It is not yet clear what role coffee will play in economic rebuilding, or if fair
trade—alternative marketing efforts that seek to assure small producers a fair return—
will account for a rapidly increasing share of coffee revenues. So far, coffee is by far the
largest fair-traded product, but it still accounts for only a fraction of coffee sales
worldwide.

The Peace Business: Global Norms and Institutions

Globalization is not just about markets or flows of labor and capital. It also includes
global norms and institutions promoting humanitarianism, human rights, social justice, and fair trade, as well as international efforts to regulate trade in blood commodities and arms, as already mentioned. The challenge is to make transnational processes
favor the peace, not the war, business.

Peace-promoting efforts, such as the convention banning land mines, the new
International Criminal Court, and the voluntary guidelines on the right to adequate
food developed under FAO auspices, play an active but not yet sufficient role in reducing the destructive forces that produce conflict and food insecurity. Improvements in
famine early warning systems and emergency nutrition interventions, which build on
the global integration of ICT and transportation, enhance the international community's ability to detect and respond to food crises. Such efforts are guided by global
humanitarian norms that assert the right to assist in zones of armed conflict and the
right of noncombatants to be free from hunger (Sphere 2003). These principles help
break the links between conflict and hunger, as shown in U.N.-authorized military-

humanitarian interventions in Iraqi Kurdistan, Somalia, and the former Yugoslavia in the 1990s.

Humanitarians, citing a global mandate and coming from all over the world, have also become important players, introducing a new, global ethic and a set of principles for distributing additional global sources of relief food and other aid in conflict or postconflict zones. Their "livelihood security" framing builds on household strategies of managing risk and vulnerability, taking into account household assets, entitlements, and possible sources of income and food (Lautze et al. 2003; compare Drèze and Sen 1989). Their closely related rights-based approach furthermore pays particular attention to gender, age, and other social divisions of labor in production, and to differences in distribution of food and other resources, to understand who gets what and who is left out while also attempting to build a framework for individual participation in rebuilding processes. In contrast to the national and global analyses treated in the rest of this chapter, both livelihood- and rights-based strategies usually involve analysis and program implementation in small-scale social units, not whole countries or regions (Schafer 2002).

From this household or small-group perspective, practitioners indicate how relief agencies and peacekeepers often contribute to the war economy. For example, programs established and implemented under humanitarian principles move food to those in need and save lives, but in the process they introduce food, vehicles, weapons, and personnel whose upkeep can also fuel conflict. Or, as in the case of Somalia in 1992, they destroy local food production and markets, because international NGO relief operations entered and would not leave. International humanitarian operations then created demand for provisioning and armed protection that favored militarized over peaceful economic interests. Food aid introduced a new primary resource available for looting and manipulation. All these developments gave advantages to agents with arms, who were able to shake down peace negotiators for resources, including land (Collins and Weiss 1997).

Humanitarian interventions and peacekeeping operations often involve external military forces in the delivery of humanitarian assistance and reconstruction activities. In so doing, these operations may usurp the roles of civil society in seeking to negotiate sustainable public services and stable relationships with government authorities (Messer 1996b; De Waal 1997). Military activities, as in the cases of Guatemala's "beans and guns" strategy to pacify highland Maya and Mexico's military-controlled food relief to Zapatista rebel areas, remind recipients about who is the dominant power and may serve directly as sources of oppression (G. Collier and Quaratiello 1999). It remains a question how U.S. plans for reconstruction in Afghanistan and Iraq will avoid such dilemmas.

International humanitarians, intending to assist, may incidentally contribute to ongoing hostilities and distrust by allowing, for example, village committees to continue to discriminate against intended beneficiaries of agricultural rehabilitation programs, thereby heightening the potential for renewed or continued conflict (Archibald and Richards 2002). In contrast, rights-based approaches analyze existing social-structural, ethnic, and power relations to deliver services and meet basic needs in ways that include all social agents. A rights-based approach begins with a deep respect for the inherent dignity of all, and it requires aid workers to work closely with communities to help people understand their rights and find ways to articulate demands for these rights through program participation (ODI 1999).

Humanitarian and human rights advocates also make use of such global communications technologies as the Internet, disseminating information about the plight and oppression of people otherwise isolated from global scrutiny. They draw attention to human rights violations and food insecurity. The Zapatista indigenous conflict with the government of Mexico thus received international attention, which arguably prevented a crackdown by Mexican authorities, at least in the short run (G. Collier and Quaratiello 1999).

But ICT can serve war as well as peace. Sierra Leone's Revolutionary United Front coordinated military operations, diamond sales, and arms purchases by satellite phone from bases in the country's hinterland while ruthlessly keeping the local civilian populace under its control (Rupert 2000). Indeed, contemporary wars seem to have moved beyond the interstate-intrastate dichotomy to a "trans-state" category, as they rely on international communications, transport, trade, and aid (Collins and Weiss 1997).

Reconnoitering Peace and Food Security

Developing countries require peace to achieve better food security and reap potential benefits of globalization. Development assistance, including aid to agriculture and rural development, can deter conflict if it is integrated into the construction of social contexts that promote equity. Our findings suggest five points for policymakers to consider in furthering this global peace and food-security business.

First, conflict and food-emergency countries overlap considerably. These countries are often the ones that cannot make good use of the "bright side" of free-market globalization—the transnational capitalist outlook of prosperity based on economic growth, liberalized markets, and democratization. However, they frequently do make good use of global networking, which sustains civil society agents working for peace. Unfortunately, such networking also sustains power-brokers associated with what proglobalizers view as globalization's "dark side"—international terrorism financed by trade in arms, minerals, other nonrenewable resources, and drugs, as well as the increasing gap between rich and poor that threatens peaceful development in poor countries. Donors need to find ways to distribute food and agricultural assistance that will be equitable and not reinforce the local and regional power structures that promise more conflict. The experience of long-term humanitarian and development aid fieldworkers in such postconflict countries as Sierra Leone can help in this regard (Archibald and Richards 2002).

Second, it is not export cropping per se but rather the structures of production and markets and the context of food and financial policies that determine local household incomes and peaceful or belligerent outcomes. Contrasting Central American experiences with coffee production suggest the important role of national government policies in assuring peaceful and equitable results. In Latin America and Southeast Asia, conflict was avoided when the prices of key export crops collapsed when there were alternative livelihood sources and peaceful outlets (such as electoral politics in Brazil) for discontent. These experiences offer lessons that should be followed up in Africa.

Third, it is essential to monitor the influences of global prices of developing countries' key agricultural exports, such as coffee and cotton. The idea, articulated recently by P. Collier and his team at the World Bank, of a compensatory fund (P. Collier 2003; see also Adams 1983 and Hazell, Pomareda, and Valdés 1986) merits further development. This fund would assist the losers from globalization in adjusting and diversifying their sources of income, so that they can get back on their feet. It remains unclear what institution would run such a fund, however. Also, as Addison and others at the U.N. University's World Institute on Development Economics have shown, it will be important to factor in monetary policies, exchange rates, and the actions of export marketing boards—all of which can compromise the incomes of small farmers and skew production (Addison 2005).

Fourth, the livelihood-security and rights-based development frameworks offer positive ways to approach conflict prevention at the local level, but these need to be linked more effectively to political-economic programs at the national level. Some development agencies have begun to think about integrating these approaches into their development activities, as have some bilateral aid donor agencies and development NGOs. At the macro level, aid donors can pressure government leaders to make sure that revenues from trade go into human resource development, such as education and health care, and not into an individual leader's bank account. Presumably, food security–related investments would also be a productive use of public resources, although the World Bank studies do not address this possibility explicitly. They do call for international sanctions to help make it less lucrative for rebels to exploit primary resources (P. Collier 2003).

Fifth, and connected to the ideas above, the particulars of any country or commodity case study can and should be analyzed in terms of Sen's theory of entitlements (that is, command over food or resources to access food; Sen 1981, 1999), livelihood security, or rights-based development. They can also be analyzed within a food-first framework, which basically asks: Who controls the food system? And what forms of democratic participation allow individual or small-scale producers, processors, and consumers to exercise control over the conditions of production, processing, and consumption (Lappé, Collins, and Rosset 1998)? These are all structural frameworks, which examine social inequalities and inequities along with principles of distributive justice and human rights.

The economic correlates of such conflict-precipitating conditions are those identified in the literature on correlates and causes of conflict that we discuss above: extreme poverty, inequality, high unemployment—particularly of young males—ethnic and religious tensions, and so on, including a history of armed conflict. As various subsequent researchers have pointed out, the correlates of conflict studies, which aggregate data, forego the significant details of individual country cases and patterns of causation. A challenge for those who would theorize or model the connections of conflict to food security and globalization (for example, Arnson and Zartman 2005; Kahl 2006) is how to move from analyzing individual cases to understanding larger patterns when there are so many environmental, political identity, historical, and other contextual variables. In addition to making sense of anecdotes, there looms the methodological challenge of synthesizing conflict narratives and political-economic numbers in ways that suggest corrective policy actions for particular cases. We need more disaggregated, commodity-specific case studies, which will move beyond the recent FAO (2006) and World Bank (Aksoy and Beghin 2005) reports on agricultural trade.

Globalization can help mitigate or even prevent violence, but activities must be undertaken with an eye to conflict prevention and justice promotion. Examining the specifics of trade in particular agricultural commodities, such as coffee, cotton, and sugarcane, provides some insight into both the root causes of hunger and conflict and their interconnections, and also into the trigger causes. Historically, more localized struggles for control over high-value agricultural commodities, and for control over the land, water, and labor resources to grow them, are part of many conflict pictures, which have included blood coffee as well as blood diamonds and white, snowy cotton, as well as "snow" processed from coca leaves. Even basic foods, including humanitarian rations and other forms of food aid, can foster competition to control the distribution. These food sources constitute important dimensions of the political economies sustaining prolonged civil wars and civil strife in the early twenty-first century, as leaders seek to feed their armies and supporters and to deny their enemies nutrition.

Ensuring fair and equitable access to scarce water and land resources are important considerations in postconflict reconstruction, which can deter the likelihood of renewed war. The trade regulations and market structure for particular agricultural commodities may also prove important where countries depend heavily on a single export crop that is subject to sudden price declines. And these factors have a bearing on more widespread human rights violations and livelihood disruptions. They need greater emphasis in development agency assessments.

We remain convinced that globalization offers positive norms and values to guide an increasingly interconnected world. However, making this bright side of globalization an intentional reality will require institutions dedicated to peace, social justice, and sustainable food security for all, linked to development processes at both the grassroots and the summit.

Notes

1. We used the definitions of armed conflict of the Conflict Data Program at Uppsala University: an armed conflict is a contested incompatibility that concerns government and/or territory where the use of armed force between two parties, of which at least one is the government of a state, results in at least 25 battle-related deaths. A minor armed conflict is one with at least 25 deaths but fewer than 1,000 during the course of the conflict. An intermediate conflict is one with more than 1,000 deaths during the course of the conflict but fewer than 1,000 in any given year (see http://www.pcr.uu.se/basicSearch/definitions_all.htm). In keeping with this definition, the current political situation in Zimbabwe is not considered a war, although it has many of the characteristics of a food war.

2. We used the Uppsala database (see preceding note) as the principal source for conflicts in 2006 as well as those in 2002–03, to allow comparability. In the earlier exercise, we supplemented the Uppsala data with Marshall and Gurr (2003); for 2006 our supplementary source was the update of the latter study, Center for Systemic Peace (2007).

3. We do not consider here appeals for humanitarian assistance based on a natural disaster (unless the disaster is coupled with a conflict or postconflict situation) or economic collapse in which significant violence is absent (for example, the Democratic People's Republic of Korea).

4. Future research should try to capture, via time-series data, the likely lagged effects on conflict of openness to trade.

5. In any event, distinctions between internal and interstate warfare have blurred (Collins and Weiss 1997). Twenty-four years of civil war in Afghanistan have featured significant Pakistani, Soviet, Tajik, Uzbek, U.S., and European interventions (SIPRI 2003a). The nominally internal conflict in the DRC, often characterized as Africa's World War, has involved military forces from Angola, Namibia, Rwanda, Uganda, and Zimbabwe, and natural resources plundered to pay for this conflict have passed through Angola, Burundi, the Central African Republic, the Congo, Kenya, Mozambique, Rwanda, Tanzania, Uganda, Zambia, and Zimbabwe on their way to market (U.N. Security Council 2003; Global Policy Forum 2005). Hostilities in the former Yugoslavia in the 1990s and early 2000s involved not only opposing Croatian, Serbian, Bosnian, Kosovar, and other troops, but also international forces for peacemaking, peacekeeping, and emergency relief, as well as Muslim volunteers from around the world (SIPRI 2003a). Many or most of the "internal" wars that occurred during the Cold War were

similarly transnational. For example, during the 1975–92 conflict in Mozambique, the government received substantial Soviet aid, while South Africa and Rhodesia backed the rebels (Nordstrom 1999).

6. Peace appears to be breaking out only if analysts intent on counting negotiated settlements as "peace" subtract the high-intensity and prolonged conflicts in Angola and Mozambique, Sri Lanka, Ethiopia, and Sudan, as well as all Latin American conflicts except Colombia (Marshall and Gurr 2003, 47 and passim). However, conflicts continue in some of these locales (such as in parts of Angola and Ethiopia) at varying degrees of intensity, promising negotiations in Sri Lanka and Sudan may well break down, ceasefires in such places as the DRC exist only on paper, and whether peace can be sustained in Angola or Sierra Leone remains an open question. If U.S.-led military involvement in Afghanistan and Iraq is included in the equation, then it seems premature at best to declare that the 2000s will be more peaceful or have fewer interstate wars than the 1990s did, as proponents of the pacific qualities of globalization frequently claim.

7. It is common to find such claims as "80 percent . . . of refugees are women and children" (Women's Commission for Refugee Women and Children 2007, 1). However, a 2000 study by the office of the U.N. High Commissioner for Refugees casts serious doubt on claims of statistically significant gender disparities in refugee populations (USCR 2000).

8. The conflict countries in question were Angola, Burundi, Chad, Ethiopia, Ghana, Kenya, Liberia, Mozambique, Nigeria, Somalia, Sudan, Uganda, Zambia, and Zimbabwe. All but Chad experienced decline in food production growth rates.

9. Wolf (1969) reviewed such revolutionary contexts with studies that suggested these earlier colonial- to postcolonial-era wars were struggles for subsistence, control over resources, and social justice. More recent studies scrutinizing the predisposing contexts of civil wars in Sri Lanka in the 1980s (Little 1994) and Rwanda in the 1990s (Uvin 1996) find much more evidence of social inequities fueled by rhetoric and violence of identity politics and further manipulated by demagogues.

10. The taskforce, now known as the Political Instability Taskforce, is made up of academic experts on conflict. Their work was initially funded by the U.S. Central Intelligence Agency (see the taskforce's website at http://globalpolicy.gmu.edu/pitf/ for more information). The first two phases of its studies also found democracy to be correlated with peaceful outcomes. These studies support the Kantian peace-promoting tripod of economic interdependence, democracy, and membership in international organizations (O'Neal and Russet 2001). They also, intentionally or unintentionally, support the Clinton administration's promotion of democracy and trade liberalization as mechanisms to foster peaceful development and prevent terrorism and "future Somalias and Rwandas" (USAID 1994). Clinton was variously cited on Internet sources as having used the phrase "the dark side of globalization" to denote terrorism or the increasing gap between rich and poor, which can also lead to war—see his talking points in the PBS program posted by Yergin (2003).

11. Peace advocates, such as the International Action Network on Small Arms, would like to see the implementation of an International Code of Conduct that would "stem the supply and mop up the surplus" of arms to countries that violate human rights standards and humanitarian norms (O'Grady 1999, 5, 10). But this action would only provide a first step to stemming the spillage of arms across borders.

12. In view of this history, it is instructive that Hamid Karzai, elected Afghan president in June 2002, stated emphatically that Afghanistan is no "banana republic" and that he intended to put millions of dollars in external aid into "stability, security, peace, economic well-being of the Afghan people, reconstruction" (Gall and Dao 2002). The reality is that post-Taliban Afghanistan is something of an "opium poppy republic," in which contending warlords vie for control of turf and profits (Constable 2003).

13. Unquestionably, an end to U.S. cotton subsidies would terminate the illogical, counter-market trade and aid policies of the U.S. government, which early in the current decade paid U.S. cotton growers US$3.4 billion a year, more than the annual income of Burkina Faso and Niger combined. The resulting glut drove global prices down 25 percent, causing West Africa to lose US$190 million in revenues and rendering an additional 250,000 people destitute in Benin (Watkins and von Braun 2003). At the same time, the United States provided Benin with US$4 million a year in food aid (USAID 2003), thus putting a double burden on U.S. taxpayers.

14. In a recent letter to the editor of the *Washington Post,* Thomas Melady, U.S. ambassador to Uganda during Amin's rule, reflected on U.S. legislation banning imports of Ugandan coffee, given the importance of coffee revenues in supporting Amin's death squads (Melady 2003).

References

Adams, R. 1983. The role of research in policy development: The creation of the IMF cereal import facility. *World Development* 11 (7): 549–563.

Addison, T. 2005. *Post-conflict recovery: Does the global economy work for peace?* WIDER Discussion Paper 2005/05. Helsinki: World Institute for Development Economics Research, U.N. University. Available at http://www.wider.unu.edu/publications/dps/dps2005/dp2005-05 .pdf.

Aksoy, M. A., and J. C. Beghin, eds. 2005. *Agricultural trade and developing countries.* Washington, D.C.: World Bank.

Araghi, F. 2000. The great global enclosure of our times: Peasants and the agrarian question at the end of the twentieth century. In *Hungry for profit: The agribusiness threat to farmers, food, and the environment,* ed. F. Magdoff, J. B. Foster, and F. H. Buttel. New York: Monthly Review Press.

Archibald, S., and P. Richards. 2002. New approaches to post-war agricultural rehabilitation in Sierra Leone. *Disasters* 26 (4): 356–367.

Arnson, C. J., and I. W. Zartman, eds. 2005. *Rethinking the economics of war: The intersection of need, creed, and greed.* Washington, D.C., and Baltimore: Woodrow Wilson Center Press and The Johns Hopkins University Press.

Azam, J. P., and N. Djimtoingar. 2002. Cotton, war, and growth in Chad (1960–2000). Prepared for African Economic Research Consortium "Explaining African Economic Growth Experience" project. Available at http://www.gdnet.org/activities/global_research_projects/explaining_growth/country_studies/.

Babu, S., and A. Tashmatov, eds. 2000. *Food policy reforms in Central Asia: Setting the research priorities.* Washington, D.C.: International Food Policy Research Institute.

Bale, C. 1998. *Faces in the crowd: A journey in hope.* Hong Kong: Chinese University Press.

Barrett, C. B., and D. G. Maxwell. 2005. *Food aid after fifty years: Recasting its role.* New York: Routledge.

Bello, W. 2001. *The future in the balance: Essays on globalization and resistance.* Oakland, Calif., U.S.A.: Food First Books.

Center for Systemic Peace. 2007. Major episodes of political violence, 1946–2006. Available at http://members.aol.com/cspmgm/warlist.htm.

Chua, A. 2003. *World on fire: How exporting free market democracy breeds ethnic and global instability.* New York: Doubleday.

CIA (U.S. Central Intelligence Agency). 2003. World factbook 2003. Available at http://www.cia .gov/cia/publications/factbook/.

Clay, J. W., and B. K. Holcomb. 1987. *Politics and the Ethiopian famine: 1984–1985.* Somerset, N.J., U.S.A.: Transaction Publishers.

Cobden, R. 1870. *Speeches on public policy.* London: Macmillan.

Cohen, M. J. 1984. U.S. food aid to South East Asia, 1975–83. *Food Policy* 9 (2): 139–155.

Collier, G., with E. L. Quaratiello. 1999. *Basta! The Zapatista Rebellion in Chiapas,* revised ed. Oakland, Calif., U.S.A.: Food First Books.

Collier, P. 1999. On the economic consequences of civil war. *Oxford Economic Papers* 51(1): 168–183.

———. 2000. Economic causes of conflict and their implications for policy. Available at http://www .worldbank.org/research/conflict/papers/civilconflict.pdf.

———. 2001. Ethnic diversity: An economic analysis. *Economic Policy* 32 (2): 129–166.

———. 2003. Breaking the conflict trap: Civil war and development policy. Available at http://econ .worldbank.org/prr/CivilWarPRR/text-26671/.

Collier, P., and A. Hoeffler. 1998. On the economic causes of civil war. *Oxford Economic Papers* 50 (8): 563–573.

———. 2000. *Greed and grievance in civil war.* Policy Research Working Paper 2355. Washington, D.C.: World Bank.

———. 2004. Greed and grievance in civil war. *Oxford Economic Papers* 56 (4): 563–595.

Collins, C., and T. G. Weiss. 1997. An overview and assessment of 1989–1996 Peace Operations Publications. Occasional Paper of the Watson Institute for International Studies 28. Providence, R.I., U.S.A.: Brown University.

Creelman, M. 2000. Central America: Land reform put off. *Central America/Mexico Report, Bimonthly Journal of the Religious Task Force on Central America,* May.

Danaher, K., ed. 1994. *Fifty years is enough: The case against the World Bank and International Monetary Fund.* Boston: South End Press.

De Soysa, I. 2000. The resource curse: Are civil wars driven by rapacity or paucity? In *Greed and grievance: Economic agendas and civil wars,* ed. M. Berdal and D. M. Malone. Boulder, Colo., U.S.A.: Lynne Rienner.

———. 2002. Paradise is a bazaar? Greed, creed, and governance in Civil War, 1989–1999. *Journal of Peace Research* 39 (4): 395–416.

De Waal, A. 1997. *Famine crimes: Politics and the disaster relief industry in Africa.* Bloomington, Ind., U.S.A.: Indiana University Press.

Dorussen, H. 2002. Trade decreases conflict more in multi-actor systems: A rejoinder. *Journal of Peace Research* 39 (1): 115–118.

Drèze, J., and A. Sen. 1989. *Hunger and public action.* Oxford: Clarendon Press.

EIU (Economist Intelligence Unit). 2003. Colombia commodities: No end seen to coffee sector's plight. Available at http://home.aigonline.com/content/0,1109,16590-653-ceo,00.html.

Equal Exchange. 1998. Hurricane Mitch devastates small farmers in Central America. Notes from the Field 1 (November). Available at http://www.equalexchange.com/news_info/notes1.html. Accessed December 2003.

———. 2005. Sugar. Posted at http://www.equalexchange.com/sugar.

Eriksson, M., P. Wallensteen, and M. Sollenberg. 2003. Armed conflict, 1989–2002. *Journal of Peace Research* 40 (5): 593–607.

Esty, D. C., J. Goldstone, T. R. Gurr, P. Surko, and A. Unger. 1995. *Working papers: State Failure Task Force report.* McLean, Va., U.S.A.: Science Applications International Corporation.

Esty, D. C., J. A. Goldstone, T. R. Gurr, B. Harff, M. Levy, G. Dabelko, P. Surko, and A. N. Unger. 1998. *State Failure Task Force report: Phase II findings.* McLean, Va., U.S.A.: Science Applications International Corporation.

FAO (Food and Agriculture Organization of the United Nations). 2000. *The state of food and agriculture 2000.* Rome.

———. 2002. *Trade yearbook 2000.* Rome.

———. 2003a. FAOSTAT. Rome.

———. 2003b. *The state of food insecurity in the world 2003.* Rome.

———. 2006. *The state of food and agriculture 2005.* Rome.

FIAN (Food First Information and Action Network). 2002. Philippines: Sugar workers face starvation in Negros Occidental/Visayas. Available at http://www.fian.org/english-version/e-0219.htm. Accessed October 2002.

Freidberg, S. 2004. *French beans and food scares: Culture and commerce in an age of anxiety.* Oxford: Oxford University Press.

Fuller, W. P., and W. A. Falcon. 1999. Indonesia at a crossroads. *San Francisco Chronicle,* May 6.

Gall, C., and J. Dao. 2002. A buoyant Karzai is sworn in as Afghanistan's leader. *New York Times,* June 20.

Gleditsch, N. P., P. Wallensteen, M. Eriksson, M. Sollenberg, and H. Strand. 2002. Armed conflict 1946–2001: A new data set. *Journal of Peace Research* 39 (5): 615–637.

Global Policy Forum. 2005. Democratic Republic of Congo. Available at http://www.globalpolicy .org/security/issues/kongidx.htm.

Goldstone, J. A., T. R. Gurr, B. Harff, M. A. Levy, M. G. Marshall, R. H. Bates, D. L. Epstein, C. H. Kahl, P. T. Surko, J. C. Ulfelder, Jr., and A. N. Unger, in consultation with M. Christenson, G. D. Dabelko, D. C. Esty, and T. M. Parris. 2003. *State failure task force report: Phase III findings.* McLean, Va., U.S.A.: Science Applications International Corporation.

Gurr, T. R., and B. Harff. 2000. *Ethnic conflict in world politics,* 2nd ed. Boulder, Colo., U.S.A.: Westview.

Hazell, P. B. R., C. Pomareda, and A. Valdés, eds. 1986. *Crop insurance for agricultural development: Issues and experience.* Baltimore: The Johns Hopkins University Press for International Food Policy Research Institute.

Hegre, H., R. Gissinger, and N. P. Gleditsch. 2003. Globalization and internal conflict. In *Globalization and armed conflict,* ed. G. Schneider, K. Barbieri, and N. P. Gleditsch. Lanham, Md., U.S.A.: Rowman and Littlefield.

Homer-Dixon, T. 1999. *Environment, scarcity, and violence.* Princeton, N.J., U.S.A.: Princeton University Press.

Human Security Centre. 2005. *The human security report 2005: War and peace in the 21st century.* Vancouver, BC, Canada: Human Security Centre.

IATP (Institute for Agriculture and Trade Policy). 2005. The July framework: Failing the development agenda. Available at http://www.tradeobservatory.org/ library.cfm?refid=73503.

Jones, P. 2003. Brazil begins anti-hunger campaign. *Chicago Tribune,* February 4.

Kahl, C. H. 2006. *States, scarcity, and civil strife in the developing world.* Princeton, N.J., U.S.A., and London: Princeton University Press.

Kaldor, M. 1999. *New and old wars: Organized violence in a global era.* Cambridge, Mass., U.S.A.: Polity Press.

Kamara, T. n.d. Diamonds, war, and state collapse in Liberia and Sierra Leone. Available at http:// www.theperspective.org/statecollapse.html.

Karnow, S. 1989. *In our image: America's empire in the Philippines.* New York: Ballantine Books.

Kherallah, M., C. Delgado, E. Gabre-Madhin, N. Minot, and M. Johnson. 2002. *Reforming agricultural markets in Africa.* Baltimore: The Johns Hopkins University Press for International Food Policy Research Institute.

Lafeber, W. 2002. *America, Russia, and the Cold War, 1945–2002.* New York: McGraw-Hill.

Lappé, F. M., J. Collins, and P. Rosset. 1998. *World hunger: Twelve myths,* 2nd ed. New York: Grove Press for Food First.

Lautze, S., Y. Aklilu, A. Raven-Roberts, H. Young, G. Kebede, and J. Leaning. 2003. Risk and vulnerability in Ethiopia: Learning from the past, responding to the present, preparing for the future. Available at http://www.tufts.edu/nutrition/ pdf/risk_ethiopia.pdf. Accessed July 2003.

Little, D. 1994. *Sri Lanka: The invention of enmity*. Washington, D.C.: U.S. Institute of Peace Press.

Markakis, J. 1998. *Resource conflict in the Horn of Africa*. Thousand Oaks, Calif., U.S.A.: Sage Publications for the International Peace Research Institute, Oslo.

Marshall, M., and T. R. Gurr. 2003. Peace and conflict 2003: A global survey of armed conflicts, self-determination movements, and democracy. College Park, Md., U.S.A.: University of Maryland, Center for International Development and Conflict Management.

Mason, J., J. Csete, and U. Jonsson. 1996. Is childhood malnutrition being overcome? In *The hunger report 1995*, ed. E. Messer and P. Uvin. Amsterdam: Gordon and Breach for the Brown University World Hunger Program.

Melady, T. 2003. A Ugandan dictator's escape from justice. Letter to the editor. *Washington Post*, August 6.

Messer, E. 1994. Food wars: Hunger as a weapon of war in 1993. In *The hunger report, 1993*, ed. P. Uvin. Yverdon, Switzerland: Gordon and Breach for the Brown University World Hunger Program.

———. 1996a. Food wars: Hunger as a weapon in 1994. In *The hunger report, 1995*, ed. E. Messer and P. Uvin. Amsterdam: Gordon and Breach for the Brown University World Hunger Program.

———. 1996b. Hunger and human rights, 1989–1994. In *The hunger report, 1995*, ed. E. Messer and P. Uvin. Amsterdam: Gordon and Breach for the Brown University World Hunger Program.

Messer, E., and M. J. Cohen. 2001. Conflict and food insecurity. In *Shaping globalization for poverty alleviation and food security*, ed. E. Díaz-Bonilla and S. Robinson. 2020 Vision Focus 8, Brief 12. Washington, D.C.: International Food Policy Research Institute.

Messer, E., M. J. Cohen, and J. D'Costa. 1998. *Food from peace: Breaking the links between conflict and hunger*. 2020 Vision for Food, Agriculture, and the Environment Discussion Paper 24. Washington, D.C.: International Food Policy Research Institute.

Messer, E., M. J. Cohen, and T. Marchione. 2001. *Conflict: A cause and effect of hunger*. Environmental Change and Security Project Report 7. Washington, D.C.: Woodrow Wilson International Center for Scholars, Smithsonian Institution.

Minot, N., B. Baulch, and M. Epprecht. 2003. *Poverty and inequality in Vietnam: Spatial patterns and geographic determinants*. Washington, D.C.: International Food Policy Research Institute.

Moore, B. 1966. *Social origins of dictatorship and democracy: Lord and peasant in the making of the modern world*. Boston: Beacon Press.

Mtonga, R. 2003. Tracing the bullets in Zambia. *IANSA News* (International Action Network on Small Arms). Available at http://www.iansa.org/newsletter/june2003/zambia_p6.pdf. Accessed December 2003.

Nafziger, E. W., and J. Auvinen. 2000. The economic causes of humanitarian emergencies. In *War, hunger, and displacement: The origins of humanitarian emergencies*, vol. 1., ed. E. W. Nafziger, F. Stewart, and R. Väyrynen. Oxford: Oxford University Press for the World Institute for Development Economics Research, U.N. University.

Nicol, A. 2000. Water rights or water wrongs. *Developments: The International Development Magazine.* Available at http://www.developments.org.uk/data/12/. Accessed May 2000.

Nordstrom, C. 1999. Requiem for the rational war. In *Deadly developments: Capitalism, states, and war: War and society,* vol. 5, ed. S. P. Reyna and R. E. Downs. Amsterdam: Gordon and Breach.

North, L. 1985. *Bitter grounds: Roots of revolt in El Salvador,* 2nd ed. Westport, Conn., U.S.A.: Lawrence Hill.

OCHA (Office for the Coordination of Humanitarian Affairs, United Nations). 2003. Consolidated appeals, country reports, and other data. Available at http://www.reliefweb.int.

――――. 2007. Consolidated and flash appeals 2006: Summary of requirements and pledges/contributions by affected country/region as of 31 May 2007. Available at http://www.reliefweb .int/fts.

ODI (Overseas Development Institute). 1999. What can we do with a rights-based approach to development? *ODI Briefing Paper* 3 (September). London.

Ofcansky, T. P., and L. Berry, eds. 1991. Ethiopia: A country study. Washington, D.C.: Federal Research Division, U.S. Library of Congress. Available at http://lcweb2.loc.gov/frd/cs/ettoc.html.

O'Grady, M. 1999. Small arms in Africa. Available at the Campaign against Arms Trade website, http://www.caat.org.uk/information/publications/countries/africa-0999.php. Accessed November 2003.

Ohlsson, L. 2000. *Livelihood conflicts—Linking poverty and environment as causes of conflict.* Stockholm: Swedish International Development Agency, Environmental Policy Unit.

O'Neal, J. R., and B. Russet. 2001. *Triangulating peace: Democracy, interdependence, and international organizations.* New York: W. W. Norton.

Oxfam America. 2004. Finding the moral fiber: Why reform is urgently needed for a fair cotton trade. Available at http://www.oxfamamerica.org/newsandpublications/ publications/briefing_papers/ cotton_brief101804.

Oxfam International. 2002. *Mugged: Poverty in your coffee cup.* Oxford.

Paarlberg, R. 2000. The weak link between world food markets and world food security. *Food Policy* 25 (3): 317–335.

Paige, J. M. 1998. *Coffee and power: Revolution and the rise of democracy in Central America.* Cambridge, Mass., U.S.A.: Harvard University Press.

Postel, S. 1999. *Pillar of sand: Can the irrigation miracle last?* New York: W. W. Norton.

Power, J. 2004. Yesterday's war headline binds its wounds. Available at http://www.transnational.org/forum/power/2004/12.03_El_Salvador.html. Accessed December 2004.

Revathi, E. 1998. Farmers' suicide: Missing issues. *Economic and Political Weekly* 33 (20): 1207.

Ross, M. 2001. *Extractive sectors and the poor.* Boston: Oxfam America.

Rupert, J. 2000. Back story: Warlord in exile. *Washington Post Magazine,* September 17.

Rupesinghe, K. 1996. Strategies for conflict resolution: The case of South Asia. In *Internal conflicts in South Asia,* ed. K. Rupesinghe and K. Mumtaz. London: Sage.

Schafer, J. 2002. *Supporting livelihoods in situations of chronic conflict and political instability: Overview of conceptual issues.* London: Overseas Development Institute.

Schlesinger, S., and S. Kinzer. 1999. *Bitter fruit: The story of the American coup in Guatemala,* expanded ed. Cambridge, Mass., U.S.A.: Harvard University, David Rockefeller Center for Latin American Studies.

Schneider, G., K. Barbieri, and N. P. Gleditsch. 2003. Does globalization contribute to peace? A critical survey of the literature. In *Globalization and armed conflict,* ed. G. Schneider, K. Barbieri, and N. P. Gleditsch. Lanham, Md., U.S.A.: Rowman and Littlefield.

Sen, A. 1981. *Poverty and famines: An essay on entitlement and deprivation.* Oxford: Clarendon Press.

————. 1999. *Development as freedom.* New York: Knopf.

Shah, A. 2003. Small arms—They cause 90% of civilian casualties. Available at http://www .globalissues.org/Geopolitics/ArmsTrade/SmallArms.asp#SmallArmsareProliferatedThrough BothLegalandIllegalTrade.

Shepherd, J. 1975. *The politics of starvation.* New York: Carnegie Endowment for International Peace.

Shiva, V. 1999. *Stolen harvest.* Cambridge, Mass., U.S.A.: South End Press.

Simler, K. R., S. Mukherjee, G. L. Dava, and G. Datt. 2003. *Rebuilding after war: Micro-level determinants of poverty reduction in Mozambique.* Research Report 132. Washington, D.C.: International Food Policy Research Institute.

SIPRI (Stockholm International Peace Research Institute). 2000. *SIPRI yearbook 2000: Armaments, disarmament, and international security.* Oxford: Oxford University Press.

————. 2003a. Database on major armed conflicts. Available at http://www.first.sipri.org.

————. 2003b. *SIPRI yearbook 2003: Armaments, disarmament, and international security.* Oxford: Oxford University Press.

Sivard, R. L. 1996. *World military and social expenditures 1996.* Washington, D.C.: World Priorities.

Smith, D. 1994. *War, peace, and Third World development.* Occasional Paper 16. Oslo: International Peace Research Institute, Oslo.

————. 1997. *The state of war and peace atlas,* 3rd ed. Oslo: International Peace Research Institute, Oslo.

Sphere. 2003. The humanitarian charter and minimum standards for disaster response. Available at http://www.sphereproject.org. Accessed September 2003.

Stewart, F. 1993. War and underdevelopment: Can economic analysis help reduce the costs? *Journal of International Development* 5 (4): 357–380.

Tefft, J. 2000. Cotton in Mali: The "White Revolution" and development. In *Democracy and development in Mali,* ed. R. J. Bingen, D. Robinson, and J. M. Staatz. East Lansing, Mich., U.S.A.: Michigan State University Press.

Toumani Toure, A., and B. Compaore. 2003. Your farm subsidies are strangling us. *New York Times,* July 11.

UCDP (Uppsala Conflict Data Program). 2007. Uppsala conflict database. Available at http://www .pcr.uu.se/database/index.php.

U.N. Security Council. 2003. Final report of the panel of experts on the illegal exploitation of natural resources and other forms of wealth of the Democratic Republic of the Congo. Report S/2003/1027. Available at http://www.globalpolicy.org/security/natres/diamonds/2003/1023 expert_panel.pdf.

USAID (U.S. Agency for International Development). 1994. Breaking the cycle of despair: President Clinton's initiative on the Horn of Africa—Building a foundation for food security and crisis prevention in the Greater Horn of Africa. A concept paper for discussion (draft). Washington, D.C. Mimeo.

———. 2003. USAID fiscal year 2004: Congressional presentation. Available at http://www.usaid.gov.

USCR (U.S. Committee on Refugees). 2000. More male refugees than previously thought. Available at http://www.refugees.org/world/articles/males_rrou_2.htm. Accessed December 2000.

U.S. Department of State. 2005. Background note: Ethiopia. Available at http://www.state.gov/r/pa/ ei/bgn/2859.htm.

Uvin, P. 1996. Tragedy in Rwanda: The political ecology of conflict. *Environment* 33 (3): 6–15, 29.

von Braun, J., and E. Kennedy, eds. 1994. *Agricultural commercialization, economic development, and nutrition.* Baltimore: The Johns Hopkins University Press for International Food Policy Research Institute.

Wallerstein, M. 1980. *Food for war, food for peace: United States food aid in a global context.* Cambridge, Mass., U.S.A.: MIT Press.

Watkins, K., and J. von Braun. 2003. Time to stop dumping on the world's poor. *IFPRI Annual Report 2002–03.* Washington, D.C.: International Food Policy Research Institute.

Wolf, E. 1969. *Peasant wars of the twentieth century.* New York: Harper and Row.

Women's Commission for Refugee Women and Children. 2007. Women's Commission fact sheet. Available at http://womenscommission.org/pdf/fctsht06.pdf.

World Bank. 2000. *Can Africa claim the 21st century?* Washington, D.C.

———. 2003. World development indicators 2003. CD-ROM. Washington, D.C.

World Shops. 2003. Food for thought—Sugar. Available at http://www.worldshops.org/activities/food forthought/sugar.htm. Accessed December 2003.

Yergin, D. 2003. Globalization and trade—The new rules of the game. Video episode 3. Available at http:// www.global-trade-law.com/video.summary. commanding%20heights.doc. Accessed December 2003.

Young, H., and A. M. Osman. 2006. *Challenges to peace and recovery in Darfur.* Medford, Mass., U.S.A.: Feinstein International Center.

National Governments: The Key to Food Security under Globalization

Robert L. Paarlberg

T his essay addresses two questions: Is globalization a threat to food security? And to reduce hunger in an age of globalization, should we first improve governance at the global or national level? In response to the first question, the impact of globalization on food security is positive rather than negative, but that impact is fairly weak. This observation leads us to the second question. Improved governance at the global level is often called for, yet in the area of food security, the greatest governance deficits are still found at the level of the nation-state. Where national governments have performed well in the developing world, hunger has been significantly reduced. In those regions where hunger is not yet under control, improving governance at the national level is now the highest priority.

Globalization and Poverty

For those worried about hunger in poor countries, globalization may not be the problem, but neither is it the solution. Consider, first, the impact of globalization on poverty. As globalization has advanced over the past 20 years, the prevalence and the incidence of poverty have both declined (Sala-i-Martin 2002a,b; review in Chapter 2).

These gains took place alongside globalization, and there is even evidence suggesting they were linked to that process. Dollar and Kraay (2001) have shown that the countries most open to globalization were those that reduced poverty most rapidly. They classified countries into two categories—the globalizers and the nonglobalizers—based on such criteria as changes in trade as a share of GDP and average tariff reductions. This work, although contested on the basis of updated statistics, shows that the globalizers enjoyed a substantial increase in per capita GDP growth rates in the 1990s relative to the 1980s, rising from 1.4 percent to 3.8 percent growth. The nonglobalizers did not do as well. Their per capita GDP growth rates were a 0.1 percent in the 1980s, and they increased to only 0.8 percent in the 1990s.

Critics willing to concede the point that countries with increased exposure to the global economy grew more rapidly tend to also say, "Yes, but the downside has been greater income inequality." In some individual cases, to be sure, income inequality has increased. Between 1980 and 1992 in China, amid rapid growth stimulated in part by exports and FDI, the Gini coefficients of income inequality did increase from 0.32 up to 0.38. But overall growth in China was so rapid during this period that the poorest quintile hardly suffered. In absolute terms, roughly 250 million Chinese citizens escaped poverty during the past two decades of rapid growth. Economic historians will probably record this as the single greatest mass escape from poverty in human history. And, as large numbers of people have escaped poverty under globalization, they have simultaneously escaped hunger and child malnutrition.

Persistent Hunger and Weak Globalization

South Asia and Sub-Saharan Africa still feature relatively weak connections to the international markets and private investment flows that define modern globalization. Food markets within South Asia are significantly disconnected from global food markets, often as a matter of national policy. In pursuit of "self-sufficiency," the South Asian nations have restricted trade so much (through tariffs, quotas, and duties) that imports cover only about 2 percent of their total grain consumption, the lowest of any region in the developing world. This restriction makes it hard to blame food problems in South Asia on the malfunction of international grain markets.

Connections to the modern global economy are also weak for many African countries. International commodity markets continue to expand, yet Africa's sales in those markets continue to shrink. Africa's total volume of exported farm commodities (coffee, groundnuts, palm oil, and sugar) is actually smaller today than it was 30 years ago. I have been a strong critic of agricultural protectionism in the United States, the European Union, and Japan, and in some markets (such as cotton) this protection does harm poor farmers in Africa. But Africa's shrinking share of world trade reflects much more than the hostility of the international marketplace toward Africa. It reflects even more the hostility of government policies in Africa toward the market—what Jeffrey Sachs has described as Africa's self-imposed exile from international markets.

Flows of FDI into South Asia and Africa have also lagged. FDI into South Asia in 1998 was still only 5 percent as large as that into LAC. Of the FDI going into the developing world as a whole, less than 1 percent goes to Sub-Saharan Africa. Multinational corporations are not exploiting Africa—they are ignoring it. Using net private capital flows as an indicator of globalization, a similar pattern emerges. In 1998 net private capital flows into Sub-Saharan Africa and South Asia combined amounted to less than one-fifth the total capital flows into East Asia and less than one-tenth of that into Latin America. The hungry regions of South Asia and Sub-Saharan Africa are not being ruined by unstable international capital flows—they are mostly being bypassed by them.

So in South Asia and Sub-Saharan Africa, where serious hunger persists, the modern forces of globalization remain surprisingly weak. Stronger international governance of global markets and investments is therefore unlikely to have a great influence on hunger in these regions.

Food Security and Strong Global Governance

In the domains where stronger international governance can make a difference for food security, consider also that global institutions with significant capabilities already exist. For famine early warning and emergency food aid, a substantial global governance capability exists within such institutions as the FAO and the World Food Programme, as it also does within some regional institutions, such as the Southern African Development Community. This international food aid system has performed well in most emergency situations, particularly since the drought in southern Africa in 1991–92. It has tended to break down only in cases where recipient-country governments conceal problems (as Ethiopia did in 1984) or block international access (North Korea after 1995), or where an internal war is under way (as in Sudan).

Global governance in international agricultural research is also quite well developed through the CGIAR. The research centers of the CGIAR have been operating for several decades now to generate scientific and technical innovations usable by poor farmers in developing countries. At the international level, this system has a strong record of performance; unfortunately, the national agricultural research systems of many poor countries have not been supported or funded adequately by their own governments to function as capable partners of the CGIAR centers.

Food Security and Improved National Governance

Particularly in Sub-Saharan Africa, improved governance at the national level is most needed today to reduce hunger. Democracy is one useful measure of good governance, but improved national governance for food security need not begin or end with democratization. Nondemocratic governments, such as in China, or predemocratic ones, such as in South Korea and Taiwan in the 1960s and 1970s, have also been able to bring large numbers of people out of the danger of chronic hunger quickly. In China after 1978, a nondemocratic regime led by Deng Xiaoping introduced market incentives and individual household land contracts into the nation's farming sector and made substantial public investments in agricultural research and rural roads. Partly as a consequence of these state actions, China's total grain output increased by 65 percent over the next two decades. Incomes in the countryside increased along with farm productivity, and the number of people in China living in poverty fell in two decades from 250 million to only 34 million.

For the purpose of reducing poverty and hunger, the most important starting point for judging good governance at the national level is a government's performance in providing basic public goods to all its citizens, including those in rural areas (Paarlberg 2002). These essentials include internal peace, the rule of law, and public investment in infrastructure and research. Where hunger is on the rise today, for example in much of rural Sub-Saharan Africa, some of the most basic public goods needed for income growth and food security are being underprovided by national governments.

Internal Peace

National governments in Africa must do a better job of preserving internal peace. Over a recent period, 13 of the world's 20 most violent conflicts were in African states. Where national governments fail to preserve internal peace, food production and access to food are compromised.

Rule of Law

The prosperity of Africa has also suffered recently because weak civil and criminal justice systems or arbitrary and corrupt governmental administrations have tended to discourage private investment. Because the internal rule of law is so weak, Africans themselves have recently opted to locate 37 percent of their wealth outside the continent.

Public Investment in Rural Infrastructure

Investments in rural infrastructure are weak in Africa, reducing the life chances of the rural poor. More than 91 percent of Africans in the poorest income quintile live in rural settings, and very few of these poor rural households enjoy the basic infrastructure needed for a healthy and productive life. Only 2 percent have in-house water, only 1 percent have sewers, and total road density for rural dwellers in Africa is only one-sixth the average of Asia.

National Government Support for Agricultural Research

Between 1971 and 1991, public spending on agricultural R&D in Africa increased at only one-fifth the average rate for the rest of the developing world, despite the worrisome fact that both food production per capita and the productivity of farm labor in Africa were declining. In Asia, where public agricultural research investments by national governments have been stronger, improved technologies have reached farmers, and average farm worker productivity and income have increased. In Africa, between 1980 and 1997, average agricultural value-added per farm worker actually declined by 9 percent.

Foreign Assistance for Public Goods Investments

When national governments lag in providing the minimum public goods needed to ensure rural prosperity and food security for their own citizens, can outsiders help make up the resulting governance deficit? International laws and norms regarding state sovereignty have traditionally restricted the freedom of outsiders to intervene in the internal affairs of other states, even when those states fail to provide their own citizens with basic public goods. Increased investments can, however, be supported financially from the outside. Affluent outsiders should do much more to help governments in poor countries finance rural roads, health and education services, and public agricultural research. Bilateral donors and international financial institutions, such as the World

Bank, have in recent decades slighted such investments, concentrating instead on loans to governments in return for promises of market-oriented "policy reform." The reforms purchased (or rented) in this fashion have too often been superficial, incomplete, or only temporary. Outsiders are correct to call for market-oriented policy reforms, but not if it means reduced assistance for more tangible investments in doctors, clinics, teachers, schools, scientists, laboratories, irrigation maintenance, electricity, and roads.

A Partnership Role for NGOs

When national governments—or donors—fail to provide basic public goods, is it possible for NGOs to step in to do the job? In the area of rural poverty reduction and food security, NGOs work best when they are partnering with governments rather than trying to replace them. If governments are willing to invest in rural infrastructure, NGOs can provide essential help mobilizing local participation in both the planning and construction phases of rural road, water, or power projects. Local participation is usually key to ensuring affordable maintenance and successful management of public goods through a greater sense of local ownership. NGO participation can also help governments target their public investments more effectively toward the poor. But in most cases both the financial resources and the authority to act will have to come from the public sector.

NGOs are good at many things, but they have not yet demonstrated an ability to keep or restore peace in divided societies, nor have they been able, on their own, to establish the rule of law or make significant investments in infrastructure and research. It was national governments and donors, not NGOs, that provided most of the essential public goods that are now making rapid hunger reduction possible in East Asia.

Conclusion

Globalization is not the cause of poverty and hunger. The most powerful causes of hunger are local, rather than global. Frequently in the same district or in the same village, some people will be poor and hungry and others will not. The poor and the hungry are often locally disadvantaged because they lack access to land, legal protection, or basic public services (from roads and electricity to health and education), or because they are victims of social bias based on ethnicity, race, caste, or gender. When famine strikes, once again the cause tends to be highly localized: floods, droughts, civil wars, or policy mistakes made in one country (say, North Korea) but not in a neighboring one (such as South Korea). These localized causes of hunger are not linked in any convincing way to globalization.

But if globalization has not been the cause of hunger, it is not likely by itself to end hunger either. If a poor country with high rates of illiteracy and disease, inadequate railroads, a high incidence of ethnic conflict, an unstable government, and no rule of law decides to open its borders to trade and FDI, the results will be disappointing: the private traders and investors will never arrive. Countries such as these will not gain as much from more openness to global markets at the border as they will from more competent government and then stronger government actions behind their own borders.

The only institutions capable of taking these essential behind-the-border actions are national governments. The international donor community can and should help with financing, but the actions themselves have to be taken by national governments one country at a time. International donors, intergovernmental organizations, and international NGOs all have a role to play, but these more global institutions are, in many ways, too far removed from the highly localized sources of poverty and hunger to take the lead. It is wise and courageous leaders at the national level in the developing world that have to do so.

If I had to put my message on a bumper sticker, it would certainly not be one reading "Halt globalization," because globalization is not the enemy. But I would also reject the well-known and fashionable bumper sticker that says "Think globally, act locally." This advice is good for some truly global issues (such as HIV/AIDS or climate change), but in the area of food security, thinking globally has its limits. Hunger and poverty have different causes in different locations.

As I have argued, despite globalization, most hunger today is still highly localized and locally generated. Local problems, such as poor rural infrastructure, little access to health services or education, gender or ethnic or caste discrimination, landlessness, governmental weakness or corruption, and violent internal conflict are all problems difficult to address at the global level. Most of these local problems must be corrected through improved government performance at the national level. So we have to think locally, not think globally. And since it is still national governments that have sovereign jurisdiction over these localities, we have to act nationally. Therefore, for the purpose of improving food security today, our first governance motto should be "think locally, then act nationally."

References

Dollar, D., and A. Kraay. 2001. Trade, growth, and poverty. Policy Research Working Paper 2615. Washington, D.C.: World Bank.

Paarlberg, R. L. 2002. *Governance and food security in an age of globalization.* 2020 Discussion Paper 36. Washington, D.C.: International Food Policy Research Institute.

Sala-i-Martin, X. 2002a. The disturbing "rise" of global income inequality. NBER Working Paper w8904. Cambridge, Mass., U.S.A.: National Bureau of Economic Research.

———. 2002b. The world distribution of income (estimated from individual country distributions). NBER Working Paper w8933. Cambridge, Mass., U.S.A: National Bureau of Economic Research.

Addressing Inherent Asymmetries of Globalization

Nancy Birdsall

Globalization has increased opportunities around the world and contributed to growing prosperity in many developing countries. But it is inherently asymmetric in its effects on the rich versus the poor. This commentary looks at this asymmetry and its implication: that globalization will not necessarily work for the poor. I begin with a description of the current debate about globalization and poverty. Then I explain what I mean by the asymmetries of the globalization process. I conclude with some thoughts on how to address these asymmetries.

Globalization and the Poor: The Debate

Globalization is a process of increased economic integration across borders, with expanding flows of goods and services, people, capital, and ideas. Mainstream economists, once reliable proponents of globalization, can now be said to have splintered into three groups: cheerleaders for globalization, cynics, and worriers. None of these groups is antiglobalization. But compared with a decade ago, there is now serious debate among them, especially about the implications of the global economy for the poor of the world, about the appropriate roles of such global institutions as the IMF and the WTO, and about what trade and

---

This essay is based on several earlier papers and speeches. Most of the sources are cited in Birdsall (2002).

other policies developing countries ought to adopt to benefit from the opportunities and escape the potential costs of joining the global economy.

The Cheerleaders: Let Globalization Roll

Most economists are, most of the time, cheerleaders for the global integration of liberalizing market-led systems. They are joined by most heads of state, finance ministers, officials of the WTO, the World Bank, the IMF, readers of the *Financial Times* and the *Economist,* and members of the corporate and financial communities. Cheerleaders note that integration into the global economy has brought rapid economic growth to China and India, growth that has pulled hundreds of millions of people out of poverty. As a result, the 1990s—a decade in which globalization and markets seemed to triumph— brought the first-ever decline in the number of people in the world living in poverty (from about 1.2 billion to 1.1 billion, according to the World Bank).

Cheerleaders invoke, in addition, the evidence that countries engaged in trade grow faster, and that faster growth reduces poverty. That was the case for Japan, beginning in the Meiji era, for the poorer countries of Western Europe during the nineteenth century, and for the so-called miracle economies of East Asia in the three decades before the Asian financial crisis.

The Cynics: Global Rules Are Rigged against the Poor

This minority group of economists is concerned that corporate and financial insiders are shaping the rules of the global system in their own narrow interests. The result is a system that is not fair (let alone efficient) and that ends up hurting the poor. Their fear is echoed by development advocates; social activists; NGOs that work on environmental, labor, and human rights issues; and by much of the popular press.

The cynics invoke as their best example the global trading system. Citing the Common Agricultural Policy of the European Union and the U.S. 2002 farm bill, they observe that political interests in the rich and powerful countries dominate good sense. Rich countries subsidize farmers to the tune of more than US$300 billion a year, six times the amount they spend on foreign aid. They restrict access to their own textile markets, and textiles and agriculture are the very sectors where the poor and unskilled in poor countries could benefit most from new job opportunities. Their industries push for phytosanitary standards and exploit antidumping rules to close rich-country markets. Cynics note that escalating and peak tariffs by the members of the OECD cost developing countries an estimated US$2.5 billion a year, according to World Bank economists, and that agricultural protection and subsidies condemn millions of poor farmers in the world's poorest countries to continued poverty (for example, Cline 2004 estimates that eliminating all barriers and subsidies in agriculture could reduce global poverty numbers by more than 100 million people, even taking into account that the price of food would increase.)

Cynics have additional good examples: the effect of pressure to strengthen patent protection, with its benefits for rich-country pharmaceutical firms, on access to medicines in poor countries, or the contrast between progress in liberalizing capital markets, with its benefits for those with financial assets, and the notably illiberal international migration regime, despite the potential benefits of greater movement of unskilled labor from poor to rich countries for both the migrants and their home countries.

The Worriers: Deeper Markets and Fair Rules Alone
Will Not Address Globalization's Downside for the World's Poor

The worriers note that China and India are exceptional. Liberalizing reforms have not reduced poverty much in Latin America and Africa. And anyway, China and India, like the "miracle" economies of Korea and Singapore that preceded them in growing so rapidly, are hardly paradigmatic examples of liberal open economies. Even in countries that opened their markets and have experienced some growth, such as Mexico and Peru, though poverty has fallen, inequality remains stubbornly high. In Latin America, the limited gains from global integration seem to be going to a privileged few with university educations and the wherewithal to shift their assets into bank accounts abroad. In Sub-Saharan Africa, many countries seem trapped in a cycle of low income and poor governance, despite more than a decade of exchange rate reform, the undoing of state monopolies (in agricultural marketing, for example), and unilateral reduction of tariffs and export subsidies.

In short, the worriers ask: why expect the market alone to work? At the same time, the worriers put little hope in better and fairer rules alone. They point out that better trade rules and increased access to rich-country markets are not likely to help much in Africa (or Nicaragua or Nepal), given the heavy dependence of those economies on primary commodity exports whose prices have been falling, their apparent inability to diversify, and the growing competition from China and other more successful low-wage economies in nonagricultural exports. Development seems to require major economic and governance reforms within countries, not just transformation of global rules to make them development-friendly.

Asymmetries of Globalization

The worriers have a point. Two fundamental problems underlie their concerns. Each contributes to asymmetry between the world's rich and poor in the costs and benefits of globalization. I use the word "asymmetry" because it is neutral; it implies no judgment. The asymmetries I describe are structural—they create problems independent of any imposition of obvious injustice. Even were the unfair rules (the concern of the cynics) to be fixed, these asymmetries would still be problematic.

The first asymmetry arises from market imperfections and failures. Markets are imperfect, which raises special problems for developing countries. Take the example of global financial markets. They are subject to the herd behavior and speculative bubbles of domestic financial markets. Emerging market economies, with their local financial markets less resilient and their creditors more wary, are particularly vulnerable to the panicked withdrawal of capital typical of bank runs. In the 1990s, in contrast to rich-country markets, these panics occurred even when the overall management of their economies was reasonably sound. Volatility in global financial markets was a likely contributor to the higher growth and employment volatility overall of developing versus OECD economies (Figure E6.1). For developing countries (the worriers note), global trade has been generally a boon, but the globalization of finance in the 1990s was pretty much a bust.

By late 2007, five years of a benign external environment and high commodity prices have reduced the resulting systemic threat to global financial stability. But inherent risks in financial markets are still also bad news for the working poor and the incipient middle class in developing countries. In emerging markets, even private-sector debt often ends up being assumed by the public sector. Then, as Keynes noted long ago, it is the taxpayers who finance the debt, not the renter class. In short, the global financial system tends to reinforce rather than offset a high concentration of assets. It is not because the overall policy approach is wrong or governments are explicitly rewarding insiders. It is just that market failures make the global system asymmetric—disproportionately benefiting the already rich.

The second type of asymmetry, ironically, arises because most markets work reasonably well. Markets reward those who already have productive assets (financial and human capital). They often leave the poor behind, because the

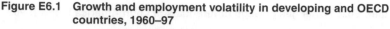

Figure E6.1   Growth and employment volatility in developing and OECD
countries, 1960–97

Standard deviation of growth and employment

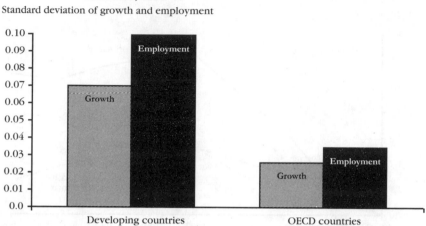

Source: Easterly, Islam, and Stiglitz (2000).

poor are not equipped with those assets. One critical asset is human capital. Figure E6.2 shows the evolution of wage differentials in Latin America, where the poor and uneducated have been left behind as the relative returns to the best-educated workers have risen rapidly in the 1990s.

The same story holds across countries as well. Global markets reward countries with effective and stable institutions. Economists assume, sensibly, that capital will get the highest returns where it is most scarce, in the poorest countries. But in fact the highest returns occur in settings with the greatest institutional assets. That explains why after more than a decade of increasing financial integration, most capital flows take place among industrialized countries. Most FDI during 2001 went to such countries (about US$600 billion), whereas Sub-Saharan Africa attracted less than US$10 billion (Figure E6.3).

For many of the world's poorest countries, their main asset is primary commodities. Their problem is that they lack critical institutional and political capabilities, not that they have failed to join the global economy. In fact, most, including those in Africa, are heavily engaged in global trade and have been "open" for at least two decades, using the conventional measure of openness— the ratio of their imports and exports to GDP. But highly dependent on primary commodity and natural resource exports, and without the institutional wherewithal to diversify into manufacturing, they have been victims (until very

Figure E6.2   Changes in wage differentials in Latin America in the 1990s

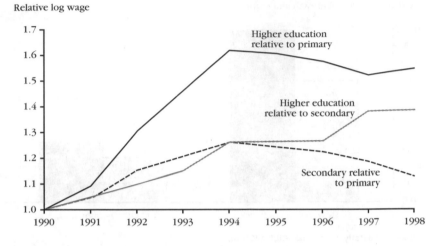

Source: Behrman, Birdsall, and Székely (2003).

Figure E6.3   Net foreign direct investment by region, 2001

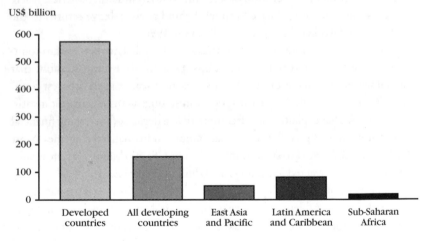

Source: World Bank (2002).

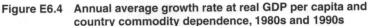

Figure E6.4   Annual average growth rate at real GDP per capita and country commodity dependence, 1980s and 1990s

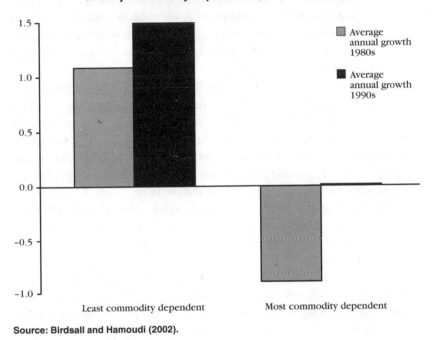

Source: Birdsall and Hamoudi (2002).

recently) of the decline in the world prices of their commodity exports (coffee, cocoa, cotton, and minerals) relative to manufactured exports. Specializing in primary commodities does not help develop the productive linkages that generate investment, the healthy pressure to exploit new technologies, and the increases in labor productivity and wages that reduce poverty. That may be why most primary commodity exporters' economies did not experience growth in the 1990s (Figure E6.4).

What to Do: Addressing Global Asymmetries

The cheerleaders are not wrong. Poor countries are unlikely to grow and reduce poverty unless they find a way to join the global economy. But cheerleaders should not be fundamentalists. Developing countries should have more—not less—autonomy and flexibility as they join the global system, particularly in managing their capital accounts. Chile's flexible use of taxes on capital inflows should not, for example, be controversial, nor even Malaysia's short-term closing of its capital market at the time of the Asian financial crisis. For emerging market economies, incautious opening of capital markets is likely to complicate exchange rate and monetary policy management in good times and to create vulnerability in bad times.

And for the poorest countries, trade liberalization is certainly not enough. The poorest countries that are heavily dependent on primary commodities, with initial handicaps of poor geography and new challenges, such as the AIDS pandemic, are not going to be transformed solely by trade and capital market liberalization. For those with weak institutions and incompetent or, worse, corrupt and predatory governments, openness alone is not going to create the kind of competition that reduces rent-seeking and predation.

In general, poor countries and the poor within countries are less likely to gain when times are good and more likely to lose (if not in absolute terms, certainly in terms of welfare losses) in bad times. That basic point of the worriers cannot be ignored.

The cynics are not wrong either, of course. The global trade regime is unfair, and especially so for the poor. But it is also true that better access to rich-country markets is not likely to help the poorest countries, most of which lack the institutional wherewithal to exploit new opportunities, nor the very poor within countries, who lack the human capital assets that matter so much in today's global economy.

In short, for the developing world's poor, more globalization and fairer rules are not enough. The structural asymmetries I have described also need to be addressed. In the case of global market failures, the rich countries need to exercise much more international leadership. These problems cry out for more effective collective action. The problem of an inadequate system for dealing with sovereign debt is only one example. (The need for an agreement to restrict greenhouse gas emissions is another.)

For the asymmetry associated with markets that work reasonably well, the challenge is to find ways to increase the ability of poor countries and poor people everywhere to exploit the opportunities of a global market. Of course, domestic economic reform and improved governance are critical. But there is also no alternative to an increase in transfers from the rich to the poor. In the industrialized economies, domestic social contracts—public transfers for investing in education, health, and housing and for social safety net programs, such as unemployment insurance and pensions—usually amount to more than 20 percent of GDP. Foreign aid to finance the equivalent at the global level is just one one-hundredth of that!

The Millennium Development Goals are the latest and closest we have come to something like a global social contract—in which global inequality of opportunity would be forcefully addressed (Birdsall and Clemens 2003). The global and multilateral institutions are our most critical bodies for managing that contract. The CGIAR is one example; the WTO, World Bank, Financial Stability Forum, Global Environmental Facility, and the United Nations itself are others. For an open global economy to benefit the poor, these must be reformed and strengthened, and their legitimacy enhanced through better representation of the world's poor. That seems to me to be the key to ensuring that globalization's deeper markets benefit from the civilizing hand of better management and fairer rules, and ultimately work better for the world's poor.

References

Behrman, J., N. Birdsall, and M. Székely. 2003. Economic policy and wage differentials in Latin America. Working Paper 29. Washington, D.C.: Center for Global Development. Available at http://www.cgdev.org.

Birdsall, N. 2002. Asymmetric globalization: Global markets require good global politics. Working Paper 12. Washington, D.C.: Center for Global Development. Available at http://www.cgdev.org.

Birdsall, N., and M. Clemens. 2003. *From promise to performance: How rich countries can help poor countries help themselves.* Center for Global Development Policy Brief, vol. 2, issue 1. Washington, D.C.: Center for Global Development. Available at http://www.cgdev.org.

Birdsall, N., and A. Hamoudi. 2002. Commodity dependence, trade, and growth: When "openness" is not enough. Working Paper 7. Washington, D.C.: Center for Global Development. Available at http://www.cgdev.org.

Cline, W. R. 2004. *Trade policy and global poverty.* Washington, D.C.: Center for Global Development and Institute for International Economics.

Easterly, W., R. Islam, and J. Stiglitz. 2000. Shaken and stirred: Explaining growth volatility. Paper presented at the Annual Bank Conference on Development Economics, April 18–20, World Bank, Washington, D.C. Available at http://sitesources.worldbank.org/INTABCDDEWASHINGTON2000/Resources/easterly.pdf.

World Bank. 2002. *Global development finance 2002.* Washington, D.C.

Contributors

Isher Judge Ahluwalia Chairperson, Board of the Governors, Indian Council for Research on International Economic Relations (ICRIER); member of the National Manufacturing Competitiveness Council, Government of India

Sartaj Aziz Senator and former agriculture minister, finance minister, and foreign minister, Pakistan

Nancy Birdsall President, Center for Global Development, Washington, D.C.

Marc J. Cohen Research fellow, International Food Policy Research Institute, Washington, D.C.

Eugenio Díaz-Bonilla Executive director for Argentina and Haiti, Inter-American Development Bank, Washington, D.C.

Ashok Gulati Director in Asia, New Delhi Office, International Food Policy Research Institute, Washington, D.C.

Corinna Hawkes Research fellow, International Food Policy Research Institute, Washington, D.C.

Tewodaj Mengistu Doctoral student, RAND Corporation, Santa Monica, California; formerly, research analyst, International Food Policy Research Institute, Washington, D.C.

Ellen Messer Visiting professor of Anthropology, Friedman School of Nutrition Science and Policy, Tufts University, Boston

Sophia Murphy   Senior advisor, Trade Program, Institute for Agriculture and Trade Policy, Minneapolis, Minnesota

Sudha Narayanan   Formerly, researcher at IFPRI; currently, Ph.D. student, Applied Economics and Management, Cornell University, Ithaca, New York

Robert L. Paarlberg   Professor of Political Science, Wellesley College, Wellesley, Massachusetts; associate at the Weatherhead Center for International Affairs, Harvard University, Cambridge, Massachusetts

Per Pinstrup-Andersen   H.E. Babcock Professor of Food, Nutrition and Public Policy, Division of Nutritional Sciences, Cornell University, Ithaca, New York

Thomas Reardon   Professor, International Development and Agribusiness/Food Industry, Michigan State University, East Lansing, Michigan

M. S. Swaminathan   Chairperson, M.S. Swaminathan Foundation, Chennai, India; chairperson, National Commission for Farmers, Government of India

C. Peter Timmer   Visiting professor, Program on Food Security and Environment, Stanford University, and nonresident fellow, Center for Global Development.

Joachim von Braun   Director general, International Food Policy Research Institute, Washington, D.C.

Kevin Watkins   Head of the United Nations Development Programme's Human Development Report Office, New York

Index

Page numbers for entries occurring in figures are suffixed by an *f* and those for entries in notes by an *n*.